# AUSTRALIAN LIVES

# Australian Lives

## An Oxford Anthology

---

### Edited by Joy Hooton

Melbourne

OXFORD UNIVERSITY PRESS

Oxford  Auckland  New York

This project has been assisted by the Commonwealth
Government through the Australia Council, its arts
funding and advisory body.

OXFORD UNIVERSITY PRESS AUSTRALIA

Oxford New York
Athens Auckland Bangkok Bogotá
Buenos Aires Calcutta Cape Town Chennai
Dar es Salaam Delhi Florence Hong Kong Istanbul
Karachi Kuala Lumpur Madrid Melbourne
Mexico City Mumbai Nairobi Paris Port Moresby
São Paulo Singapore Taipei Tokyo Toronto Warsaw
and associated companies in
Berlin Ibadan

OXFORD is a trade mark of Oxford University Press

National Library of Australia
Cataloguing-in-publication data:

The Oxford Book of Australian lives: an Oxford anthology.
    Includes index.
    ISBN 0 19 553785 8.

    1. Australia – Biography. I. Hooton, Joy W. (Joy Wendy),
    1935– .

920.094

Edited by Cathryn Game
Text designed by Design Rescue
Cover designed by Steve Randles
Typeset by Syarikat Seng Teik Sdn. Bhd., Malaysia
Printed by Kyodo Printing Co. Pty Ltd, Singapore
Published by Oxford University Press
253 Normanby Road, South Melbourne, Australia

# CONTENTS

# INTRODUCTION

I have done my best to tell the truth about what it was like, yet I am well aware that in the matter of my own feelings I have not come near meeting my aim. My ideal of auto-biography has been set by Alfieri, whose description of a duel he once fought in Hyde Park is mainly concerned with how he ran backwards to safety. Perhaps because I am not even yet sufficiently at peace with myself, I have not been able to meet those standards of honesty. Nothing I have said is factual except the bits that sound like fiction.

Clive James, *Unreliable Memoirs*

From the beginning of European settlement, autobiography has loomed large in Australian writing. The first decades of exploration and appropriation were inevitably accompanied by countless efforts to document, describe, and record, to appropriate and assimilate the continent in words as it was appropriated by other means. Inevitably, too, the act of reflecting on the new land involved reflecting on the self, on discovering that appropriation is a two-way experience. In numerous early narratives Australia is as much a mirror reflecting the narrator's perceptions of a different historical self, a self that changes dramatically in response to extraordinary pressures, as it is a subject to be known for itself.

The earliest white immigrants wrote memoirs of settlement for a variety of reasons: to explain to relatives and friends left behind the differences between Australia and the native land; to maintain familial and friendly bonds; to record for the benefit of posterity the trials and achievements of pioneering; to justify a misjudged self or to protest at injustice; or to profess reformation in the case of those who left their country for their country's good. As the nineteenth century progressed a frequent impulse was the need to conserve places and people of the past, which were threatened by the rapid erosions of time; to recover the familiarity of the recent past, once experienced in its newness as strange and made strange again as it was swallowed by the present.

The autobiographical impulse also infected fiction. The novel that was until recently generally conceded to be the first written in Australia, *Quintus Servinton* (1831) by Henry Savery, is closely based on the author's life, although its happy conclusion runs counter to actuality. If Savery was deserted by his wife and ended up in Port Arthur after a series of downfalls, his fictional *alter ego* returns to congenial retirement and connubial bliss in Devonshire. And, beginning dramatically with Miles Franklin's *My Brilliant Career*, the twentieth century has seen a continuation of writers' fascination with life-writing and autobiographical fiction. Not only are many of the novels we regard as classics, such as *The Getting of Wisdom, The Fortunes of Richard Mahony, The Man Who Loved Children, Monkey Grip,* and *My Brother Jack,* fictional autobiographies, but autobiography proper has also claimed the attention of numerous established writers.

Meanwhile politicians, historians, captains of industry, artists, political activists, feminists, actors, and theatrical entrepreneurs, journalists, military men, and prominent individuals of all varieties have provided and continue to provide versions of their life-stories. Since the 1970s Aborigines have finally surmounted Australia's culture of forgetting with narratives that document exploitation and oppression as they reflect white versions of ignorance and primitive behaviour. Another important signpost to changed interests and attitudes in the reading public was the publication in 1981 of Albert Facey's *A Fortunate Life.* Initiating interest in what appeared to be a new genre of extraordinary ordinary lives, Facey's was followed by a series of narratives from obscure individuals. Eve Hogan's in the present selection is an example.

Given the interest in life-writing on the part of publishers, writers, and readers, it is strange that the range and extent of the genre in Australia in both centuries, but particularly until the 1950s, is largely unknown. Literary critics, working according to traditional notions of aesthetic privilege, have invariably concentrated on the autobiographies of writers; practising historians have mined the mass of first-person narratives of the past as quarries for facts. Neither really literature nor really history, autobiographies as texts in their own right have either sunk from sight after a brief flush of publicity or have never risen from obscurity. Arthur Lynch's *My Life Story* (1924), for instance, the autobiography of a man whose trial for treason made him a household word in Australia, is an example of the former; Eliza Davies's 1830s paranoid voyagings and encounters with hostile places and people an example of the latter. The tendency to treat autobiography chiefly as a branch of imaginative litera-ture rather than as part of the general history of discourse is to emphasise artistic creation at the expense of the complexities of historical recreation and the intricacies of psychological and sociocultural influences.

It is interesting in this context that when Hal Porter's artful, self-conscious narrative, *The Watcher on the Cast-iron Balcony,* first appeared in 1963, it was welcomed by some critics as marking 'the beginning' of autobiography in Australia. Since then many of the bricks of Porter's carefully constructed edifice, including the cast-iron balcony, have been dismantled, to the dismay of some readers. Reading the extended representation of his mother according to the days of the week republished here, Porter's importation of snippets of social history, botany, and even familiar folksong underlines the extent to which his mother is an imaginative construction. Peter Conrad's representation of his parents has even more obvious Whistler-ite connotations. Striking and clever and even convincing as these representations are, they might sit less easily with readers now than Eve Hogan's or Jack Davis's less obvious mediations of past personalities.

Mediation is unavoidable in life-writing, however, as any autobiographer will affirm. Robert Dessaix, for instance, in *A Mother's Disgrace*, concludes with a highly enigmatic stance on the 'truth' of his telling. 'There's no operatic ending to this tale, I'm afraid,' he admits. 'In fact, to be perfectly frank, it isn't the sort of tale that has an ending. I did give it a beginning, I admit, but just for purposes of seduction.' He proceeds to provide the reader who craves straight lines with three alternative endings but undercuts them with the final words: 'I told you: this is a tale without an ending. I have told you the truth. Now trust me.'

Ti is this inalienable element of mediation that makes the genre treacherous territory for the cultural commentator. It was fashionable in the 1970s, for instance, to draw generalisations about Australian culture from life-writing, especially from such autobiographies of childhood as Donald Horne's *Education of Young Donald*, and George Johnston's *My Brother Jack*. Reading such narratives in a group, some commentators claimed to see an Australia that was overwhelmingly secular, authoritarian, racist, and philistine. Valuable as first-person narratives are as reflectors of culture, however, they are always clouded mirrors. Memory is notoriously selective, especially where the story of the self is concerned, and however sincere the desire to see the objective truth, subjectivity will invariably act as a blindfold. If seeing the truth is impossible, telling makes it doubly so in that any representation of the self is inevitably a version and a temporary version at that. What appears cogent on Monday night will appear distorted on Tuesday morning. It is an unfortunate/fortunate circumstance which has resulted in Rembrandt's innumerable self-portraits and the attempts by some writers to rediscover the past in a series of life stories.

Perhaps one of the advantages of an anthology is that it allows the reader to experience the individualities of a range of mediating personalities; the content of experience is often less interesting than the individual response. As Henry James remarked, adventures happen only to people who know how to tell them. Both Joseph Holt and Ned Kelly, for instance, write in protest at their injustices, Kelly at white-hot heat, Holt with less intensity. Kelly's pleading has an end-of-the-tether desperation, which suggests that it is an attempt to set the record straight in the full knowledge of its likely dismissal by hostile representatives of respectability. Holt writes as one who wishes to convince his respectable readers that he is one of them. Mortlock's narrative voice has another tone altogether: urbane and even humorous, he writes to emphasise his ability to domesticate the Tasmanian wilderness by turning himself into a small businessman, a successful hawker of small goods who travels the island from one end to the other.

The immigrant experience has also stimulated diverse responses. Lurie, writing of his childhood in a Jewish family, which was still tightly bonded to the old country, re-creates the costs of its claustrophobic isolation in prose that is itself narrowly focused to the point of obsession; an island of European Jewishness set down in the midst of an irrelevant Australia, the family is served for a while by the classic 'good mother' until reality breaks in. For the narrating self, meanwhile, irony lies only in the irony of circumstance. Elisabeth Wynhausen, on the other hand, finds comic material in the gulf between the parents of Jewish immigrants, the upholders of orthodoxy, and the next, more sceptical, hedonistic generation. Thorvald Weitemeyer, writing of his first experiences in Queensland in the 1870s, exploits to the full the comedy of his misapprehensions and his youthful mix of arrogance and ignorance, which makes him an easy prey for those keen to enliven boredom with practical jokes. Mary Rose Liverani plays with the comic rifts between the shrewd perceptions of lively children straight from working-class Glasgow and the banalities of the complacent Australia of the 1950s; the retrospective construction of their encounter with their first Australian is partly a revengeful dialogue between two types of ignorance, of inexperience on the one hand and unteachable complacency on the other. Similarly, reading responses to other familiar experiences such as war, death, love, or living overseas, one is struck by the unpredictable individuality and diversity of ways of seeing. Far from reflecting a monoculture, these narratives reflect a range of singular, even unrelated cultures.

This is not to suggest that individuality cancels out Australian-ness, far from it, for Australia is an intangible but real presence to be reckoned with in most of these narratives. Indeed, it is the self-conscious negotiation of relationship with nation that separates Australian autobiographical writing from that of older Western democracies. Other post-colonial countries share the characteristic but in varying degrees. For Kate Jennings, for instance, memories of pastoral Australia sharpen her perceptions of chaotic city life in New York; Arthur Lynch defends himself against charges of treason on the grounds that he is an Australian, although he left the country in his twenties and never returned; Alan Moorehead is delighted to abandon the provincial atmosphere of 1930s Melbourne for London, but even his intense love affair with a young English woman is tinged with his sense of himself as Australian and therefore different; Gillian Bouras gives a new dimension to the experience of homesickness in her descriptions of adjusting to Greece, the home of her married life; for the expatriate Clive James Sydney is 'so real in … recollection that [he] can taste it' and 'it tastes like happiness'.

Oddly, given the familiar emphasis on the homogeneity of Australian culture and its notorious cultivation of the average, Australian-ness for some narrators seems to confer a confident singularity. Henry Handel Richardson unconsciously draws on her unconfessed teenage passion for the local curate in creating the main character in her first major novel, a novel set in Europe and heavily dependent on European models; her surprise when the fact is pointed out to her is less at the incongruity of the correspondence than that she had been unaware of it. Bessie Lee, after an unusual isolated childhood in rural Victoria and an eclectic education, is so convinced of the rightness of her eccentric view on sex within marriage that she leaves the WCTU and transforms herself into a one-woman army in the fight against alcohol. Stella Bowen's spirited response to the end of her relationship with Ford Madox Ford has the same quality of unconventional singularity.

Some of the narrators in this collection are not Australian in the strict legalistic sense, but they are included because their visits to Australia changed them utterly. For Havelock Ellis, his year of isolation at Sparkes Creek was crucial for his intellectual and emotional development. He writes that he acquired there 'the power of seeing the world freshly and seeing it directly with [his] own eyes, not through the dulling or disturbing medium of tradition and convention'. His mind 'was ranging freely, everywhere with a new power to grasp what it seized and to revel in its acquisitions'. Alexander Harris, while living in the bush and associating with men of no education, is led to re-examine his relationship with God. Grant Watson is similarly profoundly changed by a period of living in the bush and by his encounters with Aboriginal magic; perceiving the bush as 'a vast interrogation mark' questioning human claims to meaning and identity, he is aware that at any moment 'the veil of time seemed drawn aside, and eternity gaped in the sun's glare or in the cracking of a seed-pod'.

The impulse to find spiritual or transcendent meaning is not confined to visitors, though; the young Thomas Keneally is inspired by the poetry of Gerard Manley Hopkins to find a similar destiny in working-class Homebush. Arthur Lynch is convinced that his pursuit of thought is equal if not superior to the pursuit of adventure by men of action; as he joins the Boers, moreover, he is conscious of an assurance 'as if it had been written on high, that I would pull through, even amid all sorts of perils, and with far richer experience'.

Another common trait of Australian autobiographies of both nineteenth and twentieth centuries is a play between familiarity and strangeness. It is not surprising that narratives recording early immigrant experience should re-explore the initial strangeness of the new environment, its transformation as home, and its retrospective strangeness with the erosions of time. Something of this duality flavours Mortlock's reminiscences of his life as a hawker in Tasmania in that

Tasmania is both domesticated by his activities and made strange by his retrospective musings on their peculiarity. It is extremely common in the mass of autobiographies of childhood, which comprise almost a genre of their own in Australian writing. Jill Ker Conway simultaneously recreates the familiar rituals of her early life on an isolated property in western New South Wales and inserts her adult amazement at its extraordinary hardships and challenges. Hal Porter's celebrated representation of the social certainties of a small town childhood in the 1920s is shot through with an adult awareness of impermanence; if the child is blithely confident that it will be today forever, the older narrator is poignantly aware that his illusion is destined to be short-lived. Kathleen Fitzpatrick similarly deftly undermines the 'solid bluestone foundations' of her childhood with the educated insights of the older historian. For some narrators of childhood experience, such as Bernard Smith and W.J. Turner, the strange familiarity of the past and the gulf between past and present selves can only be expressed by presenting the younger self in the third person.

Readers will no doubt find other common traits in this collection, but it is hoped that an anthology including a selection of well-known narratives side by side with others that are less known, or even unknown, will show how much more diverse Australian autobiographical writing is than is generally realised. It is a rich body of writing, much of its richness generated by the continuing challenges of life in Australia. If some narrators express ambivalence or even hostility to Australia as their natural or acquired home, most share Clive James's sense of its persistent claims. In James's words: '... the birthplace of the fortunate ... pulsing like a beacon through the days and nights sends out its invisible waves of recollection. It always has and it always will, until even the last of us come home.'

# I

# Convicts and outlaws

# Joseph Holt

(1756–1826)

*'General' of the United Irishmen, and hero of the Wicklow rebellion of 1798, Holt was exiled to New South Wales without trial in 1799. Captain William Cox, a passenger on the same ship, offered him the management of Brush Farm. Although Holt was bent on attaining respectability and affluence, he remained under suspicion by the authorities and was arrested three times for possible complicity in planned uprisings. In September 1800 he was denounced as a conspirator during a time of tension and was acquitted, but was forced to witness the brutal flogging he describes here. He returned to Ireland in 1814 after receiving a final pardon from Governor Macquarie in 1812. His* Memoirs *were first published in 1838.*

In the month of August I had to stay continually at Canterbury. (That was the name the parson gave it.) I cut the vines and replaced the stakes, pruned the fruit trees and began to build a large dwelling house, as this place being about five miles from Sydney Mr Cox wished to have it in a stylish manner. I carried on every sort of work, and every Saturday night I use to ride to Brush Farm and settle with my men there and, on Sunday mornings I called all hands and showed them their week's work, and if I saw I would be wanted sooner than that day of the week, I came home to give further directions. My conduct was every day seen more and more to Mr Cox, and I managed the two places with such care to the satisfaction of Mr Cox that he had got very fond of me. Captain Cox bought from Captain Prentice all his horses and mares and that was a great addition to our herd.

On the fifth day of September 1800 I came to Brush Farm and measured the ground that my men had broke up for corn and settled and paid the men. I drank a little wine and water and went to bed and, at the hour of one oclock, I heard a noise about the house and I said to my wife 'I fear there is somebody going to rob the granary' when, all of a sudden, I heard a rap at door.

I asked: 'Who is there?'

A man answered: 'A friend.'

It being a strange voice, I asked him what he wanted that hour of the night? He said he had a message to me from Captain Cox. I bounced up and opened the door and, to my great surprize, in rushed eight soldiers and a sargent with fixed bayonets, and put the bayonets up against my side.

I asked them: 'What the devil are you about?'

They answered they would soon let me know.

I replied: 'You damned set of cowardly rascals, I defy you. You show yourselves a set of rascals to put your bayonets to a naked man without clothes, or armed. Why did you not come in like men, or are you afeared of one man, you cowards? Look at the piece hanging at the foot of my bed. If I had done anything that I should be afraid of I would soon send you all to Eternity.'

They took down the brass blunderbuss and found twelve fingers of a charge in it and they were going to take it away, but I dared them to take it, as it was the property of William Cox Esqr.

I dressed myself and then they knew I was of a superior rank, and they furnished my shirt wrists with a pair of steel ruffles and brought me to Parramatta to the guard house and, next day, put me in the boat and was so good to send two 'servants' to wait on me, till I was delivered up to Daniel McKay, a Scotchman. He was jailer of Sydney jail. He was convicted for picking pockets or robbing.

McKay welcomed me and told me he would learn me 'New Exercise', for he thought and wished that I might be hanged. I told the wretch I did not doubt but he did. I was put in a cell and a double sentry put on the door, orders given to not let anybody see me, nor let me get any support of any kind.

Next day, about ten oclock, there was brought me a bottle of water and one pound of bread. When I heard the key put in the lock, I set my hands aside and asked the wretches what was the news of the day?

They made answer: 'There is a few of your countrymen to be hanged by and by.'

I said: 'The Devil's cure to them if they deserve it.'

They shut the door and went away. I had neither plank, nor anything to lay my poor carcass on to rest or sleep, only the flags of the cell. I prayed to my great creator for mercy to pity a poor innocent man that did not know what I was put in for.

My Good Reader a innocent man is in most danger in one sense, because he don't know how to make out his defence and, if a villain swears against you, perhaps you may not have any witness to prove a alibi to confront him, so there the danger lies. But, if you are guilty, you can make up your defence from some part of your crime. I languished under all those thoughts and, very happy for me, I in my youthfull days read a book called 'The Innocent Sufferer' and, drawing up his words and punishments in my mind, I considered I was but a moral [sic] like him and my greatest consolation was, if I died, I would die innocent. I never grew hungry all this time, nor did I ever taste the bread or water they brought me.

It then was the second night, and being tired, I laid myself down on the flags and slept but, being incumbered with visions and dreams, I awoke and it was day. My good reader the nights is not so long there as they are in Ireland.

About ten oclock the door was opened and another bottle of water and a pound of bread was brought me, and they was very much surprised to see that I had not used any of what they brought the day before. I told them that God supported me in my affliction and they went away fuming. Whether they told the Provost Marshall or no I can't tell but, at eleven oclock, he came and Captain Aikin, a captain of a merchantman that lay in the harbour and, when he came in, he looked at me very hard and said he was sorry to see me in such a place. I told him I had a doubt of that, and I asked him would he be so good as to let me know when I was to suffer? He stared at me and said he did not understand what I meant. I broke out in this manner, and told him that I considered that, if you are under sentence of death, that it was his duty to see that I should get support till the moment of my time to go to the place of execution: 'You keep me here like a common malefactor.' And the words he says: 'Sir, If I was you I would tell the Governor what I know about this plot?'

I replied: 'Do you want me to invent a lie and then swear to it, to gain the good will of the governor? No sir, I know nothing of any plot whatsoever, for the greatest rogue knows most of all. I can say I wish you had my death warrant in your pocket, for I am ready to die and I walk with my hands aside to the gallows and welcome death and bid adieu to tyranny that is following me round the world.' I said these words with such fireiness that the tears run down both their cheeks, and Captain Aikin got me by the hands and, in an affectionate voice, said it was worse than murder to punish a man like me.

I answered: 'Sir, I don't know what is against me and, if I knew of anything, it should be my last wish for death before I would divulge or satisfy.'

'Sir' said Mr Smyth Provost Marshal 'I'll have you write to His Excellency and let him know how you are treated, and write in a forcible manner.'

I said: 'Sir pray tell me how can I write without pen ink or paper or light to do it, but I hope God will give me light in the world to come.'

He said that he would send me pen ink and paper, and said the door should not be shut any more.

Both saw the two days bread and water lying by the wall. They asked me what it was. I told them it was the allowance sent me, but I was determined to die in the cell and have done with the world for I was tired of it and, only I had the misfortune to bring my wife and childer with me, I soon would be rid of all tyranny.

He hoped I would eat a breakfast he would send me, and said, if he was to lose his commission, he'd visit me and send me support. Both begged of me not to fret, and shook hands and went away.

His servant came with breakfast and pen ink and paper, and chair to sit on. I eat my breakfast, and then resorted to my pen and wrote to His Excellency:

Sir,

I must acknowledge the great power invested in you, as I know you are His Majesty's representative. Yet and all I hope you will not disgrace your power or go beyond the power of the happy and well adapted laws made for the protection of His Majesty's subjects, and I am sorry the law, that is so ready to punish, will not step forward and protect. You know there is higher power than you. I only wish for man like usage and British law. It may, Your Excellency, come to your turn to be tried as the governor in a trial for flogging a man to death.

I remain Your Excellency's most humble and obedient servant,

Joseph Holt

Mr Smyth came and carried the letter to His Excellency and, when he read it, Mr Smyth told me he pulled off his hat and flung it on the floor, and leaped about and desired that I might be put in irons. Mr Smyth waited for his passion to be over, and then he addressed him and said: 'Now Your Excellency, if you find this man is innocent, you will be very sorry. Moreover I tell you he never eat one morsel of victuals ever since he was confined, and he is almost dead.'

These words took great effect on the Governor and he desired Mr Smyth to go to the jail and to put me along with the debtors, and to let me get wine and spirits but not take it to excess, and that my wife might come to see me whenever she liked. So my friend Mr Smyth came with the news and he and I went in to the jailer's, and he was Chief Constable but kept a publick house joining the prison, and Mr Smyth called for a bottle of rum, and we drank it, and he left orders for Henry Kable to let me come over and take refreshment whenever I liked. So you see what change I got for the better. This Mr Smyth was a North of Ireland man and so was Captain Aikin and, during one month I was confined, both of these gentlemen called to see me very often or sent Kable supplies for me, so my misery ceased.

In a few days after, there was nineteen men brought from the jail before the Governor to be examined, and eighteen of them turned informer and every one asked about me and not one man said the least thing against me so we had 'a bad clutch of troublesome rascals' and what else could we expect? There was flogging every day till some of them never got the better of it, they died at last, and some of them was so good as to bring Doctor Harold, the priest, in by their information. He was in jail and, the sixth day of October, we got orders to go in the boat. Mr Smyth came to me and brought me out of the prison and he, and a few more, went in a government boat and, when I was about ten miles from Sydney, I saw the passage boat coming down, and Mrs Holt and her young child. I told Mr Smyth that I saw her and another.

The boat rowed towards the passage boat to take Mrs Holt in. We returned back and came to Parramatta. There all the prisoners were put in to jail, unless the priest. He was left in a house with a guard with him. Mr Smyth let me go with Mrs Holt, on the honour to call on him in the morning. I did attend to the minute and we marched up to Toongabbie where all the government men was and this was the plan—to give them the opportunity of seeing the punishment inflicted on several. There was one man of the name of Maurice Fitzgerald. He was ordered to receive three hundred lashes. The place they flogged them—their arms pull round a large tree and their breasts squeezed against the tree so the men had no power to cringe or stir. Father Harold was ordered to lay his hand against the tree by the hand of the man that was flogging. There was two floggers—Richard Rice and John Johnson, the Hangmen from Sydney. Rice was a left handed man and Johnson was right handed so they stood at each side, and I never saw two threshers in a barn move their strokes more handier than those two man killers did. The moment they begun I turn my face round towards the other side and one of the constables came and desired me to turn and look on. I put my hand in my pocket and pull out my pen knife and swore I rip him from the navel to the chin. They all gather round me and would have ill used me but Mr Smyth came over and asked them who gave them any orders about me so they were oblige to walk off. I could compare them to a pack of hounds at the death of a hare, all yelping. I turned once about and as it happened I was to leeward of the floggers and I protest, though I was two perches from them, the flesh and skin blew in my face as they shook off of the cats.

Fitzgerald received his three hundred lashes. Doctor Mason—I never will forget him—he use to go to feel his pulse and he smiled and said 'This man will tire you before he will fail. Go on.' It is against the law to flog a man past 50 lashes without a doctor and, during the time he was getting his punishment, he never gave as much as a word, only one and that was saying 'Don't strike me on the neck. Flog me fair.' When he was let down two of the constables went and took hold of him by the arms to help him in the cart, I was standing by. He said to them 'Let my arms go', struck both of them with his elbows in the pit of the stomach and knock them both down and then step in the cart.

*A Rum Story: The Adventures of Joseph Holt.*
*Thirteen Years in New South Wales (1800–12) (1838).*

# John Frederick Mortlock

(1809–82)

*Convicted in 1843 of attempting to murder his uncle, who he believed had defrauded him of his inheritance, Mortlock was transported for twenty-one years to Australia. In Van Diemen's Land he ultimately won a conditional pardon in 1855 and tried various ways of making a living, including teaching, clerking, and professional billiard playing. He obtained a hawker's licence in 1854 and walked extensively through the island, becoming an experienced bushman. In 1864 he returned to England, where he published his* Experiences *in five parts (1864–65).*

The jocular remark of a friend—a grandee, Robert Septimus Price, Esq., whose brother commanded the vessel in which I afterwards completed my 'girdle round the earth,'—exercised an important influence upon my fortunes. 'I wonder,' said he, 'you who are so fond of wandering, do not take out a hawker's licence.' Struck with the idea, I sought counsel from my pillow, paid in on the morrow to Government £1, the yearly fee, and forthwith applied for one. Advice and information were acquired from a shrewd acquaintance who (his trade of brass-founder being unserviceable in the colony) had, from small dealings also as a pedlar, begun with a few shillings, grown into a thriving shopkeeper, now worth thousands of pounds. Much is comprised in Mr Room's chief maxim, 'Goods well bought are half sold,' the truth of which will from reflection and experience appear. Reserving £15 placed to my credit in the Savings' Bank at Hobart, I commenced business with £7. Oh that I had begun sooner, and had gathered in my harvest during the four past years of superabundant prosperity! The licence having been issued in August, 1854, before a twelvemonth had elapsed, I was master of £140. I am practically enabled to state that a very moderate capacity is requisite for the accumulation of money. A strong instinctive desire for getting and hoarding (such as we see in magpies and jackdaws), and a habit of saving, will generally be successful in making a 'stocking.' How many beggars, subsisting upon daily alms of the charitable, are, at their decease, found to be comparatively affluent? In fact, how can we attribute a sound intellect to the miser who regards wealth, not as the means, but as the end of living—who grudges the smallest superfluous portion of it to his fellow-creatures—who disregards the obloquy of his neighbours, the cries of his kindred, and even his own personal necessities; and clings, perhaps at the risk of his life, to the property of another? What is such behaviour but evidence of a brain positively faulty? Even if, as in the instance of Lord Bacon, an unregulated animal instinct of 'acquiring' accompanies splendid intellectual faculties, their lustre is dimmed and tarnished by its sordid operation! Is further argument needful to prove my proposition, that 'any man may, by saving and self-denial, honestly become rich?' Rambling having now become profitable as well as pleasant, hardly one square mile of the settled districts did I leave unexplored, my time being equally divided between town and country. Whilst in the former I, tolerably well dressed, attended all public sales, and watched for suitable articles on which a good per centage might fairly be expected in the bush. The investment, costing from £10 to £20, having been completed, two large bundles were enveloped in calico, tied together, and slung over my neck. These, with rug, knapsack, and latterly a gun, formed a weighty load, under which I, in humble habiliments, trudged for twenty miles before opening them, my welcome being proportioned to the distance from headquarters. After three days the heavy work ceased; for heavy it was in such a warm climate and rugged country—seventy and eighty pounds weight on the shoulders over hill and dale, from morning till night, day after day, being no joke.

I may here suggest that, in India, European soldiers should be allowed to march and fight in their shirt sleeves, without stocks, and with light white linen or cotton caps on their heads, woollen cloth being as destructive there as the want of it would be in England. To face those first few days, during which I endured great fatigue, always required an effort. At such times my sweet temper became rather acidulated, and had I fallen across either of the knavish trustees, a severe kicking would have been his fate. To be sure, when tired I could rest; when hungry could eat, with the best of sauces; and at night could roll myself in the rug and sleep anywhere, without fear of tumbling out of bed, or of having the hill to pay. An oiled piece of calico, weighing seven or eight ounces, served to keep off the rain, and also formed a canoe to float my baggage across a stream. The ends having been gathered and tied, and my effects properly placed in it, I placed a towing-string between my teeth, and swam to the opposite bank; thus being independent of fords, boats and bridges, the many rivers on the coast or elsewhere never obstructed me. An impertinent acquaintance, the aforesaid R. S. P., Esq., to whom I mentioned my proposed contrivance, sarcastically and flippantly suggested 'the carriage of a washing tub upon my head', yet it answered admirably, and, being now a regular Robinson Crusoe, I gave to a little girl ten shillings (in goods—a sixpenny brooch and some other article equally valuable) for a long-legged terrier puppy, with very intellectual eyes; he grew apace and became my man Friday. The good-tempered though rather wilful little animal soon made himself quite at home with me, and seemed to be very happy. Our excursions were of three weeks' duration or less, sometimes more. The grand houses (whose mistresses had little else to do except to drive into town and go shopping) I avoided, but was gladly received at the smaller ones, and huts remote from stores and townships.

That mode of life, whilst occasionally painful, afforded much enjoyment; £12 being the average net profit of each trip. On one beat, whose extreme end lay ninety miles from a public-house or store of any sort, there was a ready sale for five times as much as I could carry. However, at a sheep station on the little Forrester River, the overseer's wife proved also to be a keen trader. Having herself shot and skinned all the opossums, she manufactured a handsome sable rug, for which she demanded three sovereigns, and would take no less. She often put on her husband's coat and hat—indeed, I fancy, she also at times wore something else of his. Haggling with a lady not being my forte, I gave the money to that kind hospitable dame, used the article for six weeks during a three hundred mile walk, and then, as a favour, sold it for £5 to a gentleman, a Mr Peck, on the point of returning with his family round Cape Horn to Europe. The price of such a thing in England would probably be not less than ten guineas.

During these peregrinations, I became known to a one-armed Welsh shepherd, an agreeable original sort of person, living in complete solitude on a remote sheep run—belonging to Mr Jones, at the Piper River—(of which he had sole charge) romantically situated close to the sea. Upon a pleasant open grassy declivity stood his hut, a very superior one, always neat and clean, enjoying from its door and *glass* windows, an extensive view of the coast and strait. In a pretty enclosed garden were vegetables, flowers, and bees, from whose stores he drew the 'makings' of a small cask of delicious mead. At the mouth of his little river he netted quantities of fish; the marshes were full of wild fowl, besides which, he trapped, snared, and shot kangaroo, wallaby, cockatoos, pigeons, and various other sorts of wild animals and birds; for among other functions he discharged those of head gamekeeper and lord of the manor. The carcass of a sheep was generally hanging in cut, and none could excel him in the manufacture of a capital loaf. When young, he had been in the foot guards; in Van Diemen's Land he was of forty years' standing, during the early part of which period he frequently encountered both natives and bushrangers, who severely wounded him. He always afforded me a most hospitable welcome, so that I regarded a visit to his comfortable dwelling as a treat, and used to walk fifty miles through a wild district, merely for the pleasure of stopping four-and-twenty hours in his company, on one of which occasions he regaled me with an excellent dish of hashed porcupine for supper. That charming retreat was my O[sborne], once there, I flung care to the winds; thought nothing of profit and loss, and was almost as happy as P[rince] A[lbert]. Up in the mountains, at another part of the island, I had my B[almoral] too. [...]

In January, 1855, being worth £80, I determined to shew myself in the south at the Regatta annually held in commemoration of the first landing in 1804, of the settlers from New South Wales; being rather doubtful how my friends would look upon a poor pedlar, but found that nobody esteemed me the less; the sympathy of a community, all the members of which have once been indigent, being readily bestowed upon honest industry. In all the Australian markets, then prevailed a glut of European goods, which during many months were sacrificed at auctions for half or a third of the *prime cost*. Acting with caution, I never bought too much of any article, however saleable, an assortment being preferable to suit the wants of all. For upon my memory, was deeply impressed a lesson received at the commencement of my traffic. In an out-of-the-way corner, a few sixpenny brooches, readily went off at five and six shillings each. I, wishing for seven league boots, hurried back to Launceston, a three days' march away, and in foolish ignorance eagerly secured fourteen or fifteen dozen (the whole stock of the vendor), *most of which still remain on hand, and may be had a bargain.* The expectation of rapidly coining a considerable sum by a speedy sale yielding twelve hundred per cent. profit, was bitterly disappointed; as to my incredulous surprise and mortification, scarcely anybody near home would look at the trumpery things. This taught me prudence. I never after bought anything which I did not quickly sell. Even those rascally brooches turned in something in the course of time, the purchase money being soon brought back, by the sale at such high prices, of only one or two in a trip; moreover the bush children of hospitable parents thought them very handsome presents. I never took anybody in but once; that occurred in the following manner: after half an hour's hesitation, a young lady, rather a pretty girl with a saucy turn-up nose, evidently longing for a pretty, frosted, silver brooch from India, refused to purchase it 'because the price was only one pound, had I wanted three or four she would have bought it.' In a pet, I mentally gave brevet rank on the spot to all my jewellery, and resolved not again to lose a sale for the want of asking enough. Accordingly, at the very next house, the cost of one of my sixpenny affairs having been demanded, I unblushingly answered 'two pounds,' which the good lady immediately handed to me, although I did faintly recommend a really valuable trinket, instead, that she would not have. It was shooting the sitting hare. I never think of that business, without feeling small, and should be glad to receive absolution.

Amends must be made some day, for I have never seen my fair customer since, and am ignorant whether she has found out what a rogue the pedlar was—a second Autolycus. This one thing is to be said in my behalf: money being then so abundant, especially among the farmers—a pound note, at that time, seemed of less consequence than a half-crown did a few years before.

*Experiences of a Convict Transported for Twenty-one Years* (1965).

# Ned Kelly

(1855–80)

*Australia's most famous outlaw, Ned Kelly, was executed on 11 November 1880 for the murder of two police constables, Scanlon and Lonigan, and a police sergeant, Kennedy, at Stringybark Creek, Victoria, in October 1878. Within a week of the murders the Kelly gang, consisting of Ned and his brother, Dan Kelly, Joe Byrne and Steve Hart, was outlawed but avoided capture for two years. In December 1878 the gang held up a bank at Euroa and, in February 1879, made a similar raid on a bank in Jerilderie, New South Wales. On both occasions they took more than £2000 and entertained their victims with some style. At Jerilderie Kelly gave a written statement of more than 8000 words vindicating his behaviour to a bank-teller. The original has been lost but, long after Kelly's death, copies made by a clerk in the Crown Law Department became available, and the vindication has since been known as the 'Jerilderie Letter'.*

Next day Skillion, Williamson and Mrs Kelly, with an infant were taken and thrown into prison and were six months awaiting trial and no bail allowed and was convicted on the evidence of the meanest man that ever the sun shone on. I have been told by Police that he is hardly ever sober, also between him and his father they sold his sister to a chinaman, but he seems a strapping and genteel looking young man and more fit to be a starcher to a Laundry than a trooper, but to a keen observer, he has the wrong appearance to have anything like clear conscience or a manly heart. The deceit is too plain to be seen in the White Cabbage hearted looking face, I heard nothing of this transaction until very close on the trial I being then over 400 miles from Greta. I heard that I was outlawed and 100 pound reward for me in Victoria and also hundreds of charges of Horse Stealing was against me, beside shooting a trooper. I came into Victoria and enquired after my brother and found him working with another man at Bullock Creek. Heard how the police used to be blowing that they would shoot me first and then cry Surrender. How they used to come to the house where there was no one there but women and Superintendent Smith used to say. See all the men I have today, I will have as many more tomorrow and blow him into pieces as small as the paper that is in our guns and they used to repeatedly rush into the house revolver in hand upset milk dishes, empty the flour out on the ground, break tins of eggs, and throw the meat out of the cask onto the floor, and dirty and destroy all the provisions, which can be proved and shove the girls in front of them into rooms like dogs and abuse and insult them. Detective Ward and Constable Hayes took out their revolvers and threatened to shoot the girls and children, while Mrs Skillion was absent, the oldest being with her, the greatest murderers and ruffians would not be guilty of such an action. This sort of cruelty and disgraceful conduct to my brothers and sisters who had no protection coupled with the conviction of my Mother and those innocent men certainly made my blood boil as I don't think there is a man born could have the patience to suffer what I did. They were not satisfied with frightening and insulting my sisters night and day and destroying their provisions and lagging my Mother with an infant baby and those innocent men, but should follow me and my brother who was innocent of having anything to do with any stolen horses, into the wilds, where he had been quietly digging and doing well, neither molesting or interfering with anyone and I was not there long and on the 26th October I came on the tracks of police horses, between Table Top and the Bogs, I crossed there and went to Emu Swamp and returning home came on more police tracks making for our camp, I told my mates and me and my brother went and ... ... ... found police camped at the Shingle Hut with long fire arms and we came to the conclusion our doom was sealed unless we could take their fire-arms, as we had nothing but a gun and a rifle if they came on us at our work or camp. We had no chance only to die like dogs as we thought the country was woven with police and we might have a chance of fighting them if we had firearms, as it generally takes 40 to one. We approached the Spring as close as we could get to the camp, the intervening space being clear. We saw two men at the Log, they got up and one took a double barrel fowling piece and one drove the horses down and hobbled them against the tent and we thought there was more men in the tent, those being on sentry. We could have shot those two men, without speaking, but not wishing to take life we waited. McIntyre laid the gun against the stump and Lonigan sat on the log. I advanced, my brother Dan keeping McIntyre covered. I called on them to throw up their hands McIntyre obeyed and never attempted to reach for his gun or revolver, Lonigan ran to a battery of logs and put his head up to take aim at me, when I shot him, or he would have shot me, as I knew well. I asked who was in the tent, McIntyre replied no one. I approached the camp and took possession of their revolvers and fowling piece which I loaded with bullets instead of shot. I told McIntyre I did not want to shoot him or any man that would surrender. I explained Fitzpatrick's falsehood which no policeman can be ignorant of. He said he knew that Fitzpatrick had wronged us but he could not help it. He said he intended to leave the Force on account of his bad health, his life was insured, the other two men who had no firearms came up when they heard the shot fired and went back to our camp for fear the police might call there in our absence and surprise us on our arrival. My brother went back to the Spring and I stopped at the Log with McIntyre. Kennedy and Scanlan came up, McIntyre said he would get them to surrender if I spared their lives as well as his. I said I did not know either him, Scanlan or Kennedy, and had nothing up against them, and would not shoot any of them, if they gave up their firearms and promised to leave the Force, as it was the meanest billet in the world. They are worse than cold-blooded murderers and hangmen. He said he was sure they would never follow me any more. I gave them my word that I would give them a chance. McIntyre went up to Kennedy, Scanlan being behind with a rifle and a revolver. I called on them to throw up their hands. Scanlan slewed his horse around to gallop away, but turned again and as quick as thought fired at me with the rifle and was in the act of firing again, when I shot him. Kennedy alighted on the off side of his horse and got behind a tree and opened hot fire. McIntyre got on Kennedy's horse and galloped away. I could have shot him if I choose as he was right against me but rather than break my word I let him go. My brother advanced from the Spring, Kennedy fired at him and ran as he found neither of us was dead. I followed him, he got behind another tree and fired at me again. I shot him in the armpit as he was behind the tree, he dropped his revolver and ran again and slewed round and I fired with the gun again and shot him through the right chest as I did not know that he had dropped his revolver and was turning to surrender. He could not live or I would have let him go. Had they been my own brothers, I could not help shooting them or else lie down and let them shoot me, which they would have done had their bullets been directed as they intended them. But as for handcuffing Kennedy to a tree or cutting his ear off or brutally treating any of them, is a cruel falsehood. If Kennedy's ear was cut off, it has been done since I put his cloak over him and left him as honourable as I could and if they were my own brothers I could be more sorry for them, with the exception of Lonigan I did not begrudge him what bit of lead he got as he was the beastliest meanest man that I had any account against for him. Fitzpatrick, Sergeant Whelan, Constable Day and King, the Bootmaker, once tried to hand-cuff me at Benalla and when they could not Fitzpatrick tried to choke me, Lonigan caught me by the privates and would have killed me but was not able. Mr McInnes came up and I allowed him to put the hand-cuffs on when the police were bested. This cannot be called wilful murder for I was compelled to shoot them in my own defence or lie down like a cur and die. Certainly their wives and children are to be pitied, but those men came into the bush with the intention of shooting me down like a dog, yet they know and acknowledge I have been wronged. And is my Mother and infant baby and my poor little brothers and sisters not to be pitied more so, who has got no alternative only to put up with brutal and unmanly conduct of the police who have never had any relations or a Mother or must have forgot them.

*Ned Kelly Being his own Story of Life and Times* (1942).

# 2

# CHILDHOOD AND FAMILY RELATIONS

# Kathleen Fitzpatrick

## (1905–90)

*From 1930 to 1962 Kathleen Fitzpatrick was a member of the Department of History, University of Melbourne, where she acquired a reputation as a fine teacher. She wrote the biography,* Sir John Franklin in Tasmania, 1837–1843 *(1949), and a monograph on the novelist Martin Boyd (1963) and edited a popular anthology,* Australian Explorers *(1958).* Solid Bluestone Foundations *covers the years 1908–28, ending with her return to Australia from Oxford. The title derives from the mansion, Hughenden, built by her grandfather in the 1890s.*

The dominant personality at 'Hughenden' was Grandpa, who was qualified, both by his position in the Firm and by nature, for the title of 'the Boss', by which he was known to his children. He was of medium height and weight and had an upright and sprightly carriage and a fine presence. He was handsome, with regular features, bright blue eyes and pink cheeks, and he must have had fair hair when young, but when I knew him he was bald and his pointed beard was white. Except when in his gardening clothes, which were deplorable, Grandpa was always very neatly dressed, in a pepper-and-salt suit for everyday and a navy blue for best. He had a gold watch on a chain and often took it out to check on the clocks, which he usually found inaccurate. His linen was snowy and his boots gleamed, for Grandpa held that only effeminate men wore shoes. He might have risked the shoes, really, because there was never the slightest possibility of anyone's calling the Boss effeminate. He had fathered ten children, of whom nine grew to maturity, and his voice, when raised (as it frequently was) had a decidedly bull-like quality. He was outspoken and straightforward, and both in business and in private life a man of the utmost integrity. He was capable in business and practical matters and had been, before the breaking of the Land Boom, an active and useful member of the South Melbourne Council.

Grandpa was also emotional, unreasonable, arbitrary, quick both to laughter and to sudden gusts of ill-temper, and he was what people who have never had to live with one call a fine old English eccentric. He rose and went to bed at extraordinary times and never got up for breakfast, which had to be carried to his bedroom, a long way from the kitchen, by some member of the family at whatever hour he signified his desire for it by ringing a bell. He was wont to observe that his needs were simple, merely tea and buttered toast and a dish of olives, but meeting his needs was less simple because the tea and toast had to be piping hot, despite the distance it had to be carried. The toast was put into a muffin-dish with boiling water underneath and as Grandpa did not like his tea in a pot but in a cup, ready poured and sugared and milked, the full cup had to be inserted into a covered basin of boiling water. It was quite a feat to carry these hot liquids at high speed without spilling anything, but it was possible, as I know from having carried Grandpa's breakfast many a time when I was a child. A strange feature of his bedroom was the amazing number of patent medicines, boxes of pills, and other health-promising nostrums that cluttered his dressing-table and shelves. Was he a hypochondriac or an experimentalist? Was his health so good and his life so long because of or despite all the medicines he consumed? Who can say? The Boss was *sui generis* and no one reasoned why. Sometimes he attended family lunch and sometimes he preferred to work in the garden and have it at about three instead. He did as he pleased. Once in his life [...] he had broken this rule and adapted himself to meet the requirements of others, but he had not found that it answered and never repeated the experiment.

I loved Grandpa when I was a child and although I knew that he had a hasty temper and wished he would not make scenes, I thought of him as being much like God the Father and entitled to let loose a few thunderbolts when he felt displeased. Besides, Grandpa was at his nicest with children; we were never the subjects of his denunciation and we got on with him swimmingly. He roared with laughter at primitive jokes, just like us, was a bit greedy at meals too, said whatever came into his head and was sometimes sorry afterwards. As well, his outlook on life was of the kind now called simplistic; it is an outlook which is very restful for children, to whom the whole world is new and puzzling. His politics were conservative, not to say reactionary. England was top nation and foreigners should thank Heaven fasting if England conquered them and gave them decent government, and that went specially for the ungrateful Irish, a devious, shiftless lot, a perfect nuisance, and quite incapable of looking after themselves. Although he had left England when he was seventeen and never went back, even for a visit, Grandpa never ceased to think of himself as an Englishman who happened, for his own convenience, to be living in the colonies. As for his wife and children and grandchildren, they were of course colonials and it was their duty to love, honour and obey the Mother Country[,] which knew what was for their good. Grandpa was immensely loyal to the Crown, and approved of Germans, because of the Teutonic origins and connections of the royal family. When 1914 came it must have been hard for him to take to hating the Germans whom he had always admired, and to start loving the flighty Frogs whom he had hitherto despised.

Disraeli was Grandpa's hero. He had called his house 'Hughenden' because that was the name of Disraeli's home and was so suitable in Beaconsfield Parade, named after Disraeli's title. I am sure Grandpa would have detested Disraeli had he known him; he would have found him too clever by half, not English enough in appearance nor manly enough in dress. But Disraeli had the right ideas, according to Grandpa, because he stood for the throne and the Empire, unlike the namby-pamby Gladstone, who was so weak about Ireland.

Grandpa was, in short like a stage version of an Englishman in a play written by a foreigner. He belonged to the Church of England. Low Church, he always said, but his adhesion seemed more a matter of patriotism than religion, for he did not frequent his parish church, as was pointed out in an aggrieved letter from his sister Lizzie, the wife of the Vicar. Fate played a sorry trick on Grandpa, when he was a younger man, by causing him to fall in love with Mary O'Brien, an Australian-born girl of Irish Catholic parents. He proposed and was accepted but when he learnt that he must undertake to bring up his children in the Catholic faith he refused, and the engagement was broken off. No doubt he expected Mary—or Polly as he called her in his softer moments—to give in. Grandma looked and was a gentle creature, but her principles were made of steel and she did not give in. She was a great beauty, with black hair, creamy skin, dark blue eyes, a swan neck and a wasp waist. So it was Grandpa who gave in and they were married under a cherry-plum tree in flower in the orchard behind great grandfather O'Brien's bush pub, the 'Limerick Arms' at Nar Nar Goon in Gippsland, when Grandpa was twenty-two and Grandma was nineteen. But they did not live happily ever after.

*Solid Bluestone Foundations and Other Memories of a*
*Melbourne Girlhood 1908–1928* (1983).

# Jack Davis

(1917– )

*Jack Davis was born into the Nyoongah people of the south-west of Western Australia and was brought up at Yarloop. At fourteen he went to the notorious Moore River Native Settlement, where he spent nine months and which became the basis of two of his plays,* The Dreamers *(1982) and* No Sugar *(1985). After his family broke up following his father's death, Davis made his living as a stockman, horse-breeder, and boxer. He later became an activist for the Aboriginal people and was director of the Aboriginal Centre in Perth (1967–71), first chairman of the Aboriginal Lands Trust in Western Australia in 1971, and managing editor of the Aboriginal Publications Foundation (1972–77). Davis has also published several volumes of poetry. His other plays include* Kullark *(1979),* Barungin: Smell the Wind *(1988), and* Our Town *(1992). He has also written short stories and plays for children and has won numerous awards.*

The huge jarrah tree which stood a hundred metres from our house was a real wonder of nature. It took 32 of my boyish steps to circle its sprawling girth. Years of storms had trimmed the growth of its branches, but it reared sixty metres into the blue of the sky. Year after year the kookaburras and the magpies nested and reared their offspring in the hollows of the lofty branches and we always had scraps of food for the succession of each new colony every year. There was always some reminder of me and my brothers and sisters around the tree. Scratch marks in the hoary old bark and all the odds and ends of children at play scattered around it.

I remember my baby brother, who was temporarily in my care, spied a large green caterpillar crawling in one of the folds of bark on the forest giant. From my shoulder he reached out with one small greedy hand and popped the caterpillar in his mouth. My hundred-metres-away yell brought mother from the house with a rush. She promptly rescued the caterpillar and baby Frank from probable asphyxiation. Then in fright she attempted to slap me across the ear into the bargain. When mother made a sweep at us kids the clip always had a round arm approach which gave us plenty of time to duck. Knowing the technique, I evaded the one over the caterpillar.

Father was a first class shot with a rifle and he was the proud owner of two beautifully kept .303 rifles. Occasionally he would take the rifles down from the racks, polish, repolish, clean and reclean them. He would invariably challenge mother to a shooting contest. Mother herself, from the resting position, was almost as good a shot as father. If mother accepted the challenge, a bottle would be placed in one of the folds of the old jarrah tree and the contest would begin. Father, nine times out of ten, would shoot and snap off the neck of the bottle, then mother would try for the centre of the target. Father would then shatter the base of the bottle.

Now mother was an avid picture fan and pictures were held once a week in Yarloop. That week's show was *The King of Kings*. Money for the flicks in those days was scarce and especially hard to find if you were a member of a large family like ours. But mother was shrewd and often put it over father without him knowing. This occasion was one of them. But it did turn out differently.

In the days of silent films, pictures could be rather dull if you could not read the dialogue. As mother could neither read nor write and I was considered the quickest if not the best reader, although I was the fourth eldest in our family, I therefore invariably accompanied mother on her occasional picture nights.

In the silent era, the movies, or flicks as they were called, were always of a three to four hours duration. First would be the Pathé news or gazette (often a week old) then there would be a comedy. There would then be a half-hour break, which gave the film operator time to change reels. Then the main attraction would commence. Mother and I always arrived at the flicks early so we could get a good seat, which was usually in the centre of the hall. Mother always made sure I went to the toilet before the commencement of the film because she didn't want any break in the reading of the subtitles.

Mother's favourite actress was Marie Dressler. I think it was because she was such a motherly figure that mother felt empathy towards her. When poor Marie was hard done by mother would wipe a tear from her eye. Her favourite actor was swashbuckling Douglas Fairbanks, while my favourite actors were the cowboy heroes such as Tom Mix, Buck Jones and Fred Thompson. There wasn't much dialogue in the cowboy pictures. They mainly consisted of galloping horses and popping guns, so the story line could be followed fairly easy. Just as well because I would be cheering on my cowboy hero and mother of course would be cheering along with me.

Getting back to the rifles, shooting of course, to father, was a man's sport and male-like, he disliked being beaten by a member of the so called weaker sex at anything, and of all things, shooting. Unthinkable!

The day of the contest-to-be came. Though father didn't know there was going to be one, because they were usually of a spontaneous nature. Just before father came home from work at five in the afternoon, mother instructed me to fill the target bottle with almost-boiling water. She then tightly sealed the bottle and I placed it in the open oven of the kitchen stove. Mother then placed the two rifles on the verandah table. As soon as father walked onto the verandah she called out from the kitchen, 'I've got the rifles ready, Bill. Feel like a challenge?'

'I feel a bit tired,' father replied, then added, 'Okay, you're on.' Then he put his big number nine foot on the edge of mother's snare and said, 'What's the bet?'

Mother tightened the noose a little, not daring to look at me hovering near the open oven door. 'Well,' mother replied, 'you let me have two shots and if I break the bottle completely, I'm going to see *The King of Kings* on Saturday night.' Unable to contain myself any longer I piped up, 'Yes mother, don't forget I'm coming as your reader.' 'It's a bet,' said father cheerfully, and to me, 'Go and put a bottle on the tree.'

The two contestants stepped off the verandah; father in his dungarees and flannel shirt; mother, house frock and apron attired. I turned and scooped the almost red hot bottle from the interior of the oven. Mother had already placed a kitchen chair outside, to rest her rifle on. But father scorned a resting shot. As I ran past them, juggling the red hot bottle, mother implored with unconscious reverence, 'Don't for God's sake drop it.' I thought with equal piety, 'Sure enough for *The King of Kings* sake I won't.'

I placed the bottle in the usual fold in the old forest giant. By this time the rest of the children were grouped behind the two contestants. The girls with fingers in their ears in preparation for the crack of the rifles and the boys calling out encouragement, yet still trying to remain impartial. Mother waited until I came back from the tree and joined the other children. Then I almost muffed the whole thing. As mother brought her rifle up in perfect line with the red bottle, gleaming in the western rays of the sun, I stepped within half a metre of her. The gentle pressure of her index finger on the trigger coincided with my movement and the shot rang out.

Mother stared in disbelief at the unmarked target, then made one of her round arm swipes at me and, because I too was staring at the bottle, the clip in the ear this time was successful. The rest of the family, still divided and impartial, groaned their oohs and aahs, and father, well he just roared with laughter. At that moment I felt like turning traitor and barracking for father on the off chance he would let me go and see the flicks anyway. But I thought better of it.

Mother looked at father grimly and said, 'Anyway I've still got one shot left.' He looked at mother and saw the gleam of tears of disappointment in her eyes. She angrily jerked her chair back into a new position and resting her rifle on the chair back took careful aim. By this time the suspense was almost too much for me. I was now safely ensconced on the verandah.

It was from there I saw it all happen and I will never be able to explain the wonder of it. Mother always squeezed the trigger as a good shot should do. As the pressure of her index finger on the trigger reached the point of no return, father with the quick easy flow of movement born of years of practice, brought his rifle to his shoulder and pressed the trigger. The two shots blended in perfect unison and the echo reverberated through the bush. The bottle exploded into smithereens and mother sprang to her feet and yelled with excitement, 'I did it Billy, I did it.'

Father, in seconds, had his rifle cradled in his arms. He looked at mother and said gruffly, 'Good shot love, a darn good shot. Now eject the shell and after we have had supper I'll clean your rifle for you.' My father was not the king of kings, but to me, a ten-year-old boy, on that day, he really was a king among men and we did see the movie. Mother and I together.

*A Boy's Life* (1991).

# Graham McInnes

## (1912 70)

*Graham McInnes was the son of the novelist Angela Thirkell and her first husband, James Campbell McInnes, and the brother of the novelist Colin McInnes. After his mother married George Thirkell, he was brought to Australia in 1920 and was educated in Melbourne. In 1934 he left for Canada, where he worked as a university lecturer, art editor of a Toronto newspaper, and producer for the Canadian Film Board before joining the Canadian diplomatic service in 1948. After* The Road to Gundagai *he wrote three more autobiographies,* Humping My Bluey *(1966),* Finding a Father *(1967), and* Goodbye, Melbourne Town *(1968).*

The evening ritual of reading aloud was absolutely rigid. Nothing was allowed to interfere with it—at least, no activity of ours. From it there gradually spread over us a network of fine filaments labelled 'conduct'. This code of conduct, since it was derived from books, was essentially literary; the acts which our exemplars and hence ourselves were and were not allowed to perform. These had nothing whatever to do with ordinary human relationships. We did not learn how to deal with, much less to live with, our fellow man. What we learned were basically literary postures to be assumed in fictive situations. It was a code of highly articulate cleverness rather than of intellectual honesty. The emphasis was on the skills required to solve acrostics, word games, dumb crambo, crossword puzzles. Familiar quotations, including 'capping' one's rival, were a favourite. Literary allusions encouraged the kind of conversational gambits which pass for brilliance before the less educated, but which in fact depend entirely on a retentive memory and on an unwritten law (known to you but not to your interlocutor) that those who know more or who can parrot more (irrespective of how deep their knowledge goes or on what it is based) have the right to be rude to others and to say cutting things to them.

It will readily be apparent that for a boy to assume such postures in democratic Australia would have earned him a good kick in the backside. The postures, when adopted by Mother, were less likely to be so rewarded; but her essentially literary conception of life made her dealings with Australians, and particularly with local trades people, a long cantankerous running battle. Several scenes recur almost all with Mother at the centre being rude to someone, no doubt often with justification. There was Mr Young the butcher, proprietor of Young's Meat Emporium. He had smarmy 'brush-back' curly hair, a wax moustache, a pair of evasive eyes and a bogus bonhomie which wouldn't have fooled a three-year-old. His inevitable greeting to Mother was 'Good morning Mrs—er—um—baby's looking well today.' Her reply was, 'When you can address me correctly you may take my order.' Mr Young wanted the business but he was an ex-Digger who had fought in the AIF and this kind of language made him apoplectic. He cursed under his breath and got on with the order, but he took it out on us boys if we went alone on a Saturday morning to pick up the goods.

'Here comes little Mr High-and-Mighty' was a favourite locution. On one occasion the brass letters fell off his plate-glass window so that instead of reading 'Young's Meat Emporium' the legend was 'You g's M at Emporium'. Mother's gambit as she entered the shop was, 'I see you believe in truth in advertising'. There was Mr Coughlin the milkman whose milk she found undrinkable, the clerk at the Post Office from whose precincts she would often stride forth into the street muttering 'Sold again!' There was the chemist with the respected but improbable name whom she greeted, on finally meeting him, 'Good morning, Mr Golightly; I was beginning to wonder whether you existed.' There was also the supreme occasion when we were sitting on the dummy of a cable car, and the man in the next seat cleared his throat and spat on to the street. As the globule (known to us as an oyster) arched over her and fell with a resounding smack on the pavement, Mother said in a loud voice, 'If you do that again I shall scream!' 'That's all right, lady,' said the culprit. 'Just you watch this.' He cleared his throat and spat again but it was into the wind of the onrushing car and the debris sailed back on to his own overcoat. Fortunately it was not Mother's, but she did scream. The brakeman stopped the car and we got off, purple with shame.

She met her match, though, in a tight-lipped tram conductor whom she had the hardihood to tackle on his home ground.

Conductor: 'Fez please! Hurry along there!'
Mother: 'Kindly don't push!'
Conductor: 'I ain't pushin'.'
Mother: 'And don't speak to me like that!'
Conductor: 'What's wrong with it?'

Mother: 'For one thing it's not good English.'

Conductor: 'It's good Australian; that's enough for me.'

Game, set, match and rubber.

Broadly speaking Mother looked on Australians, with few exceptions, as members of the Lower Classes. She agreed heartily with an English visitor who once told her (within our incredulous hearing) that Australia was 'a wonderful country for Warrant Officers'. The social attitude implicit in such a statement troubled her not one whit. The whole of this great grey sun-baked continent she regarded much as if it were Hornsey or Tooting Bec, and she a Kensingtonian of high degree. What made it unbearable on both sides was that in those distant days there was just enough truth in it to hurt. Mother *had* been a Kensingtonian and though never belonging to the 'establishment' had been able to arrogate to herself something of its attitudes, based on the genuine distinction of her grandfather and her father. The Australian big towns of the Twenties did bear a superficial resemblance to London suburbs and what riled her was to find suburban types and members of the Lower Orders actually running the country. It never occurred to her that she was a guest in their house, nor, I think, did she really grasp the nuggety toughness of the city dweller or the rangy, loping, deep-eyed stare of the country dweller, both of which spoke of hard horizons and a land where the sunshine got into your bones so that a runty fellow from Nottingham or St Helens became in two generations a 'white Zulu'.

On the other hand this determination to preserve literary standards did earn her a deserved reputation as a remarkable intellectual eccentric in the essentially semi-colonial society of those days. Who, without supreme confidence in themselves, could have held a literary tea-party for fifty women—artists, musicians, writers, dancers, professors' wives—in a small suburban house, and dared to mask the presence of the outside lavatory and other amenities by hanging carpets on a clothes line propped up with a stringy-bark sapling? Such brilliant improvisation argues character, and though she didn't live in Toorak or South Yarra, those who made the pilgrimage to the funny, ugly little house on Grace Street included many of the leaders of academic and cultural life in Melbourne.

*The Road to Gundagai* (1965).

CHILDHOOD AND FAMILY RELATIONS

# *Hal Porter*

## (1911–84)

*Hal Porter was born in Melbourne but moved with his family at the age of six to Bairnsdale, Gippsland, the main setting for* The Watcher *and which he later described and sketched in* Bairnsdale: Portrait of an Australian Country Town *(1977). A prolific writer, he published three novels, seven collections of short fiction, three plays, and three collections of poetry. He also won most literary awards in Australia. His other autobiographies are* The Paper Chase *(1966) and* The Extra *(1975). Porter had numerous occupations including cook, actor, hotel manager, hospital orderly, theatrical producer, schoolteacher, and librarian. His biography by Mary Lord (1993) reveals significant gaps and inventions in his autobiographies.*

In the country Mother changes. Or rather, so far as I am concerned, she appears as another kind of Mother.

Since the time I wholly saw her first, lifting the spotted veil back from her powdered face under the winged hat, the cloud earlier concealing her has thinned, shredded away, vanished. She is now a woman almost always in an apron of black Italian cloth, her blouse sleeves rolled back above her beautiful forearms which turn day by day from white to country brown, a woman labelled with the names of days.

She is Monday as she helps the washerwoman whose hands are as pleated and bleached and sodden as some tripe-like fungus, a hook-nosed, hook-chinned, toothless woman as witch-like in appearance as behaviour as she prods with the pot-stick through the smoke and steam at the outdoor copper of boiling garments.

She is Tuesday as she sprinkles pillow-slips, Father's shirt, my sister's starched sun-bonnets, and the boys' cotton sou'westers, for her flat-irons. These have already been clashed down on the top of the kitchen range so hot that a mirage almost forms above its black leaded surface. While the irons are heating, a peaceful overture to the rites begins. Mother and the washerwoman take each a bedsheet separately and, one gripping the bottom edge, one the top, retreat backwards from each other, straining the sheet horizontally taut in a version of domestic tug-o'-war, inclining their heads to scan it for signs of wear, then, this done, mincing towards each other with uplifted arms to begin the folding. On the day of this grave pavane we invariably have for dinner a succulent hash made from Sunday's cold joint. This Mother calls a German Fry—a dish her Switzer father badgered her English mother into learning how to make.

She is Wednesday, her hair concealed beneath a worn, old-fashioned head-dress, once her mother's and called a fascinator, as she shakes the little fringed furry mats that lie before each inside door, as she mops fluff from under beds, sprinkles damp tea-leaves on the Brussels carpet before brushing it, sweeps the verandas, hunts cobwebs, polishes the brass taps and door-handles, rearranges dust with a feather duster.

She is green-fingered Thursday, and happiest, dividing her violet and primrose plants; manuring her five precious azaleas with the horse-droppings I have shovelled from the road, or cow-droppings from the common; making a scarecrow that, wearing Father's old clothes, subtly resembles him, and to which, hopping about like a Pearly Queen, she sings in imitation cockney, 'I wouldn't leave a little wooden hut for you-oo-oo …'; crushing a handful of lemon verbena leaves of eau-de-Cologne mint between her palms, and inhaling the scent of her hands which must smell also of earth and thyme and toil and happiness. Thursday reveals most of all that she is country-bred, and that her passion for the country imbues her too deeply for denial: she knows a thousand delicately brutal tricks to circumvent birds and caterpillars, wasps and slugs, frost and midsummer, from despoiling her rows of peas, her lettuce and Frau Karl Druschki roses, her Lazy Wife beans and maiden-hair fern, her hydrangeas and carrots and Sweet William and chives and almost sacred camellia tree. Her bible is Mrs Rolf Boldrewood's *The Flower Garden in Australia* (A Book for Ladies and Amateurs dedicated by permission to the Countess of Jersey). Her favourite seeds come from *Vilmorin-Andrieux et Cie, Marchands-Grainiers, Quai de la Megisserie 4, Paris*. So absurd is nostalgia and my persisting desire to complete the circles of experience that when, years later, I visit Paris, I eschew the *Tour Eiffel* and other *turismo* lures first to find the Quai de la Megisserie where I compel myself not to cry.

She is Friday, curling-pinned, slap-dashing vivaciously and deftly through domesticity so that she can dress herself up, flee from her family into the after-dinner twilight, and go shopping. Friday is late shopping night. What she shops for on these evenings is nothing essential, nothing mundane. The baker, the bloody butcher in a nimbus of flies, the milkman, canter into Mitchell Street daily; the grocer, the fishmonger, the rabbit-oh, the John Chinaman greengrocer and fruiterer, the iceman and the egg-woman appear once or twice weekly; the knife-grinder, the tinker, the chimney-sweep, the clothes-prop man, the old clo' man, the clothes-peg gipsy and the Afghan pedlar drift through as regularly on time as the seasons, and the dust-laying water-waggon, and the ice-cream carts, and the swallows or their children which build their demi-cups of mud under the wooden shade over my bedroom window. Powdered and scented (eau-de-Cologne or Lily of the Valley), in her best earrings and gloves and dazzling polished shoes, her enamelled watch pinned to her bust, chewing a Sen-sen or a clove, Mother goes shopping for … for what? The tumpti-tiddily-tumpti of the Shire Band aloft in the hexagonal bandstand at the end of the Main Street? The displays of xylonite hairpin boxes of imitation tortoise-shell? The Gaby Deslys figurines with thistle-down hair? The celluloid kewpies dressed in Bairnsdale football colours? The elegantly cruel spurs and plaited whips in the saddler's? The dusty witch-balls and fuchsia-coloured paper bells suspended over the soda-fountain and marble table-tops of Russos? The glamour of gaslight, and electric light, and the passing and repassing between the wax dummies in the shop-windows and the spurred and slouch-hatted blokes rolling cigarettes and spitting with neat good manners between their feet as they lean against every Main Street veranda-post?

She returns home at nine-thirty sharp, her eyes glittering, refreshed by artificial light or moonlight or starlight, exhilarated to girlishness, crying out gaily, 'Tea! Tea! Tea!' and, taking off her shoes now filmed with the dust of roads and adventure, 'My corn is giving me Larry Dooley!' 'I heard a mopoke,' she says, prodding the fire, removing the stove-lid, and pushing the kettle over the hole. 'I saw a falling star. Someone is dead,' she says, or, 'I sneaked a piece of that variegated honeysuckle over Coster's fence: I think it'll strike,' or, 'The band was playing "The Blue Danube" tonight', and, 'One, two, three. One, two, three,' she sings whirling in her beautifully darned stockinged feet. She reveals what she has bought, other than excitement, from among the moustache cups and hurricane lamps and enamel bowls and winceyette night-gowns and glass-rubied gilt studs of Main Street. Maybe there are liquorice straps or blood oranges or little china canaries we children are to fill with water and, then, blowing down their hollow tails, make bubbling music. Whatever she buys is for us children; transfers, packets of compressed bits which expand to Japanese flowers on the surface of saucers of water, marbles of which I once knew the names, a bag of sugar-coated Paris Almonds, white and pink—simple gifts, payment that haunts now, for her several hours of freedom for the weekly promenade.

Only once does she lose her head, and buys herself a hideous white china rose, beautiful, for some reason, to her. 'When you dance tonight,' I hear her sometimes sing—oh, mockingly—as she lifts the atrocity—oh, gently, gently—to dust about it, 'wear a rose of white. 'Twill show you forgive me again ...' What is she really saying in song, for she is saying something?

She is Saturday and, breakfast over, a sergeant-major. Before breakfast, each child has had its weekly dose of Gregory Powder, a nauseous gunpowder-coloured purgative. Now, purged and fed, each child has its Saturday task. Her voice heightened, her movements brisk, she hurries about chivvying us, less because we are really of much help than that our being made to do something has its moral and disciplinary value, and is, moreover, a custom of that class in that era. Mother's humble hoard of real silver, and the electroplated silver, is cleaned with Goddard's Plate Powder and methylated spirits: the tea service, the salt-cellars and mustard-pot, the two cruets, the spoons and forks, the four biscuit-barrel rims and lids and handles, the salt spoons, soup ladles, fish-slice, cake pedestals, the rose-bowl and the trumpet vases. The fire-irons and fender are polished, and the steel knives are burnished with a sort of gritty cocoa rubbed on with a large cork set in a wooden handle like a drawer-handle. Butcher's paper is scissored into squares for the lavatory, and into cut-out filigree resembling Richelieu embroidery for the pantry shelves. Howsoever good I am, howsoever rapidly and competently I perform my part in these duties, I burn to escape and race reinless into the elm-lined streets, the Tannies, the river-flats, the miles-wide paddocks surrounding Bairnsdale.

Saturday afternoon is for baking. This is a labour of double nature: to provide a week's supply of those more solid delicacies Australian mothers of those days regard as being as nutritiously necessary as meat twice daily, four vegetables at dinner, porridge and eggs and toast for breakfast, and constant cups of tea. Empty biscuit-barrels and cake-tins being as unthinkable as beds not made before eleven a.m., Mother, therefore, constructs a great fruit cake, and a score or more each of rockcakes, Banburies, queen cakes, date rolls and ginger nuts. These conventional solidities done, she exercises her talent for ritual fantasy, for the more costly and ephemeral dainties that are to adorn as fleetingly as day-lilies the altar of the Sunday tea-table. Now appear three-storeyed sponge cakes mortared together with scented cream and in whose seductive icing are embedded walnuts, silver *cachous*, *glacé* cherries, strawberries, segments of orange and strips of angelica. Now appear cream puffs and éclairs, creations of the most momentary existence, deliberately designed neither for hoarding against a rainy day nor for social showing-off. Sunday tea is the frivolous and glittering crown of the week; there is the impression given of throwing away money like delicious dirt; there is the atmosphere rather than the fact of luxury; Sunday tea, is above all, my parents' statement to each other and their children that life is being lived on a plane of hard-earned and justifiable abundance. I watch abundance which means that I watch Mother, its actual as well as its symbolic impulse.

At this stage, astute within a vague placidity, so head-over-heels am I in harum-scarum content that my inner eye drifts away from observation of myself so that I become as blurred in outline to myself as my parents once were to me. In this mood, lasting years which all seem the same year, I appear, now, looking back, to have catalogued Mother more than any human being even though that catalogue must have been made in a by-the-way fashion. This may be the habit of sons who are driven by their natures to write, I suspect so, but am unsure. I do not even know if an eldest son, writer or shearers' cook or accountant, be the best or worst judge of his mother. I never shall know. I am discovering as I write these words that my autobiography, at this period, is my mother's biography.

*The Watcher on the Cast-iron Balcony* (1963).

# *Bernard Smith*

## (1916– )

*A distinguished art critic and art historian, Bernard Smith was director of the Power Institute of Fine Arts at the University of Sydney (1967–77). His numerous books include* Place, Taste and Tradition *(1945),* European Vision and the South Pacific (1768–1850) *(1960, 2nd ed. 1985), and* Australian Painting 1788–1960 *(1962). He has also published several collections of essays and lectures, including* The Antipodean Manifesto *(1975),* The Spectre of Truganini *(1980),* The Death of the Artist as Hero *(1988),* The Critic as Advocate *(1989), and* Imagining the Pacific: In the Wake of the Cook Voyages *(1992). His autobiography,* The Boy Adeodatus, *written in the third person, takes him to his twenty-fourth year, when he gave up painting in favour of art criticism and history. Beginning with his early experiences as a ward of the state of New South Wales, the book also focuses on the lives of his natural mother, 'Mumma Parky', and his foster mother, 'Mum Keen'.*

It was the Chinese hawkers that Mum Keen liked best. They're hard workers, she would say, and they always have a smile for you. One old Chinaman, with two heavy bamboo baskets balanced at the end of a long bamboo rod, sold only pots of ginger. But what Bertha and Mum Keen loved most were visits from the Chinaman who sold silks and satins. Out they would come, one after another, from a large old cardboard suitcase that seemed to have no bottom. He would spread his pretty treasures over everything in the back verandah; the tables and chairs, the ferns and the pots of aspidistra, and then spread them over the floor until the place began to glow like an eastern bazaar. A case without a bottom, like something magic out of the *Arabian Nights*. Always he kept smiling gently at Mum Keen, as he pulled out more and more splendid things, murmuring quietly but with great conviction, as in an incantation or a prayer, 'Something I pretty, very pretty for your daughter.' Occasionally Mum Keen bought some little thing, because she never could resist a bargain. But it was the occasion that she adored.

Mum Keen was a careful manager. Ten shillings came into the house weekly from old Dad's pension from the State Brickworks; 10s each for Valerie and Ben, and 10s rent from any young lodger who might be there. The rest of the Braeside income came from taking in washing. But the garden produced so much that they were partly self-supporting, in eggs, fruit and vegetables. Even so Mum Keen had to be thrifty. Valerie never saw a dress of her own in the seven years that she lived at Braeside. Either Bertha's old dresses, or dresses from the daughters of Mum Keen's Burwood ladies. But little Bennie did get new clothes when they felt he needed them because he was a bit of a pet in that house, and Mumma Parky sent some money down for clothes from Queensland when she could afford it. Whenever Mum Keen felt he was in need of a new outfit she would take him in the train to Central Station, then catch the tram down to Bon Marche store at the corner of Parramatta Road and Harris Street, Ultimo. It was there, she said, that you got good quality at a fair price. Once a year she took Bennie to a big building in the city. Up they would go to the seventh floor in the big iron lift, like monkeys in a cage. After waiting for a time on a long bench, they would go into a room where a man sat behind a large desk. Mum Keen always went over and talked to the man and Ben couldn't hear what they said, and when he sometimes did, he still couldn't understand. Then the man would turn to him and say always the same thing.

'Do you like your home Ben?' Smiling sheepishly at him, knowing what the answer would be. 'Always be a good boy Ben and you will get on well,' he would say as they left the room.

But Ben didn't have to be told that, because he remembered Eric flying round and round the house and Mum Keen after him with the broomstick. He sometimes wondered where Eric had gone. But the man in the big building was kind and Ben was not afraid of him. *O God, my God! what miseries and what mockeries did I find in that age; when as being yet a boy, obedience was propounded unto me, to those who advised me to get on in the world.*

Little Bennie always sat for his meals on the long brown form that was placed beneath the kitchen window behind the table. Outside the small red fuchsia bloomed through the summer in all its glory. It was Mum Keen's greatest pride, and the admiration of her Burwood ladies as they came to collect their washing or sit down for a chat and cup of tea. At the end of the table by the stove sat old Dad. A man who never raised his hand in anger. If one of Tottie's State kids sometimes annoyed him, the most he would do was to swing his hand over the top of the boy's head, lightly touching his hair. George Keen left the management of the household to his wife, and she thought him a bit of a fool at times; but she had great faith in his powers of healing. If you had a headache all you had to do was to kneel down between old Dad's knees and he would place his scarred and horny brickworker's hands on either side of your head, just touching the temples ever so softly. The laying on of hands. The warmth seemed to go through your body; the headache went away. No one was ever known, at any rate, to say that their headache hadn't gone away. 'I don't know whether it's his electricity or whether it's God,' Mum Keen would say, 'but it always works.'

Old Dad kept all the shoes at Braeside in good repair. Up in the back shed he kept his father's old boot last. It had three sides: one for a man-size boot, one for a lady's shoe, and one for a heel. On the wall nearby hung a length of good quality calf's hide leather. Whenever their boots or shoes required mending he would put on his leather apron, sharpen his fine pocket knife, which he greatly treasured, on his whetstone, and then sit to his last. Little Ben would watch fascinated as with strong hands he cut round the edge of the shoe, an even oblique stroke, as clean as through butter, then moulded the edges with crisp cuts of his sharp knife. Last of all he would nail the new sole on with small brass tacks.

When Ben first came to Braeside he was an infant, and he slept for a few months in the marriage bed of Mum Keen and old Dad: big iron double bed, a half-tester, with brass foot pillars and porcelain spindles. Later they gave him a cot. There he lay in great sweat with the measles, the design in the curtain, from which he could not take his eyes, coming at him like a fierce cat with its claws, then whirling around faster and faster. One night when he was better, old Dad gave him a small book with a brown cover. It had coloured pictures in it.

'I will teach you to read from this book,' old Dad said, 'because it is the best book in the world.' Much later, after he had learned to read, old Dad said, 'Now you must promise me to read two chapters every night before you go to sleep.' And that he did, two chapters every day from the age of six to the age of thirteen except when sick. He developed a great love of the stories in the Old Testament: of Joseph, of the children of Israel released from bondage in Egypt, of the young Samuel, and especially the book of Daniel, with that wonderful story of Shadrach, Meshach and Abednego, who would not bow down to the golden image of the king and were not consumed by the fiery furnace. The illustrations in the Bible haunted his imagination for years. One was of a city, and under it were written the words 'A city without walls cannot be hid'. It troubled him. Sydney was a city without walls. How could it hide itself from the curious, questioning, all-seeing eye of God?

One day old Dad said, 'Make up a list of the words you know Ben.' He must have known about thirty at that time. But he was proud of his Biblical knowledge and searched the Bible for the biggest word he knew. So after a string of mat, fat and sat words, after Peter the kookaburra and Mumbo the cat, and Valerie, came Nebuchadnezzar, though for a long time he pronounced it *knee bucket sneezer*.

On the opposite side of the kitchen table from old Dad sat Jeff, a quiet man, always doing crossword puzzles. Jeff was very important because he had just come back from the Front, where he had been gassed a bit, and was a little bit shell-shocked. But he wouldn't talk about the war. You could read his name on the new memorial arch they were building in Burwood Park; Clarence Jeffrey, inscribed on a grey marble slab with the names of all the returned boys, in silver. If you were killed in the war and did not come back they put your name up there in gold. One large panel was full of gold names. Little Ben liked Jeff, who taught him to do crossword puzzles and gave him books to read. He never got angry, except once. But then he got very angry.

After returning from the war Jeff began to learn a trade french-polishing. Chairs and tables with delicate joinery would appear in the back shed at various stages of sanding, staining and polishing. Now one of the Braeside pets, which Mum Keen had picked up somewhere, was a galah that talked a lot. They put him in a cage that could be moved from tree to tree. One unhappy day little Ben moved that cage up near the back shed and left it quite close to one of Jeff's highly polished antique chairs. It must have contained a kind of varnish that galahs relish because by midmorning Cocky, sticking his head through his cage, had eaten deeply into a corner of a cabriole leg. When Jeff came out to give his chair a final rubdown of wax and polish he found that a great part of the shoulder of one leg had been eaten away. He flew into a wild rage, while the wretched bird, delighted to have some personal attention, jumped up and down on his perch, first on one leg, then on the other, screeching, 'Scratch Cocky, scratch Cocky.'

'Scratch be damned, you fucking bird,' said Jeff, 'that's no scratch, you've just about eaten the bloody thing up, you've buggered up my chair. What stupid fool put the mad galah there.'

Bennie kept well out of Jeff's way for days. Shortly afterwards Jeff and old Dad built a permanent aviary for the galah and the love birds, under the big Japanese plum.

Jeff was the only boy from Braeside to join the AIF and go to France. Mum Keen wouldn't let her sons go because she didn't believe in war. But when they all came back the patriotic fever gripped Braeside as it gripped the rest of the country. On Sunday evenings they would gather round the piano in the dining room which was hardly ever used for dining, even at Christmas. It was the best room in the house, only used when very special visitors came, or for Sunday evening get-togethers. On these occasions Bertha would play a few hymns first from the Moody and Sankey or Anderson hymnals. Then she would play 'The Rose of Picardy' or 'When the Boys Come Marching Home' and end up with 'It's a Long Way to Tipperary'. Bertha's music certificate, the primary examination of the London College of Music, which she had passed on 23 November 1914 at the age of twelve, was framed above the bamboo music case. But after that Mum Keen couldn't afford to pay for any further lessons from Miss Marion Anderson, the local music teacher. On very special evenings Bertha would place candles in the brass sconces of her Beale piano and they would all gather around her and sing hymns by the candle-light and popular songs to satisfy the boys.

It was a well-furnished room for a family of such modest means; evidence enough of Tottie Keen's desire to identify herself with the respected members of Burwood's community. But in it, through the heavy curtains, the daylight rarely penetrated. In the centre of the room stood a heavy extension table, darkly varnished and covered with a thick rust-brown velvet cloth, which was never removed except occasionally to dust. Around the table were ten Austrian cane bentwood chairs—strong, light, easy to move about. To one side of the table stood Bertha's piano and on the other the rosewood sideboard that held the family tableware: silver-plated coffee pots and salvers, and a soup tureen in late Victorian rococo, heavily moulded, a pink glass biscuit barrel, and a fruit dish in open-latticework porcelain of which Mum Keen was very proud. They must have come to her from her mother after she died at Marrickville in 1903. In the centre of the sideboard stood that most precious family shrine, the three top tiers of the Keens' wedding cake, entombed in domed glass on a velvet base. The tiny columns of icing sugar still held their lintels and cornices as firmly as when Mr Blair, Burwood's finest cake man and confectioner, had first put them all together. The sugar sprigs of orange still sprouted and blossomed, the sugar flags fluttered, and sugar birds flew in the timeless air, as they did on that day when Tottie Davis married George Keen, not for love but, as she always said, for old times' sake. As a young girl Bertha dusted the glass dome each week with loving care. But after Mum Keen died, and the remaining members of the family lived more than ever in the kitchen the dome gathered dust and mildew in the dark-ened room.

There was less singing around the piano after Bert bought his phonograph. It had a long horn and little cylindrical records that were kept in a big flat wooden box lined with felt and stored in the back shed. The voices sounded faint and scratchy. The one that little Bennie remembered best began 'O the moon shines bright on pretty Red-wing'. But the kids down the street sang other words.

> O the moon shines bright on Mrs Porter,
> And on her daughter.
> They wash their feet in soda water.

Funny how kids made up silly words to songs. It had to make you laugh; and
sometimes it could make you mad. Doodie, who was always good for a lark, knew
how to make little Ben mad. He would just have to start singing:

> I met with Napper Tandy and he took me by the hand,
> And he said how poor old Ireland was,
> And how she does stand.

And Ben would run at him and start hitting him with his little fists. 'Stop singing
that song, Dood.' Then Dood would say, 'Don't get your Irish paddy up Ben. It's
just a song.'

But little Bennie didn't like that song because he knew what it meant. It meant
that he wasn't really one of them; and he wanted to be one of them. *For I was but
flesh, a wind that passeth away and cometh not again.*

The Boy Adeodatus: The Portrait of a Lucky Bastard (1984).

# Vincent Buckley

## (1925–88)

*Vincent Buckley was born in Romsey, a small Victorian country town. Educated at a
Jesuit college in Melbourne and at the universities of Melbourne and Cambridge, he was
Lockie Fellow at the University of Melbourne (1958–60) and held a personal chair in
poetry there from 1967. In the 1950s and 1960s he was an influential figure in
Melbourne as a poet, critic, academic, and editor. He published eight volumes of poetry
and several critical studies, and edited several anthologies of verse and the magazine,*
Prospect *(1958–63). He was poetry editor of the* Bulletin *(1961–63). His* Memory
Ireland: Insights into the Contemporary Irish Condition *(1985) demonstrates his
deep interest in Ireland and has some autobiographical content.*

The Depression was never entirely to be forgotten. Its demons were the shape of
acid in the very grass. It meant the whole outside pressing into a man's psychic
room, denying his relevance. It was a threat to his manhood and to a woman's sense
of possibility. 'Nobody wants a man,' my father would say despairingly. Or when
he met to play cribbage with his cronies in Carey's pub, they would ask each
other, English and Irish alike, 'Have you had any work?' This was not the inured

hopelessness of the born loser, the drunk, the semi-criminal, or even of the itinerant or the convinced solitary. It was a deep reversal of injured hopes, a loss of all that had been expected and gained—wife, family, job, car, house, standing. It broke up marriages, drove people restlessly into a kind of exile, magnified to neurosis any misfit tendencies. It was the sign of present failure, not failure feared or deferred. It was compounded by the threat of world war.

Politics was a constant thought but seldom an active possibility. You voted, but you knew how the vote would come out; my father could predict the vote within the subdivision with less than one per cent margin of error. Who cared? The party allegiances were strong, but there were no party branches in the districts. The town was run by businessmen and farmers. The electorate swung to and from Labor. At one stage it was held by the Labor left-winger Reg Pollard, and one occasion when he arrived to give an election speech in the local hall was like a nineteenth-century election procession, with banners and torches. The banners and torches were only in my imagination; for I was there, of course, with my father, savouring each rhetorical trope, engaging in every thrust at the enemy, who had not turned out for the occasion. There was a throaty rumble of applause; men crowded and surged to touch him, as if he were a victorious boxer; his name was uttered as if it were a talisman.

Such demonstrations did nothing more than attest to a feeling; it was populist politics without organization. Companionship of some sort is always available in a small country town; so is clan feeling; but nothing can provide community for people from whom far-off economic forces have taken the very notion of a perceptible, definable future. Loneliness was a common condition, and among the lonelier were the priests, ministers and nuns; loneliest of all were the priests of shy temperament. But even the ministers, for all their wives and children, were isolated in some ways. Our house stood between the shopping area and the Presbyterian manse; and over the years several of the ministers made a friend of my mother. They were interesting men; one, an Australian, was in effect a communist; the man who succeeded him, a Hungarian, was of the directly opposite stamp; they both supposed me to be of their mind, and sent me political greetings through my mother. Earlier, a minister had recruited me as companion for his son, who was passing his primary years as respectably as possible, before going to boarding school; but that arrangement was hopeless, as it was bound to be. Even the shyest of the priests visited from time to time, and of course the nuns, garrulous and spontaneous as girls, would drop in for a gossip with my mother, who was everyone's contact.

But the loneliness went, as it always does, very deep. Even Christmas was not communal with us; instead of visitors, we had Christmas cards, and we did not, as a matter of course, forgather anywhere in any numbers or do anything very rousing. I think of the Christmases of childhood as composed of heat and of a peculiar loneliness, which in turn had to do with a sense of anti-climax throughout the day itself; once Christmas Eve was done, it was all done. We were never so nuclear, so unattached to the wide world, as on Christmas Day; all its energy seemed to have been sucked out of it into the preceding days. But it was too hot, and we were psychologically too far from the sea, or from any cooling water, to make a gregarious occasion tolerable. The communal occasions were dances, football matches, fêtes, sports meetings and the occasional ball with its belle. None of these was associated with swimming; there was no usable pool, and no safe creek, in the town. Many families were like ours; they simply did not draw one another into their homes but went to some central point for their entertainment. I don't precisely know why this was: a matter of Depression shame, maybe. People whose extended families were closer to hand no doubt suffered less. But generally the poor were immobilized; at a certain point beyond the subsistence level, immobility in all its forms is perhaps their greatest deprivation.

Nor was anyone in any doubt that Australia was a class-ridden society, and that any small village could present that complex anomaly in microcosm. No manual worker or rural labourer would mistake for equality ease of manners and the occasional sense of a common purpose. The society was stratified in ways which it would be impossible to define, and which any academic analyst could misinterpret with graceful ease. [...]

Unhappiness and grievance are easily learned. I was lucky, for, while I was too close to too great a load of both during all my primary years, I was able at once to displace my sense of family injustice on to national and global evils, where it more usefully belonged, and to filter it through the terms of my own fantasy life, my psychic drama, which I interpreted in Dickensian terms or in terms derived from Scott. After any of my mother's numerous fainting spells, running for the doctor late at night up the totally silent street, I could figure it all to myself as on a par with the young Dickens's bottle factory, a present suffering which would be matter for future fame and wonder. It never did, of course. But the excitement of these crises survived their terror. Even at eight or nine years I was buoyed up by the opportunism of the writer.

This opportunist self-image is the salt that preserves poets. At nine, ten, eleven, the world was beginning for me, in books. Mussolini's gas destroyed the Abyssinian bodies, the Spanish war rolled into its second and then its third year, Hitler remained unchallenged, and the communists moved threateningly to the edge of their sphere of influence; my father continued to lose his identity; my brother and I continued to gain ours. We were pointed forward, but also, alas, away, in a repetition of that self-exiling act by which our forebears had come to this very place we were soon to leave.

Lacking grandparents, I found mentors. One was the Presbyterian widow who ran the local library and whose cows I minded; the other was the arthritic Irish bootmaker, who had fought in several wars before fetching up among the nails and sawdust of Main Street. They were for a time my wise ones, and to them I attached myself with wondering reverence. They had nothing to tell me about the spirits or powers of the land itself, or of its history or pre-history, or of its founding heroes. The land was full of 'myth', but it was as inaccessible to them as to me. Is the *whole* land mythical for the Aboriginal tribes? We are used to thinking of myth and history as interpenetrating systems or orders of psychic power. The interpenetration did not take place in Australia. Even Mt William, sacred, volcanic, where I picked up my first flints and knives, was no more than a circle for curiosity to move in. Mrs Hemphill and Paddy Moore gave anecdote, maxim, and example; they were not myth-bearers. So my experience was a mirror-opposite of Yeats's on both counts. Yet how fragmented was his childhood, really? Does the sense of his being mythically *informed* come only from the unifying force of his narrative in long retrospect?

Mrs Hemphill also lent me books from the local Mechanics Institute. I read Stevenson, Lord Macaulay, Scott, Dickens, Mrs Humphrey Ward, Buchan, Walsh, George Eliot, Orczy. But abundance was never enough. I read comics and thrillers, Hopalong Cassidy, and Sexton Blake. Satiation was not possible. For two or three years I spent the summer vacation herding cows on the long slopes above the town, and with the money I bought books. Among them was the Collected Works of Shakespeare.

Week after week, with the grass still green and the cattle wandering for miles, I read myself into a trance and talked to every stranger I met on the road. All were as harmless as I assumed they would be. The swaggies in particular thought me a curiosity. One old Swedish ex-sailor commended me gutturally for my application and promised me stores of new works: 'You're a great reader. I'll bring you some good books, really good books.' 'Have you got any on the Foreign Legion, Mr Benson?' Great excitement; surely such a world traveller would be able to duplicate P.C. Wren. What he gave me was a set of fundamentalist works commending a right-wing Protestant Christ; he was not to know that I abominated piety in its written forms. I continued to read comics and 'the classics' in the grass of the roadside.

The days became hotter, until in 1938 (when I was home from secondary school) they reached an apex of heat that resembled an explosion. For those weeks we lived in an exploded bowl. From Christmas on, the heat continued; by 9 January, forestry officers were dead in the bush, women and children were found cowering in a bush dugout, and Melbourne had reached 112.5 degrees. Towns throughout the state cowered under burning embers, and by Black Friday, 13 January, Melbourne broke a record:

ALL-TIME HEAT

RECORD — 114 DEG.!

and the Melbourne hills started to burn, with dozens killed in the fires.

This is what I could see from the slopes above Romsey as we all waited for the cool change; and when it came that time, it was with the unfamiliar smell of drench and rot, a humid pretend-cooling before the real air started to make its faint spirals on our skin. And Mrs Heffernan, in her hessian-like apron, standing by her cottage at the thick thorn hedge on the road to Springfield, continued her account of international possibilities and threats:

'He can't be that bad, 'I hey say he's cleaning out the Masons    '

'Really, Mrs Heffernan ...'

She was the midwife and the cleaner of corpses; she caught them coming and going, and coming and going they were in her hand. She said nothing about Jews, who would not have been an issue for her; it was the Masons who had taken, or might again take, the jobs, the land, the self-respect.

But by this time I was in a sense out of it all; I had gone, been sent, to school in the city. I had sat for various scholarships and won them; diminutive, puzzled, I was yet full of afflatus. The inspector who reported my scholarship results had called me a 'prodigy'. I misheard this as 'protégé', and looked it up in the dictionary. I was certainly that; for the most erect and aloof of all the priests who had served our town, and at whose lunch table in Lancefield I had sat when I took the scholarship papers, had come down quite unexpectedly to see my parents. They should be proud of me, and so on, but really he thought I would be better off going not to the scholarship school in Fitzroy but to the Jesuit school, St Patrick's. He had some contact there, and the money could be found. What about my brother, though? Well, no doubt, if we needed to stay together, the place and the money could be found for him, too.

His name was Daly, and he was an Irishman, a stately solitary of whose personal feelings no one knew anything. He was my first patron, if patronage is counted by place and money. His offer could not have been more timely, shy and decisive (in a word, splendid), or less gratefully requited. He sent me not just to school, but to the city. From that day, I was no longer a country boy.

*Cutting Green Hay: Friendships, Movements and Cultural Conflicts*

*in Australia's Great Decades* (1983).

# *Eve Hogan*

(DATES UNKNOWN)

*Eve Hogan's early childhood was spent in southern Wales, where her father had been a coal-miner from the age of ten. The family's unequal struggle for survival determined the father to migrate to Australia with his second wife, Winnie, and his six children. In 1927 they arrived in Fremantle, where another child was born soon afterwards. Eve attended two years of school at Fremantle, but when she was twelve her father was offered a contract to clear land on a property near Carribin. Eve's two elder sisters remained in service at Fremantle so that she was the eldest girl in the family of four children as they began their life as itinerant labourers.*

We duly arrived at the property which was to be our home for the next two years. We must have looked like Ma and Pa Kettle and brood as we chugged into the home paddock in our old bomb.

It did not take us long to get the house organised. After making camp we were allowed to select, chop down and cart back timber of a suitable size and thickness which would be used for the frame of our new humpy. Our few sheets of corrugated iron were bent and battered to fit onto the frame, with the utmost care being taken that holes made in previous erections were positioned in such a way that they would not allow the rain to drip through. That corrugated iron had been used so many times before that it was no easy task to assure that we would enjoy drip-free comfort in rainy weather. Our dilapidated bagging was nailed up, and here and there, where an old bag had given way, a new one was stitched to give added strength.

After we had brought in our scanty supply of furniture, the little place took on a more comfortable appearance, and we settled back on our 'woggas' to admire our handiwork. Woggas were made by sewing wheat bags together for use as blankets. They were to be found in every country home and were very warm and cosy.

Our beds were also made of wheat bags. They were threaded onto long poles which were then fitted into forked timber uprights which had been hammered into the ground. They looked not unlike today's canvas stretchers.

In the draughtiest corner of the kitchen we set up our Coolgardie safe, a fly-proof apparatus which stood on legs that were immersed in kerosene tins of water to discourage the ants. Strips of hessian covered the safe and were kept damp by a dripping tin suspended above it. Even on the hottest of days, provided we made sure not to leave the food inside for any undue length of time, it was kept cold and fresh.

We seemed to survive very well on our unvaried menu of rabbit, wild peaches, mushrooms in season, and wild honey, which we used to rob from the hives. We often got as much as eighteen litres of the rich, yellow liquid, and, as none of us were too keen on honey, we swapped at the shop in Westonia for more basic requirements such as sugar, tea, jam and golden syrup—fondly known as 'cocky's joy'. Occasionally we killed and ate one of the chooks that had obligingly multiplied from the few bedraggled birds that we had acquired earlier in our travels.

In an effort to vary our diet, we tried to grow vegetables, but turnips were the only ones that we had any success with, and they grew prolifically. I, for one, was very fond of the young turnip tops cooked in boiling water and eaten as cabbage. Sometimes a neighbour, herself the mother of a large family, would drop in with what she called 'a few eggs' and 'a drop of milk'. There were usually one hundred and twenty to one hundred and fifty eggs packed in a kerosine or tin and the milk would be in a forty-five litre drum. We would preserve some of the eggs and scald the milk for the lovely clotted cream that we poured onto our bread and porridge. Sometimes, as a rare treat, we would pour it over fresh fruit, when we had it, and now and then we would have enough to make a small amount of butter.

The old-fashioned mincer was a very important utensil in our kitchen and I am sure the manufacturers never dreamed of the uses to which it could be put. For instance, we used all four cutters at the same time to grist wheat which we sifted for flour to make our bread. The yeast was made from hops, sugar and boiled potato water, and the final product was absolutely delicious. It made today's bread look and taste a very poor substitute. The second gristing would produce porridge, some of which we would roast in the oven until it turned brown. This we used for 'coffee'.

Sometimes, someone would leave a wild turkey on our door-step. We never asked where it came from or who left it, as they were, and still are, protected birds, but oh, what a rare and wonderful treat it would be. We would cook it in a kerosene tin and quickly burn the feathers to get rid of the evidence.

The kero tin was our main cooking pot. Stews were our usual fare, with potatoes, carrots and onions added if we had them, and we were especially lucky if we had all the ingredients at the one time. We ate like kings then. Sometimes we varied the meat between rabbit and fowl, and later on, pork, but as yet those days of high living had not arrived for us.

It was about this time that my youngest stepbrother arrived. I remember Winnie arriving home in the mail carter's van, and me winning the race to see and hold the new addition. As Winnie handed the baby down for me to hold, I heard my brother mutter, 'Okay, Sis, you've got him, now you're stuck with him.' Like the prophets of old, his words held much truth. I was indeed 'stuck' with him, but, never having had dolls or other toys, nothing could dim my joy at having a real baby to look after. No baby ever had more loving attention or a more earnest defender of his rights.

The first battle began as soon as we were told what his name was to be. We were all aghast to think that such a tiny mite was to be saddled with the title of Desmond for the rest of his life, and decided that it was up to us to see to it that our new brother would not be stuck with such an awful moniker.

We faced up to my father and Winnie and stated our objections. We had decided that his name was going to be Donald, and that was that. Despite threats of beltings and supperless nights, we stood firm in our decision and refused to use the given name. Things came to such a pass that Dad brought us all before him and threatened a belting to end all beltings to the next one who referred to the baby as Donald, but my two brothers and I had had a conference and had taken an oath that we would fight it out to the end. The last one standing was to carry on the battle at all costs. In the end, our parents must have held a conference of their own, because Donald he became, and Don he still is.

Winnie could not breast feed him for long. Perhaps our plain diet was inadequate to build up a good supply of milk. Doctor Spock once wrote that babies are a lot tougher than they look, but I am certain that even he would raise his eyebrows at a baby of such tender age being taken off the breast one day and put on to rabbit stew the next. Whatever was on the menu for the day was fed to Donald, and he took his milk—when we could get it—from a spoon or a cup. There was no frilly bassinet or lovingly carved cradle for this lad. His pram was a wooden go-cart that we had made, often pulled along by our dog Nigger, who would be tied between the shafts.

My father and Winnie were away most of the time as Dad was doing odd jobs in the area until we began clearing again. This meant frequent absences which left me, a mere fourteen-year-old girl, totally responsible for the baby. My methods, hit and miss as they were, have resulted in a man standing six feet tall in his socks, and I regard him as a fine monument to stale bread soaked in water and rabbit stew.

With an innate sense of self preservation, Don learnt to walk at a very early age, and not long after he took his first step he said his first word. However, the shock of a near drowning stopped him from doing either for quite a few months afterwards. As soon as he began to toddle we realised that he was going to require very strict supervision. In a flash, his little legs would have him around a corner and out of sight. The accident happened because I trusted an adult to look after him. Harry had promised that he would keep an eye on the baby while I went to collect the eggs. It was getting late in the afternoon and I was behind with my chores, otherwise I would have known better than to leave Don in inexperienced hands. I plopped the baby down at Harry's feet and rushed off in the direction of the fowlyard.

Minutes later I returned, to find Don missing and Harry completely oblivious to the fact that he had gone. I ran out of the house and the first thing I saw was the red bank of the dam nearby. With a fearful heart I raced towards it, only to have my worst fears confirmed. In the centre of the muddy dam, one small arm was visible. I dived in, grabbed the little body and scrambled ashore, throwing him over my shoulder as I ran towards the house, screaming for Harry to get dry towels and stoke up the fire.

Harry was no help at all. He took one look at the baby's limp body and stated, 'That child is dead. I don't intend to be here when your father and mother get home,' and picking up his hat, he walked out.

I, too, was sure that Don was dead, but fighting down my panic, I struggled to remember a lecture that we had had a long time before, on the methods of lifesaving, and suddenly, every word returned clearly to my memory. After what seemed like hours without any sign of life, I gave way to my rising panic and without thinking, picked Don up and held him upside down. As I did so, dirty water poured from his mouth and he gave a weak cry. His nose and ears were packed with mud, and as I was cleaning them out, he began to cry louder and his tears washed the mud from his eyes.

I have never forgotten that dreadful ordeal and it was only after it was over that I remembered that I could not swim a stroke.

The following day I had the further ordeal of facing my father and Winnie. I was sure I would be given no opportunity to present my side of the story, and was very worried and frightened but, taking comfort from the fact that Don was alive, I prepared myself to accept whatever punishment was about to befall me. As soon as I had finished the story, my stepmother began to scream hysterical abuse at me, but to my surprise, my father abruptly ordered her to 'shut up' saying, 'This little girl has been through enough.' Taking me in his arms, he held me close while I sobbed out my fright and fear. This was the only caress I can ever remember receiving from my father.

As Don grew older, it became increasingly difficult to keep him under constant surveillance. He would have put Houdini to shame with his disappearing acts. Besides the danger of getting lost in the bush, there was also the constant fear of snakes. To make it easier to catch sight of him, I took to dressing him in bright reds and yellows so that he could be easily seen against the green of the trees and grasses. These clothes were far from being professionally sewn, but this did not matter much as he rarely had them on for very long. It seemed, that as well as being born with the urge to wander, he also had the tendency to be a nudist. To fasten clothes on him, I used every method I could think of. At one stage I sewed tapes onto his clothes that would wrap around his body and tie at the back like a miniature strait-jacket, but even this presented little problem to him. Not only did he remove his clothes, he hid them as well, and the most careful search rarely revealed his hiding places, so the monthly order at the Carribin store always included fourpence worth of red or yellow cotton.

One day my stepmother saw John speaking to a man who was humping his bluey, and she got into quite a state of nerves because she heard John tell him that the nearest town was twenty-two kilometres away and that our father was absent. She feared that the stranger would want to spend the night on the property. We always kept our dog, Nigger, inside at night, and even my father would not dare to enter until the dog was sure of his identity. Our trust in Nigger was so absolute that we could not understand Winnie's fear. However, she decided that she would keep Don with her so that she could protect him if things came to the worse.

The baby made it very obvious from the start that he had other ideas. From the day he was brought home from hospital he had slept in my room, and he screamed his rage at the alteration of his sleeping arrangements. Midnight found everyone still awake because of his yelling, and upon getting up to get myself a glass of water, I decided I had had enough, so I went into Winnie's room, gathered him up and took him back where he belonged. Winnie must have been just as fed up as the rest of us for she offered not one word of protest.

On waking up a little while later, I reached for my glass of water and realised I had left it in the other room. Taking care not to arouse the household again, I crept towards the table where I had left it, keeping my hand lightly on the bed as a guide to the table. I felt the heat of the bullet as it whizzed through my hair. Winnie had been sitting up in bed with the loaded gun, waiting for the tramp who, by that time, was probably far away from our property.

Sundays were welcome days of rest, and as each one arrived, my brothers and I took turns to make the morning 'cuppa'. It was one chore we really enjoyed, for the rules were that, whoever made the tea was entitled to a full cup for themselves.

Great care had to be taken to keep the fire small and confined to its tin surround, but one morning, when John was on duty, loud yells coming from the living room brought us all rushing out to find one wall ablaze. We knew how impossible it would be to put the fire out, for no matter how quick our actions, the scant water supply would defeat us, so our main concern was to assure that every-body was outside.

Before we had made a move, the fire was out. By fluke or design, I will never know. At John's first yell, Harry had jumped out of his bed and, gathering his bedclothes up in his arms, he rushed over and threw the whole lot at the fire. His quick thinking averted what could have been a tragedy and we were very generous in our praise for his actions. Suddenly, his look of pleasure at our words turned to embarrassment for he had realised, to our amusement, that he was bowing his thanks stark naked. Poor Harry, his rush towards his clothes had to be seen to be believed.

This near calamity made us realise how easily our hessian humpy could catch alight and how quickly the flames could race through the two rooms if ever they took hold. Soon after, Dad built a separate cookhouse of scrap iron, about fifteen metres away from where our back door would have been, if we had had one.

So it was that circumstances forced us to be older than our calendar years. We certainly had to shoulder work and responsibilities never meant for such tender years.

I remember the feelings of relief I had when night fell and we were all safely tucked inside, free of snake bites and axe-slashed legs. How lucky we were that nothing had happened that we could not cope with. We used Condy's Crystals as a disinfectant and Goanna Salve for infections.

We were alone a great deal of the time and had always been put in charge of the younger ones. My elder brother, John, upheld my authority inside the house regarding clothes, meals, bedtimes and the allotting of chores, but outside we followed where he led. Things did not always run on oiled wheels, of course, and there were often minor mutinies and the usual fights that occur in most families, but on the whole, the arrangement worked well.

We did not attend school or do any lessons at all, and I can only conclude that we got away with it because the school was so far away. Thirty-two kilometres of bush track and no transport certainly made it an impossibility for us to get there.

'The Hessian Walls' in *Selected Lives: Personal Reminiscences* (1983).

# Jill Ker Conway

## (1934– )

*Jill Ker Conway was born at Hilston, New South Wales, and left Australia for the USA in 1960 to complete a doctorate at Harvard. From 1964 to 1975 she taught at the University of Toronto, where she was vice-president (1973–75). She was the first female president of Smith College, Massachusetts (1975–85), and is a director of numerous companies. She has written several books on the historical experience of American women and, after* The Road from Coorain, *a second autobiography,* True North *(1994).*

Because it was clear that I was educating myself through reading everything within reach—a topsy-turvy mixture of children's books, my mother's books on current affairs, war correspondents' accounts of the war, my father's books on stock breeding—my parents decided not to bother with elementary school by correspondence for me the year my brothers left for boarding school. Instead, I became my father's station hand. He needed help with mustering sheep, something which needed two people on horseback to accomplish easily. I rode out with him to check the state of fences, always in need of careful attention if bloodlines were to be kept clear. We went together to clean watering troughs, carry out the maintenance of windmills, trim and dress the fly-infested spots which developed around the crutch of sheep where flies would lay eggs in the hot summer months. Dressing fly-blown sheep was hard, hot work because one had to round up the particular flock, get the sheepdogs to hold them, and then dive suddenly into the herd to tackle the one animal whose fleece needed attention. An agile child was better at doing the diving than an adult, and in time I learned to do a kind of flying tackle which would hold the animal, usually heavier than I was myself, until my father arrived with the hand shears and the disinfectant.

Much of the work with sheep involved riding slowly behind them while moving them from one paddock to another, travelling at a pace which was a comfortable walk for the animals. Often we dismounted and strolled along, horse's reins looped over an arm. Occasionally something might startle the sheep, requiring my father to shout commands to the dogs, but otherwise it was not demanding work, and it was a perfect setting for extended conversation. Why did God allow the crows to pick out the eyes of newborn lambs, I asked, as we passed a bloody carcass. My father never treated such questions as idle chatter, but tried seriously to answer. He didn't know, he replied. It was a puzzle. The world seemed set up so that the strong preyed on the weak and innocent. I would ask endless questions about the weather, the vegetation, the transmission of characteristics through several generations of sheep. How to breed to eliminate that defect, or promote this desirable characteristic. When the lambs were a year old, we would bring the sheep into the nearest sheepyards, or make a temporary one, so that we could cull the flocks, selecting the discards which would be sent for immediate sale or used for our own food.

I did reasonably well as a station hand while in sight of my father. He could shout directions, or notice that I was having trouble getting the dogs to work for me and arrive quickly to solve the problem. I didn't always do so well when we worked in the large paddocks, twelve or fifteen thousand acres in size, where we would separate, one going clockwise, one counterclockwise, turning the sheep into the middle, to be gathered into one flock and moved as a whole to a new spot. I was a long-legged seven-year-old, but not quite tall enough to remount my horse if I got off to kick some lazy sheep into motion, or to investigate a sick or lame one. Then there would be no getting back on till the next fence, or the rare occasional stump. At first I was not quite secure enough in ego to cope with the space, the silence, and the brooding sky. Occasionally I would find myself crying, half in vexation at my small size and the pigheadedness of sheep, half for the reassurance of a sound. By the family's code it was shameful to weep, and I was supposed to be too grown up for such babyish behavior. Once the wind carried the sound to my father on the other side of the paddock. By the time we were reunited, I had reached a fence, climbed on my horse, and become secure again by seeing him in the distance. 'I thought I heard someone crying,' he observed to me as we met. I looked him in the eye. 'I didn't,' I said. There he let the matter rest.

The sheepdogs were always a trial to me. They were trained to respond to a series of calls. Their trainers were station hands and drovers whose calls were usually poetic, blasphemous, and picturesquely profane. I would try to make my voice deep, and sound as though I really meant to flay them alive when I got home if they didn't go behind or get around or whatever other command was needed, but I didn't believe it and neither did they. My father would laugh at me shouting to the black kelpie whose pink tongue and nose I loved, 'You black bastard, I'll flay the hide off you if you don't go around.' 'You don't sound as if you mean it,' he said. 'Why not just try whistling, that's easier for you to do.' He tried to teach me the series of whistles used to command sheepdogs. I did better at that, but they would never obey me perfectly, as they did my father.

[...]

After the water supply was provided for the house, we built our own shearing shed. It was built of Oregon pine and galvanized iron, by an eccentric and talented carpenter named Obecue. Mr Obecue, my parents said, was a secret ladykiller, who had had a series of young and wealthy wives. This information made me gaze at him with more than usual curiosity. I could not fathom his attractions, but I admired intensely the way his fingers flew about, appearing to fabricate things so fast the result seemed to be achieved by sleight of hand. I would sit on the frame for the woolshed floor watching as he laid it, his mouth full of long nails, his hammer striking home exactly right each time, and the result a smooth floor with nails driven in in an unwavering straight line. He was an excitable man, easily upset if anyone appeared to criticize his work, and equally easily made happy by praise. He was a fast worker. The shed was up before we knew it, changing our skyline permanently.

Once the shed was built, a new excitement came into life because instead of our sheep being driven overnight to the woolshed at Mossgiel Station, our neighbour to the northeast, to be shorn, the shearing team came to Coorain. There would be six or eight shearers, a 'rouseabout'—the odd-job boy perpetually being set in action by the shouts for the shearers' needs: disinfectant for a cut sheep, a count-out for a full pen of shorn animals (anything that would speed the shearers at their piece work), a wool classer and his assistant, and a cook. I had never seen so many people on Coorain before, and I never tired of watching the throbbing bustle of the wool-shed operating at full speed, the shearers' blades powered by an impressive black engine. Everyone's movements were so stylized that they might have been the work of a choreographer. A really good shearer knew just how to touch a sheep so that it relaxed and didn't kick. Bodies bent over the sheep, arms sweeping down the sides of the animal in long graceful strokes to the floor, the shearers looked like participants in a rite. The rouseabout would pick up each fleece as it finally lay in a pure white heap on the floor, walk with it to the classer's table, then he would fling his arms wide as if giving benediction, and let it fall. The fleece would descend to the table, laid perfectly flat, and the classer, hardly lifting his eyes from the table, would begin dividing it into sections, throwing it into bins organized by spinning classifications. Everyone's hands looked fresh and pink because of the lanolin in the wool. The shed was permeated by the smell of engine oil, from the engine which powered the shearers' blades, and by the smell of lanolin.

Beyond the classer's bins were the wool press and the storage area, where the bales of wool would be pressed to reduce the wool's bulk, carefully weighed, numbered, branded, and then piled to await the contractor who hauled it to the nearest railroad station. Large woolsheds had mechanical presses, but ours, being small, had a hand press operated by an athletic giant of a man, naturally nick-named Shorty. Shorty was six feet six, weighed one hundred and ninety pounds, all of it muscle; there was no spare flesh on his body. He pressed the wool into bales by sheer muscle, operating the system of weights and ratchets which could compress four hundred and fifty pounds of wool into the size of a small bale. Then he would take metal grappling hooks and fling the bales about the storage area as though they were weightless. I loved to watch him work, and whenever I wasn't needed in the sheepyards outside, I would come into the shed, climb to the highest point on the pile of bales, and talk to Shorty. He had a wife and family of his own, farther south, whom he missed terribly, since his team began shearing in Queensland in January and worked its way south until it got to us in June. Each year when he came back, he would exclaim over how I had grown, look purposedly blank for a moment, and then with exaggerated cries of absence of mind, recall that he had brought me some candy.

In quiet moments, when he had caught up with the supply of wool and had time to sit down, we exchanged confidences. On some Mondays, he would confess to having had too much to drink over the weekend. Once, deeply troubled and exasperated with himself, he talked of going to see 'the girls'. I knew in a general way that this was not the best conduct for a married man so I tut-tutted with as much wisdom as I could summon up and said once didn't matter. It seemed to offer him some relief.

*The Road from Coorain* (1989).

# *Bruce Beaver*

## ( 1928– )

*Bruce Beaver spent much of his youth in Manly, Sydney. The autobiographical* As It Was *describes his unhappy childhood when he found consolation in comics, radio serials, books, and films. In adult life, between several periods of psychiatric treatment for manic-depressive psychosis, he has worked as a radio program arranger, clerk, proof-reader, and freelance journalist. He is a well-known poet and was influential during the rise of the 'New Australian Poetry' in the 1970s. He has published two novels and twelve collections of poetry and has won several awards.*

We had a problem in our family now, actually it was my father's problem but as he was a living presence once again among us it became a family problem. Simply he drank too much at weekends and was inclined to be irascible sometimes during the week. He knew my mother and I neither loved nor respected him despite his attractive appearance or popularity at the Saturday pubs. This was before I had to bail him regularly out of gaol each week on Sunday mornings with a ten shilling note a regular 'part of the pattern', as practising sociologists, psychologists, advertising executives and other collectors of such phrases are inclined to say.

He was invalided from the army to live with us when I was still thirteen and attending Sydney High on something like false pretences (I was quite incapable of learning anything but French phrases and passages of music by heart). I would leave in a year in disgrace, in relief. But my benighted father who was an essentially kind man could not come home to the shared asperities of insecure wife and upstart critic child so was driven on to argue almost interminably with us both, singly or together—'a classical case' as the sociologists etcetera would probably say. Of what? Of obvious incompatibility—of an innate fear of life borne with bravely enough—of an Australasian male's incontrovertible right to seek companionship verging on all but oblivion with and among his own sex as sad and sexless boys in the reiterated ceremony of mateship; all the golden hours relived of golden youth and golden beer—the iron pyrites of hangover and worse: the slow corroding ulcer, the fat-congested heart, the starved, cirrhotic liver, the self-encouraged cancer. Among these stricken boys who had behaved like men in bed, on battlefield, before the sleek or gaunt employer, yet never once within their heart of hearts; who knew the world so well, yet no jot of themselves, my father moved and had his being, and was loved.

And so it seemed my mother had no husband and I no father 'to relate to' as the sociologists etcetera and newspapers uphold glibly. Without a doubt I did not want to assume the role of manhood (hairs within my armpits and about my genitals). I unhesitantly shaved the latter's first growth clean, 'simulating emasculation' according to all the sociologists etcetera who seemed to live most of my life for the next unlucky seven years. But the prickly then luxuriant growth soon reasserted itself and I forbore merely to strip in front of younger boys. Just as preoccupied with sex as any other satyr of a similar age no exhibitionist tendencies existed for me then or now. But music. And the reading of countless books and comics. These became obsessional. And falling long and faithfully in love with certain film stars seemed to be quite apart from sex, though all were 'inter-related' as the etceteras would say.

Early on one particular mid-week evening I was sprawling on my kitchen bed which served also as a couch, placed beneath the big window. The procedure on all weekends was simple, my mother and I took flight on Saturday afternoons to my aunt's house a mile away at Balgowlah. We'd return the next morning but my father would spend the day in bed and not get up until Monday. Perhaps this night he'd skipped the evening meal. For some reason he'd begun to harangue my mother and me, but this time I refused to listen, burrowing my nose into a Buck Rogers comic in which something rather horrible had just occurred. Buck had investigated a melted rocket ship and looked down in horror and pity upon the luckless pilot whose slumped back was facing the inventive reader. I could imagine without much effort the pilot's face resembling a Christmas ham overlaid with glazed crackling, or maybe a distorted charcoal mask, the ship's instruments had dripped into stalagmites of steel and bubble shapes. I was really consciously ignoring my father's berating but was hypnotically drawn to the comic's happenings.

My father strode across the room to my bed and seizing the comic book from me, hurled it through the open window into the night outside. Without a thought I leaped after it through the window and onto the lavatory roof a foot or two below then jumped about another eight feet into the backyard, rolling on grass and clay and grabbing at my comic.

Almost immediately my father had launched himself out of the window and bounced off the roof to land beside me and inspect me for breaks or bruises, the while warning me never to do such a thing again while he, the rentpayer, was talking to me.

I wept and groaned a bit and he accompanied me up the wooden stairs and back into the kitchen where my mother made a pot of tea for us all, shaking bewilderedly her dark head at the peculiar misfortune that had landed her with a brace of aerobatic madmen.

Remembering those moments I think the mantel radio was playing a then quite popular version of the 'Spinning Chorus' from the *Flying Dutchman*. I'd learnt that year a fourth part ('Round and round my wheel goes whirling ...') but I'd envied the firsts who'd had the attractive melody. When we re-entered the room my mother had switched off the set. She wanted no background music for further melodramatics. I think the jump had shaken up my middle-aged father more than myself for he quietened down for the rest of the evening but I tucked Buck Rogers beneath the cover of the couch and drank my tea and listened attentively to my parents drinking theirs in silence.

When they went to bed I lay under the window in starwinking and moonlightened darkness. My heart raced on at the thought of my unthinking leap into 'outer space' without a flying-belt, and of how gently the grass and cushioning clay received me, and also of how not one of our neighbours had noticed the flying father and son from their seasonally opened yellow and amber lit windows. And how I had felt more protection than threat from my father's descended figure crouching above me, which no doubt was just another example of a rather predictable 'love-hate ploy' in action, as the etceteras would probably say of similar launchings and landings on that calm night in a suburb of the murderous Forties. When I slept I dreamed of melted metal and calcined faces and of flying away from it all, that is, to another ship on a flying-belt quite alone and unafraid of that future.

One day it seemed the only thing to do was to take the one pound note beneath the cut glass tray upon my mother's dressing table and convert it into brandy, lime and sodas at the nearest pub. Along the way I worked it out: the drinks were two and sixpence each and eight half-crowns made up a pound. The nearest pub was one short mile away and it was downhill going. The only thing that bothered me was stealing the pound. Yet it was then I understood one reason for stealing money: to buy oblivion with. If I could have taken only the ingredients of this potent drink from my parent's liquor cabinet I would have surely done so and knocked myself out at home. It was a day when both parents were out. But my father's liquor cabinet was the shoe space in his side of the wardrobe he shared with my mother. There he'd stowed a whisky bottle that was seventy five percent aqua no longer vitae as I'd watered it as I'd consumed it. Apparently he'd been saving it for a binge as weeks afterwards he hit the roof but only touched me with his words.

Now I was on the downhill path to Manly which meant drunkenness as then there were five busy pubs to one small harbour town and every pub did better than good business every day and better than better every wet or dry weekend whether winter or summer. But it was mainly beer that rang the till and I was out for stronger stuff and one year under age. But ennui and other modified dissipations had given me a wan and ravaged look so that I would have passed for eighteen and had no fear of canny barmen. Barmaids I liked. The best of them combined maternal feelings with the warm bonhomie of a hostess—the worst were merely distant and efficient. Most of the barmen were morose and none were young, it being towards the end of the second world war and all the young men dead and gone or coming back in bits and pieces physically and mentally.

'Flying' in *As It Was* (1979).

# Barbara Hanrahan

## (1939–91)

*Barbara Hanrahan was born in Adelaide. Her father died early, and she grew up with her mother, grandmother, and great-aunt. A painter and printmaker with an international reputation, she lectured at the South Australian School of Art and at art colleges in England, and had numerous exhibitions in Australia and Britain. She published ten novels, two collections of stories, and two autobiographies in addition to* The Scent of Eucalyptus.

Reece is my great-aunt; yet at ten I am taller than she at thirty-five. She is my grandmother's sister; yet she wears children's clothing. She has frog-like eyes with half-moon lids, sad eyebrows arched in permanent surprise, a domed forehead with wrinkles, a snout, a mouth that shows her tongue—becomes an idiot-grin when she is happy. People stare at her in the street—she is real and reality is too strong for their slumbering, narcotized lives. She is a mongol.

That was what the book with the pictures of pop-eyes, hunch-backs, Siamese-twins, swollen-heads, web-fingers, lock-jaws, wry-necks said. The cover had a stain on it like snail slime. It made me feel sick, like the mad king's signature in the *Girls' Own Annual* of 1911.

(But the medical book lied—it was evil. It made me feel ashamed of Reece. It made me see her as a case-history, a circus freak; something to be petted, pitied, locked away for ever.)

The mongol is my great-aunt, who has been given three Christian names: Laurel Gwenda Reece—and is proud of them. She boasts of a boy friend called Reggie Aire. She sings 'K-K-K-Katy' and 'Daisy, Daisy' for me. She keeps her Christmas powders and perfumes and soaps in the drawer with her handkerchiefs; when she has a cold she smells of talcum powder, lily-of-the-valley, ashes of roses. She changes her dress in the afternoon; comes back from the bedroom with smudges of Pond's Peach Powder on her cheeks, mouth touched discreetly with red, lavender-water behind her ears. She begs pardon politely when she farts and looks ashamed.

My great-aunt is a martinet whom I must obey. She flourishes her broom like some Old Testament prophet, crying 'Cease!' or 'Holy Moses!' when I talk too much. She spends her days at special tasks, carried out in a rigid, unchanging order. She sweeps the kitchen, polishes the floor, cleans the bath with Gumption, sets the table, shakes the tea-leaves onto the geraniums showing her garters, boils the hand-kerchiefs in salt, does the ironing.

She likes ironing. She unpegs the dry washing, collects it in the wicker basket; sprinkles a benediction over the handkerchiefs, table-cloths, bloomers, petticoats, night-dresses—reduces them to the same tight sausage bundles. Her spit sizzles on the iron as she tests its heat. She toils happily, elbow sticking out, red in the face; turning the handkerchiefs into triangles, quartering the table-cloths, folding the bloomers to sexless halves; nosing her iron through petticoat shallows of pin-tucks and pleats, guiding it to safe harbour through virginal excesses of night-dress folds.

Reece wears lisle stockings she darns on a wood mushroom, pleated skirts that stick out behind, aprons that bloom with flowers, faded winceyette nighties, a brassière Nan takes tucks in, felt slippers, patent leather shoes, a shell-stitch cocoon of cardigans. She dresses in bed on winter mornings: sits cross-legged between the sheets—an aged kewpie doll, skirts spread fanwise, mustering courage to climb into fleecy knickers.

She is at her ease in these familiar, slightly grubby garments—she looks ridiculous on special occasions costumed in her best. Then, with her body strangely stiff, her face naked from the removal of the hair along her lip, ringlets round her brow, mouth prissily pursed trying to look alert but succeeding only in looking stupid, she is Nan's despair.

Reece had a succession of celluloid dolls called always Peggy. She had as well a sewing-box, a paint-box, families of coloured pencils in plastic envelopes, a pencil sharpener shaped like the world, a budgerigar called Tony.

Reece knitted face flannels in sugar-pink and pale pea-green, crooked squares Nan sewed to patchwork quilts, bed-socks of red and yellow that tied with satin bows. Her knitting was always in plain stitch—purl was too hard; Nan always cast on and off—she did it too loose. She sat with the crinkly balls tangling in her lap, one leg tucked under, only stopping when it was time to make the tea.

Reece was a stoic: she did not flinch when the bright rose of St Anthony's fire blossomed on her face and they pulled her eye-lashes out and sheets dripping disinfectant were hung about the house.

Sometimes Reece was sick. Then, her needles silent, her hands empty, she lay in bed: her face all ashy, her cheeks gone sunken, the circles beneath her eyes swollen to ugly bladders. One day I watched her retching into the pot: shoulders shaking, brown eyes filled with tears. And I saw her in the bath: so skinny—her bones showing through sallow flesh, and withered breasts with bruised plum nipples, a beard between her legs.

When I was lazy, I ordered Reece to fetch things for me, told her she was my slant-eyed Japanese servant. When I was ill she brought me food on a tray, wiped the sweat with a flannel. I liked her to wash my arms and legs with her soft clumsy hands; dry them with pats through the towel.

I thanked her then, but sometimes I was cruel.

There were days when I taunted her, confused her with questions; scolded her when she slept in her singlet and sat on one leg—told her she was dirty, told her she would stop the blood. There were days when I discovered the pot of urine in the wardrobe and ran to tell my mother; days when I reminded her of the rattle in her belly, the smacking sound her mouth made when she ate.

She stumbled blindly away, denying she was crying—locked herself in the bathroom.

And I was pierced with lovely, painful joy.

I crept after her; stooped at the keyhole; examined her shamelessly, like a specimen under glass, I watched, as she fumblingly took off her glasses; watched, as red-eyed and gulping, she washed her poor, crumpled face. And she came out trembling, white-faced under a layer of powder, falsely smiling.

And I turned coward and tried to comfort her and soothe her—scared that Nan might find me out.

Reece remembered her mother. She watched my reaction slyly, as she told me she was in Heaven with the Angels, dropping her voice to the reverential, pious moo she thought she should.

But my great-grandmother, who gave birth gladly to Willie and Dick and Iris, was horrified at Reece's birth. It was Iris, twenty years older, who looked after her. For a while they were separated by marriage—with widowhood they came together. The relationship that both frustrated and fulfilled my grandmother's life began.

My grandmother ministers her life away in service to an eternal child.

She pares the child's corns, searches for wax in her ears, attacks her moustache with tweezers, curls her hair with spit and bobby-pins, cuts her nails when they are soft after the bath, rubs balm in her chilblains, inserts pessaries for constipation.

Nan and Reece share each other's bath water, sleep in twin beds.

When they are both old they huddle together in the room that is so cold and smells of silence. They are strangely altered: Reece, become even smaller; Iris, changed for ever from the ruddy Jewess in crêpe marocain, smiling at her future in the sepia photograph—not even any more the grandmother I knew, but a wrinkled lady who cries in secret. They sit together before the slit eye of the electric fire; before the changing images that never change on the flickering television. Sometimes they link hands over the leaves that swirl statically on the carpet. Sometimes Reece's fingers caress her sister's cheek.

They are a pair.

*The Scent of Eucalyptus* (1973).

# Peter Conrad

(1948– )

*Peter Conrad was born in Tasmania and was educated at Oxford University, where he now lectures. He has written numerous works of literary and musical criticism and a second autobiography,* Where I Fell to Earth: A Life in Four Places *(1990), the four places being Oxford, London, New York, and Lisbon. He has also written a novel,* Underworld *(1992).*

My father's job was building Tasmania. He worked for the housing department; the new suburbs of the 1950s, bulldozed into the bush or run up overnight on squelching fields of mud, were his handicraft. He began by painting the lookalike crates, walled with weatherboard and roofed with lids of corrugated iron, and ended by overseeing others—mostly gangs of 'new Australians'—who did the same. He was proprietorial about the shaky, provisional estates. On Sunday afternoon we'd often go on tours of his building sites, to look at the timber struts and asbestos ceilings and cement paths: Chigwell clinging uncertainly to its hillside, Risdon Vale cowering under the walls of the pink prison. The paling fences seemed too frail to keep uncolonised space out; the wrinkled rooftops with their skins of colour were no security against the enormous sky. The thought of living where no one had ever lived before alarmed me. But to my father, these wooden containers signified safety. They dealt so negligently with the landscape—felling trees, creating a waste and calling it a vale—because they were his escape from it. Here where all was new the old miseries of a poor rural childhood could be forgotten. Once the bush was abolished, you could cultivate a garden.

My mother's job was tending that garden. The man builds Tasmania, the woman decorates it. At first my parents grew vegetables out the front: cabbages and trellises of beans, trenches of onions and potatoes. Behind the house, they planted three fruit trees—apricot, nectarine and peach. On their little lot, they instinctively recreated in microcosm the farms they had quit. There were even hens, cackling and crapping in their coop beside the back fence. Gradually they did away with these recollections of the agricultural past. The vegetables went into hiding beyond the woodshed, and the front yard was grassed. Between the paths, my mother planted thickets of flowers. The house retired behind a red gum and a willow tree, which clutched at the water-pipes and had to be cut down for its greed. My father took to cultivating cacti in a hut of glass. The move from vegetables to flowers was a historical victory, completing that first conquest of the wild when the houses were set in their foundations. 'They make a lovely show, don't they?' my mother would say of her blowsy hydrangeas and flaunting gladioli. This was her creation, enticed from the dry black soil; her art, and her own floral barricade against the world.

My father built the house, she made the home. When he had a shower each night after work, he'd leave an anthill of silt in the tub, trophy of his day's labour among the grime of an unmade world. My mother meanwhile crusaded against dust indoors while grubbing outside to plant her seeds and bulbs and crying if they didn't grow. They made themselves at home in the country and with the land by virtue of their daily, soiling struggle with it. I lacked their courage, and ran away.

One night I was sitting with my parents in front of the television set. No doubt the programme was *Mork and Mindy*. Restless, I glanced at my father to the right of me, my mother to the left. They had settled almost sculpturally in their chairs. This evening was the exact facsimile of every previous one; for almost twenty years, with the house to themselves, they'd been fixed in their routine and in physical attitudes which summed them up. In repose, their characters were written on their unguarded expressions and in the disposition of their limbs. They occupied eternity, as in a photograph or on a tombstone. My father had one brawny leg cocked over the arm of his chair; my mother held her chin, a finger in the groove which carved her cheek between the nose and mouth. The postures were confessional. My father's sprawling leg expressed a boyish disregard for furniture and for social niceties. It was the surly statement of a larrikin who didn't like being indoors, assertively casual. My mother's hand, with her thumb propping up her chin, her index finger tracing that furrow of flesh and her forefinger lying along her lips as if to silence them, had set into an emblem of unprotesting stoicism. It held the line on her face as if comforting a pain.

Then, suddenly ashamed of being the observer looking in at their lives, I became aware of myself doing the looking, and noticed with a shock what my own body was up to. My right leg was cocked over the leg of my chair, and my left hand was holding my chin, with a finger in that same crevice on my face. We made the perfect genetic triptych: I was the superimposed image of these two people from whom I had spent so long apart, to whom I was almost a stranger. Shiftily I withdrew my leg and found something for my hand to do inside a pocket, but within that moment I had aged several years. At long last I resigned from the adolescent rage to invent myself, and quietly capitulated to a predestining chemistry. Losing faith in your own singularity is the start of wisdom, I suppose; also the first announcement of death. The recognition spread like a stain soaking outwards through the skin. And as I wriggled there in my chair, I understood that my personality was as much a compound as my posture; an unstable merger of my father's aggressiveness and my mother's nervous qualms, of paternal gruffness and maternal worry.

I apologise for the obviousness of this domestic epiphany, but until then it hadn't been obvious to me. If you are the only child in the family, you imagine yourself to be the only person in the world. Solipsistic islands and anti-social caves were my habitat. After half a life, I had to admit that I was no self-created foundling, but a haphazard amalgam of other flesh; not even the mind had been left to my choice, since it was pressed into form by the landscapes I tried so hard not to look at. Tasmania reappeared under cover in the literary scenery of England: from where else had I derived my liking for Celtic faerylands and Gothic fogs? When you leave home, it travels with you; the parents you think you can reject dictate from within your every action. You serve your sentence for the term of your natural life.

A few days later, a genetic coincidence—accidental or designed?—occurred on the mantelpiece. My father had come home from bowls, and unpinned the badge he wears on his shirt with his surname and initials. He set it down on the shelf above the fireplace. When I came into the room, I noticed it at once: it was placed in front of my framed photograph. My face wore his name as identification; I was a caption to his existence. It didn't matter that the photograph was taken among the piled snow of an American winter, and sent home to demonstrate how I was flourishing in this cold remote climate my parents would never see. Again my freedom was abruptly rescinded. I shuddered at the justice of it.

Next time I passed through the room, the badge which tagged me had gone. But the face in the photograph looked older than it did before, and no longer belonged to an individual. Behind it, pressing through the skin like a mask embedded there, was my father's and behind that the face of his father, who died in alcoholic dejection long before I was born.

This grandfather always intrigued me. His seemed to have been a very Tasmanian fate: trapped at a dead end, imprisoned and killed by circumstances. He's supposed to have had some artistic talents, but since no one ever spoke of him it was hard to discover what they were. In any event, there was no call for them in the Lachlan Valley of the 1920s and '30s. He painted houses instead, produced children, and committed slow suicide by drinking. Though the family was silent on the subject, he was its missing link: the source of all our faces, for neither I nor any of my cousins resembled his fragile, put-upon wife, who died babbling Swedish during my adolescence. The square Germanic features we all had, and those gloomy eyebrows, must be his. Yet he was a nobody—as extinct as a Tasmanian aborigine, as non-existent as one of those convict ancestors whose names were removed from the record by Hobart's burghers when they made good. He was the denied past, returning to haunt us physiognomically. I had never even seen a picture of him.

Then a cousin found two photographs to show me. They told his story in a drastic, deathly abridgement. In the first, he's dressed up for some rustic operetta, with false moustache and shiny thigh boots, posed next to the chair of a ringleted actress: one of his enthusiasms was the theatre, it seems. He and the woman stand on a ruffled flowery hedge of carpet, with a painted curtain behind. He was a Konrad then, play-acting a Bavarian or Tyrolean peasant. The second photograph abruptly drops him in Tasmania. He and my grandmother stand in their Sunday best against a row of shrubs in an unkempt garden. Over the fence, the bush begins. Their faces are bisected by dark, shadowed under the brims of their hats; their eyes can't meet mine. Only his jowl and jaw reveal what has happened to the dapper amateur actor. His cheeks are puffy yet hollow, his mouth set in a grim, terse straight line. There's no moustache to conceal the collapse of his features. His stance is the same as in the charade, left hand in pocket. But the posture the first time is foppishly lax, calculated to show off an inch of starched cuff. Here it's uneasy, awkward. The listless weight makes him buckle at the knees. In the other scene, his right hand grips the wicker chair in which the woman sits; now it droops, making no effort to touch his wife, whose own worn hands hang in front of her imploring to be occupied.

The fantasist has been trapped in reality, locked in the shabby thorny yard on the edge of the bush. There were no caves for him to find. The face erased by the hat decomposed, and then in a second biological gamble was put back together as me.

I had placed my trust, mistakenly, in the myth of self-invention. You created yourself, and did so out of nothing. The past was permitted no claim. I learned this faith in New York, where it's the local ideology. The buildings attest to it, growing recklessly away from the earth and pretending they're suspended from the sky; so do the people, attitudinising behind their shades, treating the street as their stage, each equipped with his or her own home-made mystique. Seen in Greenwich Village recently: a woman whose T-shirt loudly declared 'I'm a legend in my own mind'.

The return to Tasmania rid me of this notion. I could feel myself disappearing into the people and places I'd been made by. The person I thought I'd elected to be was an incident in someone else's mind, a convergence of other bodies, a figure grown by the landscape itself. I had no siblings to teach me that identity was shared and derivative; my tutors were my tribe of cousins. One of them, a childhood favourite whom I hadn't seen for more than twenty years, promptly co-opted me. Her every observation annexed me to the family, of which I was one more unexceptional offshoot: 'All the Conrads are stirrers' or 'All the Conrads are great readers', she would say; and once again a casual stance was classified—'All the Conrads stand with their arms crossed like that.' I was the image, she assured me, of her youngest son.

There were other claims from the competing side. When I protested that I couldn't drive because it took an effort for me to tell left from right, my mother triumphantly seized on that as evidence for her contribution: 'Your father always said the Smiths was a bit slow.' The local paper published a photograph of me scowling in the sun beside the plane which was about to take me to the south-west. An auntie told my mother that I looked just like their father, the old man who all those years ago had chased me through the orchard, convinced I was a stranger and a trespasser. I was being taken into biological custody.

I even learned that I had a double—a cousin I'd never met, son of a sister of my father's who had gone to live in Sydney before I was born. A photo album was produced to convince me: the impersonator sat in a backyard, brandishing a glass of beer. The man wearing my face was what I should have been, a me without maladjustments. He worked, I learned, in a Sydney post office. I hatched a plot, wondering whether it might end in a life-swap. I'd go to the post office, patiently queue at his window, watch for him to notice his alter ego advancing towards him; when I got to him, I'd innocently ask for some stamps. He didn't know of my existence: would he recognise himself in this anonymous walk-in? In Sydney, I did go to the post office, and paced up and down outside debating the wisdom of the experiment. I even peered in through the door. There I was, amiably selling stamps and manhandling parcels, grinning behind the counter. The sight from a distance was enough; I left without joining the line, absurdly pleased to think that someone was enjoying—as if on my behalf—the life here that I had denied myself.

*Down Home: Revisiting Tasmania* (1988).

# 3

# LIVING BLACK

# Jimmie Barker

## (1900–72)

*Jimmie Barker was born at Cunnamulla, Queensland, the son of a German boundary-rider and an Aboriginal mother. His grandmother was a member of the Murawari people. His early years at Mundiwa, on an Aboriginal reserve, and later at Milroy, were happy ones, notwithstanding economic hardship and his father's desertion of the family. In 1912, however, the family was compelled to move to a mission at Brewarrina, where they encountered harsh treatment. He worked as a station-hand at Tottenham for more than four years.*

The day before my departure the manager was still full of kindness. I decided that I must have misjudged Mr Evans, since my wonderful future and career were all due to his efforts. He told me to be ready very early the next morning as I had to catch the train at Brewarrina. He told me that he had everything organised and was also providing food for me, which I would need when travelling. Then he gave me a coat and trousers from the store. They were made of navy blue serge; all boys received this issue once a year. That night Mother removed the large brass buttons and sewed on some ordinary ones. She insisted on making me some little cakes to eat on the journey.

The next morning we were all up very early. This was near the end of March 1915; in four months I would be fifteen years old. All my dreams were coming true, the opportunity to learn many things was ahead of me and if I worked hard I might become an engineer. I was too excited to eat any breakfast. As I was leaving, Mother put a small text of St John's Gospel into my pocket. I still have this little book.

I kissed Mother and Billy goodbye and walked slowly towards the waiting sulky. The manager handed me a letter of reference addressed 'To whom it may concern'. 'Here you are Jim,' he said, 'give it to a train guard, station master or policeman if you get lost. They like to help young coloured lads going out into the world for the first time. You have a great future ahead of you, and nothing to worry about.' He handed me a sugar bag and said there was enough food for several meals in it. As we left I saw Mother and Bill standing near our hut. We waved to each other several times as I slowly moved away.

We arrived at the station and Dick, the handy man who drove the sulky, gave me my ticket. He asked me if I had any money and I told him I had three shillings; he gave me half a crown. The train drew out of the station. My excitement was mounting: there were wonderful experiences ahead of me. It was hard to believe that I could be so fortunate, and I resolved to work and study to the best of my ability. [...]

It [was] a horribly mixed up journey [...] caused by the wrong ticket being issued at Brewarrina, or it may have been the fault of the manager. My ticket should have been to Cathundral, a small siding between Trangie and Nevertire. I spent the next day with the police at Tullamore and eventually a man arrived with a motor bike and sidecar; he was to drive me to my place of employment. This was some distance away and it was late in the evening before we arrived. I had been travelling for thirty-eight hours, had eaten very little food and felt very tired and confused. Mother, Billy and the Mission seemed hundreds of miles away. I tried to forget them and made myself concentrate on the work ahead of me and my success in the future [...]

I was relieved when I was taken into the kitchen and told to sit down. The meal did not look exciting, but as this was the place where I was to be employed, the situation was sure to improve. On the wooden table was a tin of jam, a knife and fork, a tin mug and about five pieces of bread. There was also a tin of Glauber salts. A young woman came in and gave me a plate with a little meat on it. When I said 'Thank you', she made some remark about being surprised that I should have any manners. Then a man appeared and introduced himself as my boss. He was carrying a hurricane lamp, and asked if I had brought any blankets. I had not, so I just picked up the small basket Mother had given me and the manager's sugar bag and followed the boss. After about two hundred yards he opened the door of a large building, gave me the lamp and disappeared into the darkness. He had not given me much time to eat my meal, and I was still hungry and confused.

I found myself in a very large room. It was packed with chaff bags, which were stacked against the walls; there were many seed boxes, and some horses were feeding. There was something that resembled a bed, so I sat down on it and wondered about the type of work they were going to expect me to do. There did not appear to be any machinery and it seemed an odd place to be commencing my engineering career. I felt this must be a large wheat farm, because of the number of draught-horses feeding. None of this agreed with the manager's story that I would be going to a large engineering firm and would be given a good home. My dreams were shattered, and I just sat on the bed and wept. It eased me when I thought of Jesus in the lowly manger. I tried to sleep, but the chewing and bumping noises of the horses got on my nerves. In the darkness mice and rats came out in dozens. They raced everywhere, and I felt that I could not stand it much longer. I had no matches to relight my lamp, so struggled in the darkness and moved my bed about forty feet away from the building. I had no blankets, several sugar bags were the mattress and the bed was dreadfully uncomfortable. At dawn I replaced it in the building and sat there until it became lighter.

There was little else to do, so I went and sat on the doorstep waiting for instructions. A young man came in to feed the horses, and he invited me to go to the kitchen for a cup of tea. I was given the tin mug which I had used the previous night. We did not talk much and I thought he might be the son of the boss, Mr Lindsay. I wandered around for a while until I was called for breakfast. The food was exactly the same as had been given to me the previous evening. Someone came into the kitchen and told me to go to the dining room and clear everything from the table, then I must wash and dry all the dirty dishes. I had learnt a little about washing up from Mother but was not too keen on the job. I was half-way through it when I had a visit from Mrs Lindsay, the wife of the boss. She watched me and then told me that from now on I would be doing all the washing up and would also be given additional jobs around the house during the day.

That night when I had finished the washing up Mr Lindsay said he wanted to talk to me. He took me into a room where his wife was sitting and then closed the door behind us. He started by saying that his name was Jimmie, the same as mine. We could not have two people with this name on the station, so I was to be called Joe. He told me that I was apprenticed to him for four years and I must never try to run away. If I did I should most certainly be brought back again each time, or be sent to jail if I tried it too often. I must not address anyone by their Christian name, and must do everything I was asked to do. Any refusal or rudeness would be dealt with by him. He stressed that I must not raise my hands to anyone, even in self-defence. If any black touched a white man he would be shot down. He told me that I would be fed and clothed by him and my pay would be two shillings a week. This money would be banked for me. He gave me a paper to sign and then sent me back to the stable. Once again I moved the bed into the open; I did this every night until it became too cold. As I had no blankets I had to use discarded chaff bags when I needed additional warmth.

[…]

My work was constant: washing up, fixing fires, scrubbing and polishing floors, peeling potatoes, chopping wood, and numerous other dreary jobs. In a little while I had learnt to ride and was allowed to bring in the cows and milk them. I also fed the pigs and horses. I preferred the outside jobs, but most of my days were spent inside or around the house. In that first year I can remember having only two Sunday afternoons off. On one of those days I was allowed to ride four miles to a bush church meeting. I sat alone on a long form. People moved away from me and all the congregation stared at me. I suspected it must be because of my dark skin. Several weeks later I went to my second meeting, and I realised then that it was not a place for someone of my colour. There was only one class of people and I was unwelcome.

[…]

A week before Christmas, the two brothers of the boss and the women of the family went away for a holiday. This left only the boss, an assistant for the outside work and me on the property. I did the cooking as well as helping in the paddocks. There was a lot to do, but it was better than working for women who stood over me all the time.

During the morning of Christmas Eve the boss told me that he and the other man were going away too. He said that they would be away for a week, and he told me that I was to be in charge of the place during that time. They were just getting into the car when the boss said, 'Here, Joe, I nearly forgot to give you this,' and handed me a small tin of Christmas pudding. As they drove away they called out: 'Merry Christmas, Joe.' I remembered this the next morning Christmas Day 1915. There was no sound of children, no voices, nothing but the chirping of a few birds. […]

Suddenly I thought of the large room near the laundry which I always called the Haunted Room. To my knowledge no one ever went in there, and on the door was a large lock with a chain and staple. It had always appeared firmly locked, but when I investigated I was surprised to find that no key was necessary. I opened the door and found the accumulation of years. There were books, magazines, glass, crockery, old saucepans—everything one could imagine. Some of the shelves had collapsed under the weight and many things were scattered on the floor. I looked at the books and read a couple of magazines. There was a book in the corner; it seemed as if someone had left it partly open and upright. For the first time in my life I saw the golden letters saying 'Holy Bible'. I had never seen the complete book before. I took it out on the veranda and read it for a little while. Then I looked up and noticed some smoke along the tree-tops. It looked like a bush fire about a mile from the homestead. I put the book in my room and rode out to investigate.

Some grass was alight in a five-hundred-acre paddock. I rode quickly back to the homestead and telephoned our nearest neighbour and asked for help. It was not long before people were arriving from all directions. We used fire-beaters and fought the fire all day and well into the night. Someone had told the boss, for he arrived during the night. By the next day the fire had swept through several large paddocks and had moved away up into the hills. It was impossible to put out completely, and it rushed through the adjoining properties. When we returned to the homestead we were very tired and weary; there was nothing more we could do. What a Christmas that was! […]

We returned to the house late in the afternoon, and as we walked along the veranda the boss noticed all the old books and magazines which I had left there when I saw the fire. He asked me where I had found them. When I told him he became very nasty, swearing and calling me all the bad names he knew. He looked inside the old room and then came towards me with some menace: I really thought he was going to knock me down. He told me that my punishment was to make things tidy in the old room, and I must clean up all the mess as soon as I had finished my dinner. [...] Before the boss went to bed he came in to see me. It was obvious that I would be spending most of my night in there. He asked if I had removed anything, and I told him that I had put the Bible in my room. He told me to bring it to him immediately. When I gave it to him he turned over a couple of pages and then asked if I really wanted to read it. When I assured him that I did, he said I could borrow it provided I read some of it every day while I was working on his property. Somehow from that day onwards he treated me a little better.

*The Two Worlds of Jimmie Barker: The Life of an Australian Aboriginal 1900–1972* (1977).

# Glenyse Ward

## (1949– )

*Glenyse Ward was born in Perth. She was taken from her parents when she was a year old and placed first in an orphanage, then in the Wandering Brook mission run by a German Roman Catholic order. At sixteen she was sent out into domestic service for a white farming family, named the Bigelows in* Wandering Girl. *Ward's subsequent autobiography,* Unna You Fullas *(1991), describes her years in the mission.*

I fell asleep, only to be awoken by the shrill ringing of the alarm clock. I turned over and groaned, thinking I could stay in my bed for a week.

As I lay flat on my back for a minute to get my brains ticking, it suddenly dawned on me that she was taking me to town. I quickly jumped out of bed, had a wash, got into my working clothes, just skimped through my jobs, then went inside to prepare breakfast.

She came in just as I had finished cooking it, and told me to get the boys' break-fast ready too, as they were also going to town and would be joining their parents at the table.

Seeing hers and her husband's ready, she took the plates of food in. As soon as I had cooked the boys' breakfast, I was to knock on the door and bring it in also. They would be waiting. So I hurried up and made the toast. By that time the bacon and eggs were sizzling, so I served everything out on their plates, put them on the trolley and knocked on the door. She called out to come in.

The boys were there as I pushed the trolley in. As usual, everything was quiet. All eyes were on me. Suddenly the phone rang. To my surprise, she turned to me and told me to answer it. As I said before, I had never used a phone, so I went over feeling very nervous and shy. Everyone was looking at me. I picked the phone up off the hook and said, 'Yeah!' I could not hear anything, except a lot of noise from the other end.

She slammed her knife and fork down on the table and came rushing over to me, snatched the phone out of my hand and pushed me out of the way. Never had a girl working for her been so stupid and humiliated her so much! She wondered whether I had any sense at all.

Holding her hand over the phone, she pointed out to me that I must speak into the speaking part, not the listening part, then she ushered me out of the room.

As I went back and sat down to eat my weeties, I wondered why I had heard someone talking at the other end of the phone?

When I finished those weeties, I thought I'd go out to the toilet, as I was still feeling a bit shaky from her sudden outburst. Just as I was ready to open the door to go out the back, she rang the bell. I made out I never heard it, snuck out quietly and ran flat out to my own toilet. I just made it.

When I got back to the kitchen, she was standing there fuming. She shouted at me, 'Where have you been?' She had given me strict orders never to leave the kitchen while her family was still in the dining room.

I apologized, and told her where I had been. 'Next time you want to go to the toilet, come and let me know—and did you wash your hands after?'

I said, 'Yes,' and she told me to get a move on, as she wasn't very happy with me or my attitude towards her; and when everything was done, I was to comb my hair and put clean working clothes on, then meet her outside near her car. With that she strutted out the door.

I sat down on the chair to collect myself again. I felt like having a good cry, but I soon rose up, wiped my eyes and got stuck into my work.

After I completed everything I went out, washed myself, put a clean change of clothes on, and wondered—why working clothes? Then I tripped out to her car, which was standing in the driveway.

She wasn't there, so I tried opening the doors, only to find everything locked up. So I waited patiently.

It was a couple of minutes before she came out. She opened her door and gave me her keys to open the back door. I did so, climbed in, then handed the keys to her. We were on our way.

Despite the hurt I was feeling inside, I felt glad to be going to town, although Mrs Bigelow was as usual quiet in the car.

Soon as we reached the outskirts of Ridgeway, she veered off in an unexpected direction. I saw a sign saying *Hospital* and I was thinking, 'That's funny, we're not going to the shops,' when she turned to the left, and stopped outside this beautiful home. The gardens were so colourful. Every flower seemed to be in bloom.

I noticed that the house was built high up. And from here I could see all the township as I looked back over my shoulder. I was still sitting in the car waiting for her, as she made her way up the garden path.

A couple of kids ran out to her singing out, 'Nanna', as they grabbed one of her hands on either side and walked with her. It was then that I realized this was her daughter's house. The one that came to see her every now and again.

Then her daughter Janet came out to greet her. They stood talking for a while. I wished that she would hurry up, as I wanted to go to the shops! I felt hot in the car and could have done with a bottle of cool drink.

In the meantime, while they were still talking, her grand-kids were coming down, peeping into the car at me, then running away laughing and sniggering. I felt like a monkey in a cage.

Then I saw them both coming down the path. When they reached the car, she told me to get out and follow her up to the house. I was beginning to get confused, and wondered whether I would go into town at all.

When I reached the house, her daughter asked me inside. It was beautiful. Just like her mum's. Then she came over to me with a list of duties to be done. I looked at it, then at her, and it suddenly dawned on me why I'd been brought to town a day early.

Mrs Bigelow explained to me, in front of her daughter, that every fortnight she was bringing me in to clean Janet's house, while they both went shopping.

With those instructions she left me. Janet called for her kids, and they all trooped outside, climbed into their car and drove off.

I sat down on the chair in her kitchen. As I went through the list of jobs her daughter had given, I felt very down-hearted. The chores weren't anything new. They were just what I did for her mum; but where to start, where to begin? The whole house was a mess!

I began with the kids' bedroom. There were clothes everywhere. It took me nearly two hours to get through the room. I wondered whether I would finish the rest of the house before they got back. I looked at the time. It was twelve o'clock.

I went and looked in her fridge. There was a jam sandwich on a tin plate. I presumed she had left that for my lunch. I didn't feel like a jam sandwich, so I helped myself to cold meat and salad, then I went down to her backyard to see if she had chooks. She did.

Screwing the sandwich up, I chucked it to them. They were quite pleased to get it too, as they scrambled over one another for every bit of bread.

Feeling worn out, I went back into the house to continue on with my work. It was nearly half past three by the time I had finished cleaning. The whole house smelt fresh and clean, as I had used plenty of Dettol to freshen the place up. I looked around the house and felt something was missing.

'Oh yes, that's it. I'll go and pick some flowers and put them around the rooms.'

So I went to find some vases, which she kept in the laundry—put them on the shelf in the kitchen, then got some scissors out of the drawer, and went outside. I cast my eyes over her beautiful garden then went over and snipped some red, pink and white carnations. I held them to my nose. 'Mm they are beautiful'—and I breathed in deeply the fragrance.

I added a few other types of flowers, snapdragons, hollyhocks. Now that I had bunched up a variety of flowers in my hand, I went back into the kitchen to place them in the vases and arrange them around the house.

I felt pleased with myself, as the flowers made the rooms so much more alive, and I thought I'd take myself off on a bit of a walk, seeing I had done my jobs. I strolled down the garden path, casually taking in the scenery all around me. It sure was a pretty town. The green hills towering behind the houses reminded me of those around Wandering Mission.

While I stood there gazing around, I had the feeling I was being watched. I looked to my left and right and saw a couple of ladies out in their front garden talking together and pointing at me. When I looked over the road the same thing was happening. There were ladies everywhere over the fences in the front yards—all eyes were on me!

Being used to talking to old Bill, my shyness having worn off me, I thought I'd better go over and ask the ladies if something was wrong? I made my way over to the nearest house and when I got to the fence, glanced up. There was no-one in sight. I sang out, 'Are you there?'

Then I caught a glimpse of someone peering out from a window. They reminded me of a mob of chooks in a cage.

I went back inside the daughter's house and had just sat myself down comfortably on a chair in her lounge, when I heard a car door slam. I quickly got up, ran to the kitchen and made out I was busy wiping the sink.

When the door opened, her two grandchildren came in, laughing and sniggering. They said, 'Nanna wants you!'

I left them there laughing as I went out the door. As soon as the boss saw me, she told me to hurry up and take the shopping in, since she had to take me back to the farm to get tea on for the family.

Janet hardly ever spoke to me on those fortnightly working days in town. The only time she smiled was when I caught her off guard and she had no choice. It was only when I looked after her kids that she had to face me, to tell me what times to send the boys in for their washes or meals.

Mrs Bigelow and her daughter walked past me, as I quickly began unloading the shopping, took it into the house and put everything away. By then she was saying goodbye to her daughter.

She told me to get into the car! As we made our way back, I had a notion she was going to tell me something.

*Wandering Girl* (1987).

# 4

---

# WILDERNESS, SEA, AND BUSH

# Eliza Davies

(DATES UNKNOWN)

*Eliza Davies was born in Paisley, Scotland, and made two extended visits to Australia in the 1830s and from the 1850s to the 1870s. Her autobiography includes an account of Charles Sturt's disastrous 1839 expedition, which she accompanied and which resulted in the death of Henry Bryan. She subsequently worked in Adelaide with G. F. Angas in education. Although Davies writes as if she is the social equal of Julia Gawler, the Governor's daughter, it is possible she had a more menial role.*

The brightest days have clouds sometimes; so it was with our party at the Bend. Pleasantly as we were situated, dark clouds were looming on our horizon. Four days were over and gone and our explorers had not yet returned. We thought of course that they had found water and were all right. On the fifth day, I as usual was up early and standing at the tent-door inhaling the fresh morning air, when I saw four horsemen ride into camp. Who are these? I mentally asked. I was not long held in suspense, for I heard Captain Sturt's voice. I ran to meet him as I was the only one astir in the camp. How strangely the captain looked. He was swaying back and forth and sideways; one hand hanging listlessly by his side, the other resting on the pummel of his saddle. I saw a strange look in his face. He threw himself out of the saddle and asked me:

'Where is the governor and Bryan?'

'I do not know,' I said.

Then, he muttered something, I did not know what. His words and looks were wild; I was afraid that he was out of his mind. I ran to awake Mrs Sturt and Miss Julia. They both dressed in a hurry and came out. The captain was still calling,

'Where is the governor!'

His wife's arms were soon around his neck. Poor Julia screamed out:

'Oh, where is my father? where?'

The captain tore himself from his wife, and ran to his own and the governor's tent, calling loudly for the governor and Bryan; but they gave no response. Mr Pullen ordered a search-party to be got ready, to go and find the missing men, and bring them to the camp.

'Great God, where can they be?' exclaimed the captain.

Many were the questions asked about the missing men, but none could answer. The three gentlemen who had ridden into camp with the captain were lying on the floor of the dining-tent in a state of perfect exhaustion, but were tended well by willing hands. Captain Sturt was raging wild, and poor Julia, like a stricken deer, could do nothing but weep and wring her hands, and call:

'Where is my father? my dear, dear father?'

I had no time to think. I went to the cook and had him make a strong coffee, and I gave it to the captain, and it worked like a charm to quiet him. He was able now to talk coherently. Mr Pullen said to the captain:

'I have a search-party ready to start off to look for the missing ones.'

'For God's sake let them go at once, and find the governor and the noble young fellow who is with him; they ought to have been here yesterday.'

'Where shall they go? in what direction?' was asked, and the captain told them as well as he could.

The party started, but they had not gone more than a hundred yards in a north-west direction, when he saw a solitary horseman approaching the camp from the west. The search-party had seen the equestrian, and turned back just in time to catch the governor in their arms, as he fell senseless off his horse, and was carried to his tent, where he received the needed attention. They gave restoratives, but his mind was wandering. He did not know where he was; he could tell nothing of poor Bryan; did not know where he left him. Captain Sturt ordered the search-party to proceed on their search for Bryan, and off they started toward the west, the direction whence the governor came. We had harrowing accounts of the sufferings endured by the explorers. They found no water the first day out, as they had expected; and their water only held out to the second day. Still hoping to find water, instead of returning, as they ought to have done, they continued their search, but it was fruitless. They went still farther inland, till their food, as well as water, was exhausted; then they began to retrace their steps. The governor showed signs of great suffering; his tongue began to swell and turn black, his head was affected. The captain became alarmed when he saw these signs, and he told the governor that he had better ride with all haste to camp. He was incapable of taking care of himself, so Mr Bryan accompanied him, and they both started straight for the camp, and ought to have been in more than a day before the others. After the two left; the others were still diverging from the direct route in hope of finding water. The heat was fearful; the glare of the sand was blinding. The horses were showing signs of 'knocking up,' as they say. Their tongues were hanging out of their mouths and dreadfully swollen for want of water. One very valuable horse, worth $700, fell exhausted. The sufferings of the men were so terrible, that they fell from their horses, and my two countrymen wished to be left in the desert to die; they said they could go no further; they became delirious. Captain Sturt felt the symptoms of delirium coming on himself, his tongue was beginning to swell; and as he desired to save the others if possible, he cut the throat of the dying horse, and gave each of the men a quart of the blood to drink. This they drank, disgusting as it was, and it saved them. It acted as an opiate, and they all slept a long sleep, and awoke refreshed, but with singularly wild feelings. Their half-dead horses could hardly bear them to the camp. The poor horses suffered dreadfully. A little water at a time was given them, their feet and legs were well bathed with water, and then they were fastened up to keep them from the river. One of the finest of them went mad, broke away from his fastenings, ran to the river, rushed in, looked around in triumph, then began to plunge, and finally to drink, and drank, and drank, and then fell dead. Poor Georgie! Our provisions were getting low; we had not all we needed, but we could get no fresh supplies. Meantime, the governor was as well attended as he could be under the circumstances. Only at times was he rational during the first day. His invariable answer to the question,

'Where did you leave Bryan?' was:

'I do not know.'

By close questioning at the right time, it was ascertained that as soon as the governor and Bryan left the party, the governor grew worse, and fell from his horse. Bryan did everything he could to help him up, and on his horse again; but the horse, as well as the rider, was showing signs of exhaustion, and Bryan, fearing lest the governor should die, insisted on an exchange of horses, Bryan's being the stronger and fresher. The exchange was made, and the last that was seen of Bryan was, when he told the governor to hurry to the camp while the horse had strength to carry him.

'I looked back when I left Bryan, and saw him walking slowly, leading my poor, sick horse; but I do not know where that was. Soon after I left him, I fell from my horse again, and became unconscious, or slept, I know not which, and how long I lay I do not know. When I returned to consciousness my clothes were very damp. My horse was quietly standing by me, and my arm through the bridle. I succeeded in getting on my feet, and I tried to call for Bryan. I thought he could not be far from me. I cooeed, and cooeed, but received no answering cooey. How long since, or where it was, I can not tell.'

When this exciting day drew to a close, all were anxious for the return of the search-party. When it came in sight several ran to meet the men, and see or hear of Bryan, but there was no intelligence; he could not be found. Captain Sturt was nearly frantic. He said he would go himself, and search for the youth till he was found; but he was prevented from making the attempt. He ordered another party to be formed, and to start in another direction, and to search and find Bryan, dead or alive, and bring him to camp. The party started before sun up, taking black Bob and Tom to follow up Bryan's trail, if they could find it. They could follow a trail over a naked rock. They had the sight of the grayhound, and the scent of the bloodhound. We were all hopeful that Bryan would be brought to camp this day. They got up to where the governor parted with Bryan. They tracked Bryan in a different direction from the track the governor took to get to the camp. Another day of anxious suspense passed, and the party returned, bringing with them a slip of paper, on which was written these words in pencil: 'I take a southeast direction from this place.'

They had found this paper stuck in the saddle that Bryan had taken off his horse and left on the ground, with bridle and blanket and tin pannikin. His linen coat, vest, necktie and socks were folded and placed beside the saddle. They saw the horse's tracks, where he had been turned loose, going one way, Bryan's going another. It was asked why they did not follow up the youth's track? They answered: the day was far spent when they found the things, and they had neither food nor water with them. Another party started off early next morning for the spot where the paper was found, with orders to take a southeast direction till the river was reached. Another party was despatched down the river, to where the two parties would form a junction, and they both were to search all round the country for the missing youth. Sundown brought them all to camp without Bryan or any tidings of him. His saddle, bridle, blanket and other things were brought to camp. The Blacks tracked him through scrub and brush, till they came to a great sand-flat, but beyond this not a vestige of poor Bryan was ever seen. With the instinct of hounds, Bob and Tom crossed and recrossed the sand-flat, and went round it, but beyond it no trace could be found. For one week parties were sent out every day in different directions, but all efforts put forth to find the lost one were futile. Conjecture was busy at work. Where could Bryan have gone? As far as the sand-flat, he had followed the direction indicated on his paper; the same direction would have taken him to the river; but beyond the sand-flat, there was no trace of him. There was no quicksand in the flats or he might have disappeared in it. If the savages had got hold of him and killed and ate him, we should have found his bones and vestiges of fire. Twenty-four hours after he parted from the governor, he could not have lived without water, and if he died for want of water, we ought to have found his body. Whether his grave was in the stomachs of the savages or elsewhere was never known. His end was shrouded in mystery. His spirit had flown to God, and none but God knew where his body lay. It would have been a mournful satisfaction to us all could his body have been found, and more especially to his brother, his only relative in the colony. He was good and brave, but he fell a sacrifice to government policy. The young, handsome, noble youth sleeps a dreamless sleep, which will last till a better day dawns. When poor Bryan was lying faint and low on the burning sands, with swollen tongue and closing throat, praying for water, we in camp, all unconscious of his despairing cry, were full of enjoyment. While his poor body lay blistering in the sun, his eyes starting from their sockets in mortal agony, we were talking of the time when we should all be in Adelaide recounting our travels. His brother was devoted to him, and for months party after party was sent in search of the lost one, but all to no purpose. The horse he rode was found three months afterward alive and well, but very thin.

*The Story of an Earnest Life* (1881).

# Edward Eyre

## (1815–1901)

*Edward Eyre migrated to Australia in 1832 and became an overlander, droving sheep and cattle into new country. In 1840 he began an epic journey of exploration into central Australia but was blocked by Lake Torrens. Instead he decided to attempt an east–west crossing of the continent. In February 1841, accompanied by three Aborigines and his overseer, James Baxter, Eyre set out from Fowler's Bay to attempt to reach Western Australia by the Great Australian Bight. The extract describes the death of Baxter in April 1841. From 1841 to 1842 Eyre was a magistrate and protector of Aborigines at Moorundie on the Murray River and later served as a colonial administrator in New Zealand, St Vincent, the Leeward Islands, and Jamaica.*

April 27 [1841]. [...] We had now entered upon the last fearful push, which was to decide our fate. This one stretch of bad country crossed, I felt a conviction we should be safe. That we had at least 150 miles to go to the next water I was fully assured of; I was equally satisfied that our horses were by no means in a condition to encounter the hardships and privations they must meet with in such a journey; for though they had had a long rest, and in some degree recovered from their former tired-out condition, they had not picked up in flesh or regained their spirits; the sapless, withered state of the grass and the severe cold of the nights had prevented them from deriving the advantage that they ought to have done from so long a respite from labour. Still I hoped we might be successful. We had lingered day by day, until it would have been folly to have waited longer; the rubicon was, however, now passed, and we had nothing to rely upon but our own exertions and perseverance, humbly trusting that the great and merciful God who had hitherto guarded and guided us in safety would not desert us now. [...]

April 29. [...] The horses having been all hobbled and turned out to feed, the whole party proceeded to make break-winds of boughs to form a shelter from the wind, preparatory to laying down for the night. We had taken a meal in the middle of the day, which ought to have been deferred until night, and our circumstances did not admit of our having another now, so that there remained only to arrange the watching of the horses, before going to sleep. The native boys had watched them last night, and this duty of course fell to myself and the overseer [James Baxter] this evening. The first watch was from six o'clock p.m. to eleven, the second from eleven until four a.m., at which hour the whole party usually arose and made preparations for moving on with the first streak of daylight.

Tonight the overseer asked me which of the watches I would keep, and as I was not sleepy, though tired, I chose the first. At a quarter before six, I went to take charge of the horses, having previously seen the overseer and the natives lay down to sleep, at their respective break-winds, ten or twelve yards apart from one another. The arms and provisions, as was our custom, were piled up under an oilskin, between my breakwind and that of the overseer, with the exception of one gun, which I always kept at my own sleeping place. I have been thus minute in detailing the position and arrangement of our encampment this evening, because of the fearful consequences that followed, and to shew the very slight circumstances upon which the destinies of life sometimes hinge. Trifling as the arrangement of the watches might seem, and unimportant as I thought it at the time, whether I undertook the first or the second, yet was my choice, in this respect, the means under God's providence of my life being saved, and the cause of the loss of that of my overseer.

The night was cold, and the wind blowing hard from the southwest, whilst scud and nimbus were passing very rapidly by the moon. The horses fed tolerably well, but rambled a good deal, threading in and out among the many belts of scrub which intersected the grassy openings, until at last I hardly knew exactly where our camp was, the fires having apparently expired some time ago. It was now half past ten, and I headed the horses back, in the direction in which I thought the camp lay, that I might be ready to call the overseer to relieve me at eleven. Whilst thus engaged, and looking steadfastly around among the scrub, to see if I could anywhere detect the embers of our fires, I was startled by a sudden flash, followed by the report of a gun, not a quarter of a mile away from me. Imagining that the overseer had mistaken the hour of the night, and not being able to find me or the horses, had taken that method to attract my attention, I immediately called out, but as no answer was returned, I got alarmed, and leaving the horses, hurried up towards the camp as rapidly as I could. About a hundred yards from it, I met the King George's Sound native (Wylie), running towards me, and in great alarm, crying out, 'Oh

Massa, oh Massa, come here,'—but could gain no information from him, as to what had occurred. Upon reaching the encampment, which I did in about five minutes after the shot was fired, I was horror-struck to find my poor overseer lying on the ground, weltering in his blood, and in the last agonies of death.

Glancing hastily around the camp I found it deserted by the two younger native boys, whilst the scattered fragments of our baggage, which I left carefully piled under the oilskin, lay thrown about in wild disorder, and at once revealed the cause of the harrowing scene before me.

Upon raising the body of my faithful, but ill-fated follower, I found that he was beyond all human aid; he had been shot through the left breast with a ball, the last convulsions of death were upon him, and he expired almost immediately after our arrival. The frightful, the appalling truth now burst upon me, that I was alone in the desert. He who had faithfully served me for many years, who had followed my fortunes in adversity and in prosperity, who had accompanied me in all my wanderings, and whose attachment to me had been his sole inducement to remain with me in this last, and to him alas, fatal journey, was now no more. For an instant, I was almost tempted to wish that it had been my own fate instead of his. The horrors of my situation glared upon me in such startling reality, as for an instant almost to paralyse the mind. At the dead hour of night, in the wildest and most inhospitable wastes of Australia, with the fierce wind raging in unison with the scene of violence before me, I was left, with a single native, whose fidelity I could not rely upon, and who for aught I knew might be in league with the other two, who perhaps were even now, lurking about with the view of taking away my life as they had done that of the overseer. Three days had passed away since we left the last water, and it was very doubtful when we might find any more. Six hundred miles of country had to be traversed, before I could hope to obtain the slightest aid or assistance of any kind, whilst I knew not that a single drop of water or an ounce of flour had been left by these murderers, from a stock that had previously been so small.

With such thoughts rapidly passing through my mind, I turned to search for my double-barrelled gun, which I had left covered with an oilskin at the head of my own break wind. It was gone, as was also the double-barrelled gun that had belonged to the overseer. These were the only weapons at the time that were in serviceable condition, for though there were a brace of pistols they had been packed away, as there were no cartridges for them, and my rifle was useless, from having a ball sticking fast in the breech, and which we had in vain endeavoured to extract. A few days previous to our leaving the last water, the overseer had attempted to wash out the rifle not knowing it was loaded, and the consequence was, that the powder became wetted and partly washed away, so that we could neither fire it off, nor get out the ball; I was, therefore, temporarily defenceless, and quite at the mercy of the natives, had they at this time come upon me. Having hastily ripped open the bag in which the pistols had been sewn up, I got them out, together with my powder flask, and a bag containing a little shot and some large balls. The rifle I found where it had been left, but the ramrod had been taken out by the boys to load my double-barrelled gun with, its own ramrod being too short for that purpose; I found it, however, together with several loose cartridges, lying about near the place where the boys had slept, so that it was evident they had deliberately loaded the fire-arms before they tried to move away with the things they had stolen; one barrel only of my gun had been previously loaded, and I believe neither barrel in that of the overseer.

After obtaining possession of all the remaining arms, useless as they were at the moment, with some ammunition, I made no further examination then, but hurried away from the fearful scene, accompanied by the King George's Sound native, to search for the horses, knowing that if they got away now, no chance whatever would remain of saving our lives. Already the wretched animals had wandered to a considerable distance; and although the night was moonlit, yet the belts of scrub, intersecting the plains, were so numerous and dense, that for a long time we could not find them; having succeeded in doing so at last, Wylie and I remained with them, watching them during the remainder of the night; but they were very restless, and gave us a great deal of trouble. With an aching heart, and in most painful reflections, I passed this dreadful night. Every moment appeared to be protracted to an hour, and it seemed as if the daylight would never appear. About midnight the wind ceased, and the weather became bitterly cold and frosty. I had nothing on but a shirt and a pair of trowsers, and suffered most acutely from the cold; to mental anguish was now added intense bodily pain. Suffering and distress had well nigh overwhelmed me, and life seemed hardly worth the effort necessary to prolong it. Ages can never efface the horrors of this single night, nor would the wealth of the world ever tempt me to go through similar ones again.

April 30.—At last, by God's blessing, daylight dawned once more, but sad and heart-rending was the scene it presented to my view, upon driving the horses to what had been our last night's camp. The corpse of my poor companion lay extended on the ground, with the eyes open, but cold and glazed in death. The same stern resolution, and fearless open look, which had characterized him when living, stamped the expression of his countenance even now. He had fallen upon his breast four or five yards from where he had been sleeping, and was dressed only in his shirt. In all probability, the noise made by the natives, in plundering the camp, had awoke him; and upon his jumping up, with a view of stopping them, they had fired upon and killed him.

Around the camp lay scattered the harness of the horses, and the remains of the stores that had been the temptation to this fatal deed.

As soon as the horses were caught, and secured, I left Wylie to make a fire, whilst I proceeded to examine into the state of our baggage, that I might decide upon our future proceedings. Among the principal things carried off by the natives, were, the whole of our baked bread, amounting to twenty pounds weight, some mutton, tea and sugar, the overseer's tobacco and pipes, a one gallon keg full of water, some clothes, two double-barrelled guns, some ammunition, and a few other small articles.

There were still left forty pounds of flour, a little tea and sugar, and four gallons of water, besides the arms and ammunition I had secured last night. [...]

At eight o'clock we were ready to proceed; there remained but to perform the last sad offices of humanity towards him, whose career had been cut short in so untimely a manner. This duty was rendered even more than ordinarily painful, by the nature of the country, where we happened to have been encamped. One vast unbroken surface of sheet rock extended for miles in every direction, and rendered it impossible to make a grave. We were some miles away from the sea-shore, and even had we been nearer, could not have got down the cliffs to bury the corpse in the sand. I could only, therefore, wrap a blanket around the body of the overseer, and leaving it enshrouded where he fell, escape from the melancholy scene, accompanied by Wylie, under the influence of feelings which neither time nor circumstances will ever obliterate. Though years have now passed away since the enactment of this tragedy, the dreadful horrors of that time and scene, are recalled before me with frightful vividness, and make me shudder even now, when I think of them. A life time was crowded into those few short hours, and death alone may blot out the impressions they produced.

*Journals of Expeditions of Discovery into Central Australia and Overland*
*from Adelaide to King George's Sound, in the years 1840–41* (1845).

# James Armour

(DATES UNKNOWN)

*James Armour, a Scotsman, spent three years in Victoria from 1852. He was unsuccessful at the Bendigo and Avoca diggings and was often destitute, sometimes obtaining work as wool-baler, butcher, camp cook, carter, stockman, and yard-hand. He later wrote several books on technology.*

At sundown I camped about four miles from the Avoca diggings, and in the morning entered on them with the intention of passing through for the bush on the other side, should no friendly face meet me on the way. I had barely reached the inner circle of tents, when I observed a little man apparently eyeing me with rather more than ordinary interest. My breakfast had been anything but stimulating, and my gait in consequence was perhaps a little pensive, but I quickly mended that on drawing near him. His face somehow did not invite me to seek close acquaintance with him, yet I was glad when he asked if I wanted work, and soon engaged myself to serve him with stones and mortar in the building of an oven, for fourteen shillings a day and my rations. Taking me to his tent, he introduced me to his wife and child. The place looked clean and tidy, and wore an air of comfort I had long been a stranger to. My employer told me his name was Watty Scott, and that I would find him a good man and true if dealt fairly with. After much talk about the perfidy of former mates, he said that on the completion of the oven, he would take me for a partner and go digging; that meantime he thought he had read me sufficiently well to know me; I might consider the partnership already entered into, and might look upon all he possessed as half my own, all except—here he drew his wife tenderly to his side, and looked prayerfully in my face. I knew not what to say to this, and was perplexed about what might be coming next, so rapidly had events developed within two hours, but as he sat between me and the door I could only ask how he could think it of me, and look reproaches at him. Meanwhile the wife never spoke, but disengaging herself from him, went outside. He laughed, and laying his hand upon my shoulder, said, 'it's all right, Jamie'—he had already familiarised my name—'I was only trying you, come let's take a walk.' He does not care about beginning work that day, but next, meantime I can take a look about me.

Evening comes, and Watty is not sober. I try to guess his age, but fail to satisfy myself; he has no whiskers, seems never to have needed shaving, and has a crop of jet black curly hair. He seems to be between thirty and forty-five. His wife seldom speaks, seldom looks at either of us, and appears very sad. Watty regrets that I have no tent with me, but thinks an arrangement can be made for my accommodation.

The night being too chilly and damp for camping outside under a bush cover, I was only too glad at the offer of a strip of bark upon the floor of their tent to make my bed on. The wife made up a pillow for me, spread a spare quilt upon the bare hollow of the bark, and then my own blankets over all, in so quiet and kindly a manner, that I felt moved with respectful gratitude, while somewhat ashamed of my intrusion on her privacy. On making some remarks to that effect, Watty poohed and bade me never mention it. I was to consider myself one of the family now. When bed time came, he and I discreetly went outside to the fire. A drunk man's talk is none of the most edifying, and I had become weary of his during the long evening, but had borne with it so patiently, and so followed up his humours, as at least to delay his very evident desire to quarrel with his wife. To this fact I in part attributed her motherly interest in the comfort of my bed. The little while we remained outside, he talked more rationally, but as the topic was mainly of the weather, with which the passions have but little concern, little positive conclusion could be drawn from the circumstance regarding the man.

On re-entering, we found as we expected the wife and child in bed. They lay upon a rude bench raised some eighteen inches from the ground, and which occupied at least one-half of the tent floor, which measured only about ten feet by eight; a narrow space of some twelve inches wide separated my humbler couch from theirs. I could not get to sleep for Watty's talking to or rather at his wife, who maintained a singular silence, save once or twice when she ventured on a brief meekly-spoken answer; somehow this meekness did not suit him, but only excited him the more, until about three o'clock in the morning, his delirious abuse became outrageous. Sense and reason, judgment and humanity forsook him in the paroxysm he had wrought himself into, and I could only hear the ravings of a madman. I tremble for the wife and child—by the sounds he seems to be gathering himself together, and while I am still holding my breath in doubt about what he means to do, they are pushed bodily out of bed and fall heavily on me. The case was beyond my help, so I lay still; the cries of the child made it a hard task to do so. The madman's delirium seemed to calm considerably on getting the whole bed to himself, and it might be towards four o'clock he muttered himself to sleep; the wife then taking courage rose from the floor, and ventured in again beside him. On waking at break of day, I found him up and dressed; hearing me move he bade me good morning more heartily than I could answer him just then; a habit he had of raising his eyebrows, and which seemed to say 'look within who may, there is nothing to conceal,' lent a certain air of candour to his face, that at first shook my faith in what had passed being more than a troubled dream. He got the fire lit, and the kettle boiled, and addressed his wife Eliza in accents so subdued, that I was almost inclined to doubt the evidence against him.

We commenced the building of the oven. I was not a weak man, but he proved so good a workman, that my back was never off the bend keeping him supplied. In an hour or so however, greatly to my relief, he became thirsty, crossed the road to a grog tent for a drink, and came back no more till dinner time. After dinner he said that this being now a broken day, he would wait till next day, and then begin work in earnest. I fetched water and firewood from a distance for the wife and began to talk with her, and keep the infant in amusement, and when Watty came home in the evening, continued to keep him in at least peaceable humour. His prodigious self-esteem made this comparatively easy to do so long as I continued feeding it, but I found it at times disposed to froth up into arrogance, and, at intervals, my ready consent to all he said and did, seemed likely to take a wrong direction. Taking my hand in his, and falling away into a whining mood, he said he had been an unfortunate and ill-used man all his days, that he ought to have been, and would have been an independent gentleman long before now, had he not been deceived, and robbed; and kept down among the dust by—here his eye glanced over to his wife, as she bent her head over some piece of sewing for the baby, and I felt uneasy at the glare of malice that reddened in his face. At haphazard I broke in upon him with as lively a sally as I could muster at the sudden call; for a moment he hung in the balance, I prepared myself for some extremity, but happily the fell grimness of his look relaxed, his overweening pride was recovering its seat. I had touched him rightly, and to my intense relief he broke out into a laugh, and for the present contented himself with merely blowing out the candle she was working by. I felt it dreary work, but for the woman's sake I persevered, and so passed our second night together. I thought the drink that he had taken would surely overpower him when he went to bed, but the warmth seemed only to make him worse, and the frightful words that poured from him made it like a night in a cell of hell. He appeared to have lost all recollection of my presence, so that what I suffered I feared was but a little of what the poor wife would call her daily life with him. It had been taking place before I came to them; it could not go on so for ever, but the end I never knew.

The oven was not progressing, and on the fourth day I found him in the company of two slouching fellows in a beer shop. He introduced me with due form, for he liked to do things respectably, then taking me to one side, begged the loan of half-a-crown, but I could only promise him the loan of one when I received the wages due to me, and took the opportunity of calling his attention to the condition of my boots, the soles of which had quite loosened from the uppers, requiring some little management when walking to keep my toes within. My appeal was ill-timed, and he seemed for the moment ashamed of my dilapidated appearance, the eyes of his friends being at the time directed towards us. Having respect for my feelings, however, he said no more there, but led me out to the road, and reminded me of our partnership agreement, and that talking about wages was as good as mistrusting him. The oven he said would be soon finished, and then boots and whatever else was needed I would receive to my heart's content.

Late in the afternoon I returned to the tent, and found the wife sitting pale and trembling, her eyes fixed with evidently unobservant gaze, and her lips twitching nervously apart. As I stood for a moment in the doorway, looking in at her, there fled once and for ever from my mind all doubt of the reality of broken hearts. For such distress I had no consolation adequate, but mute though I was at first and disconcerted, it seemed as if my coming had broken the rigour of her grief. I was sad with very pity for her, and my manner may have revealed that much as I quietly seated myself inside the door. I made an attempt to speak about something I had seen on my way back, but was stopped short by an indescribable working of her features, and while I was yet looking—my half-told story fast dropping out of mind—the tears started to her eyes, and for a few minutes I heard nothing but sobs, the like of which I had never before known. When her grief had somewhat spent itself, she told me I had better leave, or I would be getting into trouble, as Watty was after no good with the men I had seen him with, one of them she knew to be a common thief. After a fresh outburst of crying over her poor infant, she told me further with many an outbreak of shame and sorrow between, that he had brought this man to the tent for her specially to entertain, and had menaced her with his eye, because she would not, and that she looked for nothing short of death on his return. Her arms encircled her young child, and her eyes were at times bent sadly on its small upturned face as it lay innocently asleep upon her breast.

The day was already near its close, there was barely time to seek out and prepare some sleeping place in the bush, even did I start at once, and the weather was too wintry for an unsheltered bed upon the ground. I had not yet determined what to do when there came to the door one of five rough looking men who had erected a couple of blankets for a tent early in the day a few hundred yards from Watty's. Being acquaintances of Watty's this was a friendly visit. After a little talk, making known to him my intention of leaving, he kindly invited me to pass the night with him and his mate. I gladly accepted, and left with him shortly after. On getting among my new acquaintance, I found that one of them, called Bill, had only the day before returned, the victor in a prize fight at Tarrangower. He was a short but strong and heavy-bodied man, with a dark stolid-looking eye, and very deaf. He no sooner learnt that the little mason was ill-using his wife than he swore he would have her from him in the morning. He appeared to have no thought of her objecting to the change; his faith had very likely grown to this assurance by considerable practice in similar disinterested knight-errantry among the distressed wives of the society he moved in. By their conversation I learnt that they were all old convicts, that Watty was one also, and that they were mostly natives of the town of Paisley. One of them had only half served his sentence of seven years in Van Diemen's Land, and had stolen away in a passenger ship bound for Melbourne. On this account he was living as quietly as circumstances would permit. There seemed no lack of money, for liquor was in plenty, and they appeared fond of it. I was luckily in time to hear how Bill had fought and won his battle, in which he had received but little damage. His opponent, a 'new chum' fresh from England and conceited with excess of science, had looked on him as an unlearned bumpkin upon whom his subtleties of art would be almost wasted. In part this estimate was right, Bill was brute enough not to see the beauty of the other's fence, and being of the old barbaric school had at once rushed to blows and buttocking, feints and manoeuvres he snuffed at, and going in straight at his man was ever quickly bringing him to grief. His knuckles were his pride, he had before now driven nails up to the head in pine boards with them, and cushioning one blow upon the new chum's stomach quickly brought to light what he had been eating last and all but broke his back, a feat that he gleefully styled 'doubling him up'.

It was my general habit to be civil and conciliatory in strange company and I felt no inclination to be otherwise now—whichever way my 'fur' was rubbed, I made that the right way, and so succeeded that when bed time came there were two who claimed me to lie next them. Our sleeping place was the floor on a litter of brushwood; each rolled his blanket round about him, but the space was so limited, that one had scarce room to turn without jostling his neighbours. On the one hand I had to fend my face from the long greasy uncombed hair of the Vandemonian, and on the other from the sour beery breath of Bill's brother.

Breakfast was scarcely over, when Watty came tumbling in amongst us with an air of muddled defiance, and yet with an evident desire to put himself on the best of terms with us. Slapping as many shoulders as he could well get at, and ruffling one head of hair, by way of provoking the owner to say something pleasant, and failing in his object, the situation was becoming awkward for us all, when the dish of beef and bread from which we had been eating caught his eye. With a 'hie Joe reach that dish here, the very thing I wanted,' he took it on his knee, and without uncovering commenced with his knife upon the victuals. Regardless of the coolness apparent in his hosts, he called on one of them for mustard, saying 'that beef was nothing without a relish', then nudged another with his elbow to see if there was any tea left in the billy. Wiping his lips when he had at length taken his fill— and that was not a little—he replenished his pipe with borrowed tobacco, and set himself to talk. He had a perfect command of words, and a pointed manner of expressing himself that readily attracted attention in his more earnest moods, so that the discussion he now entered on soon found interested listeners. He began by drawing a picture of their defenceless condition were misfortune or sickness to come upon them. Pointing to the disordered brushwood of the beds, and the damp dirty looking piles of blankets huddled together at the far end, he painted them lying there through days and nights of sickness, dependent on chance friendships for all those little attentions that a sick man needs, and when he had apparently sobered them to think how it might be thus, he shifted ground, and asked them to look at the men of Manchester and Liverpool, placed in like circumstances with them, but banded together in a common cause against bad times—relieving their needy, and from their mutual sympathy and support, never knowing want, while they of Paisley went their ways in solitary pairs or single tentfuls, stretching no helping hand to save a brother in distress, but with close-fisted narrow meanness with a single eye to self, leaving fellow townsmen, old schoolmates even, to fight with their troubles as they best could, and drift away on their necessities if they could do no better. His heart, he said, was pained at the estrangements and cold-shoulderings of those whom a long life of misfortune such as theirs should rather have drawn together in the fellow-feeling of fellow sufferers—it led him at times, through very shame, to disown being a native of the town that had raised men possessed of so little generosity. The times in short were so grievously hard upon the working man, that with the counsel of a friend he advised the establishing of a fund, from which relief might be given as need required, and contributions from the more successful among the brethren might for this purpose be deposited in the hands of some well known party. As his subject grew upon him, his manner became more earnest, till at the close he bore the look of one ready to sacrifice himself to any extent in the good enterprise; his pipe had gone out in his enthusiasm, his eyes sought to gather the feeling of the company, but a more stolid lot of faces I never before saw grouped together. Vexed by their apathetic treatment of the scheme, he stretched his hand to them saying 'Well now men, how is it to be, for the honour of our town how is it to be,' on which the Vandemonian broke the spell by crying 'to blazes with the town, much reason have we to mind its honour.' The others fell back in a roar of laughter. Watty in a fury dashed his pipe into fragments in the beef dish, and cursing their stupidity hurried from the tent in the direction of his own, the cries that shortly afterwards arose from which made known to us that his gentle partner was expiating our indifference, on which Bill, recollecting his vow of the previous night, to see to her relief, abruptly rose and catching Watty as he was coming out of his own door with the air of a conqueror, thrashed him well, but only with his open hand, for 'he never made his hand a fist,' he said, 'but when he had to do with men.' The wife cried bitterly when she saw it. It was not likely to help her any, and I could not help thinking that the sight of suffering under the chastisement reanimated her old abused affection for him into throbs of tender but timid compassion. The weather was stormy and wet, which made me glad to accept my friends' hospitality for at least twenty-four hours longer. I repaid their kindness by becoming hewer of wood and drawer of water to them. [...] About two hours after sundown we were all inside, playing at cards by the light of a slim candle, when Watty appeared at the door in company with a tall, robust, rough-bearded and unwashed man, rather past the prime of life, whom he introduced in rather a stiff manner as his friend 'Scottie Stratton'. They seemed both the worse of liquor, but as regards that, the others were fairly on equal terms with them. My impression was that the mental habits of the company tended little to reflection, and that the things of the passing moment were generally sufficient for their attention, but I detected an air of wariness in Bill, attributing it to his small transaction with Watty in the morning, and to his deafness, which called for the more active use of his eyes. However that may be, room was made for the new comers and the cards were reshuffled that a new game might be begun to include them. All went well enough for a while, and the bottle passed freely from hand to hand, the absence of a glass obliging them to measure their takings in their mouths. At length a hitch occurred, Watty declared that Stratton was being imposed upon, on which Stratton knocked the candle out, and in the darkness all struggled to their feet. I was farthest from the door, and for a moment thought from the shaking of the tent pole that a fight had commenced upon the spot, and was glad on hearing Bill in the midst of the stumbling and confusion say with steady voice 'O if that's your little game I'm ready for you, come, get outside.' A couple of candles were got and lighted. The two men, Bill and Stratton stripped, Bill shorter by a head than the other. The candles glared in the damp breeze, as they were held high above the level of our eyes. The places were taken, the word 'all ready' was given, and I heard a rush and the dull sound of blows upon a face, then a lumbering fall upon the ground. Again and again was this repeated, till I began to wonder how much beating it took to kill a man. Stratton's height and length of arm were of no avail against the determined energy of his opponent. I saw the bustling and the rushing leaps; I heard the deep muttered curses of the losing man, and the shouts and imprecations of the others, and felt as if accessory to a mad revel of damned spirits. Could I have got my blankets out unseen, the dark bush that night would have been my bed. When becoming faint with compassion for the man whose flesh was being so bruised, I heard another fall, followed by a third, and an 'ugh' exclamation, that plainly told me the uppermost man had fallen with his knees upon the body of the other, but before I had time to think there came a succession of mashing sounds that needed no interpretation. Stratton was being beaten on the ground, Bill's blood was up, and had not his fellows rushed in and taken him off, there would have been murder done. Bill was forced into the tent, Watty with difficulty getting his man raised to his feet, staggered off with him, and I saw him no more.

When after a time, I ventured in among them, the bottle had resumed its work. Bill was singing ballads, and the others were so elated with his fighting merits, that daylight was close at hand before they went to bed—possibly they would not have lain down at all had the liquor lasted. In the morning, after breakfast, I bade them good-bye, and wandered forth, not caring whither. I had now tasted of both frying-pan and fire, and felt truly thankful on finding myself once more breathing the air of solitude among the ranges.

*The Diggings, The Bush and Melbourne; or,*
*Reminiscences of Three Years' Wanderings in Victoria* (1864).

# Emily Skinner

## (1832–90)

*Emily Skinner came to Australia in 1854 to join her future husband, William. In May 1855 she joined him at the Owen diggings in Victoria. Her account of their experiences on the diggings is one of the most graphic and reflective of goldfields narratives. Hamilton, who is mentioned in the extract, was a friend of the Skinners who first persuaded them to try the diggings.*

Winding slowly down hill, we soon passed the pretty waterfall of Reid's Creek and came in sight of the white tents of the new diggings. A very large number of them were clustered in a hollow or basin among the hills, with the creek running through the midst. No longer a stream of clear water as in the days when it was used for sheep. The whole place had formerly been a large sheep station, and I believe the gold had just been discovered by the shepherds or stockmen—I forget which.

There was every variety of tents, from the large framed ones which did duty for hotels and stores, to the small tents of the single miners. It was into one of these latter that I was introduced. Close to the spot on which our party were already busy erecting a good sized frame for one. The owner of this small house, being an acquaintance, had kindly placed it at my disposal, till our own should be ready, as I steadily declined to avail myself of hotel accommodation. So here I and the little one rested and watched the process of building. In a few hours it was finished:

a neat frame firmly fixed, of strong wood covered with stout unbleached calico tightly stretched. It was divided into two compartments, a place left for a door and windows to be put in next day, which, alas, were not of glass, but calico again. A second roof stretched a little distance above the first, was called a 'fly' and helped to make the tent much cooler (great fun it used to be on a windy night, when the flies would become loose from their fastenings and break away). There was no fireplace, that was a luxury to come, and for the present the cooking must be done on a stump burning in the open air. The floor was roughly pared and then the furniture moved in, but by this time night was falling and there was not time to put up bedsteads, so spreading first oilcloth, then whatever we could find, under our mattresses on the somewhat damp ground, we were glad to rest so. The others of the party had their tents nearby. I have wondered since how people did not get their deaths from rheumatism in those times, but we seldom heard of such a thing then. Perhaps they were all too busy and eager for gold.

In a few days' time we had a fireplace built of turf sods, cut evenly and laid like bricks one above the other. We lined the tent with green baize, and it was really pretty and comfortable, only much hotter than our old bark house. The place itself lying so low and sheltered, was much warmer than Spring Creek. Now, for the first time, I saw a new rush in all its glory. Such a rowdy place it was, by the way. I think I heard the word 'rowdy' for the first time on the Woolshed, and it is very expressive. It is wonderful how quickly one gets to use these colonial expressions too. The ground was mainly taken up in very large claims, and the fortunate owners were called 'bosses', some of them employing a large number of men, each of whose wages was from £7 to £9 per week. When 30 or 40 men were paid, it must have taken a nice little sum, but they were nearly all getting immense quantities of gold. It was very fine here, and always found in black sand or tin ore, which of itself, was very valuable. William's party, being late on the spot, had to go lower down for their ground, and though pretty fair, was nothing like as good as the upper part of the creek.

Extravagance seemed the order of the day. It was no uncommon thing for one or two of the richest bosses to give a champagne shout; that is, to stop in the middle of the day and treat all their men with champagne, then £1 per bottle. Everything was very dear. But few women and children as yet were there, and hotels and restaurants did a thriving trade. There were numbers of them, and at most of the former, five or six or even more girls were kept who did the work in the day and in the evening were expected to join in the dance. Billiard markers and musicians were kept. Concerts and amusements of all description going on. Generally, the dances were open to all, but sometimes a special ball would be given, admission by guinea tickets. On one of these nights, being curious to see how they looked,

William took me down and we stood by one of the open windows of the ballroom for a few minutes. I was surprised to see how really well and appropriately the girls were dressed—not gaudily, as I had expected, but some, most beautifully. Many of these girls made very good marriages, and in a few years were the leading members of society in the town. Of course, there were exceptions, one in particular comes to mind of a girl marrying a well-to-do hotel keeper, and after living in great style for a year or so, who should walk in but wife No. 1. She had come out unexpectedly from home. Many others made hasty matches that turned out wretchedly enough and the old story of man's treachery and woman's folly and faithfulness was too often met with. But at first, women were rather scarce, so much so, that when one first made her appearance out walking, she was sometimes greeted by the men working in the claims with loud cries of 'Jo Jo', the old derisive cry with which the police had been greeted in the hunt for the miners' licenses a year or so previously. (These had now been superseded by miners' rights, a much less harassing procedure.) The first time I ventured out to make some purchases, I heard these cries, but having my baby in my arms, took no notice till their prolonged repetition forced me to look around. To my horror I found they were directed at me. That was the only time, though, and soon the practice wore off.

One night there was to be a grand free ball and the supper at an hotel near. We heard an account of it next day from one of the guests. He told us he never saw such a scene of confusion. A splendid supper had been prepared, every dainty procurable. Of course it was expected that drink consumed would amply pay for all expense, but I daresay it did, for they got too much beforehand and as soon as the supper room was opened a regular rush was made. In a few minutes the table was a perfect wreck, one seizing a ham, another a fowl, and so on. The last he saw was the poor hostess lying on a sofa, kicking and screaming in hysterics and frantically hugging a roast suckling pig to her disconsolate bosom. She had not expected her nicely prepared supper to go off so. I do not think such bad behaviour happened very often though, rowdy as the place was.

The summer there proved to be an intensely hot one, and the fever, which then often appeared on newly opened ground, broke out very severely. The local doctor and druggist must have made a fortune. Deaths were a frequent occurrence, especially among the young people who made up most of the population. The children were quite young. It was a treat then to see an elderly couple. William and I both fell victim to the prostrating low fever and both at the same time, so that we were in a hard case, as it was impossible to hire anyone. All were too busy with their own affairs, and but for our good angel of a little woman who lived near, we should have fared worse than we did. She, poor thing, was not strong, had her child to attend to beside her husband and his mates to cook for, yet contrived to give a good deal of her time to me, especially to the poor babe. My husband got over it in a much shorter time than I, and then he was able to help me a little, for I lay many weeks almost at death's door, raving in delirium in intense weakness. In the midst of this the dear child, from a fine healthy babe, became sick and passed from us. So utterly worn down was I that I was almost indifferent to it; and not till partly restored to health did the anguish of the loss come upon me.

[...]

I rose from this sickness after many weeks, the shadow of my former self, hair fallen out, teeth loosened and a figure shrunken and bent with weakness. I had to use a stick to totter about with at first; but by degrees, youth and a good constitution overcame in a measure the effects of the fever. As strength returned the time began to hang heavily, having only Hamilton boarding with us. Among the several people who had done little kindnesses for us in our time of need was one to whom I felt especially drawn. She was a middle aged lady, who, with her husband, son, and two young daughters, had just come out from home. She had been an only daughter and reared in luxury, but had chosen to accompany her husband to the diggings. To see the way she accommodated herself to the new way of life and strove to help her husband, who was not very fortunate, made me feel a useless creature. She opened a small school so that she could instruct her own girls with others. She gave lessons in music and French to a few aspiring pupils, and not content with all this, she also undertook needlework, such as children's dresses, flannel shirts etc., for the stores. One day she proposed that I should help her with the sewing, as she could get very much more than she and her girls could do. I was very glad to take her offer. Besides giving me a fresh interest, the money, which I thus received, was my very own. Many happy afternoons we passed, sewing together. Sometimes we would take our work and a book for one of the girls to read aloud, and, after school was out, go up to the top of the hill that overlooked the country for miles around, with glimpses of the Buffalo and mountains of New South Wales in the distance. Here in a huge granite armchair, formed of immense boulders of blocks of granite, we would sit until the lengthening shadows spoke of supper time. Sometimes the men folk would come and meet us, but generally they were too tired after their hard day's work in the claim. How hot and tired they used to be in those long summer days, and what quantities of tea and hop beer I used to make for them. It was an intensely hot place, like an oven, and the nights were nearly as bad as the days, especially when the surrounding hills were covered with bushfires. It was alarming to hear the crackling of the fire in the night time, but it seldom did any damage as there were no farms or fences near. Sometimes, though, some horses turned out on the hills would get burnt, poor things.

*A Woman on the Goldfields: Recollections of Emily Skinner 1854–1878* (1995).

# Morley Roberts

## (1857–1942)

*Morley Roberts came to Australia early in 1877 and worked in Melbourne and on stations in the Riverina. He recorded his experiences in two volumes of autobiography,* A Tramp's Notebook *(1904) and* Land-Travel and Sea-Faring. *The author of more than eighty books, including stories of the sea, historical romances, novels and studies on psychological, medical, and literary topics, he drew on his Australian experiences in many stories and romances. He returned to Britain in 1879. The following extract describes his voyage to Australia.*

Few incidents of importance occurred from the time we were well to the eastward of the Cape, until we were south of Cape Leeuwin, the most westerly point of the great Australian Bight, beyond a few rows among us in the steerage, which was becoming, for unspeakable reasons, almost uninhabitable by a person of any cleanliness, and the broaching of the cargo by the second-class passengers, who, by drawing some nails with great skill, managed to steal several cases of the finest Irish whiskey.

Strange as it may seem from what occurred off the Leeuwin, our captain was a total abstainer. But to make up for this sobriety, his wife, a fine handsome woman she was, invariably took too much to drink when it blew heavily, and increased her doses in proportion to the violence of the storm. [...] But never until the gale off the Leeuwin did she entirely lose control over herself and finally become insensible, which shows that the weather there surpassed in violence anything we had experienced in the Bay or off the Cape of Good Hope. And indeed this was so.

It had been Mr Mackintosh's middle watch that night, and not liking the look of the weather, he took in some of the lighter canvas just before he went below at four o'clock. The second mate, Mr Ladd, although the weather grew worse yet, did not shorten sail further, and when the captain came on deck he ordered those sails to be set which Mackintosh had stowed four hours previously. The second officer stared a little when he received his superior's orders, but of course said nothing, although the wind was now coming in heavy puffs from the west, and the sea was rising rapidly. By this time, from my own experience and from the face of Ladd, I could see we were probably in for a heavy gale, and boy-like, I was pleased at the prospect. For within certain limits a storm at sea always exhilarates me in a most marked degree, and I am never so merry as when it blows hard. This, too, promised to be a sight worth seeing, for there was no sign of rain, and the sky was not quite overclouded until noon, by which time the wind was reaching its maximum. […]

At eight o'clock Mr Mackintosh came on deck again, and as he stood near me I could see he was angry at the conduct of the captain. I suppose Ladd told him what had happened, for he only greeted his superior officer with a rather surly 'good morning', and made no remark to him. With the skipper on deck taking an interest in matters, it was no part of his duty to shorten sail, and within a quarter of an hour it was beyond any one's power to again furl the sails he had taken in at first, for the sky sail and three royals suddenly disappeared, leaving only a few fragments attached to the yards. Every one who was on deck expected to hear the order to shorten sail, but our unmoved skipper hardly took notice of what was happening, and walked up and down the poop, smoking his pipe in the most undisturbed manner. I am almost afraid that sailors will not believe that any one in command of a big vessel could act as he did, but I am ready to vouch for the truth of every word I set down here, and can even bring corroborative evidence. For not one sail did the captain order to be stowed save the mainsail, which was driving her almost under the water. That was taken in with infinite labour at ten o'clock, but though the force of the wind momentarily increased until it blew a hurricane, he never even tried to reef the topsails before they went. Before that, the three topgallant sails vanished one by one, and then two of the three upper topsails were blown out of their bolt-ropes with a report like thunder, and inside of half an hour the mizen and main lower topsails followed suit. Then the cro'jack sheets parted, and the cro'jack flogging the yard in ribbons. The only sail we saved in fair condition was the upper main topsail, and that the two mates, the Serang, two quarter-masters, Broome, Salton and myself took in. For by this time I was quite accustomed to go aloft, and we volunteered because most of the Lascars and Malays were fairly frightened and would not leave the deck. They stowed themselves away in every hole and corner they could find, and out of forty-five there were only three in the topsail yard with us.

I have said it was blowing a hurricane, and I mean what I say. Since then I have seen it blow hard, and I had known some bad weather, as I have said, in the Bay and off the Cape; but this fairly came out ahead of anything I have ever known for violence, though it scarcely rained during the whole thirty-six hours it lasted, and still remained warm. The torn and driven sea, under the rainless canopy of low drifting clouds, was cruel and ghastly to look at, and the waves were as big as the rollers off the Horn. […] As we pitched, the water came in over the bows and poured in a white and green cataract over the fok'sle head; as we rolled, it came in great masses over the rail, until it filled up the main deck and escaped through the stove-in main deck ports and scupper holes. Sometimes the following sea even overtook and pooped us, that is, came in over the stern, and poured down on the main deck. It was fortunate for us that we did not injure or lose our rudder, for if we had come broadside on to the wind, it would have been good-bye for all of us. When we had the topsail stowed in some sort of a fashion we went down and got some whiskey, for, strange to say, our teetotal captain let us have as much as we wanted. And some of us appeared to want a great deal, for about three o'clock, Mackintosh, Ladd, Salton and Broome were all very drunk indeed. [...]

Shortly after four o'clock I quitted the deck for a little while to put on another coat, and came up again in less than five minutes to see Mr Ladd sitting in the main hatch, smothered in blood. I ran to him in great alarm and asked what the matter was. He emitted a tremendous volley of oaths, and ended by roaring, 'Mutiny! mutiny!' I left him and went forward. Just by the cook's galley I met Mr Mackintosh, in a worse plight, if possible, than the second officer, for the blood was streaming from a cut in his head, one eye was quite closed up, and the rest of his face was hardly to be distinguished. He too was swearing, and, holding on to the deckhouse, he likewise roared 'Mutiny!' I caught his arm, guided him to the main hatch, where a sea presently washed over him, and ran to meet Salton and Broome, who were coming forward, telling them what I had gathered vaguely, that the mates had gone into the fok'sle to turn the men out to work and had got severely thrashed for their pains. We all looked at each other and at the Lascars, who were standing in a crowd at the port door of the fok'sle armed with handspikes and belaying-pins, and without further enquiry Broome rushed into the cook's galley on one side, seized a long carving-knife, and emerged from the other uttering a howl like a fiend's. Salton produced a sixshooter, and I, not to be behind-hand, grabbed an iron belaying-pin. I had no distinct notion of what we were to do, but I followed Broome, who sprang into the fok'sle at a bound. There were some forty men inside, and we were three; but I verily believe Broome would have charged an army at that moment, and our audacity carried the day. To say the Lascars ran like sheep would be to put it mildly; for they yelled with terror, and fled like smoke before the wind. In half a minute they were crowded on the deck outside. Broome was threatening to have the life of any one who murmured, and Salton made first one and then the other cower and shrink by pointing his sixshooter at him. I came near getting my skull cracked, and was hit slightly on the shoulder. But when I was in the open again I recovered some slight degree of common sense, and rushed off for the captain. Surely the man was the strangest mixture of courage and cowardice I ever saw, for though he was white and almost trembling, he came forward without a weapon. [...] The captain ordered them into the fok'sle again, and they went like lambs, for Salton joined in with his weapon. [...] Then the captain and I escorted the mates to their respective bunks, and all was quiet except the gale, which was now at its height. I stood under the break of the poop, and watched it for some time. It was now past five o'clock.

The sea was a wonderful sight, and the ship, as it drove through the waves with most of its sails torn in fragments, which whipped and knotted themselves into ropes on the yards, seemed like a flying creature tormented by strong invisible hands. The decks of the *Seringapatam* were continually full of water, and the main deck ports having been wrenched and beaten out, it was hazardous in the extreme to venture forward. Yet at such a time the captain's wife and the young girl passenger came out of the saloon on to the main deck.

Mrs — was as pale as death; the girl was flushed fiery red; both were most disgracefully intoxicated and could scarcely stand. I was really shocked beyond measure and ashamed; but being the only person then on the main deck, I did not think it right to allow them to stay in a place where even a sober man was in danger; so I opened the saloon door and pushed the girl in first, and after her the captain's wife, who fell down, and for a moment prevented me shutting the door. Just at that moment a heavy sea came on board and poured into the open saloon, thoroughly drenching the two women. I rolled the eldest in unceremoniously, and jamming the door to, left them struggling to rise.

I have got so far in the narrative, and in spite of what I said some pages back about my fearing lest some should disbelieve me, I have now to relate something still more incredible even to myself as I recall it, than any thing that I have yet written. Perhaps it is not quite impossible that a captain should obstinately stand to lose almost a whole suit of sails, although it is foolish enough, but that the same man should go below, when both his officers were drunk and incapable, and leave his ship to the care of the carpenter, who was not a sailor, seems like a fable. And yet it is just this that our skipper did. He ordered 'Chips' to stay on deck from eight to twelve, and call him at midnight, and then coolly went below and turned in. At midnight the man duly summoned the captain, who did not turn out, and without waiting to be relieved, went to his bunk. Thus from twelve till two there was nobody on deck but the men at the wheel, for the Lascar whose look-out it was remained in the fok'sle, taking advantage of there being no officer of the watch. And we nearly paid a dreadful penalty for the criminal negligence our commander displayed. At three bells, or half-past one, the helmsmen were so near losing control over the vessel, that she almost came broadside on to the waves, and shipped a tremendous sea on the starboard side, as if the whole ocean were coming on board. I heard a terrific shock over my head, and then the rush and roar of the water as it washed over the rail, and poured down through every crack in the hatch into the 'tween-decks. It was some ten minutes before she cleared herself sufficiently of the sea for us to get on deck, and then we could see what had happened.

The after boat on the starboard side, which had been lifted some ten feet above our heads by 'skids' or 'strongbacks', was lying on the deck in fragments, and the skids were smashed and splintered as well. Some well lashed 400-gallon tanks had disappeared overboard and with them the harness casks where the salt meat was kept; a kind of bridge, running from the poop towards the main-mast, which carried a large standard compass, had gone too, together with its valuable burden, and some of the iron stanchions, which were beaten and twisted out of all shape. The brass rail on the starboard side of the poop was gone, and the box where the signalling flags were kept. It was only the task of a moment to take this in with the eye for there were loud bellows for help from the mate's berth. It seems that the wreck of the boat had been launched against his windows, staving them in, and admitting sufficient water to fill the berth up above the level of the highest bunk. The cold bath had roused him from his drunken slumbers, and he, fearing to be drowned like a rat in his hole, was imploring aid from all and sundry to help him to open his door, which was jammed hard by the great weight of water inside. It took three of us to release him, and then we went into the saloon, which was fairly afloat, for one of the doors had been burst open by the same sea. It was a melancholy sight and not a little disgusting for the captain's wife was sitting in pronounced *déshabillé*, in a foot of water, vowing she should be drowned, and imploring us to dive in, so to speak, and bring her to dry land. As for the captain, he was now on deck.

In the early morning, when I went up, although it was still blowing fairly hard, it was no longer a tempest, and the sea was rapidly subsiding. But the vessel looked a wreck, even if she had lost no spars, with the torn sails, the flying gear, the broken skids, and stove-in ports, while the second mate looked worse yet, being ornamented with two black eyes and innumerable scars. He grinned at me in a somewhat shamefaced manner, but said little. When Mr Mackintosh came on deck I could have roared with laughter to see the two together eying each other as if to say, 'He's rather worse than I am myself', and as if calculating how much difference in value there might be between two badly swelled lips and a nose apparently knocked on one side. But the Lascars, the very men who had beaten these two for trying to get them to work the day before, were now as obsequious as slaves, and hurried to do the bidding of their officers, without a smile on their faces, although I dare say they chuckled inwardly at the aspect of their superiors. I never knew if the captain reprimanded them, but I think not, as he was to blame for allowing every one to drink as much as he pleased, nor was his own conduct extremely praiseworthy, as any one, I think, will allow.

*Land-Travel and Sea-Faring* (1891).

# William Linklater

## (1867–1959)

*William Linklater left his family in Adelaide in his late teens and headed for northern Australia. He worked as an itinerant on stations all over the Northern Territory and into Western Australia and spent some time pearling and gold-digging. The following extract deals with some of his experiences on a 400-square-mile property owned by Jack Frayne. He argues from both the white and the Aboriginal points of view in the conflict in the Northern Territory, but concludes that the white settlers were arrogant, greedy, and cruel, shooting down the 'blacks like crows' during the cattle migration and the gold rush to the Kimberleys.*

The settlers in the vicinity warned us to take no chances whatever with the blacks, for they were always ready to show a very practical belligerence towards the occupation of their country. One day as I was riding alone, intent on tracking a mob of cattle that had broken away from the main herd, a blackfellow suddenly let go a spear at me. I felt the wind of it on my face as it flew past my jugular vein. I jerked the Winchester and fired a haphazard shot in his direction, but my horse was startled by the suddenness of the attack and played up. Though he had no spears left, the black made capital of my disadvantage by picking up a huge basalt stone and letting it fly at me from ten feet. It was coming at my forehead, but I bent and got it further back on my head instead.

I saw thousands of vivid stars and lost my reins. As I fell back, my head hit the rump of my horse, but fortunately I did not fall off. If I had, there is no doubt but that the black would have bashed my brains out. I recovered myself almost instantly, pulled myself up in the saddle, caught the reins, let out a blood-curdling yell and raced the horse right at him. At top speed he bounded into a large patch of silver-leaved box trees and disappeared among the long grass and ant hills.

Jack Frayne, who had heard and seen the encounter from a distance, came galloping up, and we rode back to camp where he cut my hair. When the lump as large as a goose's egg went down, there was a small dent in my skull. Now so many years later, when rain is coming I feel a pain there and my thoughts go back to the attack on the plain, and I shudder as I feel the wind from the stone-headed spear which was such a near miss.

Perhaps the most nerve-racking times I ever experienced were when I became camp sergeant for Texas Kelly at Bedford Downs, a new holding he had taken up under the King Leopold Range.

Although Kelly had asked me to take on the job because I 'didn't mind the blacks', he said that Hastie Burns, the stockman, was not to camp out leaving me alone for more than one night at a time. He gave Hastie instructions to that effect before going off. After a week, however, Hastie said he had some business in Halls Creek and that he could do the 108 miles there and back in six days. I guessed that the business was just an excuse for a booze.

Shortly after Hastie left, a gin whose duty it was to look after the goats failed to come back with them one evening. About three days later her dog appeared and would not leave my side. I knew then that the wild blacks had killed her, or the dog would not have been acting so strangely. Night and day my Winchester was always by my hand.

As the weeks went by I became very anxious about Bob Sexton, Kelly's partner, who was by this time five weeks overdue at our station. I imagined that he might have been speared, or that his horse might have fallen with him, and that he might be lying somewhere, helpless and alone. Worry on his account helped to unnerve me. One day seven blacks came boldly into view, and were waving for the gins to come and join them. In an effort to discourage them, I put on the shirt, hat and skirt belonging to one of the gins, walked apparently aimlessly towards them, and then, from the closer range of some rocks behind which I could shelter, I fired to frighten them, and had the satisfaction of seeing them disappear, if only temporarily.

One evening I heard the milking cows bellowing as they ran along the creek in front of the hut. Picking up the Winchester, I dashed outside to see the cows running to the yard in which they were milked. One young heifer had a spear stuck in her back, and the eight-foot haft was dragging along the ground as she moved. I put them into the yard, then caught hold of the spear. The cow still continued to run, bellowing with pain and fright. At last the spear came out.

By this time it was dark, so I returned to the hut. It was dangerous to sleep inside, as the roof and walls were thatched with grass, and the blacks could tie a bunch of grass to the end of a spear, light it, and throw it from a hundred yards into a thatched building. Naturally they would be waiting to spear the inmates as they escaped.

When Mr Sexton turned up after another three or four weeks, I showed him the spear I had pulled out of the heifer, and told him I was certain that they had killed the gin who had been tailing the goats.

Shortly afterwards we shifted to that part of the holding known as New Bedford. While the men rode round the cattle for ten days at a time two gins and I thatched the house, using a method I had learned by watching the Chinese on the mines out of Darwin. I made a big wooden needle which served to thread through the thongs of greenhide used to tie the swathes of grass together, and the gins proved very clever at the work. These thatched walls were very dangerous where the blacks were hostile, but since the wet season was setting in, they were an absolute necessity.

When finished the house was seventeen feet by fifteen, with a six-foot verandah in front. I had to do the cooking at an open fire, almost an impossibility in the rainy season. Anyway, we were fully occupied, and when the others came back they built a framework for a kitchen, ready for thatching while they went off riding round the cattle again. This was a continuous job, both to prevent them straying, and to keep the blacks from spearing too many.

One day the gins and I sensed that the wild blacks had watched from their eyrie 600 feet up on the Durack Range as the men rode away. That evening both gins brought their swags and made a bed on the verandah.

They said, 'Bulka, might blackfellow come up tonight. Supposem we hearem, we wakem you.'

I told them that if they did hear anything not to make a sound, and not to shake me if I happened to be asleep in case I should be startled and call out, but to pull my hair very gently. I put a box beside my bunk, and laid my Winchester on it. If the blacks set fire to the thatch I would have to turn out, so I also put a dozen cartridges in each of my trouser-pockets.

It was after midnight and I was asleep when I felt someone very gently pulling my hair. I woke soundlessly and breathed, 'What name?'

Jenny whispered as softly, 'Blackfellow, me bin hearem.'

I crawled out on to the verandah and listened, almost without breathing, and presently I heard the sound of spears clicking together. The blacks hold three in their left hand and a wommera in their right, and they can ship a spear in the wommeras in a split second, daylight or dark.

After a time one of the gins breathed in my ear, 'You hearem spear?'

I knew then that they must be as close as seventy yards, so I let fly a salvo of cartridges. Then I waited for a long time, but everything was quiet. It happened that I was ill with fever, so I decided to lie down for a few hours till daylight, because I knew that I could trust one gin to watch while the other slept.

When it was light enough Jenny and I had a look round, and within seventy yards of the house we picked up six spears with stone heads cemented to the hafts with spinifex gum, a couple of boomerangs and two firesticks. If the two gins had not been so watchful I would certainly have been killed, and the place looted.

This was typical of what one could expect at any moment in those days in that country. Had it not been for my reading, past and present, I think that I must have succumbed to the continual strain. It was odd how, whenever the tension mounted, my mind would dwell on the stories from the Iliad and the Odyssey with which it had been stored when I was a child, and one could scarcely default utterly in the remembered company of heroes.

I was well enough off for reading matter, with Motley's *Rise and Fall of the Dutch Republic*, Macaulay's *Essays* and poetry, and, of course, Shakespeare. I had a Bible, too that I had found at Old Bedford. When I was in the mood, I would read the Psalms aloud for hours.

Sometimes Jenny would ask, 'What name that one tellem you?'

'Why?'

'Well, me look longa your eye. Me bin think it tellem you longa pretty woman.'

There came a day, though, when the sheer isolation became so oppressive that I cast the Bible away and felt with Wordsworth:

> I find nothing great;
> Nothing is left which I can venerate;
> So that a doubt almost within me springs
> Of Providence, such emptiness at length
> Seems at the heart of things.

I sent, by paper yabba, to Albert's bookshop in Perth for Adam Smith's *Wealth of Nations*, Darwin's *Origin of Species*, and the works of Haeckel and Locke. They came eventually, carried on the head of a naked Aborigine. Locke's *On the Knowledge of Understanding* proved too much for mine, but the others without doubt helped to preserve my sanity.

Afer I had put in a year, I asked Bob Sexton to find a man to take my place, so some time afterwards Jim McKenzie rode up with his lubra and a blackboy of about fourteen. That night while I was listening eagerly to news of the outside world, a lubra who was talking to her Munjong consort just clear of the verandah let out a terrific scream.

I picked up my rifle, and fired three shots in succession to scare away the lurking figure I saw in the distance in the bright moonlight. Back in the hut, Jim looked thoughtful.

'Well, go on with the tale,' I said, but Jim wanted to know what the firing was about. 'You'll get used to that,' I said, but by morning Jim had decided to go back to Turkey Creek. The lubra and the boy were frightened. I reminded him that blacks only need a good lead in such a situation, but Jim had made up his mind.

When Mr Sexton heard the news he groaned and said that he would never get another man. Of course, I had to stay and it was six months before I was relieved. Later I met Mr Sexton in Wyndham and went out to Bedford Downs again. This time Macaulay's *History of England* was a great standby, and when the men came in I used to read it to them. They never tired of hearing how Horatius held the bridge, and those who could not read would ask for it again and again.

Sometimes out on the Durack, where the blacks were a very bad lot indeed, when the day's work was done I would walk up and down in front of the camp fire, revolver in pouch at belt, rifle in the crook of my arm and Shakespeare in hand, declaiming favourite passages.

The gins would double up with laughter and cry out to me, 'Billy, you mad fellow.'

*Gather No Moss* (1968).

# G. W. Broughton

(DATES UNKNOWN)

*Gordon William Broughton, a third-generation Australian, spent his childhood in the country towns of Tamworth and Cootamundra and worked first as a bank clerk in Sydney, Maitland, and Scone. In 1908 he obtained a position as bookkeeper at Lissadell, an East Kimberley station owned by the Durack family, and fulfilled an ambition to become a bushman. He later travelled in the Philippines and China. His subsequent autobiography,* The Sliprails are Down *(1966), extends his story to his service in World War I.*

The arrival at Lissadell of 'M.J.', alias 'Long Michael', alias 'Black Mick' Durack, galvanized the place into burning activity. After sacking Favell he turned his attention to getting every ounce of work out of all of us, the manager included. Nothing was ever right and no praise was ever given. If Sunday found the men at the homestead, he fumed silently over what to him was a wasted day, and on Monday morning he would be up even earlier than was customary in that land of pre-dawn rising. He was a childless man, with a wife in a big home in Fremantle, and there seemed to be about him an inner unhappiness. As a lad he had had little opportunity for advanced schooling, and as a young man he had worked hard and long on Queensland cattle stations. His tough life had developed in him an abhorrence of waste, either in material or in labour paid for; and even in Kimberley he was regarded as a 'hard' man who gave nothing away. As I knew him then, M.J. was in his early fifties, tall and spare. His hands were hard and calloused with years of rough bush work, and the ravages of fever and dysentery showed in his face. When angry his words were punctuated with a spasmodic stutter.

After a week or two during which everything I did appeared to be wrong, M.J. announced that he would see if he could make a stockman out of me. Brusquely he said, 'You might have the makings of a cattleman, but by God I'll work you hard, young feller. Fred Hill is too bloody soft, and I'll see that he keeps your head down to it after I've gone.' He then said that from now on I was to get thirty shillings a week! So it was in great enthusiasm that I joined in several days of boundary mustering along the borders of Argyle and Rosewood. These stations sent riders to join us and to sort out their branded cattle running free with Lissadell stock. But more urgent and important was the equitable division of clean-skin (unbranded) cattle, whose ownership was anybody's guess. They were usually found in wild and difficult country where they had been led away by old scrub bulls, and through the years had escaped the branding iron.

There was a saying in the bush that 'a bullock has two calves a year in Kimberley'. This remark was meant chiefly as an ironic reference to the unbelievably rapid increase in the herds of certain small station owners who had taken up land on the far outskirts of the larger properties. But it also gave sarcastic emphasis to the fact that even the most high-minded managers were ready to assume that every clean-skin found on their land or along its borders was their fair and just possession. To steal a man's watch was an unpardonable offence, but to claim a border clean-skin—well, if you did not, the other man did!

A few days after M.J.'s arrival the wagoner pulled in with his annual load of stores brought out from Wyndham one hundred and eighty miles away by the only vehicle route. Fred Hill had hopefully ordered a case of Johnnie Walker whisky from the Wyndham store, but all the wagoner could produce was one partly emptied bottle, explaining with gruff bravado, 'Well you see, Fred, me and me offsider started off with two cases of our own, but she all got drunk on the track. So help me Gawd, mate, we hung off your booze for two days and then we bust into it. Put it down in yer books agin me, and better luck next time!'

About this time also came news that Macdonald, a quiet old settler on a small lease near the Ord River station, had been shot. Then came word that Nipper, a black boy who had once worked on Lissadell, and Major, another native stockman, had cleared out from a neighbouring station, taking with them a rifle and revolvers. These two men had rather a bad reputation, but we heard later that one of them had been abused and knocked about several times by a rather brutal stockman. Thus, one night, they took to the bush armed and ready for murder. Any white man would do, and harmless old 'Scotty' was shot as he sat in his stockyard milking his goats in the early dawn. The killers departed without robbing his hut, and a black gin, with a loyalty that Aborigines sometimes, but rarely, show, caught a horse and helped the sorely wounded man into the saddle. There he clung for twelve miles or more while the gin led the horse until at a station homestead he was carried inside by friendly hands. But they could only watch helplessly while the old man died.

After the news that Nipper and Major were 'loose' in the bush, and when every man looked to his firearms and slept uneasily at night, a stranger jogged into Lissadell. He asked me where he could camp and I pointed over to the creek and he said, 'That'll do me, mate.' As an afterthought I called out, 'We buried a stockman down there lately.' 'Holy Jesus!' yelled the stranger, 'I'm not goin' to camp near that bloke,' and he jingled away further up the creek.

Jim Davidson was the stranger's name, and next morning, there being no other white men at the homestead at the time, he came along to the store and asked me if I thought he might get a job. I told him that a cook was needed up at the outstation at Blackfellow's Creek, and after I had given him the customary supply of free salt beef, he camped by the creek until the boss and the big mustering party returned. He got the job and rode away to join George Fettle, the out-station manager.

A week later there was death again at Lissadell—this time grim and bloody. Two black stockmen had been sent up to the out-station with stores loaded on packhorses. They had departed early, nervous and fearful of the killers now loose somewhere in the bushland wilderness. On the night of their departure, as we at Lissadell were about to take to our bunks, we suddenly became aware of the distant sound of galloping horses. The nightly crooning of tribal songs and the rhythmic tapping of the yam sticks had ceased abruptly down at the native huts. There was a taut stillness as we all sat and listened. Then out of the darkness burst the excited yabber of the station blacks as two horsemen pulled up in the compound.

Quick steps approached us into the light of a hurricane lamp. The two boys who had been sent at dawn that day to the outstation had returned. They were momentarily breathless and incoherent, but M.J. calmed them and asked what had happened. Their words tumbled out in the limited inadequate 'pidgin': 'We bin reachem Blackfeller creek longa sun-down. Too much quiet fella allabout; we thinkit everybody gone away. We plenty fritint fella. By'n-by we walk longa hut belonga George Fettle. We bin look in winder, George he dead fella longa bunk. Old Jim [Davidson] we no findum; blackboys, lubras, piccaninnies— everybody gone away. We too much fritint fella; leavum packhorse and clear out longa Lissadell.'

The moon had gone down and the night was black. I lay awake for a long time with a .32 rifle beside me, and then only slept intermittently. At dawn M.J. and

Fred Hill, with Black Andy and Willy, the two Queensland boys, departed for the out-station. The other white stockmen were away at a distant mustering camp and native women and children and Jimmy Long Die, the very frightened Chinese cook. That night the yam sticks and the crooning were silent, and the dark bush seemed uncannily still. I felt taut and apprehensive, but in the end sleep came and dawn brought the comfort of sight and sound.

Late that day M.J. returned alone. They had found Fettle on his bunk in the hut shot dead and outside on a stretcher, Jim Davidson, brained with a wagon-wheel spoke while he slept. The hut had been ransacked and the dead men's firearms taken. The station natives had all gone, either scattered into the bush or with the killers. Hill sent Black Andy to a bush police depot and stayed on at the hut to await the rough and ready inquest.

At dinner M.J. was taciturn and grim. A little later, after giving me brief details of the slaughter he rather abruptly said goodnight and went to his room. It was by then a night of high moonlight. The crooning and the yam stick tapping had all died away, and there was only the silence. The outlaws Major and Nipper were somewhere in the wide bush, but no man knew where and when they might strike again, even though they were now being hunted by both bushmen and police. Sleep came over me, and then suddenly there was a crash like a gunshot, and a low groan. Wide awake and tensed, I snatched up my Winchester rifle and lay for a moment listening and breathless. There was no sound from the blacks' huts, nothing but stillness and the brilliant moon. I felt certain that M.J. had been shot in his bunk and was even at that moment in urgent need of help, but sure that as soon as I moved into the moonlit passageway I also would be shot down. But with great caution I crept, rifle in hand, along the passage to his room. He lay on his side, his back towards me, breathing heavily and as I watched, tensed, he suddenly heaved over on to his other side. As he did so his elbow bumped hard with a crashing sound on the galvanized iron partition wall, and without waking he groaned loudly, muttering in his dreams. Sweating, I stood there for a moment or two, barefooted and clad only in my shirt and as the tension eased and the absurdity of the anti-climax overtook me, I crept back to my bunk.

Two weeks later Nulyeree, a lubra whose copper-hued skin denoted Malayan ancestry somewhere, betrayed a secret all the gins had been hiding. We learned then that on that moonlight night when M.J. and I slept alone at Government House, the two outlaws had in fact spent several hours with the Lissadell gins. All the boys were still away, and it was a night of sexual savagery, primitive and uninhibited. The outlaws had crept up late at night, calling softly to the lubras from the shelter of the creek. Then the 'party' had been held in subdued whispers, a hundred yards or so upstream on the soft sandbed of the creek. Long before dawn the blacks had gone silently away into the bush, and the gins, drowsy with sleep, had lain down again by their huts. M.J., partly by cajolery and partly by bluff, extracted this story from Nulyeree, young and slender, pert and straight as a reed, and commented grimly to me, 'Well, young feller, you and I would probably be dead now if those bloody niggers had come for murder. Luckily for us they wanted lubras.'

As the days went on the hunt for the outlaws grew in intensity. Rumours came in of their tracks having been picked up at such widely separated points that not all could possibly be true. Cattlemen and police hunted them, led by trusted black-trackers who sometimes picked up their tracks, only to lose them where a rain storm blotted them out. In every station homestead and musterers' camp men went about their work with senses tuned to menace.

Five weeks or more after the outlaws had killed Macdonald, a small party of police and stockmen ran them down in a patch of rock and scrub. There was a savage exchange of shots and then a sudden silence from the fugitives except for the wail of a black gin. One of the police rushed forward and found the outlaws dead—Major with a shot through his forehead. A wounded gin lay whimpering beside the dead men. One of the bushmen tore his shirt and they roughly bandaged her wounds. When her terror had subsided she told how she had loaded Major's rifle for him after a bullet had shattered his wrist.

Such was more or less the account given at the inquiry later held in Wyndham by the resident magistrate. In the bush however there were conflicting stories, and out of all these emerged the accepted contention among the cattlemen that the pursuing parties had mutually agreed there would be no prisoners, but only two very dead outlaws.

This bloody episode was just one of many—the outcome of which could often be traced back to some form of harsh treatment of the station Aborigines by a white man. In general, the station owners and managers were benign but firm, but cruelty came from some rough men who combined contempt with brutality in their handling of these primitive people. Men's actions can only be judged as in and of their time. And life was new and raw in Kimberley in the period of which I write. Colonialism was very real and widespread among the ruling powers of the world, and in general the subjugated races were exploited, little heed being given to their cultural integrity, their tribal laws, or their future place as a people.

[...]

One night as we sat on the steps of Government House, M.J., in a rare mood of reminiscence, related to me the story of the founding of Lissadell and other Durack properties in Kimberley. First, in 1881, there had been a long talk in Perth between Alexander Forrest the explorer and two of the older Duracks. As a result of this interview, several huge leases on the Ord and the Fitzroy rivers were tentatively applied for. They were 'paper' leases, uninspected and vague as to boundaries, the course of the Ord being as yet unknown to any man. Then followed the perilous expedition from Cambridge Gulf to Beagle Bay in 1882 and early next year preparations for the great trek of Queensland cattle began. They were grouped into several mobs totalling over seven thousand, M.J. and two of his brothers taking charge of one of these.

The historic overland drive began in 1883 and ended twenty-five months later on the banks of the Ord River on a day in September 1885, when M.J., riding on ahead of his party and the remnants of the original mob, had chosen a site for the homestead of the station to be called Lissadell.

He had spent that day alone in a hostile land, with wild blacks' smoke signals here and there in the sky. Playing the old bushman's trick, he had pitched his mosquito net, and then, after dark, had crept off some distance to spend a long night of taut watching and listening, plagued by sleep and mosquito hordes. At dawn he had gone back to his net, but to his amazement no spears had been hurled into it, although all around were Aborigines' tracks.

In words terse and devoid of imagery, he recited to me grim details of the terrible hardships of that journey of nearly three thousand miles; of fever and dysentery, Barcoo Rot, and cattle and horse sicknesses; of long weeks and even months of monotonous camping to rest the weary herds, and of the death of some of their party.

The short cut to Kimberley, pioneered by Nat Buchanan in 1886, and in time to become known to all drovers as the 'Murranji Track', was too dry and perilous for the great mobs of Durack and other pioneers' cattle all slowly moving westward. They had to take the long and devious route which cut the western rivers of the Gulf of Carpentaria until they came to the Roper River, which borders Arnhem Land. Thence they worked across to the Katherine River, moving then south-west until they crossed the upper Victoria, and at long last, passed over the divide into the valley of the Ord.

*Turn Again Home* (1965).

# 5

# NEW CHUMS AND NEW AUSTRALIANS

# Charles Stretton

(DATES UNKNOWN)

*Charles Stretton, the youngest son of a wealthy Welsh family, came to Australia in 1852 in search of fortune. He was then in middle age, although his friends, especially Edward Carroll, were younger men. Stretton tried numerous ways of making a living, such as shepherding, brick-making, gold-mining, and working for a Jewish watch-maker, but was invariably reduced to indigence. His fortunes revived after he was introduced to John Price, the Inspector-General of the Penal Department, and was appointed chief warder on a convict hulk. In 1858 he returned to England, assisted by Price's financial aid.*

Walking one day, accompanied by Carroll and his brother, some two miles from Melbourne, by the side of the Yarra Yarra, and talking over our intentions, we came upon a log-hut, situated in the midst of the tea-scrub which there borders both sides of that river; it was one of those frightfully hot days. Being very thirsty, from having our mouths filled with dust, we entered the hut to beg a pannikin of water.

The owner of the log-cabin was a fisherman; that is to say, he was the possessor of a seine-net and a whale-boat. In the course of conversation, we learnt from him that he plied his occupation at night-time, in the bay, from eight to ten miles distant from where we then were. I remarked that I should like to live altogether on the water, during the prevalence of the 'brick-fielders', as the north winds are called; when Carroll said—

'Stretton! you understand netting, do you not?'

'Yes,' I said; having some years back, had a great deal to do in that way, both with trammel and pitching-nets.

'What will you take,' said Carroll, addressing the owner of the hut, 'for the seine and the whale-boat?'

'Seventy pounds,' answered the man.

'How many yards is it in length, and how many in depth?' I asked.

'It is upwards of seventy yards long, and two yards and a half deep; the mesh is an inch and a half, and it is quite new,' was the reply.

Telling him that he was asking more than three times its value, we proceeded to stretch the net out for inspection by the side of the river. The net was in good order, as was the boat; and, in an hour's time, the whale-boat and seine-net were the property of Edward Carroll; he paying down fifty pounds, in notes of the Union Bank.

There is no doubt that Carroll would have given the whole sum demanded, rather than not have had it; it was a fresh hobby, and how well the speculation turned out, the sequel will show.

The reader may think it odd that a young fellow, in Australia, above all countries in the world should wander about with so much money in his pocket; but such was his habit, and it would have been the same, had he at the time been the possessor of a thousand pounds.

It was laughable to see Edward dive down into his breeches-pocket, and draw forth a bundle of notes, a quantity of loose silver, pieces of tobacco, ditto string, and a large clasp-knife, all jumbled up together. He, poor young fellow, seemed excessively delighted with his purchase; and although I might not have felt equally sanguine as to the success of our undertaking, the idea pleased me much.

It was agreed that we were to commence operations the night following, if we could succeed in finding a fourth person to join us, for it took that number of hands to 'work the oracle,' as Edward would call it.

We returned at once to Collingwod, in order to rake up whatever we could find in the shape of warm clothing, and to lay in a small supply of necessaries, for the work we were about to undertake was of a very cold nature, being all night-work. It is true that when we arrived at the spot at which we purposed camping, we should only be two miles from Sandridge, where everything necessary could be procured by paying for it.

We were not long in finding a fourth to make up the boat's complement; which consisted of Edward, his brother, Landon, and myself.

So sanguine was my friend of success, that he began talking of the wages that he was to pay us; but I recommended him to delay any settlement upon that head, until after two or three days' trial.

The weather, the day following the purchase of the net and boat, was heavenly; and with pleasurable anticipations we started for the log-hut, each carrying his own blankets and necessaries, with a portion of the general stores that we had purchased. So fine was the weather, that we scorned taking any tent, intending to lay ourselves down in the day-time among the tea trees which grow luxuriously all along the sandy bay.

At three o'clock in the afternoon of that day, we jumped into our boat, having stowed everything away, and suffered her to drift down the river, merely dipping our oars now and then to keep her head straight. In rounding a well-wooded point, we came upon at least twenty pelicans. The huge birds were standing all together on an island of mud, and suffered us to come within twenty yards of them. We had no gun with us, and if we had, it would have been only a piece of barbarous cruelty to kill any of them, as we could not have put a foot upon that treacherous mud. We continued to drift on until at last we reached a beautiful little sandy bay. The tea-trees came down close to the water's edge at high tide; but one little nook was discovered, which was immediately fixed upon by general consent, as the spot on which to camp. Hauling the boat upon the sand, we commenced arranging everything, intending to make some stay at that pretty spot.

There was no lack of fire-wood about us, and thus a collection was soon made which we considered sufficient to last two days. Could any of our relations have seen us then, they would have said that there never was a happier party. We had some few hours to ourselves before we commenced work. The steaks were frying in the pan, and the potatoes were being roasted among the wood ashes; the bottles of grog were all placed where no sun could reach them, and above all, we had found a little trickling stream of tolerable water. Thoroughly believing, that we had neglected nothing that could conduce to our comfort, the plates and dishes were produced and filled, when lo! to our consternation, it was discovered that there was no salt. The change in each countenance may be fancied: we were at least two miles from Sandridge, and not a hut near us. Eat my meat without salt, and plenty of it too, I never could, so I at once volunteered to walk to Sandridge and procure a supply.

'Never, old fellow!' said Carroll, jumping up; 'Dick and I are younger than you; we'll go together, for I cannot swallow those tough steaks, which had life in them half a-dozen hours ago, without that well-known seasoning. Come along, Dick.'

In spite of my entreaties they would go; and in an incredible short space of time we saw them returning, evidently loaded with more than that useful condiment.

Of course, neither of us who remained behind thought of commencing dinner before the return of our friends, and which, by-the-by, was in consequence fearfully over-done, which did not take away from the toughness. Had it been a slice out of Lord Darnley's boot that is shown to all visitors at Holyrood Palace, it could not have withstood the attacks of our teeth with greater success. Nevertheless, with the aid of pickles we all managed to allay our hunger; and the circling glass and never-failing pipe brought the meal to a close.

At sunset (there is little or no twilight in those regions) we commenced our operations. Richard Carroll was to remain on shore and hold one end of the cork line; Edward and Landon were to row the boat whilst I paid out the net. All went on smoothly enough, and our first draught was a good one. Five more draughts we made that night; and we pronounced our first attempt a decided success. Fishing by night is decidedly cold work, even during the summer months of the Antipodes, and it was with great difficulty that I could get my friends to make the two last draughts. As for myself, I was wet through to the waist, and so cold that I could not have worked any more.

Leaving the net and fish in the boat, we again hauled our little Norwegian craft upon the land, and commenced taking off our wet clothes, which done, and the fire replenished, we threw ourselves upon the ground with our feet towards the flames to sleep away the time until the fish carts would come down from Melbourne which we were informed would be the case at four o'clock every morning.

The sun rose brilliantly, and almost as soon as the fiery god showed his round face, were the fish carts perceptible, advancing towards us along the sands. There were numerous fishing parties up and down the bay; and decidedly the Melbourne purveyors of that article were not choice in their selection: anything in the shape of the finny tribe was sure to sell and Edward made three pounds [and] odd shillings by the first night's work. Yet that sum would never pay, thought I, considering the price of provisions, and the number of the mouths that were to be filled.

The fish carts had no sooner left us, than we shook out our net and spread it upon the sand to dry; the tide was on the ebb, and therefore this could be done in perfect safety.

Nothing could be more tediously idle than the manner in which the day was spent; and one day was like unto the next. As there was no use attempting to work the seine before darkness came on, all were at liberty to amuse themselves as it suited them, so long as one remained to take care of the property. Now idleness invariably begets mischief: I do not mean to insinuate that I was one whit better than the rest of my companions; but having nothing to do we used to wander to Sandridge, at that time a large township, and now, I hear, with that of Emerald Hill, boasting of a population over twenty thousand; so I am given to understand. There were two or three very large hotels at the former, and to those accursed places of resort we constantly went. No good could come from it; it naturally rendered us quite unfit for work, and when the time came for real drudgery, accompanied with darkness and wet, I could see amongst the party a slight disposition to flinch.

That night, as soon as the sun went down, we were again on the water: about the same success attended us, but with all my entreaties they would only make three hauls.

'It is so deuced dark and cold,' one would say.

'Confound it! It's all very well working by light, but hang me if I like this work,' another would chime in.

Edward said nothing; and as there was no light in the boat I could not tell how he looked. I tried my utmost to keep them up to their work, but failed.

It was the sixth or seventh night that we commenced our distasteful task (and I may as well now say our last), when we fell in with a misadventure which put the *grand coup* upon the fishing speculation. It was this: the night was fearfully dark;

we had made two hauls which were tolerably successful, when on making our third and last compass the net fouled; ordering the rowers to pull gently back whilst I tried the cork line to find if possible where the hitch could be, I discovered that our net was firmly grappled by some huge piece of timber. Telling Edward and Landon to pull out gently towards the middle of the bay, I, by the merest chance imaginable, got it clear; I then told them to pull gently to shore whilst I drew the net into the boat: of course there were no fish, but the net was saved, for there was not one mesh broken.

Everybody appeared heartily sick and tired of the work; I endeavoured to prevail upon them to drop down, at daylight, a few miles further down the bay, but no—they struck, not for want of wages but for warmth. Making all safe for the night, and attending well to our fire, we again stretched our shivering limbs before the burning scrub; but not before our clothes had been changed, and a nobbler of rum had been handed to each.

I felt annoyed, and could not sleep; I knew Edward's temper so well, that I was confident he would not brook a failure; and I made up my mind that our fishing speculation was at an end.

When the carts came round in the morning; they found but a scanty supply of fish from our party; and few were the shillings that Edward put into his pocket.

As usual we all went to work; one cooking, another gathering fuel, whilst Carroll and I spread the net to dry.

'I tell you what, Charlie,' said Edward, 'we will make no hand of this fishing game, and you must allow that it is uncommon cold work. Hang me! if I would not rather break stones at ten shillings the square yard. Then again there's no fun in it; you cannot see what you are about; you are wet from the beginning of the business to the end of it; and to crown all, there's no profit. Charlie, we must cut it.'

*Memoirs of a Chequered Life* (1862).

# Thorvald Weitemeyer

## (1850–?)

*Thorvald Weitemeyer was born in Copenhagen, the second son of a builder. At the age of twenty-one, resentful of his father's iron-handed discipline, he left home without notice for Hamburg, where he joined an emigrant ship bound for Queensland. After fourteen years of silence he wrote to his eldest brother for news of the family and received letters by return mail from his brother and father. Now a married man and a father himself, he felt conscience-stricken and set to writing down his experiences for his parents' information. A copy of his manuscript arrived in Copenhagen the day after his father's death and was buried with him. Well written and as an early narrative unusually reflective, Weitemeyer's autobiography is also valuable as social history. This extract describes his arrival in Queensland and his attempt to sell a large number of bottles he had accumulated on the voyage in the belief that they would be valuable in Australia. Thorkill, an Icelander, was his close friend, whose death is the subject of a subsequent extract (see p. 202).*

Meanwhile, a number of the immigrants had gone ashore, and Thorkill and I were getting the bottles out of their hiding-places and putting them on the table. Some Queenslanders came in. They looked on a little. I said, 'How much money you pay me for one bottle?'

'Have you got all these bottles for sale?' inquired one.

'Of course,' said I.

He did not answer, but went outside and called out 'Mick'.

In came the man who had sold me the bananas.

'Do you want to buy any more "dead mariner"?' asked the first.

'Has he got all these bottles for sale?' inquired the banana man.

'Certainly,' cried I. [...]

'No,' cried he; 'he did not think he wanted any more just now.'

'How much money you think I receive for one bottle?' inquired I.

'Oh, plenty money,' cried he, 'my word, ready market; any one buys them.'

'What do they say?' asked Thorkill of me.

'They say the bottles are worth a lot of money.'

'See if you can find out what "dead mariner" is.'

I took a porter bottle up, and then said, 'You name that one "dead mariner"?'

Queenslander: 'Yes, certainly; that is one "dead mariner".'

I took up a clear bottle and inquired, 'This clear thing, you call that empty bottle?'

Queenslander: 'To be sure that is an empty bottle. But if you are willing to sell, you take them all up to that large hotel you see there. They give you half-a-crown apiece for them.'

I then asked, 'Which one is most costly, "dead mariner" bottle or clear bottle?'

Queenslander: 'Oh, that fellow—"dead mariner"—very dear; three shillings, I think.'

'Heavens! here, we have made our fortune already, Thorkill,' cried I. 'Three shillings apiece for these bottles and two-and-sixpence for those. And it appears any one will buy. Are we not lucky?'

'Oh, but,' said Thorkill, 'I shall never feel justified in taking half of all that money. It was your idea. I should never have thought of it. I shall be very thankful to receive just a pound or two.'

'Oh, no,' cried I, 'you shall share half with me whatever I get. But, excuse me for saying it, you are so unpractical. Why are we not up and stirring? Why are we sitting here yet? Remember time is money in this country.' Then I ventured to ask the Queenslanders if in the town there was any one whom I might ask to assist us in carrying the bottles ashore.

'Oh, yes,' they all cried, as if with one mouth. 'You go up in town and get hold of a couple of blackfellows, and then you take them all up that street you see there. Any one will buy there.'

Thorkill remained on board keeping watch over the bottles, while I went ashore to see what I should see.

Just as I came to the end of the long jetty I saw standing there an aboriginal and three Gins. […] I began to explain to them that I wanted them to work—to carry burdens from the ship. That was soon made clear to them. Then the 'gentleman' of the party was very particular to know what I would pay him. I had thought to get them to carry the bottles up, and, having sold them, to pay them out of the proceeds; but, as he seemed anxious to make a fixed bargain, I said, 'I give you one bottle.' In case he should have refused that, I intended to have gone one further, and to have offered a 'dead mariner', but to my joy he accepted the offer with evident satisfaction, which again more thoroughly convinced me of the value of my bottles. I and the black fellow with his three Gins accordingly went back to the ship, where Thorkill sat keeping watch over our treasure.

I loaded the four blacks with four bags, in each of which were two dozen assorted bottles, and now we started for town in earnest. I thought it beneath my dignity to carry any bottles myself. I had exhorted so many of the immigrants that it was our duty to one another to try to make a good impression when we first landed, that the least I could do I thought would be to set a good example. Therefore I was faultlessly got up, in my own opinion, or at least as well as the circumstances of my wardrobe would permit. Still, my attire was not very suitable to this country, and indeed, when I think of it now, I must have cut a strange figure. I had on my black evening-dress suit, which so far would have been good enough to have gone to a ball in, but my white shirt, I know, was of a very doubtful colour, for I had been my own washerwoman, and it was neither starched nor ironed. Then my tall black hat, of which I was so proud when I got it, had suffered great damage on the voyage, and brush it as I would, any one might easily have seen that it had been used as a footstool. My big overcoat, I, according to the most approved fashion in Copenhagen, carried over my arm. In one hand I had my handkerchief, with which I had to constantly wipe the perspiration off my face, because it was very hot. Still, I felt myself a tip-top dignitary as I stalked along in front of the four blacks, who came, chattering their strange lingo, behind me.

We marched up to the main street, and I saw at once a hotel, that pointed out to me from the ship as the place in which to sell my bottles. In the bar were two or three gentlemen of whom I took no notice. Behind the bar stood the barmaid, whom I profoundly saluted, also in Copenhagen fashion. I had what to say on the tip of my tongue, and indeed I have never forgotten it since. So I spoke to the barmaid thus: 'I have bottles I will sell to you. Will you buy? Three shillings every one.' She looked bewildered, not at me but at the gentlemen in the bar, as if she appealed to them for assistance, and they began to talk to me, but I did not understand them at all. I could feel myself getting red in the face, too, but I manfully made another effort. I called in the blacks and ordered them to deposit their load inside the door. Then I said with great exactness, 'I—do—not—ferstan—the—thou—ferstan—me. I—sell—this—clear—bottles—to thee—for three shillings every one. This—dead—mariner—I—sell—three—shillings—and sixpence every one. Will thou buy?' Meanwhile, I had taken out of the bags two samples, a clear and a dark bottle, and placed them on the counter, and I now looked inquiringly around me.

Oh, the mortification which became my portion! The girl seemed to faint behind the bar, and the gentlemen made not the slightest excuse for laughing right out in my face. What they said I do not know, but it was clear they did not want my bottles. I felt insulted, and I determined to pay the blacks off and to leave the bottles here until I could find a German Queenslander to whom I might explain my business, and who might help me to sell them. So I took the clear bottle which stood on the counter, and handed it to the black as payment for his service. He looked viciously at me and said, 'That fellow no good bottle.'

I said, 'Very dear bottle that.' Then I decided to satisfy him at any cost, and gave him the other one, too, and said, 'Very dear bottle this, dead mariner.'

Now began a scene as good as a play. The blacks appealed to the gentlemen, and the gentlemen howled with laughter, and I wished myself a thousand miles away. What did they laugh at? Why did these scampish blacks not feel satisfied after having received double payment? What did it all mean? More people came in and seemed amused and happy, but I was not in the swim. Something was wrong. But what was it? I began to suspect that my bottles could not be so very valuable, as the blacks had thrown both the bottles out into the gutter. Anyhow, for me to stand here to be made a fool of would not do, so I went out of the bar and down the street. But to get away was no easy matter. In fact I found it impossible. The coloured gentleman with his three ladies were in front of me, behind me, and on both sides, crying, howling, yelling, cursing, and appealing to every one who passed, or to those who came to their doors, 'That fellow big rogue. That fellow no — good. He b— new chum. He say he give me bottle, he give me no good b— bottle; dead mariner no b— good.' This was more than human nature could stand. I threw my overcoat and bell-topper into the gutter, and went for the black fellow straight. I got on top of him in a minute, but the battle was not nearly won by that, because the black ladies were tearing at my coat-tails, which just formed two fine handles for them. They split my coat right up to the shoulders, pulled my hair, and belaboured me in a general way. Now came a policeman and grabbed me by the neck. All the 'ladies' ran for their lives out of sight, but I suspect their spouse was too bruised to follow their example. Anyhow he stuck to his guns yet, and while the policeman tried to march us both down the street, he kept appealing to him, declaring his innocence, and my villainy. That I should have spent the next few days in the watch-house I am sure enough, had not an elderly man stepped out of the crowd of onlookers and spoken to the policeman. Then he addressed me in German. I learned then, through much merriment on his part and heartburning on my own, that empty bottles are in Queensland just so much rubbish. Indeed, after the policeman let me go, he took me round to the back yard of the hotel, and there I saw bottles lying by the thousands, some broken and others sound, ready to cart away. But how was I to have known that? Was it easy to guess that a bottle, which might pass for twopence English money in Copenhagen nearly as readily as cash, would here in Queensland have absolutely no value? It is like all other things one knows, easily explained: here there being no distilleries or breweries for making liquors of any kind, they are all imported, hence empty bottles become a drug in the market.

But I was not out of trouble yet. The German who had in so timely a manner come to my rescue, seeing the state of mind I was in, tried to console me by offering me a glass of spirits. I accepted his offer very readily, I admit, and coming into the bar again, which so vividly reminded me of my former shame and all the indignities heaped upon me, I poured out a whole tumblerful of raw brandy—which I should not have done, considering that I came from a ship on which nothing of that sort was served out. But I will draw a veil over the rest of this miserable day. Not but that the worst is told. Intemperance was never my weakness, but I will leave the reader to fill out the picture, and to think of me as I returned to the ship, bleeding, torn, and battered, and there I had to face poor Thorkill, who, in his mild surprise and disapproval, was to me more terrible than if he had stormed and raged ever so much.

*Missing Friends, being the Adventures of a Danish
Emigrant in Queensland (1871–1880) (1902).*

# Andrew Riemer

## (1936– )

*Andrew Riemer was born in Budapest, Hungary, and came to Australia with his parents when he was ten. A distinguished Shakespearean scholar and a well-known book reviewer, he was a member of the English Department of the University of Sydney until 1994, when he retired to write full-time. He has written two further volumes of autobiography,* The Habsburg Café *(1993) and* America with Subtitles *(1995). He has also contributed to literary controversy with* The Demidenko Debate *(1996).*

By the autumn of 1947 my parents could no longer justify keeping me away from school. We had been settled in our rented rooms in Hurlstone Park for some weeks, and an attempt had therefore to be made to introduce a measure of normality into what had been a markedly vagrant existence for a child. For the first time, a month or so after my eleventh birthday, I began attending school regularly. I was enrolled at Canterbury Public School, a few minutes' walk from where we lived. My first days there provide some of my most bizarre memories of our early months in Australia.

My appearance in the potholed school playground on a stifling morning in late March caused a sensation. This was due largely to the clothes my mother considered it appropriate for me to wear. In New York, where we spent a few weeks on our way to Australia, she had stocked up at Macy's New Year sale. Her choice of items was probably governed by those Carmen Miranda fantasies that my parents had entertained about life in Australia. On this particular morning she rigged me out for school in a coloured summer shirt, a pair of blue cotton shorts, and brightly-striped socks worn with sandals. The socks, especially, made me the centre of an incredulous circle of onlookers. I was a garish parrot amidst a flock of drab sparrows.

In the late forties Hurlstone Park and Canterbury represented the quintessence of working-class Australia. The rows of mostly single-fronted cottages in the streets of our neighbourhood were separated at the back by rusting sheets of corrugated iron and at the front by flimsy picket fences. At weekends sallow-complexioned men wearing sparklingly clean cotton singlets sat for hours on brown-stained front steps, with bottles of beer perched beside them, addressing the odd laconic remark to their counterparts next door. On weekdays, as they were leaving for the factory or the railway yards where many of them worked, their wives were already out the front, clad in faded dressing-gowns, their heads wrapped in scarves, watering the inevitable hydrangeas that grew beside the steps of most of these houses. Before they had finished watering, their children would be leaving for school, the boys in heavy grey woollen shorts, their hair, like their fathers', brutally 'short-back-sides' (as in the terrible indignity suffered by the central character in Patrick White's story 'Clay'), the girls in equally inappropriate blue serge tunics. Girls usually carried Globite schoolcases; the boys considered them too prissy—their books and sandwiches were often conveyed in mustard-coloured shoulder bags which you could buy at disposal stores. My parents never allowed me to have one of those badges of manliness—I had to be content with a sissy Globite.

The bemused boys who surrounded me on that first morning, staring in wonderment at an overcoloured scarecrow, were all lean and sinewy, their faces old for their years, many of them barefooted, their clothes crumpled and dirty. Small eyes looked suspiciously out of freckled faces; thin lips were pursed in disapproval. Even the girls, separated from us by an inviolable *cordon sanitaire*, had become aware of my presence: they stood in little groups inside the white line painted across the playground, craning their necks to see better. The teachers—all male, I cannot remember a single woman teacher at that school—were equally curious, stealing surreptitious glances at me as they strolled around the playground ostentatiously in pursuit of their arcane supervisory duties. They wore heavy, shabby suits, some with a waistcoat, reeking of tobacco and sweat. They had the gnarled, hollow-cheeked look of our neighbours who spent their weekends sitting on doorsteps slowly pouring beer into thick glasses.

Almost no communication was possible; my knowledge of English in those early days was limited to the few phrases I had picked up during our weeks in America and on the three-week voyage of the *Marine Phoenix*. I was isolated in the middle of a circle of curious faces, an outsider even though I was standing in the middle of that circle. Several well-meaning boys and teachers attempted to engage me in some form of conversation, but it proved futile. [...] It was then, I think, that I began to recognise an aspect of Australian culture which I did not acknowledge fully until many years later, at a time when I began to think a good deal about the differences betwen cultures and about the impact of an unfamiliar culture on the outsider. It was this: Australians, at least the children and adults of the inner western and southern suburbs of Sydney in the 1940s, employed a very restricted repertoire of gestures—body language, in the jargon of the seventies and eighties. The faces staring at me, even those that attempted to draw me out of that circle of isolation, were impassive, their hands immobile. You could not 'read' their intentions, especially if you were the product of a culture which habitually employed exaggerated gestures, smiles and other facial expressions. Those sinewy children and gnarled middle-aged men were inscrutable in their curiosity, just as I no doubt proved incomprehensible to them in my brightly coloured parrot-garb.

At length a boy pulled on the school bell. I was shown where to stand for assembly while we saluted the flag, promised to honour the King and to obey God— though I understood none of that at the time. We marched into a classroom where someone showed me where to sit. My education had begun.

I cannot adequately describe the sense of total desolation that descended on me during those first days. I can state my condition: I understood almost nothing of what went on around me—none of the instructions the teacher seemed to be giving; nor the significance of the map he unrolled in order to explain something; nor the radio broadcast to which we had to listen. These things may be stated; but I find it impossible to convey the experience of living in a state of almost total incomprehension, of being cast into a group governed by elaborate rules and mechanisms which you cannot comprehend. I was surrounded by a world where things happened, where things were done, where certain actions had consequences, without possessing any ability to discover what was expected of me. What was the strange chant that the class took up at one point? Why did one of the boys get called out to the front to receive a couple of whacks with a stick? What was the point of the teacher's joke that sent the whole class into gales of laughter? Of course there was some trickle of understanding: I realised that the chanting had something to do with numbers; I knew that the boy got whacked because he had been making a great deal of noise. The joke, on the other hand, remained totally incomprehensible—like many migrants and aliens, I was beginning already to nurture a healthy crop of paranoia: was I the butt of that joke?

*Inside Outside: Life Between Two Worlds* (1992).

# Mary Rose Liverani

## (1939– )

*Mary Rose Liverani was born in Glasgow and came to Australia at the age of thirteen
when her family migrated to Wollongong. Her autobiography compares the highly
charged life she lived in Glasgow as the daughter of a ship's rigger and the bland life the
family discovered in Australia.*

I am waiting for Australia to enchant me. To distract me from the past. To become
the hypnotic present.

Today I had my very first Australian cut. The first in the family. A sliver of raw
steel was sticking out from the side supports of the gangway and it pricked me on
the left calf as I put my right foot down on Terra Australis. Two gouts of blood
blotched the concrete in tooth-edged circles before a path was found down my leg
and into my sock. 'Take care,' my father warned, when I yelled 'Hey, look!' Cuts
cannot be neglected here. The germs are ferocious in this water-sodden heat. I
licked my finger and rubbed at the slit skin carelessly. What was the use of having
a cut in Australia if it didn't develop its own unique characteristics? I would see
how terrible the germs are.

Boys were punting a ball in a side street we passed on the way up from the ship.
My father insisted they were ordinary kids like us, nothing special, and he wouldn't
stop to stare. I wanted to see their faces close up and listen to their voices, but he
loped away from us, bobbing up and down on what Mammy called his two left
legs, opening and shutting them like scissors cutting up yard after yard of space.
'There's a train waiting,' he panted, when we grumbled in line behind him, straggling in and out like the tail of a kite.

He was wrong. The train had gone when we reached the station.

'Damnation. Two more hours.'

We consumed square pies with interest rather than hunger, prising open the lids
and examining the gritty meat curiously.

'There's a lot o' empty space in here.'

'That's for people who're no' very hungry,' my father joked.

Bits of meat and gristle bloodied with red sauce began to dribble down best
clothes.

'Christ, you eat like a pig. Here you, take him tae a bubbler and wipe that mess
off his clothes.'

We couldn't find a bubbler in the Ladies' Waiting Room where eating food was
strictly forbidden, but rows of wash basins with peeling taps and flaky porcelain

were perched like cranes on single legs underneath dulled mirrors. Most extraordinary were the toilets with two bowls plonked side by side.

'This might be a toilet for twins,' Margaret suggested.

'Or best friends,' whispered hungry Susan who was always hiding at keyholes.

Margaret placed her two hands side by side between the bowls.

'Look at the wee space between them. Two fat women would be touching each other. Ugh.'

We looked at each other horrified. Nae peace tae read a book, even.

Then, reluctantly, for we might need it again and would then have to pay another penny, we let the door slam and 'vacant' rushed round to shove 'engaged' into the lower half of the dial.

We wandered aimlessly over the station, stopping to read the headlines on the newspapers. [...]

Robert, who was gazing around him, suddenly grabbed my father's arm.

'Hey, Da, there's an Aborigine!'

We all stared at the little dark man he was pointing to pushing an empty trolley. My father put down the paper he was reading (it was called the *Common Cause*) and glanced quickly at the little man.

'Don't go pointing at people like an ignoramus,' he snapped. 'And that man's no' an Aborigine. He's a Greek or an Italian. Jesus, did they no' teach ye anything at school, in geography?'

We played games in a frenzied squandering of time. Half an hour was spent, heedlessly running and taking wide stretched leaps over Susan's or Robert's bent back. But sometimes we ran, only to stop abruptly on the points of our shoes, pawing the air and holding in our stomachs to prevent a collision with a frozen-eyed man or woman whose sight was fixed on things inward.

My mother was fretful.

'Ye'll have tae stop playing leapfrog. Ye're getting in people's way and they're staring at us.'

And when we looked, so they were. Brown paper carrying bags lying on their ankles or smallish suitcases with the corners pulled back and thick, ochre coloured cardboard exposed, clamped firmly between long, thin thighs and sharp chin. They were gaping at us. All along a red-brown seat. Sadie stuck her tongue out.

'Oh,' my mother said, affronted, and gave her a slap.

[...]

'Here, there's only twenty minutes left,' my father announced standing up.

'The train'll be in. We can go and sit in it.'

It was leaving from platform 11. All stations to Gullawobblong.

'It's a slow train,' my father said.

And we all tried to push through the barrier at once.

'Christ, ah'm goin' tae kill that lot,' my mother swore.

In the train, however, she beamed happily when she came to inspect and found all the younger ones asleep, lying across each other like kittens.

'Thank God for that,' she said to Margaret and me. 'Ah can relax noo.'

And down the aisle she went to her own seat beside my father.

Though it was getting dark we could still see out of the window. Margaret had the window seat, so I watched from crab eyes the man sitting opposite us. He wore a cardigan and a hat. The skin on his face looked rough and tough and he had thin, drained lips. He sat with his knees spread open and his hands hanging between them, the fingers tapping each other restlessly. A few minutes after the train left the station he tapped his fingers together with a last flourish, one after the other as if he were running them down piano keys, and leaning forward, said:

'You kids mind if I smoke?'

Well, I nearly died. To ask us if we minded anything! The only time that was ever said to us was in the tone that meant quit it or I'll punch your nose. Do you mind, with a filthy look. Meaning, I blooming well mind what you're doing.

Margaret didn't hear him but I said:

'Good heavens, no.'

[…]

Then the man spoke again. It was clear he felt comfortable with us now.

'Where are you kids going?'

'Gullawobblong.'

'Nice town. Lots of beaches. And steelworks for making money.' He flicked some ash on to the floor. Dirty thing. 'Poms, aren't you?'

What were Poms? Margaret never liked to show her ignorance.

'We're Protestants,' she said.

It was a useless attempt. I could see by the quick flicker of the man's lips that she'd said something stupid. He tried to cover it up.

'Then you're Protestant Poms.'

There was little point in going on with this game. It was like twenty questions. So I confessed that we weren't familiar with the word.

'Poms are short for Pommies. People from England.'

'From England or Britain?' I asked quickly.

He shrugged his shoulders and stared out of the window.

'What's it matter? They're all the same.'

Then he saw by my face I was annoyed and added:

'It's the English really. They're the Pommies.'

'Well,' I said, 'we're Scottish and there's a big difference, you know. But you haven't told us what Pommie means.'

He tapped his teeth with his long fingernail.

'I don't really know, kid. Something to do with their skins.'

'Is it good or bad?' I persisted.

He shook his head from left to right in a negative gesture.

'Bad. It means "I don't like you mate"!'

Then he changed the subject, wrenching it out of its ugly shape.

'What do you think of the bush?'

I felt anxious to please him somehow, so I looked along his wiggling fingers that pointed outside the window, and tried to single out particular leaves. It was impossible.

'Which one?'

'Which what?'

'Which bush?'

Oh dear. It was easier to talk broken English with Frank, the Italian fish shop owner. The man was exasperated. He made a queer sound in the back of his throat and withdrew into himself. His lids, drawing down over his eyes, said 'the end' and I folded my hands together on my lap, irritated because I didn't know what I'd done to be so annoying. From time to time I looked over at the man. A fine, dark glitter, sharp across his face, told me his eyes weren't perfectly shut. But he was sleeping, quietly soughing through his teeth. I nudged Margaret. She was dozing with her cheek on the hand that rested against the glass.

'That man,' I whispered, trying not to move my lips, 'that man is queer.'

She didn't answer.

[…]

Then I felt fingers tapping on my knee. It was the man. He was leaning over to get my attention.

'It's the lot,' he said.

'The lot of what?'

'The lot—' He swung his arm widely this time. 'The grass, the trees, the ferns.' He swung again like a drunk man. 'Everything's the bush.'

'Och, is that what ye mean?'

He nodded deeply, pleased that I understood at last.

'Yeah, well what do you think?'

This time I did the shrugging. Grass and stuff. What could you say? […]

'Everything seems to be coming or going,' I said, finally.

He sat up straight, his face watchful, and I sensed he was preparing to do battle for his bush. He was listening, not with interest but with ammunition.

'What do you mean?'

I swung my arm the way he had.

'The trees and the little bushes. They're all young, just growing, or they're all twisted, just dying. There don't seem to be any tall straight trees that are in the middle. Look at those,' I said, pointing. 'That tree's like an old hand springing out of the earth without a wrist, even. It hasn't got a proper trunk in the middle.'

'Maybe it's not a proper tree,' he argued craftily. 'It may be just scrub. But we've got mighty trees, you know. How do you think we get our telegraph poles?' he cried, delighted with his inspiration. There was nothing I could say to that. 'The bush,' he went on like a salesman, as if he wanted me to buy it, 'goes on forever so that it never seems to move at all. All together, it is always there. Nobody saw its beginning, and it'll likely see our end. So you're wrong, you see. Got no understanding of it at all.'

*The Winter Sparrows* (1975).

# *Morris Lurie*

## (1938– )

*Morris Lurie was born in Melbourne into a Jewish family from Poland. He has lived overseas for extended periods and has published in Australia, the USA, and Britain. He has published six novels, six collections of short stories, five collections of prose pieces that he refers to as 'reportage', three plays, and several children's books.*

There was once a family with a miraculous servant. Heavensent, a worker of magic, there was nothing impossible for her, there was nothing she couldn't do. Returning from the markets, say, to the house cold and dark, she had only to step inside for everything to be in an instant transformed. Her presence was sufficient. She scarcely needed to kindle the lamps, to put a light to the stove. One foot in the door and straight away the whole house sprung alive, ablaze with light, inviting and warm.

But the family would be hungry, ravenous. They were starving. They were dying. Their stomachs shouted shrill with pain. From the servant's baskets tumbled meats, loaves, delicacies, fruits, her hands already slicing, spreading, plucking, peeling. In minutes the kitchen would sing with head-swimming smells, the choicest aromas. There was absolutely no waiting. It was ready at once. In the blink of an eye food flew to the table, steaming soups, stews, tastes beyond imagining, all manner of marvellous things.

The kitchen would be like paradise, the centre of the world.

The servant herself ate little, the merest mouthful, a bite here and there. She didn't require more. Her pleasure was in serving, the family attended to, the family fed.

Strangers she fed too, guests, whoever came to the house. Invited or otherwise, it made no difference. She bustled. She laid extra places. She rushed in spare chairs. Even without notice she was always prepared. No one left hungry, there was always something, there was always enough. How she did it was a mystery, even the family didn't know. From empty cupboards she could conjure dishes in endless procession, spicy and scented, nourishing puddings, egg-rich cakes.

And for everyone a smile, a welcome, a warming word.

But don't imagine her extravagant, a spender, a waster, a squanderer, a fool. In fact, the opposite. Quite the reverse. She was masterful with money. She understood it, bargains, economy, true value, a penny saved is a penny earned. She was careful, shrewd. She was parsimonious, even. She was exact. She lit a dozen fires from the one match, could keep the kettle sweet all day with a single pinch of tea. She was cunning. She was sharp in her blood. She knew how to spin her miracles without heedless outlay of cash.

And where the father of the family had no head for figures, was almost oafish in that regard, in fact, certainly slack, slovenly, couldn't care less, she was not. She took stock. She kept check. Her accounts were immaculate. She knew what was coming in, what was going out. And all done in her head, never a figure committed to paper, there was no need, her mind was clear, she knew where she stood.

It was a point of honour with her to pay each bill on its due date, if possible earlier, certainly never a minute late. She owed no one. She was never in debt.

Similarly the future she accorded its rightful respect. She set aside. She put away. She calculated. She planned. She would not be caught napping. Brick by brick she made solid the family's essential dreams.

She was smart.

She was dauntless.

She was exemplary in all things.

Her cleaning, for example, her care of the house.

When she washed a floor it shone like a mirror. The furniture too, the windows, the walls. She stood on tables, ladders, frightened of nothing, leaning wide, reaching far, cornices, dados, the tops of cupboards, the furthest corners, even the ceilings she ransacked for dirt. She was scrupulous. She was fastidious. She was always with a rag in her hand, a cloth, a mop. You would search her house in vain for a single speck of dust. Whatever she touched, knobs and handles, shelves and sills, lamps and ledges and vases and plates, all objects, all surfaces, stone and glass and metal and wood, she made brilliant, she made gleam.

Spotless was her ultimate accolade, her highest praise.

Clothes she boiled in a copper, stirring with a pole. Blankets, sheets, the family wash. She plunged her hands into scalding water. She worked in steam. Her arms blossomed red as roses, her shoulders, her neck, her cheeks, her face. She glowed with work, aflame. She rubbed, she squeezed, she twisted, she wrung. Load after iron load she ran outside to hang under the sky. And then the reverse, wind-stiff now, sun-blown, down it came again, in the one lyric movement stretching, folding, whisking it inside.

In the evening when she ironed, she warmed the whole house with a fragrance like fresh loaves.

And if a sock needed darning, a collar turned, a hem taken up, a patch, a pocket, a button, a zip? You had only to ask, and usually not even that. She was alert to such things. Her eyes were fast. Nothing escaped her. She saw. She noticed. She attended. Her needle swooped like music, fleet as a bird. In a trice her golden fingers restored better than brand-new.

She embroidered too, tablecloths, pillowcases, napkins, doilies, the tiniest stitches, the most delicate things, spun their surfaces with intricate patterns, sprinkled flowers of every colour on their linen fields.

When she whisked out a tablecloth, for visitors, for afternoon tea, it covered the table like a work of art.

She was tireless. She required no sleep. She would work fourteen hours at a stretch. Then a sip of tea, a scrap of bread, and she was ready for a further four. At three o'clock in the morning, the family safely and soundly asleep, she would still be working, catching up, jobs, neglected chores so far not done. In the hush of the house, her sewing machine would hum and whirr.

And should a child be injured, a bump, a bruise, she was instantly prepared. She knew all the right remedies. She knew what to do. A swelling on the forehead she softened first with butter, then pressed down gently with the flat of a knife. She was expert with sties too, with chapped ears, cracked lips, all scratches, all scrapes, she knew the steams and flannels for every ache and fever and chill, for when a nose bloomed like a flower, for when a chest rattled, for when a throat rubbed sore, though she herself was never sick, never ill, never a single day absent from her duties and work.

Whoever needed her, at whatever hour, she was immediately available, she was always there.

She was a treasure, a jewel. The words don't exist properly to describe her. She was without equal. She was entirely unique.

And everyone knew her, the entire community sang her praises. The way you were always welcome in her kitchen. Her open-heartedness. Her selflessness. Her instant generosity. She was unparallelled, a model servant. In the city where she lived, her name was synonymous with virtue and goodness, with thoughtfulness and love and care.

She was lauded.

She was famous.

The family, of course, loved her too, worshipped her, cherished her, doted on her. And in the way of all families with servants, miraculous or otherwise, they exploited her. They used her up. They pressed her to work even harder, to do even more. They accepted her miracles as commonplace. They deserved them, they said. They were their due. She was their very first servant, you understand. They had never had another, had nothing to compare.

They took her for granted.

And the servant did it, whatever was asked. She never once complained. She did as she was bidden, whatever was required. Her back was like whale bone, like steel. She carried any load.

A pretty woman, you saw, or had been, however briefly, once. Small. But the eyes forever lovely, dark and soft. And of course her selfless smile.

And then one day she was called away. It was very sudden. One minute she was there and the next she was gone. She had duties elsewhere. She was summoned. It was not so much a request as an order. The word was announced and that was that. There was no question of saying no.

One minute she was there and the next she was not.

The family was stunned. They were numbed. They were disconsolate. They were totally bereft. For the first time they realized how much they had relied on their servant, how much they had needed her for even the slightest thing. They would never find her equal. It seemed to them impossible even to try.

In particular, the father. Of the whole family, he seemed the hardest struck. His grief was palpable and visible. His mouth hung open, his eyes stood forth wide and glazed. He looked baffled, stupefied. It was as though he had been hit by a hammer. The moment the servant had gone, he began to lurch around the house, from room to room, bumping into furniture, into doorways, into walls. He was like a blinded bull. He was like a rudderless ship.

No one could help him. He didn't want to be helped. He wouldn't listen. He was deaf to every word. Around and around he went, hands stuffed into his trouser pockets, slump-shouldered, head down, from this room to that room, lurching and bumping, around and around the house. He wouldn't stop. He couldn't stop. He did it day and night. He had always been untidy, the father, unkempt, uncaring of appearances, a bit of a slob, but now you could see it clearly now that the servant was no longer there to look after him, to keep him clean. His trousers became at once rumpled and shapeless, crumpled like bags. Dirt sprang to them everywhere, droppings and spots and flecks. And on his shirt too, the front, the sleeves, ingrained into the cuffs. The collar pointed out like twisted horns. His scuffed shoes trailed laces knotted and broken. Wherever you looked the father was begrimed, befouled, besmirched with stains and grease.

He neglected his toilet. He was unwashed, uncombed. Grey hair in a tuft arose on his head, a spike of icy grass. His body smelled sour. His teeth turned yellow. The nails on his fingers stood out rimmed jet black.

Sometimes he paused, in this room, that room. He stood in the passage. He switched on a light, switched it off again. He stood in the dark. He blinked. He gaped. He rubbed his stunned face, the grey bristles roaring. He panted hard through his open mouth. He sighed. He breathed. And then again he lumbered, he resumed his journey, he lurched, from this room to that room, around and around.

When he sat it was temporary, a makeshift mooring. His chair creaked like a sail.

He was like this for fifty days, this extraordinary behaviour, fifty days and nights, while his family helplessly watched.

And then the father too received a summons, an order. He was instantly excited. He understood it at once. He was to see the servant again, his beloved servant. He was to go where she had gone, the very same place. He laughed. He sang. He clapped his hands. He shouted with joy. He was jubilant. He was like a horse scenting water. He whinneyed. He neighed. He stamped his hooves. He kicked and jumped and bounded and thrashed. It took him ten days but there was no question, no doubt, there was no holding him back. It was so close. There was only one last fence to hurdle and then he was there. He braced himself. He was ready. He took one final breath and over he bolted, made it, gone.

And twenty years later his son, his elder son, the son whose story this is, this hard history, in hopeless depression, awash with tears, driving to see the psychiatrist who has been trying to help him twice a week now for almost two years, this son curses the servant and her husband the slob, rails against their dumbness, their blindness, their unfeeling stupidity, and in his black rage all he can think to do—and would have done, had there been the slightest point, had it been of the slightest use—is to drive to the cemetery where they are buried and piss on their graves.

*Whole Life: An Autobiography* (1987).

# Elisabeth Wynhausen

(1946– )

*Elisabeth Wynhausen was born in the Netherlands and migrated to Sydney with her family at the age of four. She is a well-known journalist and has worked for the* Age, *the* Bulletin, *and the* National Times. *References to the Betarim in the extract indicate a Zionist youth movement called Betar, which attracted some of the more aggressive Jewish youths. A shul is a synagogue.*

Though I had severed most of my connections with the tribe, on one occasion, in 1968, I found myself surrounded by its elders. It was my brother's doing. He was marrying the English Rose, whose father was not only a rabbi, but the bossiest man we had ever met. One immediate result was that the wedding could not have been more traditional—our families went to war, and Manischewitz supplied the so-called wine.

The guests were already gossiping in the squat little synagogue on the outskirts of Sydney's western suburbs when hostilities broke out in the kitchen of the house next door. 'You're wearing Homburgs and that's all there is to it,' the rabbi shouted. 'I'm not,' his future son-in-law said mildly enough to get under anyone's skin. Jules, who looked unnatural in a suit, kept fingering the collar of the perfectly-fitted shirt, as if he might choke to death at any moment. He remembered looking down on a surge of Homburgs when he was a nine-year-old choir boy at the Great Synagogue in downtown Sydney, where manufacturers whose grandfathers had been pedlars in Bialystok acted like English gentlemen. 'No way.'

'We can't,' said the rabbi's son, Ian, who had hidden the hats on the chairs tucked under the kitchen table. 'They've disappeared. I've looked everywhere, even in shul.' At seventeen, Ian towered over his father. He seemed to be about to pat him consolingly on the top of his head, or perhaps to swipe the kippah and hide that as well. 'It's time, dad. We'll have to go without them.'

The rabbi thumped the table, something fell over, and his wife crept in, looking helpless. She would have liked to finish fixing her corsage and wig, but did not dare. 'Harold …'

'This,' said the rabbi melodramatically, 'is easily the worst day of my life.'

They relented, of course. It was his day. In the first of his starring roles he strutted down the short aisle, with Eve on his arm, his eyes sternly fixed on the Homburgs up ahead, and with a two-step of ceremonial gravity, he popped up under the Chuppah and waited for silence. Though it was a cool day in June, the synagogue was stifling. Swathed in a bridesmaid's dress in dark-green velvet, I stared sidelong at the front pews, inspecting the boiled faces under hair lacquered in place, until I caught my mother's eye. She winked. Ordinary Jews used to caper for joy at an affair like this. If you couldn't have a Rothschild in the family, a rabbi was the next-best thing. But we thought it was a nuisance. Harold was a conceited little fellow so used to having his own way at home that he tried to bully us as well. Every single word he had said about the wedding emphasized that it was his show, from beginning to end. He had telephoned often, in recent weeks, and he only had to say, 'Harold, here …' for my mother to start giggling. I winked back.

Now he was saying something about a 'fifty-fifty partnership in marriage' and one or two of the guests looked downright sceptical, as if he were going against the grain. Not that Harold had got off scot-free. Though his wife was anxious, apologetic and devout about the least of his needs, his daughter could match him for intransigence down to the final bitter words as she fled into marriage at the age of twenty, unable to stand one more interminable Saturday afternoon out in the dreariest of suburbs. Harold couldn't stop himself from mentioning it, when he alluded to the lucky couple at long last. 'In fact, there's plenty of room for improvement …' Cathy, the other bridesmaid, glanced at me in alarm. She was not Jewish, and Eve had forgotten to warn her that no occasion was too exalted to wash a bit of dirty linen in public. The rabbi was restrained, however, allowing only that the lovebirds still had a thing or two to learn about good manners towards their parents.

He had claimed that he had to invite about three-quarters of his congregation and half the rabbinate. It left our side with a reduced guest list, which was just as well. They might not have said so, but Aunty Nan and her friends considered themselves a cut above the Jews who lived on the edge of civilization (an hour's drive from the Cosmopolitan in Double Bay), and who probably went to the sort of shul where no-one noticed if you wore a cardigan.

Not even our nearest and dearest had bothered to fake much pleasure at the prospect of driving out to the sticks to hear Harold's nasal East End intonations, before driving back, pell-mell, for the festivities in a hall in Woollahra. The balloons looked a little limp by the time that we reached the place, and the classy gardenias in the floral arrangements reeked of stale perfume, but these were details lost in the crisis of the moment.

Though he presided over a shul where people were sometimes to be seen in white twinsets, even on Yom Kippur, highest of the High Fashion Days, Harold had managed to turn the tables, socially speaking. Nevertheless, he seemed surprised that my mother objected to a seating plan which had her guests at the two tables at the back of the hall, with the Betarim. For a minute, she was speechless with rage, and then she spluttered, 'Chutzpah, Harold, what chutzpah …'

seizing handfuls of the place cards, as if to redistribute them. The argument continued out the back, in the kitchen, where Mrs Goodkind, the caterer, was supervising the preparation of the usual boiled chicken. Referees were called in, the English Rose burst into tears and mum threatened a walkout, but by then it was all over bar the shouting, and my aunts, uncles and honorary relations roughed it with the rowdies down the back. I could hardly believe their luck.

The bridesmaids were at the High Table, and I was with the geriatrics. On my right was a venerable great-aunt of Eve's who spoke only Yiddish. On my left was the Chief Rabbi of Sydney. Our conversation was strained, after the opening gambit. I had started to light a cigarette. 'Not before the toast to the Queen,' he hissed, closing his hand over mine like a vice. I played at being deaf, but it was boring. 'Do you speak Yiddish, Dr Porush?' He looked startled.

'Why do you ask, my child?'

'Oh, this lady here doesn't speak English.'

They conversed, and I leaned forward politely, scanning the room to see if there was a single person I could have considered screwing. [...]

Harold, the Master of Ceremonies, had grabbed the microphone by his plate to introduce himself, with a modest chuckle, as the father of the bride, before explaining that this was only an introduction because we would be hearing from him later in the afternoon. 'Of course, you've all met my wife, Yetta,' he said, 'and as you are undoubtedly aware, we are especially honoured by the presence of the Honorable Dr Israel Porush ...' I stole a glance at Porush, dipping his heavy old head to a scatter of subservient applause.

Harold was a lightweight, but Porush had this way of looking into the middle distance, and I couldn't help conjecturing about his hotline to a God I didn't believe in. 'I beg your pardon?' Jesus, he was asking where I went to synagogue. Talk about tactless. 'My parents are with Cremorne shul,' I said carefully, 'but I live in Balmain. It's nice, Balmain, near the old wharves, almost European, with those winding little streets ...'

'Yes, I know.' He smiled encouragingly, and turned to the person on his other side. What did I tell him about Balmain being European for? No-one said that except my mother, who was dismayed by it.

'Balmain,' she had snapped, in the last act of the drama played out on the day I said I was leaving home, 'who ever heard of Balmain?' It had happened in the summer, a couple of weeks after I left Frensham. [...]

My mother acted as if there had been a death in the family, wailing that decent Jewish girls did not run away from home unless they had something to hide. 'I'm pregnant,' I said, 'can't you tell? It happened last night when dad left us alone for eight-and-a-half minutes.'

'Don't speak to your mother like that.'

'Like what? Mind your own business.'

'If you speak to your father like that again, you can get out of this house ...' Before long, she was considering the shame of it all. What would she tell the family? She could just hear people talking about it at B'nai B'rith. Only in moments of stress did she resort to such arguments; fortunately she was herself again by the time we went off to inspect the terrace house in East Balmain.

In fact, she was rather quiet, and Tante Ali did most of the talking. I had dragged Ali along because she was known for her modern outlook on life, but even she paled a little at the sight of the grey stucco slapped over the exterior of the dark, narrow fronted house. The real estate agent, Balmain impresario Reggie Window, seemed to overreact to the presence of a pair of Dutch matrons, because he kept tapping at things to show that the house wouldn't fall down. Someone else was moving into the attic, but the second-floor bedroom in the front had a varnished wood floor, an improbable plaster rosette in the ceiling, and iron-lace on a balcony which hung slightly askew. If you stood on tiptoe, you could see the inner harbour. 'All these bedrooms for only twenty-five dollars a week,' I said excitedly.

Depressed or not, my mother couldn't tolerate this soft headed enthusiasm, and she quizzed the agent about the plumbing and the gas, as she ran her hand over one dusty surface after another. 'You'll never keep this place clean.' It was her only triumph. All I could see was the patina of age, and I was thrilled. [...]

Eve's great-aunt was tugging at my elbow. She had lapped up the tinned fruit salad, and seemed to be jiggling her shoulders in time to the music. 'Herbie Marks Trio,' she said in impeccable English.

'I know.' [...]

'You dance,' she said.

Everyone else was having a high old time. My brother's friends had moved some tables and were dancing. They must have tapped a stash of hooch. All I had got my hands on was kosher wine, and kosher wine is the Jewish answer to holy water— you could drown in it without getting drunk. Did Porush really say that anyone could dance? The old guard was ganging up on me, and even mum and dad were out on the floor, doing the foxtrot, while I sat there submerged in self-pity, pulling petals out of a manufactured-looking carnation.

'Your sister-in-law looks lovely,' Porush said.

'I think they're going to sing.'

Jules had lost the struggle for the microphone, and Harold announced that he had a special treat for us, a return engagement by the Bridal Couple and their friend, Henry Berkovic, who was back from Eretz Yisroel where he had gone as a volunteer. In its heyday, two years earlier, the trio had materialized at parties in the

Hakoah Club or the Maccabean Hall, often to the surprise of the guests, who seemed to be expecting the likes of Daniel Barenboim instead of a few straggly-looking folk singers in duffel coats. [...]

The trio was huddled around the mike. Jules strummed an experimental chord on his guitar. His eyes were half-shut, and as usual, he looked to be in an existential stupor, dark suit or no dark suit. [...] Getting the crowdpleaser in early, the trio had launched into 'To Life, To Life, L'chaim'. [...]

Out the back, in Mrs Goodkind's domain, the sound of breaking glass was followed by an ominous thud. Some of the Betarim were paralytic. Harold stayed at his post. So did I. Down below, almost everyone had joined hands to circle the room, because the trio was finishing off with 'Hava Nagila'. Now and again, Dr Porush gazed at me with patriarchal reproach, as if he had somehow divined that I had strayed. Until the previous week, in fact, I had been involved with a creep whose occupation as a truck driver for Coca Cola should have made the first of mum's questions about him redundant.

'No, sorry, he's not Jewish,' I had tried to be polite, 'but it's okay, I'm not going to marry him, or anything.' For once I regretted having issued the usual gazette on my love life. 'He's all right, really; I met him at the Piccolo.' She had not looked reassured. [...]

'Normal people don't spend every night in the Piccolo Bar,' my mother had said, and dad gave her a glance of admiration.

I couldn't stand it for another second. 'Excuse me,' I muttered to no-one in particular. The great-aunt had disappeared. Porush, who was deep in conversation with another rabbi, looked relieved to be talking shop. 'Do you want to dance?' said a friend of my brother's I hadn't seen in years.

I was aggrieved. 'I don't care. I've been up there two hours with the rabbis inter-rogating me about where I go to shul, and there wasn't even any booze, except that disgusting sweet wine ...'

'Listen, he's going to make a Speech!'

'Bullshit, Jules never made a speech in his life!'

I was wrong. Harold had just announced that his son-in-law had the floor. 'Only Harold could take five minutes to introduce someone else's speech. What a pain in the arse ...'

'Shhhh.'

My brother finally looked as if he meant business. He tapped the mike, straight-ened up, and stared over our way. 'Thank you,' he said, and walked away.

*Manly Girls* (1989).

# Christos Tsiolkas

## (1965– )

*Christos Tsiolkas is a graduate of Melbourne University. His first novel,* Loaded, *was published in 1995.*

Memory is a duty. I remember Linda. We are dancing to Human League 'Fascination', in Tasha's lounge room. Eighteen, and we know everything. High on speed. Her hair is dyed, shaved at the sides and gelled on top. This is how I remember her.

She is dead at twenty-two. A suicide, swinging on a beam.

At the Greek Orthodox funeral, the priest chants. Tasha can't stop sobbing. My eyes are dry for the moment, angry at the priest who prays over her body. The Church refuses to give her the rites of burial. Suicide, a sin, buried in Springvale's Cemetery's unconsecrated ground, away from the Orthodox and the Catholics who have been graced by the Last Rites.

A plain white cross marks her grave.

At the wake, I am suspended between two worlds.

In the house, aunts in black are crying. A timid cousin passes coffee around. On the lawn, Linda's friends drink beer and get pissed. I sit on the verandah. I join neither party. The Greeks in the house are silenced by shame. One of her brothers is locked up in prison, a murder committed in a drunken rage. Her sister is up north, on heroin. *Poutana, alitis,* losers.

I watch friends get drunk. Linda's father is speaking broken English. I jump off the steps and crack a beer. The gambling father and the poofter cousin are not welcome in this house.

The violence of migration spans two generations. The parent has had to lose a homeland in order to create a life; the child has to create a life without ever knowing home.

Thinking of the sluts, whores, junkies and losers I have known in my life, when the histories of our time and place are written, we won't be in the cast of characters. Migration is a success story. Multiculturalism. The history books will talk of parliaments, republicanism, technology and economics. This is what they won't tell, that my mother cries herself to sleep thinking of Greece.

My aunt, at fifty-five, starts work at three in the morning to pick scallops out of their shells so they will be fresh for the markets. She has been doing it for thirty years. Thirty years is all of my life.

My father, working the assembly lines at the Rosella factory, has witnessed friends being crushed to death, or losing limbs, working the machines.

For three years Maria lies to her parents that she is studying, unable to face their anger if she tells them the truth. She flunked and got chucked out of La Trobe University. The night before the graduation she drove her parents' car into the Yarra River.

Dimitri stops by a travel agency, dreams of flying to Greece, but he knows, once there, he will only feel he is Australian. That's why he quotes the words of poets, Cavafy, Seferis, Palamas, in Greek, to boys in nightclubs.

Have they ever been translated, he is asked?

He never tells them that they've won a Nobel Prize.

In a tavern in Patra, I dance with Linda's ghost, she the light around me, dancing to a bouzouki.

This was the first music we were ever touched by.

*Jump Cuts: An Autobiography* (1996).

# 6

AUSTRALIANS OVERSEAS

# Alan Moorehead

(1910–83)

*Alan Moorehead grew up in Melbourne and was educated at the University of Melbourne before working for five years for the Melbourne* Herald. *He left Australia for Europe in 1936 and in London joined the* Daily Express. *During World War II he established himself as the outstanding correspondent of the North African war.*

When I came to England in 1936 one of my companions on the voyage was a boy named Frank Sullivan with whom I had been friendly at the university. He really had wretched luck; he dressed himself up as a fairy for the fancy dress ball in the Red Sea, and he grew very heated as he danced the Black Bottom and the Charleston. Then he made the mistake of cooling off on deck in his flimsy costume. Halfway up the Mediterranean he took to his bed, and by the time we passed through the Straits of Gibraltar his illness was diagnosed as pneumonia. At that time there were no antibiotics to cope with the disease; it rose steadily to a crisis and on the ninth day the patient either died or made a rapid recovery. In the Bay of Biscay it seemed quite likely that Frank would die, and the ship was diverted to Plymouth so that he could be landed and taken to hospital. A launch came out to meet us in the harbour and he was lowered into it on a stretcher. I followed down the gangway feeling very conscious of the doleful faces of the hundreds of other passengers lining the rails.

It was a dismal ending to all my expectations of a gay and exciting arrival in England, but the staff at the nursing home were very kind; they even provided a bed for me so that I could be called if Frank died in the night, and I felt a little less alone with my responsibility after I had got off a carefully worded cable to Frank's family in Melbourne. Then I set out on foot to inspect the town. Up to this point I had hardly noticed my new surroundings, but now I did take note, now I looked around and unconsciously compared my preconceived notions of what England would be like with what was actually before my eyes. It is a very fragile and fortuitous thing, this moment of the first impression, but with me it is indelible, and no matter whether I am dealing with places or people I seldom altogether forget it or perhaps see so clearly again. I walked down a steep street towards the centre of the town, and it was marvellous to me that the houses could be so closely huddled together, terrace after terrace, all alike, all so cosy, so regimented, so unnautical. After four weeks at sea the ground rose and fell gently beneath my feet, and my dreams of Plymouth were of smoke-wreathed cannon and of Drake and Nelson setting out in their glory from Plymouth Hoe—not these grey and sober houses with their complacent chimney pots. Those canary birds in the bay windows should have been oath-screeching parrots. Yet there was a solidity here, an earth-based-I-am-what-I-am-ness, that was reassuring.

I turned into a park with iron railings around it. Why railings? There were no railings around our parks; they were as open as the bush. And then arrived my moment of mild revelation. I found myself in front of the green and mossy bole of an immense tree that spread out its dense foliage some forty feet above my head. I stood there in the gentle rain and studied this object with close attention, for I had never seen such a thing before. It was the dampest and greenest tree in the whole world. I reached forward and felt the clammy smoothness of the trunk, I picked up a piece of moss from between the tangled roots, and I gazed upward at the thick canopy of leaves above, the abode no doubt of Squirrel Nutkin and a suitable hiding place for Robin Hood. My Australian eye was adjusted to thin grey leaves with hard sunshine in between and the hard dry plain beyond, and now, by contrast, this explosion of lushness and greenness was delightful. It enveloped one, hid one away, gave one a sense of lazy virility. And in the same way the warm and gentle rain enveloped one and so did the terraced houses. It was the harmony of suburbia and the jungle, a painting by the Douanier Rousseau. Later on in London I grew to detest the warm and gentle rain, and I longed for the sun and a distant view, but I never got tired of the greenness, and still after thirty years or more it is impossible for me to think of England without some gadget in my brain turning a light upon a long row of houses all alike, and a burst of jungle greenery dividing them from the street.

When Frank recovered and we went up to London I had a similar experience among the crowds, the first permanent crowds I had ever known. I loved the march of faceless strangers in the street. To be known by no one, watched by no one, to join the ant-like anonymous processions—this was a new and exhilarating kind of privacy. Somewhere in his *Voyage au bout de la nuit* which I was reading at that time Ferdinand Celine says that he screamed and yelled out of the open window of his bedroom when he reached New York, but no one heard him, and he was made frantic by that indifference. I did not feel like yelling at all in London. We had rooms in Bloomsbury in Mecklenburg Square (25s a week for bed and breakfast), we ate in Lyons cornerhouses, we drank in the Fleet Street pubs, and we were a part of the town.

Perhaps best of all was the feeling I had that at last I was in the centre of the world instead of being on the periphery; you could observe events with your own eyes as they were happening instead of forever hearing about them at second-hand. Here was Edward VIII proposing to abdicate and you could actually see him driving out of Buckingham Palace and find in the paper a photograph of

Mrs Simpson that had been taken that very day. It was not too difficult to get into the House of Commons and hear Anthony Eden making a speech about the Nyon Agreement, and the Spanish Civil War itself was only a day's journey away. If you wanted to see young Laurence Olivier making his first appearance in *Hamlet* there he was in the Old Vic just across the river; and if you were in funds you could nip across the channel to Paris and go to the *Folies Bergères* where Josephine Baker was executing her celebrated dance wearing nothing but a girdle of bananas round her waist.

Then too there was the feeling that one was entirely free, one could go anywhere and do anything.

*A Late Education: Episodes in a Life* (1970).

# Donald Horne

(1921– )

*Donald Horne is well known as a commentator on Australian culture and public affairs, as one-time editor of several major journals, and as an academic and university administrator. His most influential book is* The Lucky Country *(1964), which was followed by a sequence of similar books, but he has also written novels, accounts of his travels, and two further autobiographies,* The Education of Young Donald *(1967) and* Portrait of an Optimist *(1988).*

There was no doubt I would go 'overseas', of course, although how I would get there was not a matter to which I had given any connected thought. 'Overseas' had been waiting for me since I had discovered it as a child in my father's war souvenirs (photographs of soldiers on the Great Pyramid or posed before the Sphinx ... a postcard of a Cairo belly dancer ... pasted on a card, a leaf from the Mount of Olives ... snapshots of Jericho, the Jordan Valley, Bethlehem, the Holy Sepulchre, the Garden of Gethsemane, the Dead Sea) and in the eight volumes of *Cassell's Children's Book of Knowledge* where the essence of 'overseas' was in the photographs and captions of the entry on India, almost all of which I still remembered more or less in their original wordings: *the allure of exotic beauty in the dream-like Hall of Winds at Jaipur, a vision of radiance and dainty loveliness ... the oriental sense of mystery in the calm disdain on the face of the giant bull of Siva at Mysore, beneath whose great left hoof lies the fate, it is believed, of many a poor worshipper.*

Above all: *in the dense throngs of pilgrims washing away their sins in the sacred waters of the Ganges River near the city of Benares and then returning to their villages and spreading the diseases they had acquired in the waters of the Ganges, there is a reminder of those age old customs of the East before which Western civilization stands almost helpless.*

When I was a child receiving these images of the exotic, they seemed images of an 'overseas' I was unlikely ever to see since only the richest of the landed families in the Hunter Valley could afford to go abroad. Now that there was no doubt that I would travel I could scarcely be expected to be concerned, at least publicly, with the *Cassell's Children's Book of Knowledge* kind of sightseeing. I was not likely to speak now of the exotic beauty of the Hall of Winds but of seeing James Joyce's Dublin, or, in New York, the kind of bar the New Yorker people might drink at, or, in Paris, the great post-impressionist collections, or, in London, the West End theatre; but, emotionally, as well as these public desires there was still the secret pleasure of imagining that one day I might actually see the calm disdain on the face of the giant bull of Siva.

But while there was no doubt that I would travel, there was great doubt as to who would pay the fare.

'Just go to London and get a job'. As we were drinking in the saloon bar at the Castlereagh, Ronald Monson's brave explorer's face would look at me in its kindliest way, as if he were explaining that it was as easy to get a job in Fleet Street as it was to learn the rudiments of Swahili, but I felt a kind of modesty about exposing myself to a foreign newspaper. Why would anyone in London want me? I was, after all, an imposter; I was so unlike a true journalist that there were still times when I was afraid I would drop my mask, 'come back without a story', and resign. Surely, over in London, with their sharp English eyes, they would see through my disguise? and even if I managed to trick them, as I had deceived the *Telegraph*, it would only be because I would have to learn new indignities in the style of some other newspaper and in some other way of not being 'myself'. What was the point of travel if it meant moving from the *Telegraph's* enormous room to some enormous room 'overseas'? Sam White spoke of the 'opportunities' there were in Fleet Street. What 'opportunities' were there for me, when it was journalism I wanted to get away from?

I could feel a kind of timidity about earning a living: my father had existed within the bureaucracy of the state schools and now received two pensions for his services to the state, as schoolteacher and soldier, and, despite past surface uproar about the 'servility' of the welfare state, there was one quiet, submerged and indestructible part of me where it could still seem that money should forever be growing modestly on small trees as a reward for those who had behaved themselves. In another part, also indestructible, there was even, still, a primary school vision that my career would be assured because, year by year, I would pass from classroom to classroom and come top in all the exams. In other parts of me there were other indestructible memories of daydreams—of how I made my fortune as a liberal lawyer, or of how I had gone down to some celebrated defeat as a bold political leader; I had never imagined myself as a wage plug signing a duty book. I had imagined great liberal causes lost in court, defeats in parliament, suppressions in the street by the Cossacks, books maliciously reviewed, even being mown down in battle, assassinated as a ruler or executed as a rebel: there were all misfortunes that must be nobly sustained—but the idea of being sacked aroused, simply, fear. [...]

I would strike a bargain with my daydreams and imagine that I was successful as an author, but only very modestly to begin with: a room in London would do, or a small country cottage without water laid on. To write novels it was, however, essential to be 'overseas'. We all knew that there were no real markets in Australia for serious work, nor any good publishers, but there was more than that to it—there seemed something so dull about Australia that it might not be possible to write well while living in it (except verse, of course: I still imagined that, despite being Australians, [Alec] Hope, [Harold] Stewart and [James] McAuley would make their world reputation). It didn't have to be England. Some cheap country in Europe would do: I could be like [Brian] Penton, live in a European village on rough red wine, cheese and bread while I got on with my novel—or, like Elliot Paul in *A Narrow Street*, hide in a European city and turn one small part of it into a book.

But I didn't have the fare to get to any European country, however cheap. I couldn't save money. It would cost at least eighty pounds to sail to London, and every week my salary leaked out into restaurants, bars, bookshops; sometimes I had to borrow to get into the next week.

*Confessions of a New Boy* (1985).

# Gillian Bouras

## (1945– )

*Gillian Bouras, who was born in Melbourne, went to live in Greece with her Greek husband in 1980. She has written further accounts of her experiences of living in a foreign culture,* A Fair Exchange *(1991),* Aphrodite and the Others *(1994), and a novel partly based on the same experience,* A Stranger Here *(1996).*

Autumn advances. Yellow and brown leaves drift from the vines and a chill creeps into the morning air. September is wine-making time and the smell of must lingers along the village lanes for days. Mitso, Vaso's husband, *Yiayia's* son-in-law, backs his utility truck into his backyard, lines the tray with a huge sheet of clear plastic, heaps it full of grapes, dons new rubber boots and proceeds to tramp for hours. Romance is definitely dying; when George was small the children used to leap bare-foot into a stone trough and squish and squash with the greatest of pleasure. There is nothing quite like an ooze or trickle between the toes. But Niko loves turning the wine-press. None of the boys is interested in retsina, but would walk miles for *Yiayia's mustalevria* (must and flour) sweet. She boils grape juice and then adds flour, crushed almonds and cinnamon to make a kind of jelly.

Back into routine at last, I take the blankets and rugs to be washed in the river. The village women have always used the river. They used to slap their linen on stones, using soap they made themselves from olive oil. For stubborn dirt they had an implement somewhat like a rounders bat. *Yiayia* still has one and she pounds away at rugs and blankets every summer, the whack and thwack resounding like gun shots in the early morning air. But now a washer-man secures my blankets in a whirlpool and the water does the work.

Dozens of items hang under trees to dry: old, soft-hued handwoven rugs contrast with garish acrylic blankets, and occasionally a saddle rug of intricate pattern flaps on the line.

The river runs through another village, not ours. Although barely two kilometres separate them, each community sees itself as being quite distinct. Anybody not of one's own village is automatically foreign.

'Who are they?' I ask *Yiayia*, on seeing unfamiliar faces in the street.

'They're not ours,' she answers, firmly. 'They're foreigners,' and she names a village perhaps ten kilometres away. For older Greeks there are only two places on Earth: Greece and *exo* (outside). Their idea of *exo* is often hazy. One old priest is convinced I come from Africa, while another has no idea that Christian denominations other than Orthodoxy exist. On hearing that I was not Orthodox, one relative assumed that I was Muslim.

Today I meet one of the teachers.

'How did you enjoy your holiday *exo*?' she asks.

Similar ideas prevail about language. There is Greek and there is *ta xenna*, the foreign, as if there are only two languages spoken in the world. People have come to me, wanting me to interpret Russian.

'But don't you speak *ta xenna*?' they protest, in bewilderment.

We have been back here barely four weeks, and although I have taken up the threads of day-to-day living, I feel oppressed, closed in and very foreign. Even the food seems strange again. It is such a small world, a confident, complacent, even smug world of which I can never really be a part: there is no return to the womb here for me. But that is as well; it is dangerous to feel too comfortable.

Once, though, in 1980 and 1981, all I wanted was security, safety and comfort, having lost all these things fairly unexpectedly, having lost my past, my tradition and my identity. Even my name was strange to the villagers. By the end of September 1980, George had found a job which excited him, the holiday was over, we knew we would stay. It was then I realised: we are born, we die, and we migrate, alone. For months I walked round with homesickness and anxiety sitting like a lead weight on my chest. The weight went away, but it always returns; it is here now, and all I can do is read my new books, write my letters, work in the garden and talk to Gregory, Panayioti, Spiro, Uncle Vangeli and the others until it retreats.

My mother gave me an enormous book of quotations for my birthday. I could not bear to post it surface mail and so I lugged it on to the aeroplane in my carry-all. I turn to the Scottish proverb which leapt out from the page during the first reading:

'Time and thinking tame the strongest grief.'

So do reading and writing.

*A Foreign Wife* (1986).

# Clive James

## (1939– )

*Clive James, who is well known as a television broadcaster, interviewer, and performer,*
*was born in Sydney and left for England in 1962. He is a prolific writer and has*
*published books of reviews and literary criticism, selections of television journalism,*
*selections of verse, travel accounts, and novels. He has also published two more autobio-*
*graphies,* Falling Towards England *(1985) and* May Week Was in June *(1990).*

The longer I have stayed in England, the more numerous and powerful my memories of Sydney have grown. There is nothing like staying away for bringing it with
you. I have done my best to tell the truth about what it was like, yet I am well aware
that in the matter of my own feelings I have not come near meeting my aim. My
ideal of autobiography has been set by Alfieri, whose description of a duel he once
fought in Hyde Park is mainly concerned with how he ran backwards to safety.
Perhaps because I am not even yet sufficiently at peace with myself, I have not been
able to meet those standards of honesty. Nothing I have said is factual except the
bits that sound like fiction.

By the time this book is published I will be forty years old. When I left Sydney I
boasted that I would be gone for five years. I was to be gone three times that and
more. During that time most of those who came away have gone back. Before
Gough Whitlam came to power, having to return felt like defeat. Afterwards it felt
like the natural thing to do. Suddenly Australia began offering its artists all the
recognition they had previously been denied. It took a kind of perversity to refuse
the lure. Perhaps I did the wrong thing. Eventually fear plays a part: when you are
too long gone, to return even for a month feels like time-travel. So you try to forget.
But the memories keep on coming. I have tried to keep them under control. I hope
I have not overdone it, and killed the flavour. Because Sydney is so real in my recollection that I can taste it.

It tastes like happiness. I have never ceased to feel orphaned, but nor have I ever
felt less than lucky—a lucky member of a lucky generation. In this century of all
centuries we have been allowed to grow up and grow old in peace. There is a
Buster Keaton film in which he is standing around innocently when the façade of
a house falls on him. An open window in the façade passes over his body, so that he
is left untouched.

I can see the Fun Doctor juggling for us at Kogarah Infants' School. One of the
balls hits the floor with a thud. Then what looks like the same ball lands on his
head. I can hear the squeak that the mica window panels of the Kosi stove made
when I scorched them with the red-hot poker. When Jeanette Elphick came back

on a visit from Hollywood they drove her around town in a blue Customline with her new name painted in huge yellow letters along the side: VICTORIA SHAW. On Empire Night when we threw pieces of fibro into the bonfire they cracked like rifle shots. Every evening for weeks before Empire Night I used to lay my fireworks out on the lounge-room carpet, which became impregnated with the smell of gunpowder. Peter Moulton kept his fireworks in a Weetabix carton. On the night, a spark from the fire drifted into the carton and the whole lot went up. A rocket chased Gail Thorpe, who was only just back from therapy. She must have thought it was all part of the treatment.

At the Legacy Party in Clifton Gardens I got a No. 4 Meccano set. On hot nights before the nor'easter came you changed into your cossie and ran under the sprinkler. At Sans Souci baths I dive-bombed a jelly blubber for a dare. If you rubbed sand into the sting it hurt less. Bindies in the front lawn made you limp to the steps of the porch and bend over to pick them out. Sandfly bites needed Calomine lotion that dried to a milky crust. From Rose Bay at night you could hear the lions making love in Taronga Park. If the shark bell rang and you missed the wave, you were left out there alone beyond the third line of breakers. Every shadow had teeth. Treading water in frantic silence, you felt afraid enough to run Christ-like for the shore.

At the Harvest Festivals in church the area behind the pulpit was piled high with tins of IXL fruit for the old age pensioners. We had collected the tinned fruit from door to door. Most of it came from old age pensioners. Some of them must have got their own stuff back. Others were less lucky. Hunting for cicadas in the peppercorns and the willows, you were always in search of the legendary Black Prince, but invariably he turned out to be a Red-eye. The ordinary cicada was called a Pisser because he squirted mud at you. The most beautiful cicada was the Yellow Monday. He was as yellow as a canary and transparent as crystal. When he lifted his wings in the sunlight the membranes were like the deltas of little rivers. The sun shone straight through him. It shone straight through all of us.

It shone straight through everything, and I suppose it still does. As I begin this last paragraph, outside my window a misty afternoon drizzle gently but inexorably soaks the City of London. Down there in the street I can see umbrellas commiserating with each other. In Sydney Harbour, twelve thousand miles away and ten hours from now, the yachts will be racing on the crushed diamond water under a sky the texture of powdered sapphires. It would be churlish not to concede that the same abundance of natural blessings which gave us the energy to leave has every right to call us back. All in, the whippy's taken. Pulsing like a beacon through the days and nights, the birthplace of the fortunate sends out its invisible waves of recollection. It always has and it always will, until even the last of us come home.

*Unreliable Memoirs* (1980).

# Kate Jennings

(1948– )

*Kate Jennings was active in left-wing politics and radical feminism at Sydney University in the late 1960s and early 1970s, a period that saw the publication of her edition of contemporary women's verse,* Mother I'm Rooted *(1975). She has published two collections of her own verse, another collection of essays, some of which are autobiographical,* Bad Manners *(1993), a collection of short stories,* Women Falling Down in the Street *(1990), and a novel,* Snake *(1996). The title of* Save Me, Joe Louis *is taken from the last words of a young Negro before he died in an American gas chamber.*

Winter in New York. It has been snowing. The sky, what I can see of it, is a dirty yellow, the colour of a sweat-stained singlet. Lexington Avenue is ankle-deep in brown slush. As I step off the curb to cross at Seventy-First Street, a station wagon stops at the traffic light next to a brand new black BMW. Apparently the station wagon is too near the BMW for the driver's liking because he leans across and yells, 'That's too damn close!' The lights change. As the two cars proceed up Lexington, the driver of the BMW swerves and bounces his shiny car off the side of the station wagon. The people in the station wagon are a picture of astonishment. Again the BMW bounces off the station wagon. And again. The cars jitterbug slowly up Lexington. Then the BMW speeds away, spurting slurried snow into the air.

What am I doing here? I say to myself, not for the first time. What am I doing here, daughter of Edna and Laurie, grand-daughter of Madge and George, Phyllis and James?, as if this litany of familiar names will ward off New York's deranged nastiness. All New Yorkers have stories that illustrate the seething neuroticism of the city. The best of them pass from person to person, a kind of tribal story-telling. My favourite is about a woman on a bus who was complimented on her eyes by a man. 'You have the most beautiful green eyes I have ever seen,' said the man. 'Thank you,' replied the woman. 'I'd like to impale them on a stick,' said the man.

I am on my way to have lunch with my friend Virginia, a dealer in black opals. Virginia has the mobility and money most women would give their eyeteeth for yet she is unhappy. She longs to live in the country and indulge her passion for horses. New York leaches the life out of her. The idea of spending a Sunday in the city— Central Park jammed with joggers, bicyclists, and people 'making do', as Virginia would put it—fills her with disgust.

Virginia's father was a wool classer. She grew up near Balmoral outside of Sydney in a lovely colonial house flounced with a wrought-iron-trimmed veranda.

We have rural Australian childhoods in common and often understand each other when nobody else does. When an acquaintance spent $700 on a veterinarian bill for a sick cat, we were appalled. Country girls, sensible about pets, we would never do that. Several weeks after this conversation, my own cat became dreadfully ill. Frantic trips to the animal hospital, medication galore, X-rays, an operation, more X-rays … and a $700 vet bill. 'How could I not?' I said to Virginia, sheepish as could be, and we fell about laughing at our former self-righteousness.

We have lunch in a café in the underground concourse at Rockefeller Center. For a change, Virginia's face is shining. On her last trip home to Australia, she started negotiations to buy 25 acres in the Mandalong Valley, and the deal has gone through. She has brought along photos to show me, and her acres are beautiful, a Hans Heysen landscape of pencil-straight ghost gums, the antithesis of the environment bearing down on us. Huddled over the photos and our pasta salads, we begin to plan the house Virginia will build. 'I want five bedrooms, three baths, lounge room, library, a dining room with a table that will seat at least twenty people, stables …' she says grandly. 'That's a bit big,' I interrupt. 'You only get to build a house once,' she bridles, comical in her seriousness.

I ask after a recently acquired boyfriend. Much to the despair of her friends, Virginia was in love for years with a fellow who could charm the birds out of the trees but was careless when it came to affairs of the heart. Virginia doesn't answer my query. Instead she shrugs her shoulders, shakes her head, sighs, and stares off into the middle distance, which would also be comical if courting nowadays in New York weren't such a painful, unspontaneous business. Most of my friends, I reflect, are partnerless, made as bleak as the Ancient Mariner in their attempts to give and receive affection.

Her happiness over her land in the Mandalong Valley has eclipsed Virginia's big worry, a lump in her breast. Although her doctor assures her there is nothing to worry about, she is understandably panicky because her mother died of breast cancer. I say soothing things, but I am thinking, thank God it's not me.

Invariably our conversation comes around to AIDS. Like many New Yorkers, we have gone from shock and anger to numbness. Three of Virginia's friends have died from AIDS; others are in the early stages or have tested positive to AIDS antibodies. She was particularly close to two of the men who died, nursing them in their last days. One of them, an ex-Green Beret who had a hard time admitting he was gay much less he had AIDS, died a horrible death. His family, stricken with shame, pleaded with Virginia to marry him so his hometown wouldn't suspect anything. Our conversation about AIDS today, like all the others we've had, goes in circles, as if we can't grasp the viciousness of the disease despite firsthand experience and the media yabbering in fear all around us.

We take the escalator up to the street level and part. I watch Virginia as she makes her way, head down and frowning, into the crowds that gush through the Diamond District, black fedoras and yarmulkes eddying this way and that. I lose sight of her as she enters the doorway of her building, where she will catch the elevator to the tenth floor and buzz herself through the elaborate security system into her office. What *are* we doing here? [...]

The windows of our apartment on East Seventy-Second Street face north, so the light is milky and dreamlike. My desk is at a window which looks out over carriage houses, ailanthus and ginkgo trees, the green copper dome of St Jean Baptiste, and apartment houses of pre-war vintage topped by homey wooden water tanks, none of them very high by New York standards, a human cityscape unmarred by the monstrous towers that cast their doomsday shadows all over town.

To the west is Park Avenue with its dowager apartment buildings and ever-present doormen, Madison Avenue and merchandise guaranteed to give you an immediate attack of acquisitiveness, and Central Park. A short walk from the Seventy-Second Street entrance to the park is an esplanade sheltered by long rows of oaks, and at the end of the esplanade, a bandshell. The last time I walked by *Peter and the Wolf* was being performed with a full orchestra and Dustin Hoffman as one of the readers. Beyond the bandshell, the newly restored Bethesda Fountain terrace. This stately area attracts lone violinists and flautists as well as jam groups of blacks playing African music.

Next to the terrace is a small lake, where families and lovers take the air in rowboats. Early one recent Sunday morning, my friend Bob and I, addled by work and the porridge-like humidity for which New York is notorious, hired one ourselves. Our oars kept slipping out of the rowlocks and snagging on slimy aquatic weeds, but we felt better for it. In the middle of all this ersatz pastorality, we came across a scene totally unexpected in the middle of New York and one of heart-warming optimism: a fellow fishing.

To the east are modern apartment buildings honeycombed with studio apartments for singles. These young people, so jaundiced they refer to love as the 'L word', hang out in Second Avenue restaurants with names like Ciaobella, Tuba City Truck Stop, and Camelback and Central.

There are sights and faces worthy of Breughel in this neighbourhood. Most of all I love to watch the dog walkers, the professional ones, who at any given time have upward of fourteen dogs on leashes that fan out around them like streamers on a maypole. You name it, there are poodles, pugs, beagles, spaniels, collies, terriers, huskies, Labradors, Egyptian salukis, even mutts, all trim and well groomed. The walkers seem to be in telepathic communication with their charges, who sail by like a miniature armada, impervious to distractions and lesser dogs.

I used to think being a dog walker would be an idyllic occupation, a naive notion. Many of them, apparently, are martinets, impatient of interruptions and delays, sympathetic only to the dogs, and even those are exercised at such a brisk pace they fall over when they get home and sleep all day. To make matters worse, the world of dog walkers is rife with more feuds than an English department. 'See that?' said one dog walker of a rival's pack. 'Terrible. No rhythm and no regard.' In retaliation, the rival accused his critic of the most heinous dog walking crime of all. He said, down his nose, 'She drops her leashes.'

Late one summer afternoon, Bob and I set out for Central Park. We keep passing festive Puerto Ricans instead of the usual button-upped burghers. What were they doing here? The reason soon became apparent. A jubilant parade to celebrate Puerto Rico Day was proceeding up Fifth Avenue, turning the decorum of the neighbourhood on its head. The first float we saw, sponsored by the Hotel Tropicana, was a knockout—a dozen cha-cha-ing big-bosomed showgirls in gold lamé swimsuits. There was applause but surprisingly no catcalls or wolf whistles. I looked around. The men in the crowd were in a seventh heaven, a mixture of awe and lust on their faces. They stood quite still, feasting their eyes, shaking their heads as if the sight of these beauties was almost more than they could bear. Then, after the float had gone by, their faces broke into big, lazy, cat-got-the-cream smiles.

The Tropicana float was followed by a contingent of women from the garment workers' union. They carried placards announcing 'A Woman's Place is in the Union'. Much cheering. Behind them, the longest stretch limousine I have ever seen, the kind that is rumoured to have a swimming pool. Loudspeakers affixed to the roof of the limo blasted that corny Frank Sinatra favourite, 'New York, New York'. In Spanish, of course. *Si triunfas aqui, triunfas en cualquier parte.* If you can make it here, you can make it anywhere. The crowd joined in at the top of their lungs. I wouldn't like much to be a Puerto Rican trying to *triunfas* in this city.

*Save Me, Joe Louis* (1988).

# 7

---

# WAR

# Brian Lewis

## (1906–91)

*Brian Lewis was Professor of Architecture at the University of Melbourne for twenty-five years. He was the foundation chairman and later president of the National Trust. He wrote another autobiography about his Melbourne childhood as the youngest of eight children in a middle-class family,* Sunday at Kooyong Road *(1976). In* World War I *all four of his elder brothers enlisted, and one, Owen, was killed.* Quo Vadis *is a film made in 1913.*

There was a strange feeling at Lawside on that first August Monday of the war; every one of us came from homes which were excited about it and we brought that excitement with us to school. The Boer War had meant little to our parents: it could not have been lost and Australia was not really involved. This new war also could not be lost, but it was much bigger and we were in it officially, right from the very start, and the German colonies were close to us.

In the first week a change came over us and we boys had a new importance, for it was only the males who were fighting. Soldiers marched and we marched every day; we marched for pleasure, not with hands behind us but hard at our sides, and we stamped our feet, as we were sure soldiers did. The girls surrendered their pre-eminence in marching and concentrated on being Red Cross nurses. In that middle-class community, it was an unlucky girl who did not have a white apron with a red cross on the front, before many days were out.

The orderly division of the playground broke down and it became the joint property of the two sexes. The boys fought their battles in their old playground but went to hospital in the summer-house on the girls' side where the nurses attended to them.

We gathered that the Belgians were holy and beautiful, but we did not know what the Belgians were. We learned that they were people rather like the early Christians, and most of us had been to 'Quo Vadis' and knew what the lions did to Christians. Now the Germans were doing far worse things to the Belgians.

Belgium was 'Gallant Little Belgium' and the people were the 'gallant starving Belgians' and from now on, if we did not finish our porridge we were told how much the Belgians needed it. In February of the next year the *Argus* described how they were getting it: 'Food is not at an extraordinary price. Bread is sold for about 2d a pound—Meat is fairly cheap and plentiful—Milk is about $2\frac{1}{2}$d a quart. Eggs are very scarce, vegetables are cheap: butter is about 1/6d a pound'. But we still saved our pennies for the gallant starving Belgians.

The Germans were unspeakably horrible. We had known Germans and they had seemed nice people, but all the time they had been wicked and we had not recognized it. Marion Schneider had been head-girl not so long ago and it was a shock to know that all the time she had been a secret German. Her name showed it and if we had known that her mother was an unspotted Australian and that her father had been born and lived all his life close by, it would have made no difference.

[...]

Max had a German name but it did not seem to worry him or affect his position at school. He was Austrian, and although Austria was on Germany's side, they were not fighting England, not yet.

In fact, Max seemed to feel rather superior to us. He came from Europe with its glittering Kings and Emperors whose soldiers fought real wars, not sordid amateur ones like ours in South Africa, and they fought them in splendid uniforms, not like the dull khaki forced on us by those amateur Boers.

His Austrians dressed in spotless white and his Hungarians galloped along with flashing sabres, nothing meanly utilitarian like our troops. They were far more attractive than the French infantry with scarlet trousers and blue frock-coats, or the Belgians in a similar get-up, but with top-hats instead of the French peaked caps. The French cavalry was good: they had shining helmets, like our firemen, but trailing a brush of horse-hair and they wore shining breast-plates, but even they were vulgar compared to Max's Austrians.

My ideas of war came from the *Boys' Own Paper* where a young officer, pathetically but not mortally wounded, was propped with his back against a tree with a bandage around his head and one arm in a sling—for war-wounds were confined to gashes on the head and holes in the arm—whilst he was touchingly comforted by one of his faithful men. Those wounds, suffered for the glory of his country, seemed a small price to pay for being transformed into an interesting hero.

We were not completely ignorant of military affairs at Lawside because last year Jack Wilkinson had been a fellow student and his father was Colonel Wilkinson and lived in Denbigh Road quite near the school. They were a martial family: Jack was hoping to go into the Australian navy as a thirteen-year-old trainee officer, and Colonel Wilkinson was important—I think he was the top army engineer.

[...]

Quite recently I had had direct contact with the Australian army. Last birthday Alan Gibbs had been given a tricycle and I badly wanted one. I had got it last Christmas. Uncle Sam sent an annual Christmas gift to mother of £5; it was divided amongst the family and my share was five shillings but mother made up the rest and I got a tricycle costing fifteen shillings. Maybe it was not as good as

Alan's: the big front wheel was badly set and cut into the enclosing fork; but still, it was a trike.

One Saturday afternoon Neil and I met another eight-year-old on his trike, and Neil arranged a race for us down the slope of Kooyong Road from Wattletree Road, my rival on the footpath on the other side of the road and me on ours. Off I went, down the six-foot strip of asphalt, and I had reached maximum acceleration when out stepped Major and Mrs Johnston from their front gate.

Major Johnston may have retired from the army but he was still a fine erect soldierly figure, with a well-pressed grey suit, grey Homburg, a flower in his buttonhole, gloves and a walking stick. Mrs Johnston was ample and fluffy with a wide hat and veil and a sunshade. They were out for their usual 3.30 promenade.

There was not a chance of missing them and I went slap into Mrs Johnston's backside. She was very outspoken. The major was very considerate and excused me to her and calmed her down and we parted friends. It had been almost worth it to have had this consideration from such a fine man, through contact with his wife.

[…]

By the end of the first week we all carried flags to school. Everybody seemed to produce a flag from somewhere and quite a reasonably sized Union Jack could be bought for threepence.

In the streets flags were everywhere. They flew from buildings in the city, cars carried them, and even our baker's cart had a little one beside the driver; they blossomed from previously bare poles in front gardens. It would be suspicious to have a flag pole and no flag.

The most patriotic flag of all was carried by a girl riding on a horse; nothing could be more patriotic than a girl with a big Union Jack and she rode astride, like Joan of Arc, and not side-saddle like a lady.

[…]

All four brothers sent home postcards of the places they had been. We took the family cards out of the fattest album and put in the new war postcards and still more came until there were three albums on the wickerwork fitting in the corner.

[…]

On the mantelpiece among the vases were two miniature shells, only about an inch in diameter, possibly high-velocity anti-tank ammunition; they looked very well when they were highly polished. There was also the rather ugly nose-cap of a much bigger shell with a bit of jagged metal around it.

Athol sent home a bundle of magazines which never got to the drawing room but were kept under the curtain in the study. They were from Paris and I think they were sent to tease mother; they were not a bit like our patriotic magazines and I gathered that I should not look at them.

A twelve-year-old friend and I were on the balcony with *La Vie Parisienne*, trying to translate it with our school French. We got the meaning 'He who goes hunting loses his place'; it went with a picture of a luscious young woman starting up from her bed, an officer in only his pants getting out of the side of the picture and a furious old husband with white moustaches, in hunting clothes and a gun slung over his shoulder, entering the room. We were puzzled about what it meant. Phyllis came out and caught us.

[...]

Ralph was on the way home. All we knew about it was that he would not lose his leg. Now after six months in different hospitals he would be safely home with us. We were told that his hospital ship would arrive in February and the censor even allowed us to know the actual date.

[...]

The ship pulled in to the grey wharf where a quiet clump of relatives waited in silence. The gangway was put down and men with empty sleeves, men on crutches and men hobbling with sticks came down it; at least their kit-bags were carried down for them. Then down came the stretchers and parents were able to talk for a minute or two before they were put into the ambulances.

Ralph came down, getting along with a stick, and was allowed to travel with us in the car. Off we went in a miserable procession through the unnoticing streets of Melbourne and along to the Victoria Barracks in St Kilda Road where Ralph limped off whilst we waited to take him home to a late lunch.

He had always been quiet. Now in the car he seemed very quiet and a bit shaky; in the next war we would have said that he was 'bomb-happy' but in this war only officers got 'shell-shocked' and it was not creditable, even for them. He looked different. His face had little scars and dents where the shrapnel had got him and in his curly black hair were a couple of pure white streaks which made him look very distinguished.

At home we had done our best for him and he was able to have Keith's old room; he had never had a room of his own before, and each of us had done something towards furnishing it especially for him. He had to put up with a wastepaper-basket which I had made out of a wooden soap box with drawings pasted on the outside, things like the Rising Sun of the AIF and the badge of the Tunnelling Companies, but I had done my best.

As he settled back into the family he spoke of things not mentioned in his letters. The Belgian hospital had been very good, but not the people of the Belgian villages, dirty, money-grubbing people who were not a bit concerned with who won the war and would be quite as happy with the Germans as with us. They were willing to sell anything to either side, including military information.

On his ship were some men who had been badly wounded before capture, so badly wounded that the Germans allowed them to be repatriated. The Germans had treated them very correctly, but they had had a bad time in hospital because of the shortage of anaesthetics—a result of the British blockade. The Germans had shown no resentment towards them, but whilst they were being carried through Belgian towns, the Belgians had spat on these desperately wounded men. A few years ago we had thought of the Belgians as only a little lower than the angels.

Next morning Ralph was helped into town by Phyllis and got to the Repatriation Office before it opened in the morning. He waited whilst others were escorted in by important people, he waited all morning. Just before lunch the office was empty of visitors, but he had not been called. He knocked on the door and entered. 'There seems to be one too many in the room,' said the civil servant. Ralph said that he was very tired and had waited all the morning. 'I won't see you now, come back after lunch.'

After he had hobbled off to lunch and hobbled back, there was a notice on the door: 'No more cases will be seen today.'

Ralph really was nervy and this upset him so much that he had to go to bed for a week to regain his confidence. By the time he was able to return to his civil servant, the university term had begun and it was decided that he was too late.

Repatriation could not get him a job in which his training in chemistry, geology and mining was of any use, but he was offered a course in wool-sorting in the Working Men's College and told that if he did not take it, he would be crossed off the books. He did not take it. Nothing from Repatriation for him.

In some weeks he was fit enough to get a temporary job in the Commonwealth Patents Office and he stayed in it for over forty years. He made a remarkable recovery in the quiet of home and even the great hole behind his knee filled out. In time, he was able to play football again.

We got very friendly with the new people next door who had replaced the Rosenfelts, a widow with two little girls younger than I, nice people who got on particularly well with Ralph. One evening some few weeks after his return he limped in with his stick to feed their fowls—they were away for the afternoon. When he came back through our front gate someone had fixed a white feather on our letter box for him.

At first he had to attend hospital occasionally but at the end of March he had his last visit, was discharged from the army and his pension stopped. The army got rid of him very cheaply.

*Our War: Australia During World War I* (1980).

# A. B. Facey

(1894–1982)

*Albert Barnett Facey grew up on the Kalgoorlie goldfields and in the wheat belt of Western Australia. His autobiography,* A Fortunate Life *(1981), which relates his survival of a series of serious misfortunes, has often been described as a microcosm of the earlier life of Australia.*

After the best part of a week we arrived at a place called Lemnos Island and entered a harbour. At first sight it didn't look much, but as our ship sailed in we were all surprised at the size and beauty of the place. Some of the ships anchored there were enormous—must have been at least sixty vessels of all sizes and kinds: transport ships, battleships, cruisers and many smaller craft, but there still seemed to be plenty of room for movement. My brigade—the Third—and other troops were already there in their ships.

Some time after we arrived motor launches began to come alongside and take off troops. Finally the corporal who was in charge of us (the twenty-four replacements for the Eleventh Battalion) ordered us to get into full battle dress and fall in, as our turn to be taken to our battalion would be soon. We got ready with our full kit and then climbed down into a motor launch and were taken to one of the transports.

When we had been put aboard, an officer called us to attention, and from a list of names, assigned us in small groups to the various companies of the Eleventh. Seven, including me, had to go to 'D' Company. A sergeant said, 'Follow me men', and took us to the major in command of our company. The major told us that he was glad to have us in his command, and that we would be going into action soon. We were then taken to the sections that were in need of replacements. I was attached to No. 4 Platoon 'D' Company.

The men in my section were from different parts of Western Australia. Quite a few came from the seaport of Bunbury, south of Perth. They were all strangers to me and were anxious to know how things and the folks at home were. I told them all I could but it wasn't much more than they already knew, as I had left Australia only about six weeks after they had. Then a sergeant came and called my name, and took me to the top deck where all the replacements had assembled. We had to wait a few minutes, then an officer told us to gather around and lectured us on what was expected of us when we went into action. He told us that he didn't know at that moment when or where that would be but it was likely to be soon. We were then examined by the battalion's medical officer before returning to our units.

While we were waiting in our troopship the main topic of conversation was where we were going and who we would be fighting. We were nervous now that we were so close to going into battle, but glad too that the time had finally come.

It was very calm in the harbour and there was a peaceful kind of feeling, at least to me. Many of the men settled down to write letters but I had written already to the only two people I wrote to—Grandma and Laura.

In the harbour there were French and British ships and several of these had brass bands aboard. While we were there, as if someone had given the signal, all the bands commenced to play 'Sons of the Sea', then followed this with some beautiful waltz tunes. This was a wonderful thrill; it was simply beautiful.

We left the harbour—Mudros Harbour I had found it was called—on the afternoon of the twenty-fourth of April. We were nervous and excited, knowing that we were finally on our way into action. We sailed all afternoon through a calm sea. That night we turned in to sleep in hammocks. I was very tired and despite the excitement, went to sleep.

The next thing I knew, I was being shaken awake by a corporal. The ship was moving slowly, some lights were on, and everyone was busy packing up and getting into battle dress. I noticed that stripes and rank markings had been removed from uniforms. One of the sergeants said, 'It's not far now. All portholes are blacked out and no lights on deck.'

The officers and sergeants were called to report to the Company Commander. Now excitement ran high. A few minutes later they returned and told us that we were to land on the Gallipoli Peninsula in Turkey.

When we were called to our sections our officer gave us a briefing on the proper instructions for landing. We were told that our ship would move as close as possible into shore but would keep out of range of the enemy's shelling. He said, 'They will throw everything they've got at us as soon as they wake up to what we're doing. Now, when the ship stops you will be called to the side and lined up. On the side of the ship is a rope net already in place. A destroyer will come alongside and you will climb over the side and down the rope onto the deck of the destroyer when ordered. When the destroyer has enough men it will pull away and go towards where you are to land. Close to shore you will be met by a small motor boat towing rowing-boats. You will climb into the rowing-boats and the motor boats will take you as close to shore as possible. There will be sailors in the rowing-boats and they will take you into the beach. Now you are to get ashore as best you can and then line up on the beach and await further instructions.'

This was it. We were scared stiff—I know I was—but keyed up and eager to be on our way. We thought we would tear right through the Turks and keep going to Constantinople.

Troops were taken off both sides of the ship onto destroyers. My platoon and other 'D' Company men were on the same destroyer. All went well until we were making the change into rowing-boats.

Suddenly all hell broke loose; heavy shelling and shrapnel fire commenced. The ships that were protecting our troops returned fire. Bullets were thumping into us in the rowing-boat. Men were being hit and killed all around me.

When we were cut loose to make our way to the shore was the worst period. I was terribly frightened. The boat touched bottom some thirty yards from shore so we had to jump out and wade into the beach. The water in some places was up to my shoulders. The Turks had machine-guns sweeping the strip of beach where we landed—there were many dead already when we got there. Bodies of men who had reached the beach ahead of us were lying all along the beach and wounded men were screaming for help. We couldn't stop for them—the Turkish fire was terrible and mowing into us. The order to line up on the beach was forgotten. We all ran for our lives over the strip of beach and got into the scrub and bush. Men were falling all around me. We were stumbling over bodies—running blind.

The sight of the bodies on the beach was shocking. It worried me for days that I couldn't stop to help the men calling out. (This was one of the hardest things of the war for me and I'm sure for many of the others. There were to be other times under fire when we couldn't help those that were hit. I would think for days, 'I should have helped that poor beggar'.)

We used our trenching tools to dig mounds of earth and sheltered from the firing until daylight—the Turks never let up. Their machine-guns were sweeping the scrub. The slaughter was terrible.

I am sure that there wouldn't have been one of us left if we had obeyed that damn fool order to line up on the beach.

*A Fortunate Life* (1981).

# Martin Boyd

(1879–1972)

*Martin Boyd, a member of the distinguished Boyd family, lived partly in Australia and partly in Europe. In World War I he joined an English regiment and served in France in 1915–18, first in the infantry and then in the flying corps. He later spent a period in an Anglican Franciscan community. His verse collection,* Retrospect *(1920), expresses his post-war disillusionment as do his autobiographies,* Day of My Delight *and* A Single Flame *(1939), and the second novel in his Langton tetralogy,* A Difficult Young Man *(1955). As well as sixteen novels, he published an autobiographical travel book,* Much Else in Italy *(1958).*

After a few days at Étaples I was sent to join the first (regular) battalion of my regiment at the front. With two or three other subalterns and a draft of men we set out in a semi-derelict train for Béthune. It was snowing, and it took us from eight in the morning till dusk to make the short journey. When the train stopped the men got out. It all somehow suggested a journey in the Middle Ages, particularly to me, to whom snow was unfamiliar, as were the ancient farms and churches we passed, and the French names on the railway stations.

After a few days I was sent off with a guide to the trenches. For a while we walked along an open road. Nowhere around us was anything left standing. One or two broken tree-trunks stood up from the snow. A chink of light came from the basement of a shattered house. My guide with relief descended into the communication trench, which was called Piccadilly or Savile Row.

I felt a mixture of curiosity and depression, but also rather grand at being at last in the trenches. Occasionally a shell whined and exploded, but not near at hand, and now and then a Very light hung in the air and shed its sickly light on the snow-covered ground. Later, I had to censor letters, and I found that nearly all the new arrivals felt grand at being in the line, though none of them appeared to have any enthusiasm for the war. Certainly my own depression and hatred of the whole condition of this wrecked countryside were greater than my curiosity or sense of grandeur, and I had no 'spirit of the offensive', nor had any of the men. Their courage was that of endurance.

At last we reached the front line. I lifted a piece of sacking, descended some steps, and entered the dug-out which was 'A' company headquarters. It was about fifty yards from the German front line. Brown, my company commander, and his only other subaltern were just about to dine at a table illuminated by two candles stuck in bottles. They were expecting me, and an extra place was laid. We had fried sole, pork chops with vegetables, apple tart and cream, a hot cheese savoury, white wine, Vichy water, whisky, and coffee. This meal was prepared behind a sacking curtain by the two officers' servants, who were named appropriately Butler and Pantry. Brown was correct, efficient, and gentlemanly. He was killed in April while I was on a Lewis-gun course.

God tempered the war, but not the weather to my shorn, pacifist, nature. For the first three months my battalion was in a very quiet sector of the line, but the cold was intense in that 1916–17 winter. For three weeks there was a black frost. Apart from the desultory shellfire to which one became accustomed, there was little more than the discomfort of living underground and of the nightly two-hour watches to make one realise that there was a war. Occasionally one had to duck while machine-gun bullets rattled along the parapet. One morning 'B' company had to do a raid to capture some specimen prisoners. I saw the walking wounded coming back down the communication trench. They were still wrapped in sheets they had worn to make themselves inconspicuous in the snow. Some were bleeding, with broken arms and bandaged heads. One man glanced at me with pain-drawn eyes. It was my first glimpse of the accumulated agony of the war.

Up till about the end of March we held the line peacefully. Our battalion did a week in the front line, a week in the second line, and a week in reserve in one of the semi-shattered villages. No palace could ever seem as luxurious as the back bedroom of a miner's cottage on the first night out of the line.

I was sent on a course to a château near Béthune, the historic old town, which a year later was smashed to rubble. One evening with two fellow subalterns, I went there in search of women, strangely unsuccessful. The next morning a padre came to the château and held a communion service which my two companions attended. One said to me afterwards: 'I like to go whoring on Saturday night and to communion on Sunday. It gives me a cosmopolitan feeling.'

When I went back to battalion Brown had been killed, and I inherited his servant Butler, who had been footman to the headmaster of Eton. Harvey James, an old Etonian actor, was now in command of my company. He was full of charm and courage, but he was too humane to be a satisfactory soldier. When, with his walking stick, his revolver, his gas-mask, and his Mills bombs in his pockets, he climbed up into the slimy deathly trench for an afternoon tour of inspection, he turned and said:

'I shan't be long. If the vicar's wife calls tell her I'll be back to tea.'

He was killed in April 1917, while making one of those noble gestures divorced from murderous intention, which are anachronisms in modern warfare.

A man named Wells, a year younger than myself, was then given command of the company. He had been wounded and had just returned to France. He was a regular, and very conscious of the fact. He felt it a disgrace that territorial officers should be drafted to the first battalion, and said so. In the line he was very timid, for which no one who had once been wounded could be blamed. My own courage I found depended almost entirely on my liver.

One morning the Germans put down a barrage of trench mortars a quarter of a mile to the right of our sector. They were mostly 'minnies' which made a nerve-shattering 'crump'. My knees began to tremble and I had to go round a traverse to compose myself before giving orders. A few days later a barrage descended on our own bit of line. An aeroplane came flying low and dropped a bomb on the parapet which blew off my tin hat, just as I was trying to light a rocket. Stuff was flying everywhere. I felt exhilarated and began to laugh. Wells put his pale face up from the dug-out entrance and found me laughing and picking up my tin hat, which made him think I had iron nerves.

Though for a while I was his only subaltern, he stayed in the dug-out all night and would not take his share of the watch. In the daytime he complained that I slept too much.

One morning at 'stand-to' the sun came up like a red orange, in an enamelled, unbroken sky. There were small field-flowers growing in no-man's-land and behind the trenches. The sun rising on this stricken land was beautiful, like a sunrise at sea. At five o'clock it was broad daylight and the men were relieved that we had passed the dangerous hour of another day. As the order to stand down was given a five-point-nine burst behind the trench. From five o'clock until eleven, every two minutes, one of these shells burst on the hundred yards of line held by our company. I was on watch for most of that time. Wells sat in the dug-out wondering nervously if this was the prelude to an attack. My own nervousness had become a sick dread. Every now and then a man came to me saying that so-and-so had been killed or wounded. A Lewis-gun section had been hit. I saw the men to whom I had been talking with forced cheerfulness a few minutes earlier, now hardly recognisable as human, their blood mixed with the earth under which they were buried. There was every possibility that the fatigue detailed to dig them out might soon be in the same condition. I walked about the hot, sunbaked trenches, thinking every time a shell burst: 'Well, I'm alive for another two minutes', and wondering which way to go, not knowing whether I was walking towards or away from a danger spot. I had been in more dangerous situations, but in none that strained my nerves more than that six hours, when the leisure to think was combined with the certainty of the next explosion.

One day a subaltern was standing by the wire bunk where I was resting. He had his hair cropped and it stood up on his head like plush. I stroked it as I would a cat, and he was very cross, though there was no more intention behind my gesture than there would have been towards the cat. I think his reaction was sad, as this was the last caress of his life, his last human touch, a sort of viaticum. A day or two later he was killed by a stray shell, and I took his place on the leave roll, setting out at the beginning of July for ten days in England.

*Day of My Delight: An Anglo-Australian Memoir* (1965).

# A. Tiveychoc

## (1897–?)

*'Tiveychoc's' real name was Rowland Edward Lording. He enlisted in the AIF in 1915 at the age of 18 and saw war service in Egypt and the Western Front. In July 1916 he was severely wounded in action and transferred to military hospitals in England. In February 1917 he returned to Australia and was discharged in October that year. In the extract he refers to himself in the third person as 'Ted'.*

The voyage so far had each day seen an improvement in Ted's condition, and the interlude at Durban put him on his feet. Had authority been content to let this state of convalescence continue, the patient would no doubt have been in a comparatively fit condition to face whatever surgical treatment was deemed necessary at the conclusion of the voyage. Authority, however, had other ideas and insisted on removing pieces of bone from the arm. Heedless of Ted's protest that Colonel Ryan and others had advised that no further operation be performed upon him until arrival in Australia, the 'sawbones' brought pressure to bear by threatening that a pension might not be granted if the operation were refused. There was no immediate necessity for the operation—the patient's condition was improving—and the shipboard facilities, no matter how good, could not equal those of a general hospital. Furthermore, owing to the patient's chest condition, there was a distinct danger of subsequent complications. Many were the complaints of those who were practically shanghaied to the operating table. Ted was one of five who, on the morning of his operation, attended the orderly corporal's 'boogee' parade. Something of a humorist, this NCO called it the 'physical works parade,' and, lining up his victims, he proceeded to carry out the manoeuvre in burlesque regimental style.

Ted's operation was not a success—it resulted in a bad haemorrhage, increased pain in the region of the wound, further loss of feeling in the hand, and his return

:o the DI list. Incidentally it was also responsible for the loss of a souvenir wristlet watch which disappeared from his person while he was under the anaesthetic.

Affixed to the bulkhead immediately in front of Ted's cot was a copper steril-zer. The 'nut' case whose particular fancy it was to polish this every day for hours on end, and gape at his inane reflection therein, was even more irritating than the pain and illness following the operation. Still Ted might have found it worse had he been located in the ward where one of the 'nuts' chanted the Lord's prayer continuously for two days and three nights ere he died.

As soon as Ted felt able to stand the journey, he one evening prevailed on Fireman Thomas, though without the sanction of the MO, whom he was determined to ignore—to carry him to the foc's'le where he enjoyed an extra bottle of stout and a few dips in the 'black pan'—a tin sent to the foc's'le crew after the officers' mess and containing the assorted leavings of their menu. Thus, ere the ship reached Fremantle, Ted was again able to get about, though not with official consent.

Not more than a few hours were spent by the ship at the various ports of call in Australia. Those disembarking took what might have appeared to be casual leave of their shipmates, but the parting was in fact deeply felt by all. They did not make promises to write, but just flung a 'Cheerio', 'So long', or 'Good luck' to one another or banteringly remarked: 'Keep your legs together,' 'What do you think of our 'arbour?' 'Don't get stuck in the Yarra,' 'See you at the next war.' Ted's Durban creditor did not even bother to let anyone know he was leaving the ship at Melbourne—he just went.

Words, what words were there that could express the feelings and thoughts of these men? None. They were members of a freemasonry that had endured many partings—partings from loved ones at home, with old cobbers, with English and foreign brothers and sisters of the craft, with those 'gone west.' But their bonds of friendship, moulded in an atmosphere of mutual suffering, sympathy, and good fellowship, would endure. Words were unnecessary. Materially, they had parted—were parting; spiritually, they were together. Life would see many reunions, and in passing they would but part to meet again.

The evening of the last day found Ted alone on the boat-deck. He had gone there to see the sun set, and in the tranquillity of its fading light and changing hues his thoughts went fleeting over the days he had been absent from home. Lingering here and there to hold the happy memories; passing quickly over the sordidness, the horrors, the sufferings, and his own maimed state; yet ever mindful of those who, like the setting sun, had gone west, he felt not the glamour of heroics but rather the pathos of this eventide that signified the passing of so much—the venture, the great experience, had ended—the sun had set.

Contemplation of the future did not extend beyond the morrow. Would he be granted leave? No, he was marked down for transport by ambulance to Randwick Hospital. Still, he would have to work it somehow, if only for a few hours, so that the folk at home would feel less the shock of his condition. Would his mother and father reproach themselves for having allowed him to go away? Surely not, it was not their fault, they did not start the war—but, once started, someone had to go. The fault—yes, there must be a fault—belonged to civilization generally. Did he himself regret having gone away? No, that would be tantamount to his repudiation of all the personal compensations and associations, but he did regret that civilization permitted war and so robbed itself of its best material—its youth.

But the morrow. Would they have a car to meet him? He hoped so. Would there be a lot of fuss? He hoped not, and prayed that his first day at least would be spent only with his own folk. There would be lots of time to see the others, and to listen to their foolish questions and be embarrassed by their hero worship. How disappointed some of them would be to hear that he had not killed a Fritz, yet how horrified if they learnt that he was credited with having dispatched a Gyppo. And there were other things that would horrify them. There was, thought Ted miserably, nothing to justify his appearing in the role of a soldier who had heroically served his country. Explanations would be futile—folks would not understand, but would put it down to his modesty! Yet, if it were possible to give adequate expression to his experiences and thoughts, he would, if believed, be branded a blackguard and a coward. Better then to say nothing. Let them think him a modest hero, let them continue to paint glamorous pictures of the war and their cause, at least until the rotten business was over—one way or the other; then, perhaps, the old soldiers of the world would join together in one great army to oppose tooth and nail those who upheld war as a means of settling international disputes. Yes, he would enlist in that 'army' if it came into being, but, at present, his voice would only fall on unheeding, if not deaf, ears—if perchance they were noticed, he would probably be put away in some concentration camp or other for making seditious utterances. For the present, therefore, it were best, if unable to encourage enlistment, not to hinder it, so that the bitter end might come the sooner. And, for one who was of no further active use, well there was nothing left but to make the best of a bad lot, have a good time, try and find a place in civilian life, keep smiling and—forget.

*There and Back: The Story of an Australian Soldier 1915–1935* (1935).

# David Martin

## (1915–97)

*David Martin was born in Hungary and brought up in Germany, which he left at the age of seventeen. After some time in Holland, where he worked on the reclamation of the Zuider Zee, and a year in Palestine, where he lived on a kibbutz, he served as a first-aid orderly in the International Brigade in the Spanish Civil War (1937–38).* My Strange Friend *deals in part with this experience. He subsequently worked in London as a journalist and writer and in India as correspondent for the* Daily Express. *Since 1949 he lived in Australia, where he was one of its best-known writers. He published eight collections of verse, six novels, two collections of short stories, plays, film scripts, a travel book, and numerous books for children. He also wrote another autobiography,* Fox on My Door *(1987).*

Over the distance of years I am trying to touch the thin fellow who is standing on that square in Morata, leaning on a rolled-up stretcher. He really is thin. His hair is ample but won't be so for much longer. His nose sticks out. His spectacles are steel-rimmed and have thick lenses. He looks unsoldierly as he listens to the wood-pecker tack-tack of the machine-guns. He understands nothing of the strategy of the battle, but he's curious and hopes he will not continue to stay so ignorant. If nothing else does his poems (the only writing he brought out of Spain, for he kept no diaries) tell me that he had some talent and a great faith. Whether he thinks of himself as a *voluntario* first and only in the second place a poet I cannot say, but I imagine it would be so, since he wrote practically no verse until the fighting settled. Poet or volunteer: they clearly are the one and the same for him. Or does he already sense they might not be? It is hard for me to get into his skull. This young man could be my son or grandson.

I marvel at friends, writers who at seventy-four calmly declare that they have no trouble comprehending themselves as they were when they had just turned twenty-one. Can it be true? Or is their gift for fiction colouring reminiscence? And is not this the problem for all novelists who write autobiography? I am the one who stands there in Morata, shivering in the dawn and hoping to get through unscathed, and I am not the one. Certainly, I cannot hear what his ears are hearing and feel what his heart feels.

I do remember, however, what happened that day, because I wrote a factual story about it as early as 1945. It appears, slightly changed, as a chapter in a later book, sketches from my life for young readers. I do not want to repeat it in detail: too much like the *ancien combattant*. But I pretty much went through it all while the light lasted. I had my first sight of the dead, one of whom, as he came in on a stretcher without any sign of a wound, I tried to bring back to life. I carried out frantic dressing and sometimes redressing of the wounded, always worrying whether my bandages, in particular my capelline bandages, should stay on during the terrible drive over pot-holed roads to the hospital at Chinchon or Colmenar. I unwrapped the field-dressing on the left hand of a conscript, a man who looked elderly to me. His palm had the tell-tale powder marks. I did not let him through—think of it what you like. The White House [the central dressing station of the Dimitrov Battalion where Martin was stationed] was briefly shelled. I cleaned but did not carry stretchers and helped in the loading of ambulances. One of our bearers got hit in the throat, doing the same. I watched new recruits march up in broad daylight, singing. An English officer (Tom Wintringham?) stood on a knoll, pointing with a swagger stick. Looking out from a tank's turret was a Russian; at least it was a man with very fair hair. There were aerial fights; we did not seem to be short of planes. I sterilised needles, prepared but did not give injections, poured hydrogen peroxide to get rid of caked blood. In the afternoon some Spanish of the XVth gave way and were turned back. They protested that the Moors were behind them, which they were not. I was too tired to feel hungry and too busy to be very scared. [...]

When the battle was over I was sent to where my languages could be used, a dressing station farther back on the road to Colmenar. It had been a flour mill. It was a quiet place, though in artillery range, and peasants on burros clip-clopped by to work in the fields. Our main job was to check the ambulances on their way from the front, making sure the wounded were all right. Usually no first-aid men travelled with them. Sometimes the men had to be taken out. A few times when heart action threatened to fail, we injected a powerful stimulant—adrenalin perhaps, or some early version of cardiazol—directly into the heart, a terrifying process even under direction. Our techniques were not novel. I do not believe I had heard then about Norman Bethune and his frontline blood bank.

We relieved first-aid men in the now established trenches or volunteered for night-time pick and shovel work. We were issued with tools and moved up to the line to dig, either just in front or just behind it. The ground was hard and stony and we were kept warm without touching the anise in our flasks. We got to know men in various battalions and companies: Polish miners from France and the Borinage, British and Irish, and the Franco-Belges who belied the rumour that they were good only for attack. I liked best the Abraham Lincoln boys. Onto their native brand of unmartial spontaneity they grafted a cheerful, reliable discipline. They had a happy gift for making themselves comfortable in uncomfortable sectors. They had designed re-heating stations on the road by which the field kitchens had to come, so that the food entered piping hot into American stomachs. There were a lot of Blacks and a lot of Jews among them.

The *Volunteer of Liberty* carried an item about me in which I was called 'General of the Shit Brigade'. It referred to my latrine-building passion and was a title of honour. A soldier saved from the dysentery ward is a soldier fit for combat. We did better with the men's bellies than with their genitals. The VD hospitals were always full, in spite of propaganda and prophylaxis. A man who was given the means to protect himself and did not do so could face a charge of self-mutilation, but I know of none that was brought. Only first-aid men were expected to shave, and I was threatened with punishment for not always setting a hygienic example. The warmer weather brought body lice. To have them in the pubic hair was torture. We issued ointments, but the dangerous technique of singeing was not unknown. I saw it practised with an infested man using a lighter and cupful of kerosene, while a mate stood by with a bucket of water. Mobile showers were taken forward as far as was ammunition, and underwear was collected for steam laundering in the rear.

Boredom became an enemy. Every few nights heavy barrages were laid down and there was a steady trickle of casualties. But for four months the front did not change. The International Brigade were shock troops and should have been pulled back into reserve. To leave them in the trenches for so long was a blunder.

A Spanish cavalry squadron had been stationed in Morata. When it was withdrawn we were ordered to ensure that their quarters were fit to be occupied again. Spaniards are clean in their persons but sanitary habits are not their strong suit. The rooms stank of faeces. We carted them away by the barrowload from the cellars where they had dried solid. Shovelling and cursing we came upon pathetic bins and vats in which scarce produce had been secreted that should have been declared. The people who had done this were not hostile, they were simply storing up against uncertainty.

Two wars, not one, were being waged in Spain, which for some of us was hard to understand. Our fight was against European fascism; the fight of those peasants was the continuation of one in which, openly or stealthily, they had been engaged for centuries. They called themselves anarchists, and we thought of Tolstoy and Bakunin. They thought of the *alcalde*, the *guardia civil* and the theft of their harvests. On the whole they liked us and were glad we had come to help them, but they seemed puzzled. Franco's Radio Burgos may not have been solely responsible for the fact that sometimes we were called Russos. When a man volunteers for a patrol and straps on dynamite you can tell what his real feelings are. It is not so easy to read Sancho's mind when he trots home to his plate of *garbanzos* and, if he is lucky, his sour wine. We learned *no pasaran!* and *pasaremos!* but not that *sufrimiento* is Spanish for endurance. We lit our cigarettes from flint lighters with cords of loosely twisted hemp and when we could not scrounge Gauloise or Gitane we smoked a local brand which we dubbed anti-tank. We ate garbanzos, chick peas, until we farted. [...] But to break a Spanish wind does not make you a Spaniard.

*My Strange Friend* (1991).

# Barney Roberts

## (1920– )

*Barney Roberts was a prisoner of war in World War II. Captured in Greece at Megara, he was taken to Salonika, then to Marburg in northern Yugoslavia, and then to Eichberg in southern Austria. Roberts has also written verse, short stories, and an autobiography of his Tasmanian childhood,* Where's Morning Gone? *(1987), and has won several literary awards.*

MEGARA Corinth. We had been at Corinth for three weeks. It was no improvement. If anything it was worse. So far we were not impressed with being prisoners of war. If only our diarrhoea would clear up. It was better than it was at Megara, but both Stag and I still had the runs. There was always the chance that by next camp we would be better; that the camp itself would be better. Just to be moving was something. And there was some consolation in knowing that everyone around was tired, lousy, hungry, and just as miserable as we were.

It must have been part of the treatment. The Germans woke us at 2 a.m. to gather all our gear and start walking. We marched about seven miles before arriving at daybreak beside a long train.

We moved in a long, slow line through the station yard. I counted twenty-seven trucks—box trucks with the doors open on one side, and high up on the other two openings, about big enough for a skinny man to crawl through.

A huge black engine squatted quiet on the rails; quiet apart from the low hushing of controlled steam. Two coal-dusty figures stood with hands on hips watching us. Their expression was one I had grown familiar with, a dull-eyed stare that gave nothing away. Friends or enemies? Friends most probably. Themselves prisoners, at least doing exactly what they were told.

A blond-headed German, pink-faced, thin, who looked no more than sixteen, flashed his rifle around with his bayonet fixed. A *Feldwebel* came striding down the line. The boy slapped his heels, threw up his hand, said 'Heil Hitler', and the sergeant major shouted a guttural stream of orders.

We were a mob of cattle to be herded into pens. Five, ten, fifteen, twenty—hit with rifle-butts, pushed, prodded up into the trucks, where we stood listening to but not understanding the strange shouting which forced more and more bodies into an impossibly small area. Forty-five, fifty, fifty-five, and one over. Somehow the fifty-sixth man was pushed and pulled into the truck and the doors were closed. I heard the bolt latch being slid into place.

'Look out, Germany', someone said, 'here we come'. The voice lacked conviction. Nobody laughed.

We stood for a long time, not moving, listening to the noises of other trucks being loaded; of doors being slammed. I could see through the small window a patch of blue sky and a branch of a tree that kept waving rhythmically into view and out of view, up and down, up and down.

**Have I ever climbed that one? It looks a bit like the one next to the poplar tree down on the middle flat. And is that smoke? The old man is burning rushes just over in the swamp. He used to love his football once, but I bet if you ask him now what he likes doing best, he will say burning rushes.**

Everything that mattered in the world was happening outside that window. As long as the window remained open, everything would be all right. A window on the world. A window that could not be shattered. A world that I knew nothing could change. They had shut me in away from the world, but I had taken the world in with me.

This, inside the truck, was another life beginning. I noticed that most of the men had dropped their haversacks or packs at their feet. Some were sitting on them. I tried to jam mine down where I was standing. 'Go easy', the man in front growled. 'There's not much room', I said.

'Half standing. Half sitting.' Someone took on the role of leader. 'The ones up now can sit down later.'

There was no reply, apart from a mumbled aside which I guessed reflected what most thought: 'Who bloody said?'

The few weeks I had been with this crowd at Megara and Corinth had taught me there was only one law, the law of the German gun. Hunger bred in many a single-minded sense of self-preservation which seemed to thrive on distrust and larceny. I was made aware of this at Corinth. Because of the incredible extent of thieving in the camp Stag and I never left our gear unguarded, yet once when I was washing my face, during those few seconds when I had my eyes closed, my precious soap was stolen.

Men who had never stolen anything in their lives before suddenly became thieves without conscience, and generally the more intelligent the man, the more cunning the thief. It may have been that these people who had never wanted for anything found it more difficult to have nothing and consequently the incentive to steal was relatively greater. Whatever, it became apparent that there was no parallel between the so called 'well-bred' person and basic honesty. But I guess that principle may still apply in any normal peacetime society.

The train started and stopped again. Someone was running—two people—running down the track. There was shouting. Germans shouting—and the sound of a shot. There was a noise like a belly-shot in a milky-doe rabbit. Another shot. More talking. 'What's going on?'

A man at the window turned. He was a tall Maori. 'They got him', he said. 'Second shot.' He clipped his words, but his voice was soft, unconcerned, almost as if he were saying: 'We scored another goal'.

Footsteps walking back the crunching gravel. The engine started up again, spitting and shuffling.

**The same sort of thunk. Hit her as she runs—across the river at Cullen's. She's crawling on her belly towards the blackberries—squealing all the way—my brother shoots her through the eye.**

I kept changing the hand that was pressing against the roof to stop me swaying too much. A man behind me said, 'Hey Aus, have a seat. I'll stand up for a while'. I looked at the New Zealander. 'Thanks, Ki', I said and sat down. 'You can put your hand on my shoulder', I said, 'it's easier than holding on to the roof'.

Suddenly I could smell a new and foul smell. The man to my right was squatting, both hands on the shoulders of the man in front of him. His head was down, chin tucked into his chest. I knew he was shitting, and I knew that even if he knew he was shitting, he didn't care. I hadn't thought about it before, but fifty-six men would all have to piss and those with dysentery, like this man—there was no way—except in a tin hat.

Tom Corney, stocky Queenslander, shearers' cook, offered his.

Backwards and forwards it went; to and from the window, from hand to hand. The padding on the sides tended to stop the slop.

Lippiting-lippiting-lippiting-buffeting. I could be—it could be anything—anywhere—pleasant—so pleasant

**standing on the sledge with legs braced—reins tight—Kit cantering and bits of flying grass—the jinker with old Star, trotting down the track from the Red Hill—a goods train steaming down from Allen's Siding—the shrill double whistle as the driver draws level with Bobbie Jackson ploughing near the line—the horses swinging out of the furrow—Bobbie laughing in spite of**

himself—the driver—the fireman—black caps white teeth—the guard waving waving—laugh

'What's so funny fer Christ sake', said Nark.

Again there were fifty-six men in a truck and the air stank.

The Maori, I noticed, had not moved from his position. Hour after tedious hour, he had stood. Another New Zealander, small, thin, sat on the deck at his feet. Twice, three times, I heard him tell the Maori to keep his knees out of his back. Then again, 'For God's sake keep your bloody knees to yourself, you black bastard'. The Maori glanced down at the top of the little man's head and without any apparent malice reached down and picked him up by the neck. The fingers pressed tight. The eyes, the tongue protruded. The face went grey, then the Maori dropped him unconscious at his feet, where he lay jiggling with the movement of the train. No one spoke.

I found my eyes kept returning to the Maori's face. He was looking out of the window, unmoving except for the train-trembling of his body.

Soft brown eyes—soft brown skin—fat-smeared—shedding water—drops sparkling from paddles—seas running on from the horizon south of the sunset—like his ancestors six generations before protected by the Tangaroa—THE WARRIOR—in Tahiti—New Zealand—Greece or was he travelling to Te Po, the underworld beneath the sea, where he could live his life in peace—sweet tongue-tasting names—Rotorua—Wakatipu—Taranaki—Wanganui—names—like that—at home—soft—native names—Preolenna—Myalla—Montumana

Nabageena

Wayatinah

Lia weneee e e e.

TRINITY SUNDAY. Eighth of June 1941. The Father, the Son and the Holy Ghost. Trinity Sunday. Three in the morning, and the train slowing down. Stopping. My God, it's stopping! Only the starlight and the dark shapes of mountains.

It has stopped. We have stopped. To shoot us here on the lonely hills. Torches waving in the hands of demons, writing in the night and against truck walls. Picking out faces with white teeth. Criss-crossing. They all seem to have torches in one hand and a bayoneted rifle in the other. Shouting. Why do they shout? Is it to frighten away the demons? Undoing of trucks, one at a time. An officer, surrounded by bayonet-jabbing soldiers, shouting, almost screaming, '*Aus! Aus! Marsch!*' He must be an officer, with his braid and flat-topped cap, not the *chapeau de feutre* of the common soldier. '*Marsch! Marsch!*' And guards delighting in pricking skin through the khaki trousers.

The bridge is blown up. There is no bridge. Someone says, 'We blew it up when we withdrew'. *'Marsch! Marsch! Aus! Marsch!'* We march, mate. Happily we march. Anything for a change. Away from the stink of the shit and the ache of cramped muscles. They are even counting us out *'Zwei, vier—'* Do they wonder we are still alive? Fifty-six in one truck. *'Marsch!'*

Someone translated—forty-five kilometres to the station. How many miles?

Down a steep goat-track to the river bed. Struggle up and up to the far side. Up and on. The mountains stay with us and the stars. There is no longer any shouting. The guards are walking too beside us, spread out along the line, the long shuffling line of prisoners planting feet, one in front of the other. A gritting of teeth. Now there's something; a gritting of teeth, something to bite on to. Take a bite of the granite hills. He's got grit. Grit to stop the shit which keeps coming in a thin, urgent stream. Or bubbles of green, from the herbs we pick on the way. Our arses are red hot. Careful to wipe them dry, to wash them when we come to a stream.

*Marsch. Marsch. Marsch.* Nobody says it any more. At the end of two hours a spell. At the end of three hours. And four. Some people want to die. To lie down and die. They are prodded. Their packs or bundles are thrown away. Others, like people in a three-legged race. Or lovers with arms around waists and shoulders. They are not allowed to die. Some die in spite of the prodding.

The sun touches the tips of the mountains. It is a warm sun, full of promise, and love. I find I am smiling at the golden-tinted rocks. I want to say something about it to Stag, but I don't because I can see he is heavy with his own thoughts.

The hours are ticking over slowly. There is a problem. Forty-five kilometres is how many miles? Multiply by five over eight. Divide by three to get hours of travel. The answer is between nine and ten. We should arrive at our destination by 1 p.m., which is approximately twenty shits away.

I'm glad I decided not to talk to Stag. I'm glad Stag doesn't want to talk to me. He has probably just started out on a walk from Scottsdale to Launceston. He can have it. I know where I'm going. I'm going to walk across the paddocks to the railway line, down to the Preolenna turn-off back up the road past Norton's, Bassett's, Smythe's, Cullen's; cross the river on the log at Jackey's Bend and back home across the railway bridge. It's not very far but I'm going to take it slowly. There are hundreds of things to look at and as well I'll check out any fresh rabbit burrows, to go ferreting later. If I'm very quiet I may even see the platypus coming out of his burrow down by the crossing-log.

In that other world there are people lying face down on the track verge. There are eyes full of emptiness and despair. We tell our legs not to stop. But they are no longer under our control. They move systematically and conscientiously forward.

We pass a huge sailor carrying pick-a-back a small sailor whose head is lolling over the huge man's shoulder. The small man's trousers are stained green where his arse-hole is. The huge man doesn't look to left or right, only to the ground in front, where he is to plant his feet. While his pace is slower than ours he leaves me with the impression that he could go on for ever.

But nothing is permanent. Even the rock walls, with stunted trees growing sideways out of crevices, change. And suddenly, quite suddenly, they are not there any longer. Not in front of us, that is. A deep chasm gouged out of the mountain has at its foot a winding grey-brown stream which snakes down to a river running through miles of flat, fertile farming land.

Someone said that the railway station is at the other end of the plain.

Free-wheeling down the hill. Stag's long legs. He's scenting the end. Another four, five, six miles.

We arrive at the stream. It is rest time. Two German guards sitting on the bank by the bridge are staring at us. I look directly at one of them. He looks as tired as I feel. He motions me to rest. I smile. He smiles back. Stag and I go down below the bridge. There are others already there. We shit, then splash and wash in the yellow water. We take out a small piece of bread and eat it, then return to rest with our backs snug in a hollow on the side of the road.

I am wakened by a whistle and German voices shouting. I glance at the German who had smiled at me. He shouts '*Auf! Auf!*' We move across the plain. There are shell-holes in the fields. Several men and women in a crop of maize stop work to watch us go by. I look back across the plain to the straggling line of prisoners. The Germans have commandeered a wagon to carry the very ill and their belongings. I wonder is my small sailor one of those jolting on the bottom of the cart.

The sun is getting hotter. My feet are dragging. Stag tells me it is not far to go. Only a mile past the village. I must shit again. We have become expert. One minute and it's finished. A small piece of precious paper ready, trousers undone, down and up again. But here are Greek women watching. I move off to squat in the maize. My German guard shouts and raises his gun. He beckons me back. I squat where I am and hurry to catch Stag. A Greek woman smiles at me.

A civilian offers us small pieces of bread and fruit. I see there are others with stone jars and glass jugs handing out water and wine. I am very thirsty. Stag gargles and swallows a mouthful and moves on. He says it is only a mile to go. I let him go. I fill my tummy, gulping mouthful after mouthful as I pass through the village. It's only a mile.

The liquid settles like lead in my boots. Only a few hundred yards now. People are passing me, yet they seem to be walking very slowly. I try to hurry to catch them. Still others pass me. I want to ask them to wait.

Now I see him. Already he has a small fire going, a dixie of water simmering and the smell of fish cooking. 'Strip off', Stag says, 'and they'll give you a shower under the water hose where they fill the engine'. 'Later', I say, and stretch out on the ground with my head resting on my pack.

I open my eyes when he says, 'Get this into you'. I look along the train, standing stationary, the engine quietly hissing steam. A couple of men are standing naked under the spurting water. The doors of the box trucks are open, ready and waiting for their human cargo. 'We made it', I say.

*A Kind of Cattle* (1985).

# *Patsy Adam Smith*

## (1924– )

*After a childhood in rural areas of Victoria, Patsy Adam Smith served with the VADs in World War II. She subsequently worked as a radio operator on an Australian trading ship, as an adult education officer and as manuscripts field officer for the State Library of Victoria. A prolific writer with a keen interest in the Australian experience of war, the outback, and the railways, she has written numerous documentary and historical books. She has also written two more autobiographies,* Hear the Train Blow *(1964), and* There Was a Ship *(1967).*

The wives and mothers and fathers and the children on No. 2 platform at Spencer Street railway station, Melbourne, began to wave and cry out to us and to sing:

> *You are my sunshine, my only sunshine;*
> *You make me happy, though skies are grey.*
> *You'll never know dear,*
> *How much I miss you,*
> *Please don't take my sunshine away.*

The civilians sang all the while as the long troop train began to pull out slowly from the empty No. 1 platform where no civilians were permitted when troops were being moved.

> *The other night dear,*
> *While I lay sleeping,*

*I dreamed I held you in my arms.*

*When I awoke dear,*

*I was mistaken,*

*And I hung my head and I cried*

*You are my sunshine ...*

The Regimental Transport Officer (we knew him as the RTO) and his men had directed the groups of naval men, army, air force, nursing sisters and us—enlisted VADs (nursing aides) to the sections of the train that we would occupy for many days and nights to come as the steam train rattled northwards.

Many of us were escapees, young men and women happy to be leaving behind the memories of the depression, that period that had almost wrung the pride out of us, some of us were under-age, all of us were glad to be leaving.

There was little disorder, each of our groups had been given their marching orders before being bussed in, men in trucks and steam trains, nurses and aides in ambulances, each of us kitted out with tin helmet, gas mask, kit-bag, shoulder bag, waterproof ground-sheet, and emergency rations, as well as a small, splendid leather suitcase. And, coming from a heavy tea-drinking family, I had tied on to my kit-bag a 'silver' teapot—'EPNS to prove it', as Matron said when she looked for the brand—and smiled as she came along the corridor to see we were safely packed in.

And packed we were. Some girls had already climbed up and claimed the string-bottomed luggage racks, but they eventually swapped with us tinier, younger girls; there was much to be said for being small, nippy, fit and young in the army. As for the teapot, it stood me in good stead for the whole of my army days and I have it still, the broad-based, non-drip, sensible style symbolic of the great days of railway refreshment rooms.

There was scarcely room to move in the carriages, the floor was thick with kit-bags, the floor of the corridors just as deeply covered with gas masks, tin helmets and the rest strung up wherever we could manage. And then we were off to 'Somewhere in Australia', as we had been ordered to tell our parents to address our mail.

These were the singing days, days before television, video, and a-radio-in-every-household took the joy from the voice and threw it back canned. But in 1941 the families and friends were still singing:

*Wish me luck as you wave me goodbye.*

*Not a tear, mother dear, make it gay.*

*Give me a smile*

*I can keep all the while,*

*In my heart while I'm away.*
*Till we meet once again, you and I.*
*Wish me luck as you wave me goodbye.*

The train moved slowly. It was long and heavily laden, and it took a time to clear the platform. All troop movements were supposed to be secret but relatives invaded No. 2 platform at Spencer Street whenever a troop train steamed out. Coming from the bush, I had no one to see me off so I didn't push my head through the open windows to look out on to that platform like everyone else did. I looked out on to platform No. 1, empty now except for the station master. 'Good luck,' he called. As the train gathered speed he shouted, 'Goodbye Girlie!' And he waved to me until I was swallowed up by distance. And only then did I know I was free.

The Second World War provided the greatest escape route in history for women and girls, while at the same time it exacted the most repressive and restrictive time for most young married women who were left at home with small children. I was one of the lucky ones—young, unmarried—I escaped. [...]

Unlike Vera Brittain, the celebrated, upperclass, young English writer who went to war in 1915 as a nursing VAD, I did not experience 'exasperation' at the breaking out of war in 1939. Vera Brittain saw her war, at the beginning, 'as an interruption of the most exasperating kind to personal plans'. She was 'going up' to Oxford. I, twenty-five years later, was trapped in the depression and was going nowhere. Like many another of my class and generation, I saw the war as my only escape, and I enlisted in the army as a nursing VAD as she had done a generation before me. Her book, *Testament of Youth,* was my lodestar.

The only things we two young women had in common was that neither of us, at the beginning, saw our war becoming a superlative tragedy, and both of us perversely volunteered to serve in the most menial toil. And both of us lost lovers. Beyond that, we had nothing in common—or perhaps everything.

Being a VAD (Volunteer Aide Detachment) was an anomalous position. Like army nursing sisters, we enlisted in the Australian Army and could be sent overseas, but we were under the auspices of an organisation that had originally been formed in England.

Our leader had the title of Commandant. The Lady Commandant, a First World War nursing sister, Alice Appleford, was married to the Doctor Appleford at Lang Lang who 'fixed' my ankle when I fell off the parapet of the railway bridge when I was eleven years old, and so I knew her when she began recruiting girls for the VAD in Melbourne. She most certainly would have known my real age as she knew my Mother well, but nevertheless she enrolled me, one year under-age. Yes,

I would study and get my First Aid and Home Nursing Certificates (in June 1941), plus working, 'getting in' 100 hours in a civilian hospital after my daily work. We country girls scarcely needed a reference: our community was our judge.

I'd already seen most of the young boys in the area escape by rushing off to war and I determined I would go too. There was a tiny private hospital in Penshurst, run by two sisters who were qualified nurses and midwives. Yes, they said, I could do the initial training as an aide here (after my eight-hour working day), and the 100 hours were spent mostly emptying pans and bottles and making beds, as well as studying for the certificates.

I went down to Gippsland where Mum, Dad, Kathleen and her toddlers were now living, and got a job in Wilkinson's grocery shop in Warragul. Mr Wilkinson asked me for assurances that I would not be enlisting. 'They just come to me until they're old enough to enlist and off they go as if they have heard a bugle blow.' 'Oh, not me,' I lied. But I had already enlisted and was waiting for my call-up, as had most of his employees under the age of forty.

But then, nothing happened. Months went by. I saw photographs in the Melbourne *Sun* of 'VADs Leaving For Middle East'. A double page spread. It seemed forever, then my time came, I was ordered to report to an office in Melbourne, swore the oath of something-or-other, told I would be called up shortly, and sent off to the Myer store to have my uniforms tailored. We were being rushed now, hurried.

The uniform was very smart: white shirt, navy-blue straight skirt, belted jacket with a woven Red Cross on our breast pocket, classic felt hat with Rising Sun badge, black shoes, small soft leather clutch bag and gloves, tie and grey stockings. Pale blue uniforms were worn in wards, and we had a fine blue mess dress for evening. On each shoulder were fastened the solid metal flashes AUSTRALIA, beneath these were our felt colour patches, the symbol of the battalion or, in our case, the hospital to which we belonged (the pale grey background indicated those of us who had enlisted to go overseas, as opposed to those who would remain in hospitals back home).

No one who has not been in the services could possibly know the tenacity with which men and women held to their colour patches, even to the degree that, on occasions, if one was transferred to another battalion permission was given for miniatures of one's original battalion or hospital to be worn as well as the new colour patch.

[...]

Behind and beyond this was a cruel jibe (but what is war but a cruel jibe at mankind?). Some men and women who had attempted to join up were unacceptable, usually because of health or infirmity. Some had been 'man-powered' and could not get a clearance. To many in the army this was seen as shirking—'He could have got in if he wanted, could have gone over the border and told a good story there and got himself in.'

(As late as June 1993 I received a sad letter from a woman who said her husband had died recently, 'but he had really died many years ago'. He had gone in to enlist but was refused 'owing to being in a protected service—munitions'. 'He never got over it, he always felt people saw him as a shirker. And many did. He couldn't join the RSL, he felt an outsider. He carried the stigma for life.')

When we first came into the service we were billeted in a great Toorak mansion which had been turned over by the owners for the duration of the war. While I was there, waiting for my uniforms to be tailored, my Mother was permitted to visit and Aunt Anastasia came down from the country with her. Aunt had been out to visit her daughters, Victoria and Margaret, who had enlisted in the air force. Mum was quite cock-a-hoop at seeing the opulent quarters in which her little girl was billeted, crystal chandeliers and all, while Anastasia's girls were in 'a stockade', as Mum described the spartan quarters those early aircraftswomen had to survive when they first enlisted. If Mum had seen some of my later quarters she wouldn't have been so cocky.

The VAD in charge of the hostel told me to 'run the hot water' to wash the dishes. Run the water? She must be pulling my leg! As far as I knew hot water came from a kettle on the wood-fire stove or, if for a bath, from the big copper in the washhouse outside in the back yard. 'It will take a while for the hot water to come through', Betsy told me as she left. I waited, wincing as the thick stream of sparkling clean water poured away down the sink and was wasted. I stuck my finger in a few times as water poured out of the tap, but it was still cold as I knew it would be—how could *hot* water come out of a tap unless the tank was out in the blazing sun, as it was back home up-country in summer? No wrigglers in this water! I waited. God knows how long I waited, but when Betsy came back she snapped, said, 'Oh, it must be turned off, don't just stand there!' I knew I looked a fool but didn't know what I had done wrong, didn't know what had been turned off. I felt like every country child has at some time felt: the universe no longer centred around the bush and it never would again for me. I grew up and exchanged one way of life for another, quick smart.

If I had thought anything at all about the army except as a place to escape to, I could never have guessed what a total change it would be from my life up to that time—for any girl's life, for that matter, because this war was the first that enlisted women other than trained nursing sisters into the services. In one sense you forgot your mother, father, sister and brother because they were now in the past and you were no longer under their control or within their ambit. You were under the total control of a machine that owned and operated you. There was no longer such talk as, 'I'll do that later, Mum.' You did it—'Now!' There was no answering back— that got you detention in barracks. And there was much more along those lines.

You were now a number and required to recite it when called upon. Few men or women can forget their service number, it stayed tattooed in our memory forever. We women had to wear our identity discs around our necks on a leather thong, as did the men, the only difference being that the letter F for female was now added to the women's identification letters, that is, I was VFX: V for enlistment in the State of Victoria, F for female, X for volunteer for enlistment for overseas service. (My friend, Phyllis, had a heart murmur on enlistment, so was denied overseas service, her disc registering only VF.) Some called the discs 'dog tags', others 'dead-meat tickets'. They were durable and would last forever under any conditions: the shower, the sweat of the tropics, or be readable for identification on dead bodies.

There was a marvellous and ridiculous use of words, language and titles in the services. When I was at 108 AGH (Australian General Hospital) at Ballarat there were WAGS and BAGS courses for airmen—Wireless Air Gunners and Bombing Air Gunners—and these lively lads, 'Blue Orchids' as the PBI (poor bloody infantry) called them because of their smart blue uniforms, didn't really swagger as the infantry swore they did. When it was their turn to get a jab in the arm or the backside before leaving for overseas, all men were equal: as many tough infantry men fell flat to the floor as did the Blue Orchids before the needle went in, and many fell while merely standing well back in the line awaiting their turn.

We VADs did nothing courageous, left no mark showing that we had even been there, had worked so hard for such long hours and days and years but no, nothing marks where we had been. But like many other groups in that war and all other stupid wars, we were there.

In a period when a girl left her father's home only to go to her husband's home, these thousands of women in the navy, army and airforce had pioneered the greatest new movement in our history.

In one sense we girls were the lowest rank, but in another we were remarkable. You can't dismiss a bevy, a great big mob of young, healthy, fit girls, many in love with someone 'over there', and all believing they were, by their labour, perhaps helping men survive.

*Goodbye Girlie* (1994).

# Jessie Elizabeth Simons

### (DATES UNKNOWN)

*Jessie Simons was one of sixty-five members of the Australian Army Nursing Service who in 1942 left Singapore after its fall in the ship* Vyner Brooke. *After Japanese bombers sank the ship off the coast of Sumatra, only thirty-two survived the bombing and a massacre by the Japanese following their landing on the beach. Only twenty-four survived the next three and a half years of imprisonment to return to Australia.*

I was deep in Ethel Mannin's *Cactus*, despite interruptions, when Matron Paschke, senior Australian matron in Malaya, summoned the sixty-five members of the AANS for a conference. Reluctantly, I closed the covers on Ethel Mannin's heroes and picked my way to the rendezvous among the prostrate passengers, earning occasional abuse for my carelessness. With Matron was Major Tibbett who was in charge of our party[,] although it was rumoured that this was merely a cloak for his real duty, a secret military mission to Batavia. Their main concern at the moment was to create some organization to operate in the event of the *Vyner Brooke* being sunk, an event they professed to regard as extremely unlikely.

It was no news to us to learn officially that the ship did not carry sufficient lifeboats to accommodate the swarm of passengers now on board. We had already surmised that in the event of disaster to the ship, our chief hope would lie in the life belts with which we had been issued the night before. Lightheartedly we assured Matron that we could swim, though many of us privately wondered whether our occasional peace-time splashings had equipped us sufficiently for the emergency of shipwreck. Our claim to the lifeboats thus disposed of, we listened to some advice which I have now forgotten, and I returned to *Cactus*.

Sometime after we had further sampled our unappetising rations at what was called lunch, for want of a really adequate term of abuse, someone really did discover a plane heading our way. In a perfect exhibition of either the stupidity or the optimism of human nature, many passengers crowded the rails in excited expectation of a salute from a friendly pilot. Singapore had made others of us more discreet and, as the distant whine of the plane droned to a roar, we took what cover we could behind the deck structures, shouting warnings to the optimists. The plane zoomed low over the *Vyner Brooke*, and the stutter of machine guns soon dispelled any doubts as the unwary watchers scuttled for shelter like alarmed rabbits. The strafing, a brief interlude to the passing plane, produced few, if any, casualties, but all the starboard lifeboats were victims, holed and useless. So much for our noble swimming volunteers, who would now have no option.

The rest of the day passed without incident, though the false alarmists were several times noisily rebuked for raising our blood pressure unnecessarily. Night brought some relief from the heat which all day had been reflected from the glassy sea, and lessened our expectations of a repeated strafing, but the *Vyner Brooke* did not make the progress which we had been anticipating. As we prepared to leave the shelter of the islands for a night's uninterrupted steaming, searchlights began to sweep across the darkness of sea and sky. We were in no mood to enjoy their shafts of silver beauty cutting through the black night but, although the groping fingers several times threatened to grasp the poor little ship, they did not quite succeed. Occasionally their unhurrying menace swept so close that our voices irrationally sank into silence. Discreetly the ship turned back behind the screen of islets and our progress, as we crept without lights among scores of tiny islands[,] was disappointingly delayed. We slept uncomfortably with the life belts as pillows. We had instructions never to move without them.

As Saturday's rising sun turned the sea to a harsh, brassy glare, we identified a low shadow, a few miles to the southwest, as the coast of Sumatra, shimmering in the morning haze. The day promised to be as hot and unpleasant as the previous one, and we mourned for the bathrooms of Singapore, mentally revelling in a hot soapy shower. Only the evidence of our eyes convinced us that the sawdust and leather which comprised our breakfast were really biscuits and bully beef. Our one stroke of good fortune was that the glassy sea was no temptation to that ultimate misery, seasickness.

The sea air, lack of exercise and the shimmering heat combined to destroy conversation and initiative as we lay on the deck half asleep, too lazy to be bothered with anything. With nothing to disturb our somnolence, I realized how easily a beachcomber's decadence began. About eleven o'clock, our peace was rudely shattered by a raucous signal which announced that enemy planes were approaching, and ordered all passengers to the lower deck. With little more than a glance at the slow moving dots high in the north-east sky, we surged towards the companionways. Lassitude vanished as we stumbled down the steep steps trying to recall the instructions to which we had listened vaguely the day before. Somehow, we squeezed like sardines into the restricted spaces of the lower deck, lying prone with tin hats on our heads as protection against flying splinters.

That all pervading odour, compounded of stale air, the smell of paint and the lingering odour of cooking, which is peculiar to ships' lower decks, mingled with the heat and the stench of the unwashed to create an atmosphere under other circumstances unbearable. The ports were tightly closed so that we could only guess at what was happening although we could hear quite plainly the steadily increasing drone of the squadron of planes.

The *Vyner Brooke* was flying the white ensign and carried one gun which suddenly barked into action in defiance of the approaching planes, dispelling our lingering hope that they might prove to be friendly. The ship's engines were now racing at full speed and she zigzagged wildly as the captain adopted the few protective measures available. To take my mind off the possibilities I re-opened *Cactus* which I had been clutching subconsciously since the alarm had interrupted my reading and, believe it or not, I became really interested in the book as I lay there on the deck with someone else's elbow in my ribs and the tin hat making my head top-heavy.

Through the shudder of racing engines and the bark of our lone gun, tensely we discerned the rising whine of a dive bomber, which soon drowned out all other sound. With the bomber's final ear-shattering zoom, came the plunk and explosion of the bomb as the ship staggered under the shock of a near miss. My breath of relief turned to a fresh tension as the second bomber screamed down; again the gallant ship shuddered, as if with relieved apprehension, as the bomb went wide. The next was closer and they followed in quick succession, twenty-seven in all, some missing the dodging ship by what felt like inches. Lying, helpless, we forgot the heat and discomfort in the excitement of our miraculous escapes and felt a little proud of the *Vyner Brooke* and her captain as we wheeled crazily, dodging bombs and barking defiance at the roaring planes.

And then came disaster! Another plane whined down and as we ducked instinctively, the ship lifted and rocked with the vast roar of a bomb exploding amidships. Fate was playing with us and, as if mocking our proud survival, the final bomb went squarely down the funnel and exploded in the engine room. Our first reaction, born of tension, was one of relief; we felt, 'Well, it's over anyway.'

It became obvious to everyone simultaneously that the lower deck of a sinking ship is very like a prison, but there was little panic as we swarmed up to the open air. One large well-fed woman grasped at my arm wailing, 'You'll take care of me, won't you, sister?' Assuming my best bedside manner, I dodged the impossible responsibility with the assurance, 'Now, you're going to be perfectly OK.'

As the thrusting passengers below belched me from the companion-way on to the top deck, another stick of bombs threshed the sea to foam, and one dealt the dying ship a last fatal blow. In the confusion of cries from the wounded, the shouts of separated friends or families and the drone of departing planes, someone roughly bound up my arm and I noticed, with surprise, that at some stage I had been hit by flying shrapnel. The chip of steel is still somewhere in my arm as a souvenir of the occasion.

To most of us it was obvious that the doomed ship was settling fast, but some incurably stolid passengers sat unconvinced on the heeling deck, stubbornly refusing to join the scramble to abandon ship. Others were frantically assisting, or hindering, the crew in lowering the sound boats or throwing overboard ropes and rope ladders, down which they could swarm to the water.

As I stopped to pull off my shoes before joining a rough queue round a rope ladder, I recalled a part of the lower deck which was open and, reasoning that the crush and the distance to the water would both be less, with two other nurses, Sisters I. Harper and L. Bates, I went below decks again. There the floor was covered with ugly-looking broken glass and, with more discretion than the occasion really warranted, I raced back to get my shoes. When I returned, my friends had taken warning from the listing ship and were nowhere to be seen. Sister Harper turned up among the prisoners later on, but Sister Bates was not taken prisoner, we presume she was drowned. She was seen on a raft during the afternoon. Somehow I always expected her to turn up and only abandoned hope when people were brought from Padang in 1944 and we were told that, 'we were all in prison now.'

Clearly, there was no time to waste and, hastily crunching through the broken glass, I grasped a rope which hung overboard, kicked off my shoes and slid rapidly down to the water, so rapidly, that I burned all the skin off my palms, although in the excitement I was completely unaware of the damage until later. I pushed off from the side of the ship and, as I swam away, I could see that a few of the boats had been successfully launched, but they were so badly holed that the occupants were bailing frantically. In one boat wounded passengers lay up to their necks in water, while others bailed desperately to keep the battered craft and its freight on the surface. Among the wounded were two of our AANS girls; another, Margaret Wilton, had been killed by a falling raft. There were many remarkable escapes as passengers made last minute leaps into the sea and swam clumsily out of danger.

I turned to float in my life belt and look back on the *Vyner Brooke*. Swiftly she settled lower in the water, then the stern lifted as if in a momentary struggle to survive, and, with a rushing gurgle and a burst of spray, the ship slipped rapidly out of sight, leaving widening circles in the afternoon sea. Within fifteen minutes of the first hit, no sign remained of the *Vyner Brooke* but a pair of leaking boats, a few rafts, scattered wreckage and scores of human heads bobbing on the oily sea. One of our ships was missing.

Despite the difficulties of distance, we held an impromptu mass meeting in the water, shouting advice and encouragement to each other and hugely amused at one nurse, Joyce Tweddell, who was still wearing a tin hat. At first, it was really pleasant, quite a 'lark', in fact, to be swimming in the cool water. We had not bathed for some time, and even a perfunctory wash had been impossible on the ship, so the clean coolness of the tropical sea on a beautiful afternoon, with the land only a few miles away, was more of a delight than a hardship to most of us. Jenny Greer started to sing, 'We're off to see the Wizard' and the girls joined in as they made towards the piece of wood she was hanging on to.

The delight vanished in a recognition of the realities of our plight when a Jap plane swooped low over us. I thought, 'We're for it,' and hunched my shoulders in expectation of a strafing, but nothing happened. The Nips were apparently satisfied that their work was sufficiently well done.

The currents were fairly strong and, aided by our attempts at swimming, they soon scattered the survivors over a wide area. I was fortunate enough to drift up against a raft upon which two British sailors and a Eurasian radio operator had clambered. There was just room for another passenger, and I was helped unceremoniously aboard. One sailor was very badly burned and clearly in a bad way, but to the other one, Stan, bombing was no new experience. While on the *Prince of Wales* and twice earlier, his ship had been torpedoed or bombed, and on each occasion he had been rescued after only a few hours in the water. Stan had an unbounded faith in his colleagues of the British Navy, and kept assuring us that we would soon be picked up.

Shortly after I joined the raft two other nurses, Pat Gunther and Winnie May Davis, were swept our way by the drift. There was no room for any more on the raft, but as Pat couldn't swim and was in a bad way, I slipped off and helped her aboard. Stan, Win and I took turns resting on the raft and, between these spells, we clung to the ropes round the sides of our inadequate but welcome refuge. The burned sailor was in very bad pain from the heat of the sun—he was practically naked and extensively burned—so I struggled out of my dress and managed to wrap it around the poor fellow to give him some protection from the blazing sun. Win was able to give him an injection of morphia from an emergency kit she had in her pocket.

[…]

Just as night fell, Stan's Navy optimism seemed to be rewarded. Several black hulls appeared on the horizon and, though realizing that we were no doubt too far away to be seen, we waved and cheered vigorously. Because my spectacles were blurred with oil and water, I took them off to see the ships more clearly, slipping them into the pocket of Stan's shorts. That was a major mistake; it was the last I saw of them. In the night's confusion they slipped out of the pocket and were irretrievably lost. A far more serious loss was the burned sailor; he slipped off the raft sometime during the night, too weak to maintain his precarious hold. Barely strong enough to keep our own grasp on the stiff ropes, we were too exhausted to do anything and did not see him again.

The on-coming darkness swiftly hid the approaching ships from our sight and we were left to peer uselessly into the night, hoping that by some miracle of fate we would be on the fleet's course. The chill which was gradually numbing our bodies combined with the gloom of night to destroy completely our earlier sense of welcome adventure. As we imagined that we heard surf breaking on the beach, or the confident beat of a ship's engines, all we asked was something solid beneath our feet and something warm to drink.

[...]

At last our peering vigil was rewarded. A black shadow crept out of the lighter darkness, carrying no lights, but the shudder of its screw in the water assured us that it was a real ship and no mocking cloud shadow. Dimly we saw a huge door open in the side of the ship and, through it, landing craft crammed with armed men chugged past us to shore.

We began to call for help. Stan's shout, 'Help! British women!' swept across the dark water several times, but in a few moments it dawned upon us with a shock that we had put our faith in the wrong navy. By a queer freak of chance we had a front line view of the Jap attack on Sumatra. All night long we bumped round Jap transports, often in imminent danger of being rammed by a landing craft as men and equipment poured ashore in the darkness. Whether we were seen or heard we could not tell, though after the first outburst we did all we could to avoid attracting attention, feeling something of the dangerous thrill of spying unsuspected on enemy operations.

If I had been alone that night, Davey Jones would have had another visitor for supper. I was numb with cold, stiff and exhausted, and my skinned hands were worn raw by the wet, coarse ropes. As if we had not enough troubles, the rubbing of the life belts took all the skin off our chins and chafed our armpits painfully in the salt water. We took turns to be hoisted on to the raft for periods of rest between nightmares of clinging with numbing hands to the unco-operative ropes. But for the encouragement of the others and Stan's croaked, 'Hang on, sister, we'll make it,' I would have let my tired arms and weakened will have their way. My impressions of the night are unpleasant and confused, but I do remember being helped up so that I could rest the upper half of my body on the raft, and so take the strain from my hands and arms. In this position, I actually slept! I dreamed that I was in a swamp with a wire fence just ahead; all I had to do, it seemed, was to put my feet down through the heavy mud, and walk over to the fence and safety. I woke trying to depth the ocean. Only the catching of my life belt on the raft prevented my following the lead of the treacherous dream.

Sometime during the night we saw a bonfire on the beach and concluded that some of the survivors of the *Vyner Brooke* had succeeded in getting ashore. With a burst of enthusiasm, we tried to swim, tugging the raft, in an effort to join the others round that beckoning fire, but the currents were too strong for our weakness. Later, we surmised that this party included the nurses who were massacred by the Nips and, in retrospect, were very thankful for the currents. [...] Dawn confirmed our surmise about the Jap landing. A considerable fleet was anchored off-shore, and the half mile of water was constantly churned by the wake of numerous landing craft taking stores and equipment ashore. We had stumbled unawares on the Japanese occupation of Sumatra, and it was obviously a major operation. [...] The scurrying landing craft paid not the least attention, and we spent the next three hours trying to swim and tow the raft to shore, but our progress was negligible. Most of us were too weak to attempt the swim unaided, and the raft represented at least a hand-hold to us all, to some the only hope of survival. At last we stopped the useless struggle, and held a council of war. [...] Our discussions were interrupted by a boat making the return trip to the fleet. It would pass very close to us, and in hurried agreement, we decided to appeal to the crew for a passage. As the blunt nosed craft smacked its way through the wavelets, in an exaggerated pantomime I pointed to the boat, to ourselves and to the shore, trying to convey by signs that we wanted to 'thumb a ride'. Somewhat to our amazement the boat altered course, and in a few moments it lumbered up alongside the raft.

One of the crew of two leaned over and dragged the women of the party unceremoniously into his craft. Unable to stand, we crumpled weakly on the rough seats in the well of the boat, wondering whether we had jumped out of the frying pan into the fire. The boys, doubting their welcome, preferred to stay on the raft which they made fast to a rope attached to the stern of the landing craft, and were towed ashore bobbing uncomfortably in the tumbling wake of the clumsy boat. The two Nips were keenly but not unkindly interested in their bedraggled find and conducted an animated conversation, of which we judged ourselves to be the topic, during the few minutes before the boat crunched heavily on the shelving beach. During the short trip, we decided that a policy of politeness and apparent submission, together with plenty of bowing and obedience, were our only hope.

At another time the beauty of the yellow sandy beach fringed with graceful palms and backed by the mysterious jungle might have made its appeal, but our attention was occupied exclusively with the hundreds of little Nips busy, ant-like, among the mountains of equipment which disfigured the beach and converted it into a warehouse of war.

As our rescue craft crunched to a stop, a squat Jap, wearing nothing but a G-string, left his ammunition shifting and waded into the foot or so of foaming water to the side of the boat. He was wooden-faced and apparently quite uninterested, as were the majority of the Japs going about their work with hardly a glance in our direction, but he held up his arms to assist us out. Weak and stumbling, I fell over the side and into his upstretched arms, too weak to avoid them and too tired to want to. It was much later that I was able to concoct the joke that I had fallen, not into the hands, but into the arms of the Japs!

*In Japanese Hands: Australian Nurses as POWs* (1985).

# Clive James

## (1939– )

I was born in 1939. The other big event of that year was the outbreak of the Second World War, but for the moment that did not affect me. Sydney in those days had all of its present attractions and few of the drawbacks. You can see it glittering in the background of the few photographs in which my father and I are together. Stocky was the word for me. Handsome was the word for him. Without firing a shot, the Japanese succeeded in extricating him from my clutches. Although a man of humble birth and restricted education, he was smart enough to see that there would be war in the Pacific. Believing that Australia should be ready, he joined up. That was how he came to be in Malaya at the crucial moment. He was at Parit Sulong bridge on the day when a lot of senior oficers at last found out what their troops had guessed long before—that the Japanese army was better led and better equipped than anything we had to pit against it. After the battle my father walked all the way south to Singapore and arrived just in time for the surrender. If he had waited to be conscripted, he might have been sent to the Western Desert and spent a relatively happy few months fighting the kind of Germans whose essential decency was later to be portrayed on the screen by James Mason and Marlon Brando. As it was, he drew the short straw.

This isn't the place to tell the story of my mother and father—a story which was by no means over, even though they never saw one another again. I could get a lot of mileage out of describing how the good-looking young mechanic wooed and won the pretty girl who left school at fourteen and worked as an upholsterer at General Motors Holden. How the Depression kept them so poor that they had to wait years to get married and have me. How fate was cruel to both of them beyond measure. But it would be untrue to them. It was thirty years or more before I even began to consider what my parents must have meant to each other. Before that I hardly gave them a thought, except as vague occurrences on the outskirts of a solipsistic universe. I can't remember my father at all. I can remember my mother only through a child's eyes. I don't know which fact is the sadder. […]

After the first atomic bomb there was a general feeling that Japan had surrendered. The street was decorated with bunting. Strings of all the Allied flags were hung up between the palm trees. The Japanese missed their cue and all the bunting had to be taken in. Finally the Japanese saw the point and all the bunting was taken out again. Everybody was in ecstasies except my mother, who still had no news. Then an official telegram came to say that he was all right. Letters from my father arrived. They were in touch with each other and must have been very happy. The Americans, with typical generosity, arranged that all the Australian POWs in Japan should be flown home instead of having to wait for ships. My mother started counting the days. Then a telegram arrived saying that my father's plane had been caught in a typhoon and had crashed in Manila Bay with the loss of everyone aboard.

Up until that day, all the grief and worry that I had ever seen my mother give way to had been tempered for my ears. But now she could not help herself. At the age of five I was seeing the full force of human despair. There were no sedatives to be had. It was several days before she could control herself. I understood nothing beyond the fact that I could not help. I think that I was marked for life. I know now that until very recent years I was never quite all there—that I was play-acting instead of living and that nothing except my own unrelenting fever of self-consciousness seemed quite real. Eventually, in my middle thirties, I got a grip on myself. But there can be no doubt that I had a tiresomely protracted adolescence, wasting a lot of other people's time, patience and love. I suppose it is just another sign of weakness to blame everything on that one moment, but it would be equally dishonest if I failed to record its piercing vividness.

As for my mother, I don't presume even to guess at what she felt. The best I can say is that at least they got the chance of writing a few words to one another before the end. In one respect they were like Osip and Nadezhda Mandelstam in the last chapters of *Hope against Hope*—torn apart in mid-word without even the chance to say goodbye. But in another way there were not. My father had taken up arms out of his own free will. In Europe, millions of women and children had been killed for no better reason than some ideological fantasy. My father was a free human being. So was my mother. What happened to them, terrible though it was, belongs in the category of what Nadezhda Mandelstam, elsewhere in that same great book, calls the privilege of ordinary heartbreaks. Slowly, in those years, the world was becoming aware that things had been happening which threw the whole value of human existence into doubt. But my father's death was not one of them. It was just bad luck. I have disliked luck ever since—an aversion only increased by the fact that I have always been inordinately lucky.

*Unreliable Memoirs* (1980).

# Terry Burstall

## (1941– )

*Terry Burstall has worked as a horse-breaker, drover, farm hand, rodeo rider, and builder's labourer. In 1965 he enlisted in the army and was posted to Vietnam, completing his tour of duty in 1967. He left the army in 1968 and spent three years in New Guinea managing a plantation. Since completing his doctorate at Griffith University in 1991, he has worked as a freelance writer and historian in Brisbane. His other books include* The Soldier's Story *(1986) and* Vietnam: The Australian Dilemma *(1993).*

A light drizzle pattered down on the 20 soldiers waiting to board the Qantas aircraft en route to war. It was May 1966 and I was 24 years old. I had joined the army 9 months before in order to help stop the 'communist aggressor from the north' from pushing over the dominoes on the march to Australia.

Wearing a set of jungle greens, with slouch hat perched jauntily on my head, I felt both proud and apprehensive as I climbed on board. Once this flight started, I thought, my life would be changed forever. I had a wistful feeling about joining a long list of family forebears who had made this trip to war before me. I was entering the unknown, but determined to acquit myself well enough to be an equal partner in their circle. The mysterious, melodious word SIGH … GONE kept sounding in my head. It conjured up images of adventure.

After a 24 hour stopover in Manila we boarded an Air France plane for the flight to Vietnam. It was an eerie feeling flying over the Vietnamese countryside and realising enemy troops might be hidden in the thick forest. When the plane circled Tan Son Nhut airport for landing, it was late afternoon. There seemed to be every sort of plane imaginable on the strip. Along one side of the airfield were concrete bays for fighters, and boxes and stores ran literally for miles.

After waiting some time in the dull, dirty concrete terminal, a bus pulled up and a warrant officer told us to get on it. A large unsmiling Negro in an air force uniform sat behind the wheel, bored and disinterested. All the windows of the grey-brown bus were covered with thick wire mesh—so a grenade could not be lobbed inside. No one missed the significance of this.

When we got to the Australian transit hotel the bored warrant officer told us to put our gear in a room and be ready to go to the Australian base at Bien Hoa at 8 in the morning. That was it, no war, no weapons being fired, no-one seemed to care in the least.

Next morning it was raining and the trip by truck to Bien Hoa was slow. There were more people in that 50 kilometre ride than I had ever seen in my life. The paddies were full of water with shoots of rice just starting to show in places. In other fields there were men wearing conical hats with their trousers rolled up above their knees, ploughing little blocks of water with dejected-looking water-buffaloes pulling old wooden single-furrow ploughs. Many of the farmers wore sheets of plastic wrapped around their shoulders in lieu of raincoats.

Near Bien Hoa City we turned off the road and headed for the airfield where the Australian base was situated. Along this road were dozens of small shanty-town bars. They were constructed of all kinds of building material, many of them covered in sheets of Coke tin foil with the labels visible to the world. Whoever sold the foil on the black market did a marvellous advertising job for Coca Cola.

The truck passed through the gate and went across to the Australian lines. It was a bleak, depressing sight. There was not a tree in the whole area, just buildings that seemed to have been put up haphazardly. The Australian lines were tents with the kitchens made of prefabricated aluminium and fly wire. I was posted to D Company and taken down to the lines.

After two weeks in the battalion I was sent to Saigon for guard duty at the transit hotel where we had stayed the first night. Part of the duties of the guard was to send soldiers out to the Australian transmitter situated on the main Saigon airfield. Across the open field from the transmitter was a shanty town full of the unwanted and unloved. Grass shacks teemed with the poor and destitute and the noise of crying, wailing, laughing, shouting and drumming from the area continued all through the night. By 2 a.m. I was deathly afraid of the place—what the hell was happening there. I was extremely relieved when the next shift came to relieve us.

That wasn't the finish of it, however. On another occasion I found myself inadvertently going into a refugee area in downtown Saigon as I tried to take a short cut between two main roads. The conditions were appalling. I turned a corner in the narrow lane and confronted the most pathetic sight I have ever seen. A woman sat on a small piece of rotting board, her buttocks just clearing the mud that was everywhere. She was dressed in rags and was nursing an emaciated infant clad only in a filthy singlet. He was almost bald and on one side of his head was a huge weeping sore. He was crying, but all he could manage was a pitiful whining whimper, as if that was all his strength would allow him. The woman was slowly and aimlessly waving her hand across his head to keep the swarming flies away. As I came toward her she put out a hand to me and spoke in a voice stripped of emotion. I looked in horror and tried to brush past her. She grabbed at my pants as I went by and the sound that came from her was more like the cry of an animal than a human being. I yanked my leg away from her feeble grip and hurried up the lane, not daring to look back at the pitiful sight of this human flotsam, abandoned and hopeless.

I needed air but, every time I breathed in, the filthy putrid air choked me. I hurried to the end of the lane where a group of South Vietnamese soldiers sat eating and playing cards. They looked at me as I came stumbling toward them and continued talking. I looked at them uncomprehendingly. Here was the army of the people we were supposed to be helping and they were sitting there as if they were on a picnic. Their weapons were scattered all over the place and there was no way they could have retrieved them had they needed them in a hurry. They seemed oblivious to the plight of their own people only several metres away.

Later I went down to Tu Do street in the central area of Saigon, where there were hundreds of bars and areas of filth and depravity. In amongst all this was the very obvious affluence of the Americans, who had private restaurants, clubs with poker machines, beer and first-class entertainment. Swirling around outside, the majority of the Vietnamese lived in squalor and degradation. Though not all Vietnamese—there were many who were reaping the benefits of the American and Australian presence and could not have cared less about the desperate circumstances of their compatriots.

When One Battalion went home I was transferred to the newly arrived Six Battalion who were then at a newly formed camp on the Back Beach on the outskirts of the coastal city of Vung Tau. After a week on the beach we flew to Nui Dat where we were to help establish the new Task Force base. It was a strange experience going to Nui Dat as it seemed that there was no war going on at all. There was, however, the constant grind of work in atrocious living conditions. The battalion's first few months at the Nui Dat base were physically and mentally demanding because of the lack of organisation and equipment to work with. Five and Six Battalions had to virtually build the base from nothing. To make matters worse the wet season started and the rain and the mud increased the discomfort. As well as the task of building the base there were security patrols and operations to be carried out and these seemed to be endless slogs through the bush.

The first operation for the battalion was the destruction of the village of Long Phuoc, several kilometres from Nui Dat. We had been told the people from Long Phuoc had been 'resettled' and tried not to think any more about it. The town of Long Phuoc was large and sprawling, with well-constructed houses built of timber and brick, nothing like the Australians' perception of grass-hut villages. The people had moved in such a hurry that they had left almost everything behind— clothes, cooking utensils, bedding, personal possessions. Where had the people gone? How were they going to live without anything to cook in or a place to sleep? How could they replace the small family treasures we were throwing on to the small fires we had lit everywhere? Don't worry, the people have been resettled[,] we were told. Don't worry! How could we? We were soldiers. The boss said pull down the town. We pulled down the town.

When we left, virtually nothing remained of Long Phuoc, two hundred years of Vietnamese history wiped away in two weeks. In ancient Chinese, the word phuoc means happy, well and prosperous. It would be a long time before Long Phuoc was ever happy, well and prosperous again.

The grind of patrolling and building the base continued and the operation into the Long Tan area in July was a portent of things to come. B Company was hit by an estimated company of main force troops and were lucky to escape being over-run. The action brought home to us that the Viet Cong forces in the area were not to be taken lightly. Still, it seemed inconceivable to us in the lower ranks that they would hit us because of the heavy logistic support we had on hand.

The VC flew in the face of this argument when they hit the base in August with an estimated 100 rounds of mortar fire. B Company Six Battalion were sent to find them, and D Company relieved B Company the next day. At 3.45 p.m. on 18 August we were ambushed in a rubber plantation just north of the village of Long Tan by an estimated regiment of the VC main force. The battle ebbed and flowed for four hours. When relief finally broke through, we hurriedly evacuated the area in order to fly out our dead and wounded. Some of them had to be left in the area overnight, however, and we returned at mid-morning the following day. The sight was horrendous—no one who was there could ever forget the horror and the carnage. Two of our wounded were found where they had lain helpless all night while Australian artillery pounded the area. We recovered the bodies of our friends who had been laughing living beings the day before. Nothing takes the supposed glory out of war more quickly than the sight of dead mutilated friends. Unfortunately it brings about a hardening of feeling toward your enemy that pushes normal human feelings of compassion to the back of the mind. It brings conflict down to a very personal level and gives you the licence to remain aloof from the suffering of others as long as your own little band of friends is protected.

These became my feelings for the rest of my tour in Vietnam. I cared nothing for the Vietnamese. I cared nothing for why we were there. I cared only for the small unit of people who shared my life 24 hours a day.

When D Company was reorganised, I was sent to Ten Platoon and took over as a machinegunner. Very little was explained to us about Long Tan and no one could be bothered asking. Life moved on, but now we knew there really was a war here. No doubt of that any more.

In September the battalion went on an operation into the Nui Dinh hills, five kilometres west of Nui Dat. The hills were an endurance test, as they were very steep and covered in trees and foliage. We came from the northern slopes and up across the eastern face and over to the south. From the southern heights you looked out over the great mangrove expanses of the Rung Sat, or Jungle of Death, and to the west you could trace the highway through the many miles of rice paddies to Phu My. At night the glow of the lights in Saigon lit up the western horizon. We had to cut down huge trees to make a helipad to resupply the company and get us off. The only flat area was a huge rock so the landing zone was made on that.

Back at Nui Dat again, the operations and patrols went on and there was no indication of whether our presence in Vietnam had altered the course of the war one bit. How did you measure success in that type of war? Perhaps by the attitude of the people. If so there had been no success as far as I could see. In the villages the people looked at us with strange eyes that seemed to smoulder. Their dislike was apparent to all but the blind. There were no young men in the villages. All the work was done by women, children and men over 40. The children went from adolescence to … who could tell? Gone as soldiers every one, but to which side? Those who did not join the Viet Cong were conscripted by the South Vietnamese army.

My perceptions had narrowed so much by this time that there were for me only two kinds of people in Vietnam: those in the villages, who hated us and showed it; and those in the towns, who hated us and didn't show it too openly because they were making a dollar and waiting to rip us off. The only way we ever met Vietnamese was when we went on leave and there they were the pimps, the bar girls, the bar owners and black market racketeers. It was a very lopsided view of the Vietnamese that we developed.

At Nui Dat we drank Australian or American beer and ate Australian or American food, watched American movies and bought American goods from the PX that was set up on the base. We transported an Australian army camp and values to Vietnam and we lived in the same environment we had known at Enogera or Singleton, except that we had to go out on patrols with live ammunition and a few of us would die and some would be wounded. […]

When we left in June I don't know what I took with me. Anger. Disillusionment. Disappointment. I certainly wasn't going to be able to join the exalted ranks of my family forebears on the equal footing I had planned on the day of my departure. I had gone to Vietnam for all the right reasons but found that none of them fitted the cause. The pride I felt for the boys I served with was overwhelmed by the uselessness of the whole year. We had achieved nothing, except the death of 37 young men and maiming of more than a hundred. We had upheld Australia's good name in the world, perhaps, but the cost of this boot-licking to an American insurance policy that might never be paid was way too high.

I was left feeling frustrated at the whole effort. The problem was that if there was anyone interested enough to ask about Vietnam, I was supposed to be an expert because I had been there. Been there! Been where? I had been to Bien Hoa airfield and some of the surrounding countryside. I had been at the base at Nui Dat and had gone from there on operations. Even then the operations never took us far. To the north I had been no further than the Binh Ba plantation, a distance of only 5 kilometres from Nui Dat. I had been east to Xuyen Moc, 20 kilometres, and west almost to Phuy My, 30 kilometres. My knowledge of Vietnam was Australian knowledge and Australian memories.

*A Soldier Returns: A Long Tan Veteran Discovers the Other Side of Vietnam* (1990).

# 8

---

# DEATH

# Ada Cambridge

## (1844–1926)

*Ada Cambridge grew up in Norfolk, England, and came to Australia in 1870 after she married a young curate, George Frederick Cross. He served as Anglican minister in various parishes in Victoria before moving to Williamstown in 1893. Two of their children died during this period.* Thirty Years in Australia *describes the vicissitudes of her experiences as a clergyman's wife and her establishment as a writer. Cambridge became one of Australia's leading writers between 1875 and 1895, publishing numerous novels, short stories, and poems.*

Sad indeed was the breaking up of that pleasant home at Y——. It followed upon, and was a consequence of, the death of our little daughter, when she was nearly a year old.

These are the times when the Bush dweller feels his geographical position most keenly—when he needs the best medical advice and cannot get it. I do not say that our dear old German doctor was not a good doctor in his way, for he was; but practically nothing had been added to his knowledge since he was young, and in this case he confessed frankly that he was altogether at fault. He had never met with a similar one—nor have I; and after looking up all the authorities at his command, even to the papers and notes of lectures of his student days, his honest mind would not pretend to have made itself up. His professional credit was not so dear to that man as truth. 'I don't know,' he said in so many words. And how often I have wondered whether, if we had been rich, we could have found someone else who did! Would a special train and a thousand guinea fee have saved her?

These are questions that shock some of my clerical friends, mothers amongst them. 'It was the Lord's will,' they say, and seem to think that settles it. A few months ago I was spending an evening with a young curate and his wife, whom I had not met before; they were ardently religious people, in their own line, and they had recently lost their only son. The mother gave me the history. He had had an internal tumour or something of the sort, a growth that steadily increased and which the doctors had plainly said must be removed if his life was to be saved. The parents replied—and they repeated the words with such proud confidence that they were the right words—'No, if the Lord intends him to get well, he will get well without that'. And instead of the operation—urged by their incumbent, who also gave me these facts, as well as by other friends—they had prayer-meetings at the bed-side. The little sufferer, described as a bright boy of nine, swelled and swelled until he died. 'The Lord needed him,' said the mother to me. And 'We feel so honoured to have a child in Heaven.' She made my blood run cold. I can never have shocked the 'good' people more than that ultra 'good' woman shocked me.

We left nothing to these chances. When whooping-cough came to the township, I took extraordinary precautions to keep my children from catching it. The epidemic was nearly over when the little boy fell a victim, and then I watched day and night to prevent contact with the baby. Quite at the last (the lady I have spoken of would have some remarks to make on this) my efforts were defeated; the baby took it in spite of me. She was a healthy and happy little soul, and at first her case seemed just an ordinary one. But after coughing for a week or two, she ceased to cough suddenly, and fell into strange fainting-fits; they seized her so silently and swiftly that I hardly once saw her go into one, although she was in the room with me, and my eye, as I thought, never off her. A cry from her nurse or somebody would cause me to jump as if I had been shot, and there lay my little one, wherever she happened to have been sitting or crawling, exactly like one dead—grey, limp, eyes sunk, lips drawn back, neither breath nor heart-beat discoverable. We would snatch her up and rub her and give her brandy; and after some minutes, more or less, she would struggle painfully back to life, and as soon as respiration returned begin to shriek in the most terrible manner, and keep it up until completely exhausted; then she would drop asleep, remain asleep for a whole day, perhaps, and awake placid and cooing, ready to be fed and played with, apparently as well as ever. At intervals of a day, or two days, she had perhaps half a dozen of these fits; then she had one that lasted nearly three hours. All the while that she lay in our arms, we having no hope that she would revive again, a thin stream of what looked like grey water trickled from one nostril; it was the only sign of life. The old doctor, having done all he knew, sat looking on, as helpless as we. However, again she struggled back, and, getting breath, began that quick, agonising shriek which was so maddening to hear and impossible to stop. The doctor put his hands to his ears. 'I can't stand it,' he said ; 'I must go outside. Call me if you want me.' After awhile he went home, but the shrieks lasted the greater part of the night, gradually, as her strength wore out, dying into hoarse wails and moaning off at last into exhausted sleep.

She slept the entire day, and I sat by the cradle and watched her, sopping several handkerchiefs with those foolish tears which I am supposed to weep for the pleasure of it and could help shedding if I liked. Then, towards evening, a little hand began playing with the cradle-frills and the happy little coo that used to wake me of a morning broke the silence of the room. I could not believe my eyes and ears. We sent post-haste for the doctor. Well, there she was, looking as if nothing had happened.

'Whatever it was,' said the doctor, 'that last attack has carried it off. You will see she will be all right now.'

At the end of the three happy weeks that seemed to prove him right, I gave a little musical party. He brought his flute, and we were in the middle of a more or less orchestral performance, when I fancied I heard a cry from the next room—a cry with that peculiar sharp edge to it that I had so learned to dread. I rushed to the cradle, the doctor after me, and we lifted the child up and examined her. 'Oh, she's all right,' we said, with long breaths of relief; 'it was only our noisy music that disturbed her.' We placed the nursemaid on guard, and went back to the drawing-room, and for the rest of the evening made less noise, while she made none, but slumbered peacefully.

In the morning she woke up as usual; that is, I did not know when she woke. She hardly ever cried to be taken up, but played with her bed-clothes and her toes, and gurgled and gabbled to herself until I chose to lift her into my bed. She was in the most blooming condition. From the time that I dressed her, until breakfast was ready, she played with the cat on the dining-room floor, and a vivid memory of the day is of the smothered chuckles of the two servants while G. was reading prayers, because of the hilarious and irreverent shouts and crows with which baby enlivened the proceedings. When breakfast came in she was carried out. At the door her nurse held her up and told her to say good-bye to her father and mother. The bright little creature, perfection in my eyes, with her sunny curls and blue eyes and the little face lit up with the fun of going through her tricks, kissed her hand and waved it, and nodded and farewelled us in her baby language, and the door closed upon our last sight of her in life.

It was my habit to take her for an airing after breakfast, while the servants helped each other with the housework, and this particular morning was a glorious one, the crisp, sunny winter morning of Australian hill country, with the first hint of spring in it. I got her little cloak and hood and went to the kitchen to fetch her. The kitchen was large and airy, opening upon the garden, and her cradle was sometimes placed in a corner there, where she could be watched by the servants, who were both devoted to her. It was there now, and she was in it. 'She seemed sleepy,' said the elder girl, 'so we laid her down.'

'She must have been awake earlier than usual,' I thought, and stooping over the cradle, I saw her, as I believed—and still believe—sleeping quietly, carefully tucked up, the little golden head laid sidewise on the pillow. It was not her bed-time by an hour or two, but her habit of not telling me when she started the day seemed to explain the too early sleepiness. I told the girls they were right to put her down, and went off to the housework on my own account. Some time later the elder servant came to me where I was busy, G. being with me. 'Oh, ma'am,' said she, gaspingly, 'I wish you'd come and look at baby. She's so pale!' G. almost flung me aside lest I should get to the door first, and dashed to the kitchen. We both knew instantly what had happened. The servants had not left her for a moment; she had not made a movement or a sound; she could not have known what had happened herself, which was something to be thankful for. One of her strange fits had seized her—the one, at last, that she would never come out of: Her father snatched her up—lying exactly as I had left her—and called for the brandy; we tried to pour it down her throat, where not a drop would go, until she grew quite cold and rigid in our arms.

It was the first of these almost insupportable bereavements, and the effect on my health was so severe that a complete change of surroundings was considered necessary—to get me away from the house whose every nook and corner was haunted by such agonising visions of what had been. G. for his part, could no longer stand the Murray journeys, involving such long and complete separation at a time when we needed so much to be together. So he cast about for a more compact parish, and one offered that fulfilled the requirements—and more.

*Thirty Years in Australia* (1903).

# Thorvald Weitemeyer

## (1850–?)

*In the following extract Weitemeyer and his friend Thorkill were working on the Cape goldfield, near Condamine Creek, Queensland.*

On one evening that is for ever engraven on my memory, we were lying in our tent Thorkill and I. It had been raining heavily all day, and we had not been able to be about. We felt pretty miserable, our usual stock of conversation seemed to be exhausted, but far out in the evening it revived again, so much indeed that Thorkill began to tell me of things of which he had never spoken before. He told me of his parents, of his brother and his sister; and explained to me where their farm in Iceland was, giving me the address, describing the road leading to it, and every detail until I said to him that if we were lucky enough now to get a bit of gold we would both go home to Iceland and settle down there. From that conversation drifted to other things, and was at last almost at a standstill when he called me by name, and, in a bashful sort of way, observed, 'I say, were you ever in love?'

This was a theme on which we had never enlarged: partly because there had not been much opportunity yet for either of us in Queensland to indulge in such a luxury, and partly because I do not know, to the best of my recollection, that it had ever been mentioned between us, so, as I recognized that he wanted to tell me something, I said, a little surprised, 'Why do you ask?'

'I have,' said he. 'While I was overseer on that farm in Alo, I knew a girl. Oh, how good she was, and how beautiful! I sometimes would go and visit her in the evening. She was only a servant girl, and her father was working there too. One evening I kissed her.'

'I am afraid,' said I, 'you have not forgotten her yet.'

'No; her I can never forget.'

'Why did you not marry her?' said I. 'I suppose as you went visiting her, she would have had no objection?'

'How could I?' replied he. 'If only I had been an ordinary working man I would willingly have asked her; but I was not that. Her father always spoke to me as if I owned a mansion yet I had scarcely sufficient salary to pay for my own clothes. No, I never asked her.'

'Does she know you are out here?' inquired I.

'No, neither she nor my parents, nor anybody; they must think I am dead.'

I had nothing to say. I was lying thinking about matters of my own. A little after this I thought I heard him crying. Was it possible? I did not like the idea. I listened again. Yes! there was no mistake. Thorkill was really crying. Deep, big, stifled sobs. I asked what was the matter. Two or three times I asked before he answered. At last he said, 'I could not help it; I cried because I know very well I shall never see Reikjavik' (the only town in Iceland) 'again.'

After that I kept talking for some time to him in a sort of overbearing way about that, saying we need not cry, surely, about that, if that was our only trouble; that we had money enough to get home now, and if we had not, what then? As for myself, if I set my mind on going home, rather than cry over it I would stow away on a ship or work my passage. But I got no answer from Thorkill. I could not sleep, and soon after the day broke. The rain had by this time ceased, and as I saw that Thorkill had now fallen asleep, I thought it a pity to waken him, and crept as quietly as I could out of the tent to make a fire and get a drop of tea for breakfast. As I sat by the fire an hour after, eating my breakfast, I saw Thorkill coming creeping on his hands and feet out of the tent, with his head screwed round, looking up in the air over the tent. I somehow thought he was looking at a bird, and wondered he had not got the gun, so I sat still and said nothing, but kept watching him. When he was a long way out of the tent he got up, and, still looking up in the air, pointed fixedly at something and cried, 'See! oh, look there!' I stole behind him and looked, but could see nothing, so I asked, 'What is it?'

'Oh, don't you see? See! a large Russian emigrant ship flying through the air.'

'Are you going altogether insane?' cried I beating him on the back. The next moment with a deep groan he fell right into my arms. I asked him what was the matter. Was he sick? Was he bitten by a snake? I do not know half I asked him, but all the reply I got as I laid him in his bunk again, was, 'Go for a minister.'

My mate was dying, and I knew it now. Dear reader, whoever you may be, if you have seen your nearest friend die, then you know how bitter it is. But if you at such time have been among others who have shared your grief, and had a doctor to take the responsibility off your hands, then you may only guess at what *I* felt when I saw Thorkill lying there perfectly unconscious. We had as it were for a long time been everything to each other, and the disappointments and mishaps we both, so far, had suffered in Queensland, had, it seemed at that moment, made him simply indispensable to my existence. How could I go for a parson? I jumped out of the tent and ran round it three or four times before I recollected that I did not know of any human habitation within fifty miles! Then I went in again and spoke to him. There was no answer; not a movement in his body. He lay as if in a heavy sleep, a high colour in his face. One of his arms was hanging out over the bunk, and would not rest where I put it, so I took a saddle and placed that underneath it, and as it was not yet high enough, I put a pint pot on that again. There I balanced it, and there it remained. I had not much medicine, only some quinine. That was no good. I thought he must have been taken by an apoplectic fit. I took the scissors and cut off all his hair and beard. Then I went outside and worked desperately at making a sunshade over the tent, because the sun was beating down on us so fiercely; next in again, and out. I did not know what to do. I could not for a moment remain still. Sometimes I carried water from the creek and bathed his head with it. Then I feared I was only tormenting him, and knocked it off again. As I sat looking at him in the afternoon I could not avoid thinking about how he had in his last hour of good health made such a complete confession about matters he always before had been so reticent about. Why? I ask the question now. Can any one answer it? It is not fashionable in our age to believe more than can be rationally explained, but I believe most people in their lives have had similar strange experiences. If I make the remark that I am superstitious, then I know I shall lay myself open to ridicule and yet it is only a form of admitting that I do not know all that passes in heaven and on earth.

In the afternoon, as Thorkill still lay in the same immovable trance, I thought I must find out whether he was conscious of my being there or not, so I knelt down and spoke in his ear, and called him by name. 'Thorkill,' cried I, 'if you *can* hear me and know that I am here, try to give me some sign.' Then as I watched him I thought he breathed extra deep, but I was never certain. Anyhow, although I had myself no Bible, and never had used one before, I got his out of his swag and began reading at the commencement and kept on until it was too dark to read any more. During the night the rain and storm began again. I could hear in Thorkill's altered breathing that the end was near, but I had no other light but a match I struck occasionally, and it seemed to frighten me when I struck one and saw his altered face. At last I knew he was dead, and in an agony of sorrow and excitement I began praying to Balder, our ancient god of all that was noble and good, to come and fetch his own. I was fearfully agitated, and remember well how I walked outside the tent singing the old 'Bjarkamsal,' and almost fancying I saw all the ancient gods coming through the air. It is a common saying of a person who has died, that he was too good to live, but if ever that saying was true of any one, it was true of Thorkill. A pure descendant from the ancient Vikings, yet how different was he from his forefathers. And all Icelanders are more or less the same. Honest, frank, and kind, he could not understand why everybody else was not also honest and good, and I know very well he declined the contest of life; he could not match his simple faith with the cunning and brutality of the ordinary set of people one meets with when the pocket is empty. Better, perhaps, he should have died then and there. Why was I sorry? Why did I not rejoice? Who knew but that I some day might not die in a great deal more lonely and in much more friendless way than he? He had lost nothing, and it was I who was the loser; but for his sake I would be glad. In this strain of mind I passed the remainder of the night, but when at last daylight came it brought with it the grim reality of death such as it is, and life such as it is, and also a sense of what was now the only favour I could show the remains of my friend. It was three or four o'clock that afternoon before I had managed, as decently as I could to bury the body, and then all my energy was expended. Yet as I sat resting myself for a moment, I was aware that I must be off somewhere before evening, far from that spot. I had a splitting headache; my legs seemed unable to carry me. Yet I must be off to get the horses. I found them, but when I came home with them it was evening and I had to let them go again. I could do no more, and not altogether with an uncomfortable feeling was it that I that evening laid myself down in Thorkill's bunk, thinking that perhaps after all we need not part. I was sick now myself, and fancied I saw fearful visions all night. The next morning I could scarcely raise myself to a sitting posture, but during the day I managed with the instinct of self-preservation to carry some water up from the creek and to bake a damper. My recollections for some time after this are very indistinct. It may have been a week or it may have been two weeks. All that I remember of that time are glimpses of myself sitting by Thorkill's grave, singing, or playing the flute. The first clear recollection of that time which I have, was one afternoon when I was lying in the bunk watching, in a lazy sort of way, some rats nibbling at the flour-bag, which had somehow fallen down from its place. The flour lay scattered about the tent, and everything seemed in glorious disorder. I lay a long time looking at the rats, and wondering where Thorkill was—whether he was making breakfast, for I felt very hungry. I had no remembrance whatever of his being dead. I called him; my voice seemed curious and weak. I grabbed a poker to strike at the rats with it—how heavy it felt! Then I got up and went outside, and stood staring for a long time at the grave before I recollected that he was dead, and that I myself was or had been sick. Everything outside the tent bore evidence of having been thrown about as if by a maniac, and I felt a thrill of horror running through me as I thought of myself, how perhaps I had walked about here at night alone, sick and delirious. I felt quite myself, however, although very weak. I was hungry, and felt that I must have something to eat, get it where I could. I staggered about looking for food. Not a vestige of tea could I find; there was no meat except a few nasty bones which I found in the billy, and had to throw away; then I discovered a little sugar, and I scraped together some flour. My next trouble was that I had no fire and no dry matches. It took me all my time to get a fire, by rubbing a hard and soft stick together, but at last I succeeded, and then made a johnny-cake in the fire. Out of sugar I made my supper, and sat by the fire dreaming and living it all over again. With the help of my gun I got some birds the next day, and stewed them in the billy with flour and figweed. I also found the horses all right, but I was too weak to think of shifting my quarters just then, much as I would have liked to do so because there seemed to me to be a sort of haunted air about the whole place. I busied myself all day, when I was not hunting for food, with repairing my clothes, but I had a great longing to see somebody of my own species again, and to sit there every day talking to or thinking about a dead man had something sickly in it that I did not like. I could not for a couple of days find either my money or the bit of gold we had got. Whatever I had done with it was to me a complete blank. I found it all at last in this way: that somehow my hat did not seem to fit me, and when I looked it over, there was all the money stuck under the lining, but I never had any recollection of putting it there.

I read all Thorkill's letters, and took them with me when I left. They were from his parents and his sister, addressed to him while he was in Denmark, telling him of all sorts of small home-news, and hoping soon to see him again. These he had been carrying with him everywhere, and I had often seen him reading them. There were also photographs of all his family, and I made them all up into a small parcel intending some day soon to write to his people.

I confess I never did write. I could not bring myself to do it. I thought of what he had said—that they must think him dead. Why, then, reopen their wound? Let him remain 'a missing friend'. As I had no settled abode for a long time after this, I carried his papers with me everywhere for many years. One photograph, of his sister, a very handsome girl, I had until after I was married, and treasured it greatly.

*Missing Friends, being the Adventures of a Danish*
*Emigrant in Queensland (1871–1880)* (1902).

# W. J. Turner

## (1884–1946)

*Walter James Turner grew up in Melbourne and left Australia in 1907 for Europe. In London he was severally music critic, drama critic, and literary editor for eight promi-nent newspapers and magazines, and became well known as a poet. A member of the Bloomsbury and Garsington cultural groups, he was friendly with such writers as W. B. Yeats, Arnold Bennett, Robert Graves, T. S. Eliot, Virginia Woolf, and Aldous Huxley. He published sixteen volumes of poetry, two plays, and several critical works on music, painting, and literature as well as some comic, semi-autobiographical works of fiction. In Blow for Balloons he refers to himself in the third person as Henry Airbubble.*

In front of the Airbubbles' weatherboard house at Box Hill was a small garden which contained two magnificent camellia trees, one red and one white, which blossomed profusely. The only other plant Henry can remember in this front garden was a cutting of a kind of daphne he has never seen since, a small plant with an intensely sweet-smelling floweret. He remembers this because his mother is connected with it in some way; possibly he helped her plant it, for he can still see it in newly watered ground.

He remembers the camellia trees for another reason. After the death of their father the Airbubbles were left not very well off. James Airbubble had always earned a large income to which his share in the dwindling balloon business had contributed steadily less and less. The bulk of his income, therefore, ceased at his death and his wife Lucy had to earn a living to support herself and her two chil-dren by teaching music. Henry, although the elder, was completely unaware of this change; for his mother Lucy was a proud competent woman who never made a fuss and it was probably her deepest desire that her children should not suffer in any material way from the loss of their father. To disguise their now straitened situation from Henry was the easiest thing possible. Henry lived in a dream-world of his own imagining and in the sharp actuality of his acute physical senses. He was hardly aware of the existence of other people and his arrival at puberty had more than ever isolated him from them. The two boys now went daily by train from Box Hill to Scotch College in East Melbourne and Henry became more and more deeply buried in his own imaginings.

Suddenly he received a shock. Struck, perhaps, by the contrast between Henry's unawareness of what was happening around him and his brother Rufus's keen apprehension of his mother's changed situation and new difficulties Lucy Airbubble one day said to Henry: 'See what your brother has brought me,' and showing him some money she also showed him two trays filled with camellia flowers, one red and one white, carefully packed in tissue paper. Henry then learned that, some time before, Rufus had gone to a florist's in Melbourne and had made arrangements to supply them with these flowers which he brought into their shop perfectly packed every morning before going to school. Henry has never forgotten this and to this day can see these two trays with their regular rows of white and red camellia flowers before him. But his preoccupation was too deep and his nature too pupa-like in its profound need for reverie to allow him to become any more attentive than before. Everything practical in the way of help to their mother in these days was given by Rufus, with Henry always doing cheerfully and willingly what he was asked to do but never initiating anything.

Behind the house was a large garden full of fruit trees between which they grew many kinds of vegetables, taught by their mother Lucy who was a keen gardener. Although she was a capable musician she had never loved music as she loved literature and gardening so very soon the boys under her direction were pruning the plums and apples, planting and growing potatoes, onions, carrots, celery—properly and carefully banked—strawberries, currants and I don't know what. At weekends and occasionally during the week they dined with their mother at their grandparents, the Tawsons', who lived not more than a quarter of an hour's walk away. In the Tawsons' garden there were several oak trees and in the orchard two fine quince trees. These trees were the favourite resort of Henry and Rufus who climbed in them, made seats in them where they took biscuits, lollies and books to sit there eating and reading for hours on end. They liked being at their grandparents'. Their grandmother Sarah was very fond of them, the servants made a great fuss of them, there was an abundance and variety of good fare that made the meals there a festival compared to the frugal living at home and their grandfather's outwardly stern behaviour was, they instinctively felt, a very thin ice-coating for they ruthlessly exploited his pride in them by borrowing many of his valuable books, taking them up into the trees in his garden from which, I have no doubt, they frequently fell. [...]

Sunday in the Tawsons' house was a riot of rich food and plain reading. All the week's newspapers were locked away, including a gay periodical entitled *Pick-me-up* in which Henry's interest was just now dawning—happily unknown to his grandfather for whom alone it was intended, nobody else ever being likely to commit the *faux pas* of opening it. The boys' grandmother read the *Quiver* and the boys were allowed to read the Bible or serious books from the library such as Addison's *Spectator*. Their mother Lucy used to play a little in the afternoon on the pianoforte but Henry does not remember that either he or his brother were particularly interested in this. Their father had not wished them to be very musical but when at an earlier age their mother having attempted to teach them the pianoforte was compelled to give it up, finding them unteachable: 'What nonsense!' their father had exclaimed, on hearing this, 'I'll soon make them learn.' After a week he confessed himself beaten since they seemed to have no aptitude for music at all and irritated him by asking questions that he could not answer and had never asked himself, for he had acquired music without knowing how and all his analytic power had developed in other directions.

On the morning of Henry's fifteenth birthday his brother presented him with a small tomato plant which they gravely planted together in a strip of ground close to the wall at the back of their weatherboard house. Henry can still smell that tomato plant and the damp exhalation rising from the ground as they watered it. Though it was only spring it was already very hot weather and the water sank into the ground suddenly, leaving a dark ring around the plant which Henry can see to this day. Shortly after this Rufus caught a chill and was in bed for a few days. Henry remembers that one afternoon during their mother's absence he was sitting looking at an old French fashion magazine with illustrations of different modes worn by fair and dark beauties and imagining to which of them he should surrender his whole being, for their femininity pierced his senses with an intense ecstasy that was like a still diamond fire within the outer blazing sunshine of that hot afternoon. If in his imagination he gave himself to a languishing fair beauty immediately the image of a proud dark rival presented itself from the turned page and for her fatally cold disdain shudderingly he forswore the other; then, perhaps, another, richer, more voluptuous white and red, a fair Venus with full rounded arms and ample torso in blue or red velvet cut low on magnificent white shoulders of an Empire period would stare at him in supercilious magnificence and straightaway he was ready to cut himself into a thousand pieces and lay them before the lovely plump feet of the new beauty. […]

In the midst of this intense preoccupation he presently heard the voice of his brother calling him. Slowly recalled out of the sensual trance in which he was absorbed he reluctantly got up and went to his brother's bedroom where Rufus, sitting up in bed, was holding a magazine. Chuckling, he pointed out to Henry a picture of Wellington and underneath were the printed words: 'Wellington, the Conqueror of Napoleon.' To understand the point of this dig of Rufus's at his brother one must know that, some years before, their mother and father had given to each of their two boys an illustrated book published by Bickers & Son, Leicester Square, London; the one in green and gold, given to Henry was *The Life of Napoleon Bonaparte* by J. G. Lockhart; the other, identical in format but in red and gold, given to Rufus was *The Life of Wellington* by W. H. Maxwell. Henry still possesses both these books. [...] It is evident that the choice of the recipient for each of these books must have been determined by the boys' own expressed predilections and naturally after such a recognition by their parents of their individual taste each became an even stronger partisan than before of the hero of his choice. Henry, annoyed at being disturbed by so trivial a matter—for Napoleon and all the boxes of soldiers with which the two boys had so long and happily played were to Henry now not worth a single hairpin—grunted some disapproval and returned to his more serious preoccupation. This may have happened on a Saturday afternoon for early the following week, perhaps on the Monday even (but Henry cannot remember exactly) on his return alone from school he was met with the news that his brother was dead. It was only many years later that he thought of inquiring the cause of his brother's death and learned that the chill had suddenly developed into pneumonia.

Everything immediately after the death of Rufus is a blank in Henry's mind. The next thing that he remembers is that a visitor at the house, perhaps not a very long time after the funeral—at which Henry was informed later that he laughed hysterically but of which he does not remember a single detail—coming to pay a visit of sympathy to his mother, who had in a comparatively short time and at an early age lost her husband and her younger son, remarked to Lucy Airbubble when Henry brought in the tea-tray, having himself prepared the buttered toast and made the tea, that she was lucky to have one boy left who was so practical and thoughtful of his mother. The loss of his brother affects Henry to this day though it is now more than thirty years ago. Perhaps he would be reckoned by many to have an unusually fortunate life were he to confess that so far this is the worst thing that has ever happened to him. But so it is.

*Blow for Balloons being the First Hemisphere of the*
*History of Henry Airbubble* (1935).

# Alan Moorehead

(1910–83)

*Alan Moorehead's three books about the war in Africa were published together, titled African Trilogy, in 1944. He wrote one other significant war book, Eclipse (1945), as well as several award-winning biographies, historical narratives, travel documentaries, and two novels. This extract includes reference to another war correspondent and close friend, Alex Clifford.*

[…] as time went on Alex and I found it increasingly difficult to get back to Cairo for more than a few days at a time, for in December the British Army invaded Libya, 500 miles away. Who can tell you now about the battle of Beda Fomm? Most Englishmen have never heard of it. Yet it was the climax of the first and perhaps the most decisive British victory in the war. At Beda Fomm, just south of Benghazi, the Italian Army was finally routed and a large part of it made prisoner. The Italians never fully recovered from this defeat, and never again after this did the British enjoy such a headlong pursuit or know such immediate and over-whelming success. These were wonderful days. All our fears were swallowed up in the excitement, and as the army overran one enemy camp after another we discovered the immense joys of looting. We looted parmesan cheeses as big as cartwheels, and tins of strawberries, barrels of wine and cases of chocolate, binoculars and type-writers, ceremonial swords and Italian money galore.

We were laden with this loot one day in the hills outside Barce, in Cyrenaica, when we ran into an ambush. There were four of us travelling in a single truck—the driver, Keating, Alex and myself—and we had gone ahead of the main body of the army to join an armoured car patrol on reconnaissance. Everywhere Italian soldiers threw down their arms and surrendered as we drove on along the macadam road to the west, but we kept on, wanting to advance as far as possible by nightfall. We went on so quickly that we surprised a group of Italian sappers laying landmines on a bend of the road, and as they ran away I heard the British comman-der in the leading armoured car shout to his gunner, 'Give them a burst.' But the gun never fired. Before the man could take aim an enemy battery hidden in the scrub began shooting directly into our little line of vehicles, and tracer bullets came down the road towards us in continuous streams of bright yellow light. The Italian gunners were only a hundred yards away on a little wooded hill, and in a momen-tary pause in the firing I heard them screaming to one another.

They blew up the leading armoured car very quickly, and at the same moment our driver, a poor quiet boy from the Midlands who never had any business to be in a war, fell sideways in his seat with a terrible wound in his arm. We dragged him from the truck into a shallow ditch, and Keating ran up and down the road among the bullets trying to find a first aid dressing. Alex and I lay with the wounded man and we saw first our own truck and then all the other vehicles destroyed. A soldier went past us dragging the torso of one of his companions, and presently he too was killed. Keating came back with the dressing and lay down with us, but he was hit twice almost at once, and each time the bullets went in his body made a little convulsive jump. He began to pray. My legs at that time were covered with desert sores, and I fumbled about with my bandages, thinking to use them on the wounded man. But it was impossible to move; the Italians could see us and they went on firing. A bullet ripped through the seat of Alex's trousers, raising a little blood, but he said nothing. It was Keating who got us moving at last. We crawled inch by inch, half pushing and half pulling the wounded driver through a prickly thicket of shrubs, and whenever we showed ourselves in the open a stream of fire came down on us again. It was growing dark and the light of the burning cars grew stronger than the sun.

This was my first acquaintance with death, and I think I can remember it very well. I never thought of surrendering. I thought only: this is too cruel, they cannot realize what they are doing to us. If they were here with us they would see it and they would stop. No one, not even a hungry beast, could inflict harm like this. There could be no hatred or anger in the world which would want to hurt us so much. I thought again and again: 'I am not hit yet … I am not hit yet.' I did not pray or think of my past life or of my family; I simply wanted to get away. If I had had a gun I doubt that I would have fired it. I did not swear, except softly under my breath, until the driver cried out pitifully that he was in agony and could go no farther, and then I shouted, 'Get on you little bastard.' If I helped my companions at all it was done mechanically and without any real volition; with all my senses I longed for the darkness so that I could crawl away and hide.

We must have covered about fifty yards like this when we came to a ditch and the firing slackened. Our driver for the moment could do no more, so we laid him down on the ground. I took a little glass phial of iodine and broke it over his enormous wound. My hands were shaking so much the whole contraption fell into the blood, the broken glass as well as the iodine. When I picked up another phial Alex took it away from me and broke it in the proper way. They he bound up the boy and got him to his feet again. It was now dusk, and although the firing had ceased we thought the Italians were coming after us on foot and so we hurried through the scrub as fast as the wounded men could go. Half an hour went by, and as my mortal panic subsided I had another fear; suppose our own troops, coming up the road, took us for Italians, suppose they fired before we could speak? We began raising our voices: 'Are you there? Are any British there?' Out of the darkness at last there was an answering cry, and presently we were riding back to a dressing station aboard an Australian bren-gun carrier.

I do not think that I ever recovered from this incident. Often afterwards we were obliged to put ourselves briefly in the way of danger, but I never again did it with any confidence or even with any feeling of dedication. Whenever I went into danger I did it as a duty or because I thought that others were watching me.

*A Late Education: Episodes in a Life* (1970).

# Ruth Park

( 1922– )

*Ruth Park was born in New Zealand and came to Australia in 1942 after some experience as a journalist and editor of children's books. After she married the writer D'Arcy Niland, they formed a remarkable literary partnership, writing for their living at a time when such a course was considered financially impossible. Park became one of Australia's best-known writers of novels for adults and children and for radio. D'Arcy Niland died in 1967 after suffering from heart disease for several years.*

When my husband died I handled grief very badly. People remarked on my calm or the capable manner in which I handled the innumerable complexities that follow a sudden death. I was unlikely to embarrass or distress them by weeping or throwing myself in front of a truck, and though their desire to console was genuine, they were secretly relieved.

'You're being wonderful,' they said.

To be wonderful is to handle grief badly. And so I nearly died. In a way I did die, as one might die of shock after an amputation or a dreadful wound.

My own character and disposition made things worse for me, terribly worse. Reserve, independence, stoicism are not the qualities needed in grief. My sorrow when Mera my father died had taught me only one thing, that I could survive that sorrow. Not *how* one survived.

Our culture knows little about meeting grief head-on. It has come to be our most impregnable Tower of Babel, the very symbol of non-communication. We stand about in tears, wishing we could assuage the pain of persons dumbfounded by woe, but mostly we don't know what to say. Better to make no reference at all? Better, more tactful, to allow them to get over it in their own time?

It is all kindness, and no help. Thus, thrown entirely upon oneself in a comfortless darkness, one has the choice either of being wonderful or falling to pieces. And if you have children or others dependent upon you, you cannot afford to fall to pieces. So mourning is not done, and the tears that run down inside turn to acid that may corrode your soul for years.

I found myself in a strange country, where no one knew the way except my fellow bereaved. There was no one in those times to tell me anything. The doctor gave me tranquillisers, D'Arcy's priest friends 'religious consolation'. I looked at these genial or melancholy fellows and thought sadly that they were, as D'Arcy had said, tucked away in a pod, isolated from the bloodstained, blissful, bawdy life of what, somewhat slightingly, they called 'the world'. Had the sword of unbearable sorrow ever pierced their honest hearts?

You can't learn about bereavement; you can't teach anyone. It is like cold. You may inform a person who has never felt cold of every scientific fact—cause, consequence, attributes—but he will have no knowledge of cold until he experiences it.

So it is the fellow bereft who help. Tears were beyond me until an Italian shopkeeper, John Quattroville, who had suffered the loss of his baby daughter in a dreadful accident, took my hands and with speaking eyes gazed into my face. That was all. After that I was able to cry, but never where people could see me.

No one ever told me that the body grieves, slows down, its systems short circuit; that the immune system becomes so unstable you become a target for the so-called 'widow's syndrome'. All kinds of small illnesses occur, in a long chain of aggravation, not psychosomatic ailments but real ones. The red vanished from my hair; in three weeks I was ash blonde. My teeth began rapidly to show small specks of decay. I had so many bodily disorders that I expected any moment to hear two sharp snaps, as the arches of my feet gave way.

Today we know of the effect of extreme sorrow or shock on the hypothalamus, and how a stressed body can succumb to much graver diseases, such as cancer. But we didn't know then.

*Fishing in the Styx* (1993).

# Roger Milliss

(1934– )

*Roger Milliss spent some years as a journalist in Moscow, where he was employed as a translator on the* Moscow News. *He also worked on* Tribune *(1966–70) and was an actor and director with Sydney's New Theatre for many years. He has written for television and radio and is the author of* Waterloo Creek *(1992), a significant account of Aboriginal relations with white settlers in northern New South Wales in 1818–40.* Serpent's Tooth *describes his political and emotional development and his difficult relationship with his father, Bruce Milliss, a successful Katoomba businessman and committed communist. Valuable as social history,* Serpent's Tooth *is also informative on the history of the Communist Party of Australia from the 1930s.*

I rang them from a phone box in the Cross just before seven one Sunday evening in July. I hadn't seen them for a week or more, or spoken to them since a few days earlier when my mother told me that my father's physician had said his heart was badly overworked and urged him to go into hospital immediately for treatment. He didn't want to go, she said; he was worried that she wouldn't be able to cope at home without him. She'd spent a couple of days in bed with neuralgia and a violent toothache the dentist had at first been reluctant to touch. Nonsense, I told her brusquely, he was sick, he had to do what the doctor said: she was better now, she'd manage all right by herself. *Will I, Roger?* she said strangely. That was almost a week ago, and I had no idea what had happened since. I didn't have the phone on, so they had no way of contacting me, but somehow I assumed that everything was still all right. Anyway, I could always count on my brother coming in to let me know of anything untoward. The day before I'd been taping up at Channel Seven, with the usual delays; when the train back into town pulled in at Strathfield station I toyed for a moment with getting off and calling in to see them, just a short walk up the road, but I was running late for a performance. I'd ring tomorrow. After the show there was a party. I picked someone up, I think, and brought her home to the flat. In the morning I impatiently made her a cup of coffee and she left about eleven. I spent the rest of the day in bed with a hangover instead, getting up late in the afternoon to play squash. I meant to ring them on the way down to the courts, but I was running late again and put it off until later. On the squash court I lathered the grog out of my system, strolled home, and then finally went out to make the call. The phone rang for some time before anybody answered, and I was on the point of hanging up. Maybe they'd gone out? Strange, at their age, on that bleak night. I'd ring again tomorrow, then. Or the day after. But at last someone replied.

Instead of my father's increasingly uncertain hello or my mother's quavering tones—God, she was beginning to sound like Grandma Clampett, twenty-three years dead!—there was an unexpected voice at the other end, but one I still knew. It was Stewart, the local doctor my parents used for the everyday complaints of old age. *I've got some very bad news for you*, he said. *Is it my father*, I shouted at him, *Is it my father?* He was patient, firm, professionally sympathetic. *No, it's your mother. I'm afraid she passed away suddenly about an hour ago. A coronary. Your brother called me. I'm sorry.* ... He meant it. He was sorry. How many times *I'm afraid your mother, I have very bad news, she passed away suddenly, I'm sorry* ... I heard him say, *I think you had better come out here as soon as you can.* I got a cab at the top of William Street. Strathfield, off Parramatta Road, just past the lights. The driver reached across and swung the flag down. Bloody freezing, brass monkey weather ... Easts done the Tigers, eh? Twenty-three-seventeen, Beetson off in the second half ... I sat looking numbly out at the city. Everything was cold, clear, terrifyingly precise. The wind bit through the lonely Sabbath-black streets. A bunch of wowsers performing at the bottom of Pitt Street close to the plonk bars and the four-dollar-a-night beds, for a drunk and two sailors with their girls sending them up, accordion, banjo, tambourines and a woman handing out tracts. In the backyard of the old cottage in the mountains town Grandpa Clampett ties up the swing all day; Sunday is for God and rest and little Edie and Ernie suffocate dumbly until evening service in the Methodist Church and tea and cakes for the faithful afterwards in the adjoining hall ... At Central a girl crosses the zebra bars yellow in the swinging lights above, skirt thigh-high and more in the wind. The University, Alma Mater, *kindly mother,* best five years of my life, the new Fisher glass-and-concrete garish as a night-shift factory below Wentworth's gothic tower, never like that in my day. The good old Governor Bourke, three more middies of new and a gin-squash, luv, get that into you Pam, bloody good leg-opener, ha-ha, if I were the marrying kind, sir, chug-a-lug. Camperdown Squash Repairs. Ellinikon Farmakeion and La Napolitana in the Leichhardt ghetto. The Petersham Inn, somewhere down there to the left she was born in eighteen ninety-nine, God, the nineteenth century, how many light years ago, horse-and-buggies, Queen Victoria and the bushmen off to fight the Boers. Colonel Sanders' Kentucky Fried Chicken at the bottom of Taverner's Hill, handy to Fort Street Boys'. She went to the other Fort Street, the real Fort Street, perched high on Observatory Hill, marooned by the expressways and Caltex and the developers now, back in the days when a girl had to battle to get beyond sixth grade ... Bob Wilson's Ashfield Autos, up there the old house where they lived for twenty years, now sacrificed like everything at the black altar of progress. Arnott's Biscuits. Go Well With Shell. Where? Somewhere a heart stops beating, another poem that would never get past the first line.

The juices have dried up in me, the song is ended. She wanted to sing, she could sing like a bird, everyone said so, a beautifully modulated voice of exceptional clarity and purity the Eisteddfod judges said, the pride of Katoomba in the nineteen-twenties at every local concert for whatever cause, *Where E'er You Walk* sung by Miss Edith Clampett soprano, proceeds to the Red Cross, on VE Day in nineteen forty-five we will now hear from Missus Bruce Milliss, the kids clap madly, that's my mum up there, the wife of the local Red sings *The Empire is Marching* under the Union Jack in the Town Hall. Who cares, a voice keeps asking. *I* care, I shout defiantly, I care about it all. Any man's death, or woman's. *I shall in all my best obey you, Madam.* But only an hour ago I'd said she'd do anything, even invent an illness, to prevent me going overseas again, over to Africa, back to the hub of the world, the borders of black and white, the crucible of struggle, away from Colonel Sanders and the new Holden Monaro and the poker machines and the hire purchase and the backyard barbecue. She'd try anything, I'd told them down at the squash courts. Only an hour ago. The old emotional blackmail bit. Don't worry about us, Roger, you go away if that's what you want to do, you may not see us again, we'll be dead soon, but don't you worry. At that moment she was already dead. Good Madam, what's the matter? *What's the matter?* ... Burwood Road. Next one left, mate. Past the home units and a brace of ageing unkempt cottages and the exclusive girls' school. And round to the right, thanks. Just here'll do fine. The house was ablaze with lights: in the downstairs flat they'd taken over for themselves and only finished doing up a couple of weeks previously she was dead, after seventy years of living through a cataract of change like all of us she'd never really understood. Had they laid her out already? What happened when somebody died? I didn't know much about it, no one close to me had ever died, only Grandma Clampett when I was a kid of twelve or so and they led me bawling out of the chapel, crying for—what? For her, for myself, for all the monstrous tragi-comedy that ends up in a rosewood coffin and a Wood Coffill parlour and a few unctuous platitudes from some sanctimonious clergyman who never knew or cared what once ticked or why in the cask before him? God knows. A dollar eighty-three, mate. Thanks, keep the change. He took the two-buck note with a grunt. A knockback, another row with the missus or the girlfriend? Maybe he even guessed what it really was. My brother opened the door without a word. The old man struggled to his feet out of an armchair.

She was sitting in the corner of the settee, her favourite position, and dressed as I'd seen her so often over the years: an old neat grey woollen twinset and plain grey skirt, and thick brown winter stockings. Her hands lay in her lap, as naturally as if she'd just dozed off, as she often did, with a magazine beside her on the couch. She seemed—what was it they always said about the dead?—composed, comfortable, almost at peace. Only a small white cotton handkerchief someone, Stewart presumably, had discreetly placed over her face gave some clue of what had happened. It was the first corpse I'd ever seen. I sat beside her and took her hands in mine. Already death had set in, her fingers were like cold, hard claws, the joints grotesquely swollen by the arthritis that had plagued her for the last ten years or more. Only the last time I'd visited them, we'd gathered around the piano after dinner as we used to twenty, thirty years ago in the mountains town and her voice had cracked on the high notes and her fingers stumbled over the keys, and she cried *I can't sing, Roger, I can't play, I just can't do it any more!* and she pounded the useless, wretched stumps down on the keyboard in a dumb cacophony of protest at life and age and at encroaching death while the tears poured down her cheeks. Sitting there now, I tried to rub some life back into those twisted talons, to bring her back for long enough to say I'm sorry, please forgive me, I didn't really hate you, I loved you, I came out of you, you gave me life, you gave me everything you could, I want you to know I'm grateful, that it wasn't wasted and that the love that life is all about was there and please, please forgive me. Bless me, mother, bless me. I wanted to take her in my arms, to lay my head on the big shapeless breasts, to stroke those thin, dry grey-and-white wisps of hair straggling down above her forehead, to pluck the handkerchief away from her face and speak the few words of tenderness and love I'd never been able to bring myself to utter, to hear her say in response *It's all right, I understand, please don't blame yourself, it's not your fault, you have nothing to ask forgiveness for.* But I do, I do. The old man stood staring vacantly at us. I wanted to say to her, there, you see, it *was* all worthwhile, you have so much to be proud of, you stood by him, with him, while he fought and battled for what he believed to be good and right, you were his pillar, his rock for forty years and he loved you, we all loved you for what you were and what you did. But I choked on the lie, I knew his enormous shadow was both her fortress and her prison, that his very achievements only served to underline the starkness of her failure, that what she was she did not want to be and what she'd done had never been enough, that the love she longed for in return for the flood of affection she tried to pour on us had never been forthcoming, and that deep inside her was a bitter spring of pain and fury at the unfulfilment of her life which only the day-by-day minutiae of home and family she sank herself in stopped from welling up and over till she pounded the piano keys and cried *I can't play, Rog, I can't sing, I just can't do it any more!* And I knew it was this I hated her for and that because I knew but never could accept that it was time and circumstance and the mountains town and the Methodist Church and the genteel pretensions of her parents that had made her what she was I hated myself and it was this I wanted her to shrive me of. So I just sat there mutely keening, blindly kneading the cold hard claws of an old inert dead woman with a handkerchief over her face, waiting for a benediction and an absolution that would never come. I looked up at the old man. He hadn't moved, his eyes still dazed with sheer incomprehension. I got up and went over to him, put my arms on his shoulders and suddenly he pulled me to him. *Rog, Rog,* he sobbed, and his big body shuddered as the grief ebbed through him. I led him to a chair and knelt beside him while he cried like a child. My brother stood quietly, almost lugubriously by the door. *A very great shock,* he said, *a very sad blow to all of us,* so gravely and sincerely I couldn't believe he really meant it. I wanted to scream, Is that all you can say, you bastard, is that all you can say? She was our mother, she bore us and brought us up and was proud of us and wanted us to love her and we never really did, and we are her sons and all you can say is *a very great shock, a sad blow to us all?* He stood there stolid in his blue corduroy jacket and slacks, the art teacher turned university administrator, the thick glasses hiding the shy self-conscious eyes, the dull black hair showing flecks of grey now in his fortieth year, and I saw his diffidence concealed a sensitivity that I would never know, that suddenly came tumbling out in the rush of colour of his landscapes. For all my passions and presumptions, he was the one with the real compassion. I shouted my emotions from the rooftops, proclaimed my deep involvement in mankind, but to me the word *humanity* was ultimately an abstraction. To him it was not even a word but a simple everyday fact. While I eschewed my parents he stood by them, in their times of crisis he supported them, as their idiosyncrasies increased with age he accepted them with almost a resigned detachment. He could see them as they were, I could see them only as I wanted them to be. When I heaped my supercilious scorn on my mother for her petty failings, for the narrowness of her vision and the emptiness of her existence, or when I assailed my father for the absurdity of his new political dogmas, my brother would say, *Look, don't you see, they're old, and they're going to get older, you've got to understand that, you've just got to make allowances for it.* But I couldn't. Yet he was right, it was obvious to him, it was obvious to anyone but me, and now it was too late. And here I was on my knees beside the old man, wallowing in a mire of grief that was really self-pity and self-guilt and standing there by the door he could see so clearly the simple fact that they were two elderly people one of whom had died two hours before and that maybe the other would shortly follow suit. *A very great shock, a sad blow.* He was right.

*Serpent's Tooth* (1984).

# Robert Dessaix

## (1944– )

*Robert Dessaix was adopted as a baby and brought up in Sydney. He lectured in Russian literature and language at the University of New South Wales and the Australian National University for almost twenty years. He later worked in Sydney in the theatre and at the ABC. In 1989 he moved to Melbourne, where he has become well known for his literary journalism and as a radio producer and presenter. He has co-edited two anthologies of Australian writing and written an earlier autobiography,* A Mother's Disgrace *(1994).*

[...] perhaps I should begin even further back still, before the idea of coming to Europe entered my head. Perhaps I should begin with the Annunciation (in a way, that's how I've come to think of it). It must be the effect of staring in recent days at all those delicate Italian dreams of a stricken, queasy-looking Virgin, in a pink or mauvish Gothic Nazareth, taking in the news. 'And ... she was troubled at his saying, and cast in her mind what manner of salutation this should be'. As well she might. But down swoops a dove on a shaft of light to comfort her. And the Archangel Gabriel, like a gaudy courtier, with his red and green feathers, on a mission to his master's mistress, raises a finger (or sometimes two) as if to admonish her for her fear and says, eyes downcast, as demure as she is: 'Thou hast found favour with God. And, behold, thou shalt conceive in thy womb. ...' Fra Angelico's is the best by far to my eye—so sumptuously grave, so graceful and enclosed, so ridden with elegant anxiety. His Gabriel's wings are a disappointing brown, that's the only thing. There was nothing gaudy about my Gabriel: he was Chinese and wore a neatly pressed shirt and an immaculate blazer. Nor were his tidings a blessing. Nor did a dove glide down towards me on a golden beam—more a dry-mouthed raven with little yellow eyes on a bolt of black lightning. It was a shock.

I remember how once, at night over Thailand, one engine on our plane burst into flame with a bang. There was dead silence in the cabin. And in the space of two seconds everything around me was seared into my memory: the hiss of the air-vent, the crumbs on my sweater, the sentence I was reading when the window lit up with flame: 'In Port Moresby overnight there were two more reports ...' It was a bit like that when my Gabriel spoke to me. I was hearing his words, his five-word fiat, but I was seeing his fine Chinese skin and reading the red label on a small brown bottle: KEEP OUT OF REACH OF CHILDREN.

It was a complete bolt from the blue. I had just thought I'd see what they had to say. It had been an ordinary Melbourne morning in September—a bit showery, a pot of tea, toast and honey, nothing special. (Again, all those museum Virgins leap to mind unbidden: there they are, just sitting around, a fat little book in their laps, nothing much going on, and then suddenly this. 'But how shall this be,' they murmur, a look of pinched suspicion on their faces, 'seeing I know not a man?')

No point in my murmuring *'virum non cognosco'*, of course. The first few seconds were like an ecstasy, a rapture, so pure I almost wasn't there. I'm writing this down because it's a moment our friends don't speak of, our writers don't write about. Characters in books, our husbands, neighbours, aunts, float in from the wings already knowing, already changed. It's a moment of such solitude, such nakedness, so utterly unlike any other, that we tend to look away from it politely as from an obscenity. If it is obscene it's because it leaves us shamelessly stripped of our learnt humanity, as animal, as instinctual as any monkey. Yet it's a moment that comes in the end to almost everyone.

Then I imploded. Some people probably explode at this point, bursting into tears, awash with anger and regret and fear and impotence. I can imagine, too, desperately wanting to drag time backwards just by a second or two and rerun the scene with different dialogue, now, before it's too late: 'It looks like that flu that's going around ... the wooziness, the lack of appetite. [...] Take a few days off, I'll write you out a prescription ...' Please say it again like that. Please. That did flash through my mind. But the seconds ticked on, carrying me with them. And I imploded.

Crumpling, foundering, caving in, I kept one eye on the face across from me. The face was alertly serene in a way I knew, even at a moment like that, I liked. Plummeting, I fixed my eyes on his eyes, as if he were peering down into the well I was falling further into. What was he thinking at this instant? What did he see? Something he'd seen many times before, obviously, right here in front of *Mosby's Dictionary of Medical Terms*. I found the name *Mosby* faintly irritating, I remember, and wondered if it should read *Mobsby*. He'd said what he had to say. Now I must say something, call back up to him. My throat was full of phlegm. I coughed, but said nothing. I felt disembowelled. And then the gentle questioning began and I tried to call back up to him, yet felt too crushed to speak.

There would need to be more tests, he said, to make quite sure. To make absolutely certain. Would I prefer to have them done in a couple of weeks' time when he came back from holidays? For some reason I thought I would. I briefly pictured him at Kakadu amongst the crocodiles and brolgas. I suppose that slowed my fall, but didn't really halt it, I was still sliding downwards into blackness. After only six or seven seconds I was already in another world. It looked and smelt and sounded the same as the one I'd just hurtled out of, but it meant something devastatingly different. Once some years ago in Tbilisi, Georgia, I went to see a spellbinding performance at Rezo Gabriadze's famous Marionette Theatre. In the darkened, crowded room only one thing was real: the brilliantly costumed medieval scene blazing with fire in a magical box at one end of the room. For an hour or two nothing existed for us but this jerky, many-hued dream-world. Its dimensions were our dimensions, its time our time. Suddenly the lights came on, a curtain was thrown back and there stood the grinning puppeteers, dangling their princes and wizards like corpses from their fingers. They were monstrous, grotesque, like fairytale giants. We shrank back in our seats, gasping in alarm and wonder—and then laughed at ourselves, of course, and shuffled and blew our noses and fitted ourselves back into our bodies. But I've never forgotten that instantaneous destruction of a way of seeing, the nauseating jolt, the feeling of foolishness, the spectacle of garish lifelessness where, only the blink of an eye before, there had been, not plaster of Paris but *presences*. Well, that's how I felt now. Is anything of what I was feeling coming across?

There had been the *memento mori* with Basil, of course, that day just a week or two before when I'd come home from work and knelt to pat him (he was in the sphinx position bassets favour, at Peter's feet) and Peter had looked down from the computer screen and said: 'Your dog's not very lively today.' Indeed not—he was dead, although we refused to take it in for a few minutes and talked about other things—Japan, I seem to remember—as if the time had not yet come to face the truth. Then I stroked his soft head, smoothing back the folds of skin I'd always loved playing with, and his eyes opened and they were dead. Helpless tenderness and grief. And when it grew dark, Peter went out and buried him in the vegetable patch behind the house, sobbing bitterly. I couldn't remember whether I'd said goodbye now from the door into the garden—'Bye bye, Bas,' it was just something I used to call out to him as I left each day. In the larger scheme of things you know it's of no consequence—in fact, death had come kindly, with no pain or fuss—but still you feel wounded and bereft. And reminded.

I thought then that for Peter there was a strength, even a comfort, in being able to say as he said to me later that evening, 'Basil isn't.'

Basil's dead eyes came back to stare at me in those first few seconds, not menacingly but as if to say, 'This is what he means.' After a while I remember saying something about not wanting to go through it all—I'd seen the slow decay and wasting away, as many of us have, watched the face become a skull and the mind go haywire and worse—and at that moment I opened my mouth and said I thought I might try to find a way to avoid all that, there was no point. At that moment, you see, I thought you had to choose between fighting and giving in, I had no idea there was another way.

It was odd walking out past people reading magazines, talking on the telephone, rummaging in their bags and peeling Mars bars as if nothing had happened. What struck me was that they all thought they were *going* somewhere, they were all *facing the front*. Don't you ever think, when you see a bus go by, with all those people sitting up in it facing the front, their hair combed, their tickets in their pockets, their shoes chosen to match their coats, that *they think they're going somewhere?* And that it's ludicrous? I expect you either do or you don't. I do.

I walked down to the car where Peter was waiting behind the wheel. I didn't want the moment ever to arrive, but kept walking towards it, of course. I could see him through the windscreen as I got closer, reading the paper. In just a few seconds I would have to wrench him out of that life he was sitting in. In some sort of way— and I don't mean to sound overly dramatic, but finding the right words is difficult—I was about to make him sad forever.

I've felt uneasy about white cars ever since, just faintly, deep below the surface. White cars and that moment are intertwined. I opened the door, got in and reached for the seat-belt. Other cars and trucks were streaming by and, in the sudden sunlight, the wet street was garish and noisy. 'Well, what did he say?' Peter asked, folding the newspaper and throwing it over onto the back seat. I scarcely hesitated. 'He says I've got it,' I said, using words that had only ever belonged to other people, out there, never us. 'He says he has to do more tests, but he's sure. I feel he's sure.'

There was—well, you can imagine—a long silence. Cars swished by in the glare, a bike or two. Someone laughed abruptly somewhere just behind us. And then, without any practice, Peter said the most marvellous two things—no squeeze of the hand, no kiss, no banal sympathy, not even 'I'm so sorry'. Much better than that he gently said—and it's given me immeasurable strength: 'Well, first of all, I'll stay beside you all the way. And the other thing is that I'll be alright.'

I blinked a bit wetly and felt a wonderful lightening. I took a deep breath. *I'll be alright.* That wasn't what you were supposed to say at all, not first off. But it was just right. Then we wheeled around and went home, teetering between saying nothing and saying everything we'd never said. At home I got sicker and it was a bit of a nightmare, especially with the dog dead. Hellish, really. You don't want to know about all that, I'm sure, not right now. Besides, it's all been said before in a thousand different ways.

*Night Letters: A Journey Through Switzerland and Italy* (1996).

# 9

---

## LOVE

# Henry Handel Richardson

## (1870–1946)

*Henry Handel Richardson (Ethel Florence Lindesay Robertson) was born in Melbourne and educated there at the Presbyterian Ladies College. She drew on her experiences at the school for her novel,* The Getting of Wisdom *(1910), as she drew on her parents' lives for her trilogy,* The Fortunes of Richard Mahony *(1930). This extract from her autobiography reveals the emotional background to her novel,* Maurice Guest *(1908). Grace is the sister of Jack Stretch, and Lil is Richardson's sister, Lillian.*

When we first lived in Maldon our Vicar was a very old man, considered by many of his congregation to be long past his duties. This feeling growing he retired soon after, and his place was taken by his son, till then curate at a fashionable church in Brighton. His father escorted him round the township, introducing him; but of the visit they paid us I remember only the two top-hats, then a droll sight up-country, that stood beside their chairs. It was not till the following Sunday that I had a real look at the newcomer—if look it could be called. Afterwards, an aunt who was staying with us let slip that he had asked who the brown-eyed little girl was, who listened so intently to his sermon.—Listened? I hadn't heard a word he said. My eyes had merely been feasting on a beauty of line and feature the like of which they had never seen—and, incidentally, were never to see in a man again. Nor can this be put down to a child's over-heated imagination. When he was studying theology in Durham, the neighbours used to gather at their windows to get a glimpse at him as he went out, strangers stand stockstill in the street to stare at him. In Brighton, rumour credited him with leaving behind a 'trail of broken hearts.' Yes, Jack Stretch was famed for his good looks. Small wonder that a child so susceptible to personal beauty should share the general infatuation. What was remarkable was its power of endurance. For this proved no short-lived fancy, of the here today and gone tomorrow kind. It overshadowed my whole girlhood; and I had still not succeeded in stamping it out when I left Australia, some six years afterwards.

The man and his actions I recall well enough. The face that worked all this havoc is now less easy to fix. I only know that the features were classic and exquisitely modelled, but redeemed from severity by a pair of laughing, dark-blue eyes, and a fascinatingly cleft chin. In a day of beards and moustaches, to be ascetically clean-shaven was a mark of distinction; and a tonsure-shaped thinning of the hair added a further exotic touch. He was also tall and slender. And merely to see this apparition, decked in coloured hood and bands, sweep up the aisle from vestry to lectern set one tingling.

The service that followed had its own excitements. For, under him, we made an abrupt swing-over from Low Church to High. Now, the altar was gay with flowers and candles, we intoned instead of gabbling, learnt to bend our heads at the name of Jesus, and to do honour to Mary the Virgin. Fasts and Festivals were scrupulously observed. On Good Friday, for instance, services went on all day long, following the Stations of the Cross, he clad in his black cassock, the altar draped in purple and bare of every flower. Brought thus home to one, religion lost its paperiness and became a real, live thing; while the colours, music, fragrance that embellished it were manna to my hungry senses. I threw myself into it with such abandon that, to this day, I cannot hear the well-known words, the familiar hymns, without a flicker of the old emotion.

Genuinely devout as he was in matters of faith and ritual—and his sincerity never came in question—out of church he was the least strait-laced of parsons. Gay, kindly, tolerant, and unconventional to a degree. For one thing he was seldom to be seen in correct clerical garb. In hot weather he went about in a white duck coat, on his head a shapeless straw hat, his feet thrust into a pair of old carpet slippers. But the whole family was like this. The two tall handsome sisters who kept house for him were as careless as he of appearances. They would scurry into church at the last moment, with their hair half-down or a placket-hole gaping. And their housekeeping was on the same level. The rooms were permanently untidy, the meals scrappy and irregular, all three being quite indifferent to food. And to comfort, too. The furnishing of the parsonage dated back to early days, and had never been renewed. Not having been born to luxuries, however, they didn't miss them. And as they were both devoted to their brother and gladly made do on his small stipend, a happier family it would have been hard to find.

Second only to 'Jack's' ministry came his passion for horses. There was nothing he didn't know about horses and little he couldn't do with them. Himself he drove a beautiful chestnut, easily the finest horse in the place. He was inordinately proud of it, and lost no chance of putting it through its paces. I have heard him fixing the details of a trotting-match on his way down the aisle, before he had shed his vestments.

How and why a man of this type came to enter the church I only learnt later—from Grace, the younger sister, who in time became my intimate friend. He had begun, it seemed, as a student of law at Trinity, and, if report spoke true, as one of the wildest. Even then he was notorious for his feats as a driver: stories ran of his prankishly setting horse *and* buggy at wire fences and other such obstacles. But chance, or fate, led him to attend a meeting addressed by Bishop Moorhouse, who was visiting Australia; and so deeply stirred was he by what he heard that he there and then made up his mind to throw up law for the church. To see him ordained had long been his mother's wish; and she was said to have died happy because of it. All I feel qualified to say is that the law was the poorer for his loss. He was a brilliant speaker, and at the bar his eloquence would have made its mark. It was certainly wasted on a country parish.

In Maldon he was mostly to be seen flying about in his light, two-wheeled buggy. We, Lil and I, often sat beside him. For he liked company on his drives, and was very fond of children, sometimes packing as many as four of us, counting himself, into a vehicle built for two. In this way I got to know a variety of outlying places—and some queer spots, too, including a leper's hut, at which he, the unfortunate's one white visitor, called from time to time with food and, I believe, other less mentionable comforts. It stood right out in the bush, encircled by scrub; but that didn't deter him, who could find a way and wheedle his horse through almost anything. I remember once being driven up a hill so thickly strewn with boulders that it would have been hard to pick one's steps on foot, he legerly guiding 'Fireworks' with his left hand.

It was on these drives, to which I looked forward through many a dull schoolterm, that I fed my dream passion—for this laughing devotee, this ascetic daredevil. It had little else to feed on. Some hours of idolatry in church, certain immodest lingerings in the porch after service, in hope of a look or a word, scattered encounters in the streets of the township. The times I was actually singled out for notice by him were but three. One came from my having been left in charge of the horse for a few minutes and Fireworks, instantly aware of the change of hand, taking it into his head to bolt, with three of us. It was the general opinion that, had I dropped the reins, we should all have been killed. For on his dash for home the creature chose the steep sides of a dam, and at one time the buggy must have hung almost perpendicular. Over this affair I was made much of; though, as a matter of fact, I had clung to the reins simply because I had nothing else to hold on to, it just hadn't occurred to me to let them go. So much for my so-called bravery.

The second incident was to me much more memorable. It occurred at one of Maldon's mixed parties, made up of both young and old. He was sitting out as usual among the elders, when somebody dared him to show that he had not forgotten how to dance. He accepted the challenge, and catching sight of me, who could be trusted not to be far away, asked if I would take him on, adding a merry 'Don't laugh if I tumble down!' And so there fell to me a bliss such as not even my dreams had soared to: I danced with him, was held in his arms. On this particular evening I wore over my white frock a little scarlet embroidered Indian wrap of Mother's, in which I rather fancied myself; and on the way home, with a group of others, I deliberately fished for his notice. As a rule I was rather shy and still with him.— The next day I overheard the same indiscreet aunt repeating to Mother somebody's remark that, had I been just a little older ... But I wasn't, was only fourteen, and all the wishing in the world wouldn't help.

The third memory has to do with the night before he went to Melbourne to be married. For of course he married, a woman of his own age and a stranger; and within a couple of years he was gone from Maldon for good and all.

On this night a few of his intimate friends were invited to the parsonage. After supper, some of us younger ones stretched ourselves out on the steps leading up to the verandah, he among us. He was in his duck coat, I in a white dress, and Grace, looking down on us from above, said casually: 'In the moonlight Jack and E. look as if they were one.' The words were like a fresh dagger-thrust at my bleeding heart. I winced, and may have made an impulsive movement to draw back; for here he took my hand and held it, and went on holding it, patting and stroking it. Why he did this only he knew. But the remembrance of it, the one ghost of a caress that ever passed between us, sustained me through many a bleak and empty month to come.

Once he had left Maldon I never saw him again. And for news of him had to depend on stray scraps of gossip picked up from others' talk. But I could not forget him, his image refused to fade; and any chance mention of his name was enough to set my heart throbbing.—Partly from a fear of what might be coming next; for such comments as I heard were seldom cheering. There were rumours of ill-health and discouragement, of a failure of energy and a lack of advancement, all sad tales to one who had known him in his prime. I shrank from verifying them.

When however the time came to leave Australia I felt that I could not go without seeing him once more. And on the Sunday before we sailed I got up very early, ostensibly for a last stroll, and trudged over to his church in outlying Fitzroy, to attend Communion. Only to find that, for this very Sunday, he had 'exchanged pulpits' with a vicar in our immediate neighbourhood. It seemed as if, in everything to do with him, fate was determined to defeat me. I could have wept with rage and bitterness; and the mood in which I went up to take the sacrament may be imagined.

Now when, in after life, I looked back on this youthful infatuation, the one thing I complimented myself on was that I had had the strength to conceal my feelings. Nobody had known or even suspected what I was going through. Or so I believed for a matter of twenty years. But during the first world war Grace—by then the wife of Dr, afterwards Sir Henry Maudsley—came to stay with me in Dorset; and as we sat over the fire in the evening we revived our memories of Maldon and its many associations. Jack's name naturally came up, and a fond, sisterly sidelight was shed on the affair of his marriage and all that had resulted from it.—At present he held a Bishopric in New South Wales; and I had long acknowledged fate's wisdom in baulking my young desires. As the wife of a Bishop I should indeed have been a misfit.

In the course of our talk, however, Grace dropped the casual remark: 'Of course it was you, E., Jack really admired.' And this was more than I had bargained for. Its effect was to bring my age-old defences of time and oblivion toppling down. In a flash I was back in the old days, the old surroundings, a prey to the old misery. Again I tossed in a hot, crumpled bed, my little heart swollen with an ache that was much too big for it; again I paced round the dam staring into its muddy yellow depths and wondering if they were deep enough to drown in; mocked at everywhere alike by the merciless southern moonlight. What wouldn't I *then* have given to know what was now so casually asserted. Even his marriage would have lost some of its sting.—Under the uprush of these supposedly extinct feelings I sat confused and silent. And when Grace went on to disconcert me still further by adding: 'You cared for him, too, I think didn't you?' all I could get out was a weak and mumbled 'Yes'.—I have often laughed at myself since for my inability to come into the open. After close on the third of a lifetime, and with a friend like Grace! What I ought to have said was: '*Cared?* I would have lain down for him to walk on!'

Another half-dozen years elapsed before I again had occasion to unearth this hoary episode. By then I was at work on the *Trilogy*, and living entirely in Mahony's world. But I had come to a part that stuck me: try as I would, I couldn't get it to move. I felt cross and tired and generally disgruntled. And one day I vented my irritation by flinging out: 'I don't know I'm sure how I ever came to write *Maurice Guest*—a poor ignorant little colonial like me!'

My husband glanced up from his writing-table, and said in his wise, quiet way: 'But emotionally very experienced.'

At the moment I rather blinked the idea, being unprepared for it, then went away to my own room to think it over. And the more I thought the more I saw how true it was—though, till now, the connexion had never occurred to me. That is to say, I had written *Maurice* quite unaware of what I was drawing on. Later events had naturally had a certain share in his story. But his most flagrant emotions—his dreams, hopes and fears, his jealousy and despair, his sufferings under rejection and desertion—could all be traced back to my own unhappy experience. No wonder the book had come easy to write. I had just to magnify and re-dress the old pangs.—But the light thrown by my husband's words did not stop there. It cleared up other knots and tangles in my life, which at the time of their happening had seemed stupidly purposeless. Now I began to sense a meaning in these to see them as threads in a general pattern. And gradually the conviction deepened that, to a writer, experience was the only thing that really mattered. Hard and bitter as it might seem, it was to be welcomed rather than shrunk from, reckoned as a gain not a loss.

*Myself When Young* (1948).

# *Stella Bowen*

## (1895–1947)

*Stella Bowen was born in Adelaide and studied art with Margaret Preston before leaving for England in 1914. She lived with Ford Madox Ford for nine years. Their daughter, Esther Julia Madox, was born in 1920. Bowen painted landscapes and portraits on commision and, in 1944, became the second female war artist to be appointed by the Australian Government.*

I don't think his [Ford's] personal relationships were important at all. They always loomed very large in his own view, but they were not intrinsically important. I don't think it matters much from whom the artist gets his nourishment, or his shelter, so long as he gets it.

In order to keep his machinery running, he requires to exercise his sentimental talents from time to time upon a new object. It keeps him young. It refreshes his ego. It restores his belief in his powers. And who shall say that this type of lubrication is too expensive for so fine a machine? Goodness knows, female devotion is always a drug on the market!

I happened to be the 'new object' at a moment when Ford needed to be given a new lease of after-the-war life. The new life was a success. For the whole nine years of its duration, we were never bored and I don't think anyone ever heard us utter an angry word. Even when we were on the brink of separating, we could still go out to dine together and have a grand argument about Lost Causes, or the Theory of the Infallibility of the Pope, or some such theme. But by that time our real relationship had become quite a different thing from what it had once been, and my education had received a big shove forward.

Four years before this, Ford had fallen in love with a very pretty and gifted young woman. He had got over it in due course, but the affair had taught me many new things. It cut the fundamental tie between himself and me, and it showed me a side of life of which I had had no previous knowledge. The girl was a really tragic person. She had written an unpublishably sordid novel of great sensitiveness and persuasiveness, but her gift for prose and her personal attractiveness were not enough to ensure her any reasonable life, for on the other side of the balance were bad health, destitution, shattered nerves, an undesirable husband, lack of nationality, and a complete absence of any desire for independence. When we met her she possessed nothing but a cardboard suit-case and the astonishing manuscript. She was down to her last three francs and she was sick.

She lived with us for many weeks whilst we tried to set her on her feet. Ford gave her invaluable help with her writing, and I tried to help her with her clothes. I was singularly slow in discovering that she and Ford were in love. We finally got her a job to 'ghost' a book for someone on the Riviera.

She had a needle-quick intelligence and a good sort of emotional honesty, but she was a doomed soul, violent and demoralised. She had neither the wish nor the capacity to tackle practical difficulties. She nearly sank our ship!

She took the lid off the world that she knew, and showed us an underworld of darkness and disorder, where officialdom, the bourgeoisie and the police were the eternal enemies and the fugitive the only hero. All the virtues, in her view, were summed up in 'being a sport', which meant being willing to take risks and show gallantry and share one's last crust; more attractive qualities, no doubt, than patience or honesty or fortitude. She regarded the law as the instrument of the 'haves' against the 'have nots' and was well acquainted with every rung of that long and dismal ladder by which the respectable citizen descends towards degradation.

It was not her fault that she knew these things, and the cynicism they engendered had an unanswerable logic in it. It taught me that the only really unbridgeable gulf in human society is between the financially solvent and the destitute. You can't have self-respect without money. You can't even have the luxury of a personality. To expect people who are destitute to be governed by any considerations whatever except money considerations is just hypocrisy. If they show any generous instincts as well, it is more than society has any right to expect.

Ford's girl was by no means without generous instincts, and her world had its own standards of *chic*. What I did not then realise was that this world, which has since found an impressive literature in the works of writers like Celine and Henry Miller, stood often for a rather feeble and egotistical kind of anarchism without any of the genuine revolutionary spirit which would seem to be the logical outcome of reflective destitution.

Life with Ford had always felt to me pretty insecure. Yet here I was cast for the role of the fortunate wife who held all the cards, and the girl for that of the poor, brave and desperate beggar who was doomed to be let down by the bourgeoisie. I learnt what a powerful weapon lies in weakness and pathos and how strong is the position of the person who has nothing to lose, and I simply hated my role! I played it, however, until the girl was restored to health and her job materialised, since we appeared to represent her last chance of survival. But it was not here that the shoe pinched most.

The obvious and banal business of remaining in love with someone who has fallen for someone else is anybody's experience and no one will deny that it hurts, or that it creates an essential change in the original relationship, however well it may afterwards appear to have been mended. And to be suddenly called upon to change one kind of relationship into another is rather like changing boats in midstream—a difficult operation, though not necessarily impossible.

To realise that there can be no such thing as 'belonging' to another person (for in the last resort you must be responsible for yourself, just as you must prepare to die alone), is surely a necessary part of an adult's education! How trite it sounds, now not worth mentioning. But what a discovery it makes!

After being quite excruciatingly unhappy for some weeks, I found on a certain day, at a certain hour, that for the first time, I was very tired—not to say bored—with personal emotions, my own no less than Ford's. This feeling recurred with greater and greater frequency, until it became perpetual.

I think that the exhilaration of falling out of love is not sufficiently extolled. The escape from the atmosphere of a stuffy room into the fresh night air, with the sky as the limit. The feeling of freedom, of integrity, of being a blissfully unimportant item in an impersonal world, whose vicissitudes are not worth a tear. The feeling of being a queen in your own right! It is a true re-birth.

The eventual waning of Ford's attachment to his girl had its distressing side. A man seldom shows to advantage when trying to get rid of a woman who has become an incubus. When Ford had disengaged himself from what he called 'this entanglement', he announced that having weathered the 'pic de tempête' nothing could ever upset us again. But of course he was wrong. The desire for freedom was already beginning to work in me, and what he really needed was another mate.

During the winter of 1926–7, and also the following winter, Ford made two visits to America, the first to lecture, and the second to straighten out a tangle with his publishers. He had a great personal success and was feted and flattered as indeed he deserved to be. For me, these periods alone in Paris served as dress-rehearsals for the time when I should be permanently alone.

After the second trip, Ford announced a sentimental attachment to an American lady whom he proposed to visit every year. He thought that our Paris ménage could go on just the same in between-whiles, but I did not. I wanted to belong to myself. I wanted to slip from under the weightiness of Ford's personality and regain my own shape.

*Drawn from Life* (1940).

# Alan Moorehead

## (1910–83)

It seems a little unfair to drag Katherine too deeply into this record—after all, I was only an incident in her life—and yet I cannot think of this period when I really began to know England without relating it to her. She haunts the scene no matter where I focus my memory, she stands there in the foreground, she is part of the view. She walks towards me at our place of rendezvous outside the Criterion brasserie in Piccadilly Circus where a hansom cab used to stand, and then we are in the foyer of the Gaiety Theatre in Aldwych where the Blackbirds of 1936 are playing, and we are riding in a bus down Fleet Street, and hanging over the wall on the embankment at Westminster, and sitting facing one another in twenty different little restaurants in Soho and Chelsea, and then we are coming back to the not-so-clean bed-sitting room in Mecklenburg Square late at night. She peels off her stockings and unhooks her belt with a quick decisive air and I feel that I am a very fine chap indeed.

She was about to marry a man to whom she was very much beholden. He was the lover who is also the father-figure. For a long time he had given himself up to her, had cherished her, had forgiven her (there was much to forgive), and he had taught her, she said, everything she knew. She on her side was devoted to him, but just for the moment she was having a last fling with me—well, perhaps fling is not quite the right word for it: what she was really doing was engaging in a little Pygmalionism of her own. Here was this eager boy from Australia who seemed to know so little about the world, not even the fact that he had a cockney accent. What fun to educate him, to be herself a teacher, just for a while, to take him to the theatres, the galleries and restaurants, and perhaps in return to feel a little of the glow of his enthusiasm. This last was a vital part of our relationship, just as it was to be later with Alex. I do not want to pose as a young innocent who went about bringing light and hope into other people's jaded lives—I was not so innocent as all that—but I do think I was able to rouse Katherine a little out of her despair.

[…] She wanted to be all things to all men and women all the time and to save nothing for herself. I suppose this made her into a bit of a tramp, and certainly she was impossible to live with since she was too gregarious to be loyal to any one person for very long. But she didn't at all look like a tramp. She had a petite, rather boyish figure, a turned-up nose, and she was very very pretty—the prettiest girl I had ever seen. I was not usually a ready giver, but just to look at her made me want to buy her flowers, and to trot around beside her and to do whatever she wanted to do. […]

I don't say that I altogether surrendered my independence—I was far too selfish for that—but she gave me a feeling of naturalness I had never had with a girl before, and I felt a little lost if she vanished, as she frequently did, for a week or two. I knew she was out with other men, but I didn't care; I wanted her back again.

We could only meet on those evenings when she found some plausible excuse to give to her fiancé and I suppose by present standards it was rather a tame affair, mostly a matter of just talking in pubs. Very occasionally we managed to get away for the weekend, and I remember one particularly happy time when we walked around Stonehenge in the snow and then came back to a warm hotel bedroom in Salisbury. Oh, the pleasure of the chintz-covered double bed and the drawn chintz curtains and nobody knowing that we were there. Just for once I had her entirely to myself, far away from her fiancé and her friends in London, and in the manner of Porphyria's lover (Browning was a great favourite of mine at that time) I might have strangled her had I loved her enough.

But to tell the truth I had no wish to marry her. By this time I had got a job with an Australian news agency in Fleet Street, but I regarded it only as a stopgap, something to tide me over till I could start travelling again, and I certainly did not want to be encumbered with a wife. Besides, there might be other girls. What I did not realize was that I was becoming much more involved than I knew, not only with Katherine, but with all the way of life to which she was introducing me. Little by little under her guidance I was beginning to change my spots and take on the camouflage and the colours of Europe. Despite myself a network of new habits was entwining itself around me, and it was not unpleasant. I began to identify myself with the events that were happening around me: I minded very much about the abdication. I was all in favour of Edward taking a morganatic wife, and I objected strongly to the sanctimonious way in which Baldwin and the Archbishop of Canterbury were manoeuvring him off the throne.

And now at last Spain started to make imperative claims. It was impossible to remain neutral. The blood rushed to the head when some arrogant bully-boy of the right asserted that Franco was simply doing his duty by putting down a lot of blood-thirsty revolutionaries in the pay of Stalin—one wanted to take him by the throat. A young Canadian friend of mine, David Holmested, came into my office one day and said he was off to join an ambulance unit on the Republican side, and I was torn with guilt when I found I could not bring myself to go with him. It was only partly cowardice that kept me back, I think. I never really wanted to fight either in this war or the world war that followed. I was a professional recorder of events, a propagandist, not a soldier. I wanted to be there, to take part in the battle, but only as an observer.

[...]

And of course I had great fun in London that winter. I moved into rather grander quarters in the Gloucester Road (bed and breakfast 35s a week), I took wine with my meals at the Rendezvous Restaurant across the street, I shared a car with a friend, and talking fiercely in the pubs was a substitute for action. It was a waiting time, a delaying for something I could not quite define, and it was only in the spring that a crisis, like some great dark bird, came winging its way towards me. Katherine announced that her marriage had been fixed for the following week.

[…] we were quite determined that we should have one final night together on the night of the eve of her wedding. It really was tremendously gay. We moved around Soho from one haunt to another, and then very late we got back to my room. She was to be married in the country at 11 o'clock on the following morning, but she had her little car and so we could safely be together till dawn, and this seemed timeless while it lasted. It was snowing quite heavily when I took her downstairs in the morning and said good-bye, and the silly girl must have driven very carelessly, for she put her car into a ditch just outside London and broke her arm. However, a doctor was found, the arm was set, and they managed to get her to the altar on time. Afterwards she set off with her husband for a three weeks' honeymoon in Switzerland.

And that presumably was that. I don't imagine that I suffered too badly; I had friends in London and at twenty-six there is a certain masochistic joy in romantic despair. But then you never could presume anything with Katherine, she simply did not act as other people do. After two weeks in Switzerland she burst in on me again.

'What's happened?'

'Nothing. Two weeks was enough, that's all.'

'Then it's broken up?'

'No. I just wanted to come back and see you.'

'You can't do this.'

'Oh yes I can.'

And of course she could. Somehow she managed it. From time to time she would reappear, we would spend a disordered night together, and then she would be off again. Had things been left to Katherine this situation might have gone on for a long time, but my nerves were not as strong as hers; I could not stand the strain. Her sudden visitations became more and more upsetting; she was irresistible but the let-down after she was gone was demoralizing, and a week or more might go by before I had a hope of seeing her again. I was sick of my job, sick of London, and sick of myself, and may even have been a little ill, if melancholia is an illness. I longed to get away to Spain and still I dared not trust myself—how would I behave at the front? Would I run away?

In the end a journalist friend named Noel Monks (how much I took his kindness for granted at the time) found a way out. His newspaper, the *Daily Express*, needed a temporary correspondent in Gibraltar, and while he knew they would engage a man on the spot if he were available, he also knew they would not go to the expense of sending a man there from England. He solved this dilemma by telling the foreign editor of the paper that he had a friend, a very promising young fellow, who by luck was just about to leave for Gibraltar. An interview with the editor was arranged, the deal was fixed—I was to be guaranteed £5 a week and minor expenses—and with Noel's help I was just able to raise the money for the third class fare by sea. Katherine was out of my life and I was on my way.

*A Late Education: Episodes in a Life* (1970).

# John Foster

(1944–94)

*John Foster was educated at Melbourne University and studied extensively in Germany and Britain. In 1971 he returned to Melbourne University to take up a position in the Department of History. His other books are* Community of Fate: Memoirs of German Jews in Melbourne *(1986) and* Victorian Picturesque: The Colonial Gardens of William Sangster *(1989).*

We were not like lovers in a novel, amazed with joy in the moment of our reunion. We had travelled too often, and too far, for that. No, it would be truer to say we were content, happy with the prospect of ordinary pleasures and a life together. And if we had known how brief this time would be, how fragile were the foundations of our contentment, we would not have arranged things any differently.

He arrived on a visitor's visa, as the GITF [Gay Immigration Task Force] had recommended. We seemed to fit so neatly into the Minister's guidelines that we didn't anticipate any problems with his application for permanent residence. The only cause for apprehension was the health tests the Department routinely administered. Would they introduce an AIDS test, either as a general policy or, still worse, targeted at high-risk applicants? There was pressure for them to move in this direction, though so far they had been deterred by concern about civil liberties or the desire to maintain the confidence of what they now described increasingly as 'the gay community'. Yet if they did introduce the test, what if he turned out to be

HIV-positive? Would they declare him a public health risk? Would they consider the care for him an unwarranted impost on the national health budget? Would they send him back to New York? And then? The sooner he submitted his application, the better.

By now the GITF people had considerable expertise in the matter of applications. They had advised on half a dozen cases and the Minister had complimented them on the exemplary documentation provided. Clearly it would be wise to follow their guidelines.

In submitting an application[,] they said, the Australian half of the committed relationship needed to show that if the permit were not granted he would suffer severe emotional hardship. But how do you talk to a bureaucracy about such things?

It seemed easier, safer, more in line with the GITF's sense of etiquette, to leave my threatened emotional stability to the representation of friends: of Susan, who had opened her house to us in Lincoln and guided us round the cold cathedral; of Jim, whom Juan always associated with the great bearded Assyrian kings in the British Museum; of Rickard, to whom I had first written about my encounter with Juan; of our neighbour, Father Jim. They composed the most supportive testimonies, saying that we had been through thick and thin, that it was costing us a fearful amount of money to maintain our trans-Pacific relationship and that I would suffer severely if the Minister didn't give us what we wanted. The combined effect of these statements was to make me sound a trifle unhinged; but Juan thought that they were perfectly correct.

There was a lot that was left unsaid. Take the question of money, for instance. There were people who wondered about that. They asked me, 'Who paid for all those fares?' And in the end, when it was all over, I was even asked, 'Who paid for the grave?' Well, of course I did. Nobody said it was a scandal, not directly. But you could tell from the way they narrowed their eyes and said 'Oh!' that they were busy making moral calculations, about Juan, and about me.

We weren't embarrassed about money, except that there was never enough. In fact, money was a subject that I had always found profoundly tedious. With the comfortable security of a tenured job and the luxury of having no dependants, I had never given it much thought. In mildly profligate reaction against the thrift of a middle-class upbringing, I spent what I had, or I gave it away, and the savings that had still mysteriously accumulated had gone to pay for that unsalaried year in Berlin. This indifference to money—or this irresponsibility—was a trait in me of which Juan entirely disapproved, and when it came to paying for those airfares and subsidising various expenses in New York, I began to see his point. It was rarely so easy as simply writing out a cheque. To raise the cash for one airfare I had to sell an antique book-case. It was an *art-nouveau* piece, but I had come to dislike its swirling lines and was happy to see it go. I had no compunction either in selling a mahogany pedestal desk. It looked magnificent but was never used because I preferred to work on the floor, so the removal of the desk was pure gain.

It was different with the icon, the Russian icon of Our Lady of Sorrows that hung over the mantelpiece. I was attached to that. But if it was necessary, as once it seemed to be, I would have sold that too.

'No,' said Juan, 'you must never sell the icon.'

'Never?'

'No,' he said, 'not even for me.'

No one could predict how long it might be before the application was processed. In the meantime Juan was not entitled to work, so that he was thrown back completely on his own resources. Sometimes, when the weather was still warm, he would cycle to St Kilda where he liked to see the palm trees, or to South Melbourne beach where he was more diverted by the bodies. In more pensive moods he walked in Royal Park, or he would turn up unexpectedly at the university for an early lunch which inevitably became a late lunch. Or he would step out, as he put it, to visit Murray, who lived in a glorified lean-to which a Maltese family had tacked on the back of their West Melbourne terrace. The approach to Murray's place was through a cobbled lane, and the longer Murray lived here, the more attenuated the lane became. Removing one bluestone pitcher after another, he transformed it into a garden, and the success of this original landscape became, in Juan's mind, the yardstick for our own. He was beginning to enjoy his patch of earth. Next summer, he said, we would grow tomatoes.

*Take Me to Paris, Johnny: A Life Accomplished in the Era of AIDS* (1993).

# 10

OCCUPATIONS AND VOCATIONS

# Alfred Deakin

## (1856–1919)

*Alfred Deakin, one of the most important figures in Australian political history, was a lawyer, teacher, and journalist before he entered politics in 1879. A prominent member of the Victorian parliament for twenty years, he was active in the federation movement in the 1890s and moved to federal parliament in 1901. He was prime minister three times (1903–04, 1905–08, and 1909–10). Deakin's other autobiographical work,* The Federal Story *(1944), describes his involvement in the federation movement.*

The gay irresponsibility with which I entered upon the contest for West Bourke was obviously very different from the gravity with which my opponent pursued his long-prepared design. A man about ten years my senior, he had with the assistance of his brothers built up a considerable business in coffee, spices and the like, and was well-known to many farmers of the district as a purchaser of their chicory. The firm had a reputation for smartness, and their opponents said for sharp practices, but all its members were young, capable and energetic. With means, some leisure and good natural capacity, Robert Harper had been able to complete what was considered a good education, to marry a daughter of the chief Presbyterian clergyman of Melbourne [Dr Cairns] and to occupy a distinguished place in the powerful Presbyterian body and in society. His country house was at Macedon and residence there had enabled him to enter into the Shire Council as a stepping stone for Parliament. He had some experience in municipal affairs and practice in public speaking, [and] many friends and hosts of acquaintances throughout the district which he knew well except in its mining portions. A man of keen intelligence, well-informed on political questions, of strong character, great persistency, marked resoluteness and untiring energy, he not unreasonably considered that he merited the seat not only by his local knowledge and services, but as superior to all his rivals in the field.

He was lacking only in one quality to which I had some claim and this was a sense of humour. When it happened during our second contest that we came to spend a night in the same hotel at Romsey and breakfasted together, he occupied most of the time with a careful contrast of our relative positions, capacities and prospects. While he admitted that I might be a clever journalist and promising but briefless barrister with some aptitude for the platform, he was convinced that it must be clear to me how much these qualifications of mine were outweighed by his fuller and longer experience in business and in municipal matters, his financial independence and social standing. I was still a juvenile theorist with unformed character and immature opinions, needing only an interval of steady application to acquire riper knowledge and thus gradually become fit to aspire to a seat in the legislature. He on the other hand was ready and qualified now, with an established position and reputation, accustomed to deal with men and things, and prepared to bear the burden of responsibility as a representative. I had everything to learn and it would be much better for me if I completed my education in a private station and at leisure instead of under pressure and as a public man, as I must if I succeeded in my candidature. Delicately but firmly he put it to me that in review of the facts I ought to recognize his right to precedence and retire in his favour. The best man ought to win and it ought not to be left to the chances of an election to pick the winner. He was the best man. My duty was plain. On the last point I was compelled to disagree with him because of party obligations. We were not the only two persons to be considered in the matter. Of course he did not ask me to resign but this was the inevitable conclusion of his argument. He left it to me dispassionately. The humour did not lie in any travesty of the facts on his part. The comparison between us was perfectly just and certainly did not underestimate my claims. He was superior in all the particulars he mentioned and I should have been the better for the period of incubation which he recommended. The fun lay in the circumstance that it was he who expounded this to me while we were rival candidates for the seat.

My equipment was certainly very insufficient. I had read largely upon abstract politics and had written a good deal upon their local application but all this was mere journalistic disquisition. Necessarily I had not had time or opportunity to test the formulas which I accepted or to study their adaptation to local circumstances. I knew nothing at first hand about either colony or constituency, had hardly ever been out of Melbourne, and was profoundly ignorant of the great industries and sources of production upon which our prosperity depended. Of the conditions of the sister colonies, our rivals and co-operators, or of the world relations which we were together building up and with whose requirements we were bound to comply, I knew nothing clearly. I probably possessed a great deal more acquaintance with first principles than most candidates but certainly knew a great deal less about practical life and affairs. I was still an overgrown lad looking at least five years older than I was, whose sporting instincts were roused by the excitement of a contest and whose love of adventure led him to regard the whole campaign as something of a picnic combined with a platform competition with my adversary and my audiences which at first amused me for its own sake. Of the machinery of an election I knew absolutely nothing, never having voted or entered a polling booth or belonged to a committee or canvassed or taken any part in such contests. Naturally I was in the hands of friends and allies. My very address was not my own, being written down by me at the offhand dictation of the Editor of the *Age*, Mr Windsor, who at once assumed the direction of that function. Needless to say I welcomed his aid, both to propitiate him and because his style was so much more nervous and vigorous than my own. Its substance was mine as it was his because at that time it expressed the policy of the paper in which we were both expounding it daily. It appeared on the Saturday morning and on the same evening I was to make my first appearance on a political platform and my first bow to the electors of West Bourke. I threw together the materials for my speech in the morning and rested in the afternoon, having somehow acquainted myself with the position of the place at which I was to speak. It was a small shire hall not seating more than 100 people and providing standing room for as many more, or perhaps 250 in all. It was packed to the doors although the notice was so short and this part of the district was then sparsely settled, the crowd being drawn partly I think because of the curiosity aroused by the first appearance of an utterly unknown young man who was described in the *Argus* as a leading article writer for the *Age*.

Although relying almost wholly upon my memory for these sketches I have looked up the *Age* report of the speech then delivered. At first beginning in an agony of nervousness, as indeed is my general experience up to the present time, but soon attaining sufficient command of myself to follow out the line of exposition determined upon, I flung myself (so to speak) at my hearers with much enthusiasm. My voice was described as pleasant, the enunciation very clear but extremely rapid, rising according to the reporters to over 200 words a minute for the greater part of my speech, and sometimes to 200–240 and even 250 words a minute when under excitement.

There was a good deal of excitement in me then, and in all audiences. At all events the reception of this, my first harangue, with its quotations from Castelar and Macaulay was most inspiriting. Ardent Liberals cheered at every pause; while in replies to interjections and answers to questions I scored, according to their thinking, off my adversaries. Practically, there were four planks in my platform: Reform of the Council, Protection, the Maintenance of the Education Act against the Catholic claims, and defence of the Land Tax. My familiarity with detail obtained in the process of writing about these enabled me to expound my views upon these topics with great readiness and fullness. The majority of those who attend public meetings are rarely seekers after novelties in the shape of ideas. They are well-content to listen to an exposition of current issues and are unduly impressed by fluency of speech and the citation of facts and figures apparently apposite to the text.

The meeting was a great success and its importance much enhanced by the presence on the platform of the Minister of Public Works, Mr Patterson, with whom I then made acquaintance for the first time. He was at this period assiduous in paying court to the *Age* and it was out of deference to the paper and because of my association with it that he attended to give me the Ministerial endorsement. The manner in which he did it was characteristic. Coming out full of zeal, attended by an old friend and political henchman, Mr Gray—a man of simple kindly straightforward disposition with whom I was afterwards more closely connected—his ardour gradually cooled as he reflected upon the possibilities of my proving a failure and the ridicule to which he might be exposed if he attended the meeting of a man whom he knew to be a perfect novice in politics, and who might for all he knew never be able to express himself articulately. Consequently he made for the nearest hotel himself and despatched Gray to reconnoitre the hall and to return with a report of the size and character of the gathering and the manner in which I was being received. Gray was back again in a few moments with the news (as given me in his own words): 'He's all right. They're cheering him like mad.' Accordingly Patterson entered, took his seat upon the platform, and at the conclusion of my remarks addressed the meeting in the slow, carefully prepared and sledge-hammer style characteristic of him. His matter was not very good and certainly not fresh but his manner was emphatic, his style forcible and his warmth infectious. His rather low-jutting forehead, stiff rebellious hair, strong cheek and jaw bones, twinkling and rather small dark eyes and powerful frame, rather stooping shoulders and heavy-footed pace all marked the weight and will of the man. They also pointed backward to his career as slaughterman and butcher. Beginning by being barely able to read and write, earning a spare living by hard physical labour, without any power of speech or knowledge of the world, he had painfully and laboriously educated himself; making his first appearance in public at penny readings until slowly and pertinaciously he made his way into notice but continued ever open to hints, ever learning and ever improving by imitation, by conversation and by enquiry until he was councillor, member, minister; and at this time becoming by sheer force of character and brain one of the leading members of the Government. Sly, tricky and untrustworthy it is true, but with a fine air of frankness; genial in personal relations; a good deal of genuine warmth of heart for his friends; great perceptive powers and a dauntless resolve to rise; his was no ordinary political aim. The most amusing and characteristic comment he made that evening was in private and to myself as we walked away. 'D— me,' said he, 'if I ever understood this blessed Plebiscite until you explained it tonight.' This from one of the authors of the Bill which proposed its adoption as a part of our Constitution! He was far from blind to the humour of his confession—but one of his strong points was that when it was safe to do so he liked telling the truth. He was strong enough for that. His consistent policy was to avail himself of every acquaintance so as to add to his own store of knowledge. At this time he did not read at all and at no time did he read more than a very few books. He was dependent largely upon journalists like the Editor of the *Age*, and afterwards Mr Willoughby of the *Argus*, for much of the matter and form of his speeches. An assiduous sucker of brains, he was able to employ the materials thus furnished to good advantage, making them his own and setting his mark upon them. His borrowings were continuous but legitimate and well-applied.

On the Monday [10 February 1879] at midday I set off on my campaign, though not having taken the precaution to look at a map my course remained a mystery to me. Leaving the railway at Keilor Road I took the coach through Melton, where two or three Liberals discussed prospects with me while we changed horses, and thence on to Bacchus Marsh where we arrived at evening. [...] My remarks were well-received and as I had taken care not to repeat much of what had been reported in the *Age* and answered many questions without hesitation and abundant self-confidence the meeting was equally successful. After this and everywhere I found that I was expected to entertain and be entertained at a friendly public house with my leading supporters and to discuss operations with them. As I was a vegetarian, a total abstainer and a non-smoker, I was not the most convivial of beings. Then again, though at this time I was a good sleeper, I was accustomed to retire early; while in the country even more than the town it was thought justifiable to prove good fellowship by drinking and discussing far into the night. Great must have been the disappointment of the many when on the plea of fatigue I retired early, though the Temperance party commenced to rally to me when my habits and practices were better known. [...] The constant discussion of public affairs of itself began to affect my mind, and so far as I could judge the addresses I delivered were improved as the contest proceeded. It was in itself an event to me to travel alone, to sleep in strange inns without friends or relations near, and much more to see for the first time rural life and manners, its hospitalities and kindnesses.

Next morning I was driven up beautiful Pentland Hills and revelled in the scenery unfolded before me, while much amused at the bucolic deliberation of those whom I encountered at our stopping places. It was a novelty to me to watch the slow assemblage of a dozen or twenty rough men who rode or drove up and were gradually shepherded into a room provided with a sleepy-looking slow-speaking chairman who introduced me, invited questions, put the vote, and then ordered in refreshments for all on his or my account. I spoke thus at Myrniong, Greendale, then driving over the mountains to Blackwood spoke there at Redhill, finishing by a drive through the darkness to a great meeting of miners at Barry's Reef, reached soon after 9 p.m., where I received a great ovation. Next day, Wednesday [12 February 1879] I was driven through endless woods to Kyneton and took the train to Gisborne, speaking there that evening and driving late at night to Riddell's Creek where I spoke on Thursday midday [13 February 1879] and at Romsey at night; launching myself after each meeting into space, going where I was told, finding someone who could show me the Hall and bring me to the active Liberals of the place, and so from strangers to strangers in an utterly unknown country, wandering in a perpetual whirl of mysterious and novel procedure. At Lancefield Road I was taken in hand by a great, fat, red-faced old warrior named Johnson, whose father had fought against the Repeal of the Corn Law and who was full of interesting stories of the old loyal Liberal party and its eventful history. At Romsey I was taken out of his hands by Kelly, a bank manager of an original type, who was Liberal in politics chiefly because the rival banker was a staunch Conservative; and by a jovial, hearty, kindly, ne'er-do-well auctioneer named Stokes who was extremely popular by reason of his wife's good qualities and his own cheery optimism and sunny good temper.

It was at the close of the Romsey meeting, which concluded auspiciously with the usual vote in my favour, that I was unexpectedly informed that Mr Woods, the Minister of Railways, had arrived with sundry officials to take a preliminary glance at the route of the railway to Lancefield for which the district had long been pleading. Of course the purpose of this sudden appearance of his was to influence votes in my favour; but as it had been devised and carried out entirely without my knowledge, though I felt some compunctions, it was with a certain degree of elation that I went across to my hotel, where he had taken up his quarters after looking in at my meeting and satisfying himself of its progress. I found him in a large room filled with a cloud of tobacco smoke and the aroma of whisky and water, his rotund form, snub nose, glistening eyes and spiky hair rendering him a rather Socrates-Silenus in appearance. He hailed me cheerfully as if an old acquaintance though I had never spoken to him or seen him before and continued his graphic and sometimes epigrammatic comments upon the questions of the day. An originally minded man, who read a good deal of serious literature, and possessed a rugged character in which the good points about balanced the bad, it was his lack of industry and self-control alone that allowed Patterson to leave him and others like him behind in the race. Egotistical, vain and dogmatic, he had a gift of phrase-making which Patterson envied and by care came to surpass, though nothing he ever coined equalled the vigour of Woods at his best or worst; as when he attacked the Sabbatarians for permitting Sunday trains merely in order that they might take 'the greasy saints to their superstition shops'. He was not sufficiently careful an administrator, though active and thoughtful and taking pride in his work, lacking ballast, tact and judgment in his dealings with officers and members. In consequence he drifted out of touch with his party and was omitted from its subsequent Ministries. At this time he was prominent but, as in this very expedition, reckless and inconsiderate even in his cunning. I did not see him again and had little speech with him.

Friday evening [14 February 1879] found me at Lancefield after making many calls upon leading farmers who insisted upon my eating and drinking in all their houses; and next morning before daylight I was on my way back to Melbourne, leaving the train at Keilor and returning through Tullamarine and Bulla without speaking, to Sunbury, where I concluded a week in which I had addressed ten meetings and travelled on my canvassing more than a couple of hundred miles. On Sunday evening [16 February 1879] I met Sir Bryan O'Loghlen at the *Age* office where he had called to learn what the prospects were of my success. On the Monday evening [17 February 1879] I spoke at Essendon and at Kensington. Tuesday the 18th February was polling day. My whole campaign had been compressed into eight days, although enough had happened in them to make them seem eighty, so great seemed the interval between the first speech and the last, and so crowded were my novel experiences between. At the preceding election Cameron had been returned at the head of the poll with 1210 votes after a close canvass of the whole district, in parts of which he was well-known and had relatives. I found that places which I had been obliged to leave practically unvisited such as Darraweit[,] Guim and Bulla gave heavy majorities against me, but heavy general returns and an overwhelming miners' vote at Barry's Reef placed me that night nearly a hundred votes ahead of my opponent. For though he surpassed Cameron and in that night's returns totalled 1287, the Liberals brought up 1384 electors to vote for me. I was member for West Bourke.

*The Crisis in Victorian Politics, 1879–1881: A Personal Retrospect* (1957).

# Mrs Arthur H. Garnsey

(DATES UNKNOWN)

*Mrs Arthur Garnsey (Ann Stafford Bird) was the daughter of Bolton Stafford Bird (1840–1924), a minister of religion, farmer, and politician. She grew up in Tasmania, which is the setting of her book,* The Romance of the Huon River *(1947). In 1922 she married an Anglican clergyman, Arthur Garnsey (1872–1944). Scarlet Pillows deals with her experiences nursing in Western Australia in the late 1890s.*

One could not be long in Coolgardie without feeling that the place was one of seething life and very great contrasts—a city in a sandy desert. Thousands of men were always hurrying about as if they were rushing to catch trains, or standing restlessly talking business, all apparently unmindful of the great heat, and their faces clearly showing the intense excitement of success, or the equally intense depression following disappointed hopes.

In the less crowded streets there were often groups of black fellows squatting under the electric light poles, playing euchre while their 'gins' begged 'bacca' from the passers-by. Black fellows and electric light poles seemed quite incongruous. The poor blacks were out of their element, and would have been much happier away by their camp fires on their own hunting grounds.

The Afghan camp settlement was on the outskirts of the town, and here sometimes a hundred camels would be loaded up with all sorts of tinned foods to be taken inland beyond the railway. The long camel train was a familiar sight, the nose of one camel tied to the tail of the other, and an Afghan walking along by the side of about every thirtieth animal.

There was no end of variety in the whole of the life, and yet such a look of dreary sameness, for over all reigned supreme the Great King Dust—a mixture of the desert sand and the mining 'dumps' stirred up and whisked together by those boisterous 'willy-willys', and thickly enveloping everything and penetrating everywhere. And, just as some animals take on the colour of the scrub in which they live, so it seemed to come naturally to the men of Coolgardie to match their clothes with the dust, and they wore chiefly khaki and assam or tussore. I must say that the miners themselves always seemed to be dressed in black, but this is hardly likely to have been the original colour—they had just 'gone black'.

The most sadly busy place of all was the hospital—a scattered collection of odd buildings with no surrounding fence. These buildings, which were the wards, were erected, as necessity demanded, on a rise to the east of the town, looking towards the well-known Golden Mile. This 'Golden Mile' stretched out as more and more mines were added, till it now reaches along most of the twelve miles between Coolgardie and Kalgoorlie.

The first hospital block was built of stone, and there were three other small stone buildings near it—the dispensary, theatre, and morgue. Then there were long corrugated iron wards built up on piles, and then a number of canvas wards. Some of these were for convalescents, and others for the isolation of various infectious diseases. A few of these were under the care of special male orderlies, and nurses were not allowed to enter them. As there were few women in the town, only one ward was set apart for them, and that was not often full.

The nurses' quarters were two rows of camps—hessian stretched over wooden framework and lined with cretonne. These rows were familiarly known as 'Rotten Row' and 'Piccadilly'. In 'Rotten Row' each camp held two beds, and had a strip of linoleum laid on the sand under each bed, and, if a bed-leg did make a hole in this and begin mining operations on its own account so that the nurse slipped off on to the sand—well, that was just one of the things one had to get used to.

The loosely-woven hessian gave us very little protection from the dust-storms, and the heat inside those camps was at times so suffocating that it was no unusual thing to throw the mattresses aside and lie on the bare wires of the spring bed, with an umbrella open over our heads, as a slight protection against the dust and sand, and a bottle of water and sponge beside us to mop our hot, dusty faces. Often, if our water dried up, the sponge had to be damped in lemonade or soda water, just to have a clean(?) face for going on duty.

The second row of camps, 'Piccadilly', was much more aristocratic. Here the camps were raised on blocks, and wooden floors! And each had three beds. But no camps had doors—there were only curtains everywhere.

The difficulties of hospital work were almost insurmountable for lack of water to cope with the intense heat and dust. Ice was brought up from Perth by rail, since the line was opened, but the only water available was the strong salt water pumped up from the mines and put through the condensers, and it was just as nasty to taste as it was costly and scarce. The hospital supply was quite inadequate, and the unfortunate patients who needed sponging and cooling suffered sadly in consequence. Lying in beds made up with grey blankets and turkey-red twill pillowcases was not soothing to poor men with high temperatures, and in despair, when the water supply ran out, nurses often tried to cool burning bodies by damping a sponge in whisky or brandy, two liquids of which Coolgardie never ran short.

In spite of all drawbacks, the men were wonderfully cheerful. There were no private wards. English aristocrats, Afghans, Italians, Australians, rough and tough miners, and Chinese, were side by side in their beds, and all did their best to be cheerful and helpful.

The supply of surgical instruments was short, and carpenters' tools, sterilized (in a sort of a way), sometimes saved the situation. An ordinary brace-and-bit was in great demand for boring holes in bones which had to be wired together. But, sad to say, in spite of all our efforts and care, the death rate was very high.

We had some delightful men attendants. The night orderly in my ward, a man in his twenties, was a very thoughtful fellow, in his way. He was always puzzling about the philosophies of life—the 'whys' and the 'wherefores'. His mind seemed full to overflowing always about midnight, when he brought me coffee and toast. Then, if the wards were quiet, he would stretch his long body flat on the stone verandah near me, and tell me all the things he was puzzling about. He said he could battle with the physical world, with what he could actually see, but the 'mind world' it was which 'floored him—that world so full of tumult in thought, and strivings, and passions, and longings'. He didn't seem upset by love in any way; said it 'hadn't hit him so far'. He was just rather abstractedly curious about its cause and effect.

We had some good talks in those midnight 'coffee' hours. He gave me lots to think about, and perhaps I helped him, too. But, really, we were both 'gropers' in philosophical reasonings.

He had a thirst for music, which seemed to be something he really needed. He said: 'Good music seems to set my soul free.' He belonged to the town 'brass band', but could rarely go to practices. He had an old flute in his camp, which often comforted him, but it could not be called by any means 'good music'.

He was reticent about his home folks, but at last he did tell me the name of the proud old English family to which he was proud to belong. He was too proud to let them know that he hadn't yet made a fortune, which he had boasted he meant to do when he came out to Australia. He asked me not to tell his right name to anyone. He was anxious that his family should never hear that he was a hospital orderly. 'That would hurt their pride too much'. It was nothing to be ashamed of. There never was a better orderly. He was tender and gentle as the best of the nurses.

He was also a fireman in the City Fire Brigade, and whenever he heard the fire-bell ring—and it rang very often, either for fires in the town or among the miners' camps—he would leave whatever he was doing at once and run off for his battered old brass helmet and crowbar. As there was no water, fire-hoses would have been useless, so all the firemen carried these crowbars and used them to push nearby houses or camps further away from the burning ones, trying to save them. After a fire my good Joe always came staggering back drunk—very drunk—because people seemed to think that they must keep firemen supplied with drinks, and there was rarely any water to mix with the whisky or rum. [...]

Another character, a really great character, was a burly Scotchman, Macdougall by name, generally known as 'Old Mac', or, by the patients, as 'Old Nick'. He had a variety of duties. One of these seemed to be to go every morning to the doorway of each ward, and in a very burly whisper say: 'Nurrse!' We all hated that sound, for it meant that we had to tell him how many graves we thought we would need by the end of the day. I objected strongly at first, and told him not to come to me. It gave me a horrible feeling like signing death warrants, and altogether did away with the idea that 'while there's life there's hope', when a man's grave was already ordered and you knew that it was out there in the heat yawning for him!

However, I had to give in. Mac won the day. He said my 'sentimentals' wouldn't hold water, even supposing there was any water, and he clearly explained to me the necessity for this premature arrangement. 'Wull, ye see, nurrse, it's this way. The Roman Catholics are fairrly easy, for their divusion is all in sand though it does drubble back as ye dig it. They Methody's we can manage weel, too: they go in clay; but it's sticky an a' that, ye ken, no aisy to warrk. But the Churrch of England, they're right on rock, an' I have to blarrst them, an' I must aye be ready. We canna keep the puir bodies waiting for burial, for Coolgardie's vurra warrum!'

We had no discussion with him; we just handed him a slip of paper. Some of the patients guessed why he came to the door and chipped at him: 'Tricked you this time, old Nick.' 'Nothing today, thank you.' 'Call again tomorrow.' Knowing he was unmarried, their favourite greeting was: 'How's your missus?'

Among all the voices that drift back to me through the years, as voices have a way of doing, I can still plainly hear that truly solid whisper, 'NURRSE!'

It hurts me to say that an entirely true picture of this wonderful mining centre must include a reference to one street on the outskirts of the town, through which I happened to walk one day, though I had not previously known of its existence. No description of this street is necessary beyond the statement that it was the street of 'Maisons Tolérées', and earned for itself the name of 'The Street of the Scarlet Stain'. The keeping of a certain number of these 'houses' was allowed by law, in spite of much pressure from public opinion. The Government hesitated to legislate about them beyond ordering frequent examinations. The question was a very diffi-cult one to solve. The scheme was considered to be a necessary evil—necessary that these unfortunate women's lives should be wrecked to satisfy men's lust!

The medical examinations did not keep a check on the awful disease which demands such heavy toll. These women were frequently in hospital, brought in by their 'bosses'—those creatures who lived by sacrificing them, and from whose iron clutch they could not escape.

A few of these unfortunates were Australians, but most were French and Japan-ese. The latter were such gentle little things, with charming ways; they should have been well cared for and protected by their men, instead of being drugged and used as they were.

One little pet of a Japanese—Oyoni—said to me: 'I not want get better, nurse. I want go sleep and no more wake up.' A few months later she did go to sleep and not wake up.

In Perth I chanced to meet one day the man she called her 'boss'. I asked him about Oyoni, and he hesitated; then told me that she was dying in Perth Hospital. I hurried along to see her. Poor little Oyoni! So wasted and so sad—just a faded flower. As I sat by her bed, I wondered how many men had helped to bring her gay young life to this dreadful end. It was an appalling revelation to me, as it would be to any girl.

She recognised me and held my hand and tried to say 'My nurse.' The nurses in this hospital did not know anything about her. To them she was just 'one of those Japs from the houses', who had to be screened off away from other decent patients. But I knew her, and to me she was a pitiful sacrifice. I was overwhelmed with bitter thoughts and feelings. When she could no longer hold my hand, I walked away with a strong desire to murder every man in the street. At any rate, I would proclaim to the world why Oyoni, that dainty, pretty little flower of Japan, had faded and died in Perth Hospital—glad to die, though quite young, having known 'life' and drugs and hated it all.

However, it was not the women only who suffered, but also their 'visitors', who frequently contracted disease. The special ward at the hospital for this kind of disease was always full, with special orderlies in attendance.

There were several cases of suicide, even among our own men friends, when they realised their hopeless condition, for the cures, now used successfully were unknown then. The kindly reason given in the inquest on these cases was always 'Insomnia'.

In 1902 an International Agreement on the operations of, and for the eradication of the White Slave Traffic was signed at Paris by nine countries, and today strenuous efforts are being made to control this dreadful evil. For humanity's sake, may those efforts by successful!

After several years of truly rampant life, a lull came over Coolgardie. 'Bailey's Reward'—the most important of all the mines—was not sending up enough payable ore, and it was decided to close down. So the noise of those batteries ceased at last. The city went to sleep. People packed up and went off somewhere else, and whenever possible they took their houses with them.

All the hospital buildings and other public buildings and offices were moved to various outback centres, where mines were working; and, sad to say, very soon there was practically nothing left of good old, bad old Coolgardie—except the sand, which, unhindered, took possession of all that was left of this 'city that had faded away'.

In those wind-swept streets, which were always crowded with thousands of men, like swarms of ants, hurrying and scurrying in all directions, just as ants do, one could now plough one's way through the loose sand in Bailey Street, and not see a soul! The only sound one's own footsteps. But to anyone who had lived there before the place was full of ghosts and dreams.

After several years of this quiet sleeping, like the 'Sleeping Beauty' life began stirring in it again. Another company took over the mine, and decided to 'give it a go', and the batteries in 1938 were roaring again, and people were gradually returning or fresh people were coming and putting up more canvas and corrugated iron houses—rebuilding, just as ants do when their hill has been kicked down. But never, never, can come back to this place again anything like

'Those days of Auld Lang Syne'.

*Scarlet Pillows: An Australian Nurse's Tales of Long Ago* (1950).

# Mary Marlowe

## (1884–1962)

*Mary Marlowe began her career as an actor, acquiring minor roles in Australia before in 1910 going to London. She achieved moderate success in Britain, the USA, and Canada. After returning to Australia in 1920 she joined the staff of the Sydney* Sun, *for which she wrote a weekly theatre column. In the 1930s she began a career in radio broadcasting, becoming an established interviewer of stage and film celebrities and a commentator on general issues. Marlowe also published several romantic novels, some of which were serialised in such magazines as the* Australian Woman's Mirror. *This extract from her autobiography deals with her experiences as an actor in Australia.*

New Zealand again and then Broken Hill. Here I was afflicted with another misdirected attack of social service. I helped a woman to run away from her husband. Broken Hill is scarcely the place for it. The area is limited and there are few places to take cover. There was, for all that, my bedroom at the hotel, and here I hid the fugitive.

Social service was working in me like yeast. Ethics were sound enough but unconventional. The husband had beaten his wife. She showed me heavy black bruises on her breasts where he had thumped her when struggling to get her salary out of her womanly pocket between them. Elsie earned more than Rupert, playing more important parts. To deceive his fellow actors on salary day, he jingled a great many loose coins in his trouser pockets. But we knew.

Why should a woman be beaten by her husband and put up with it? When Elsie fell down a rickety old stairway in the theatre, trying to run away from him, and scuttled into my dressing room, asking for help, I took her home. We both finished early in the piece and he had to stay until the end.

In the morning she was feverish and semi-conscious. I thought she would die of pneumonia or something. In Broken Hill I knew a barmaid with a golden heart. I appealed to her and she hid Elsie in her hotel—in a conscious period we got her there—and then brought a doctor. The fever condition was nerves, he said. Ice on the head and light nourishment. After a few days of this she came back to my room. Another bed was put up.

On the last two evenings, when she had to appear in a play, I policed the wings for her so she should not crash into Rupert. We scurried home as soon as possible. Every night we discussed plans for her divorce and what she would do afterwards.

We booked sleepers on the train for Adelaide. We left the hotel so as to be at the station as late as possible before the train started, but the husband was on the platform when we reached it. He stepped forward to speak to Elsie. Elsie stepped forward to speak to him. In thirty seconds they had made it up and she spent the first part of the night in the carriage in his arms. I think they had both been glad of the week's rest.

Then there was Ethel, aged seventeen. On the stage she was seductive and progressive in nakedness. Off the stage she was a chocolate-box baby. She was loved by a fellow with a brawny figure and no brains. Round about ten any morning, anybody passing Ethel's bedroom might hear her calling in infantile tones: 'Stanie! Stan-EE! Isn't Stanie coming to carwee li'le Effie to her barfee? Stan-EE!'

Ethel married Stan-EE. He had a nice mind—or none—and did the honest thing by 'Li'le Effie'. They went to America and were swallowed up in Middle West stock.

Our star, Julius Knight, was the most glamorous figure on the stage and he knew all about the technique of heroes—every variety. Combined with this, his knack of blending colour in scene or costume, his knowledge of producing and getting the best out of an artist or actor, his infallible flair for selecting the right music as prelude or accompaniment to a scene, and his resonant voice made him one of the most outstanding players who ever graced the Australian theatre. In his spare time (there wasn't much)—he knitted or made wood carvings. In both these minor crafts he also excelled. But the vision of Monsieur Beaucaire in his brocades and lace ruffles, or Napoleon in his cutaway turning a sock in the dressing room, was a rude shock.

On ships, on trains, in hotels, in dressing rooms, the men always played bridge or poker. The scene shifters played crap or nap. Somebody's rug was borrowed for a table. It covered four pairs of knees or a couple of up-ended suitcases, and served admirably.

Of all people attached to theatres the scene shifters are the best. Sometimes I stayed in the same hotels and shared their meals. Always then and now, they have been my friends.

There is nothing spectacular about the lives of the stagehands. They go on working until the job is done and, if it will make a better job, they will go on working a bit longer. They can make anything from the Eiffel Tower to the Crystal Palace, from a bunch of dewy grapes to a circular staircase to hold a hundred people. They never grumble. They are never late. They are never lazy. They always have time to do that extra something for somebody that makes the tour more comfortable. They are up with the dawn, sleep with one eye open, never ask for an alarm clock, and they often travel with the luggage—on top of it, alongside it, anywhere but under it.

It was a lovely play, *The Scarlet Pimpernel*. Julius Knight had given me the soubrette part—Sally Jellibrand. We had rehearsed it on tour. We were to open an important season in Sydney with a new leading lady, Ola Humphries. She was American cum-Swedish-French. She flitted about the stage like a willie wagtail.

First rehearsal was called in Sydney for the morning after we arrived. Before we began my old friend, the stage manager, called me into a corner. 'I hate to tell you, kid, but you're not playing Sally. The office has sent round a girl. Her father's in the Firm [J.C. Williamson's] and she has pull. Oh, don't look so tragic. I'll find a line for you in the ballroom scene and put your name on the programme.'

Several new girls were taken on for the ballroom scene. One of these was given the understudy of Sally. Another, Jean Martin, was handed the part of the ingénue to understudy. She was told to learn it quickly in case she would be called in an emergency to play it. Jean was a society girl from Adelaide, whose family fortunes had recently crashed. Exquisite of figure, Jean had poise and grace, and society had put its mark on her. She was sure of herself. At home she had many suitors.

As an extra, Jean would have been earning two pounds a week. She retained the family habit of spending lavishly, and her weekly bill for the hansom from the theatre to her society friends in Edgecliff where she was staying as a guest was thirty shillings. In our communal chorus dressing room she flaunted her understudy part.

She told me she had been promised a better one in the next play. That did not make me love her any better.

I hated Jean Martin, and all moneyed amateurs, but she took a fancy to me. She tried to be friends but I thought her immeasurably silly when she talked of her wealthy relations and associates. She found everything in the theatre funny, including us. What we thought of her did not enter her consciousness.

The Sydney season had not been going more than a week when somebody gave the company a picnic to the National Park. I did not go, being much too heartsick. The girl who was playing Sally and her understudy were both at the picnic. They were taken out in a launch on the river. The launch broke down. Word came through by telephone to the theatre that they had missed the train and could not be back in time for the start of the play.

A ring came through while I was at dinner. The stage manager told me he was coming for me in a car. I would have to play Sally that evening, and he couldn't find the spare part. Could I do it? Could I!

We ran through the lines in the car going to the theatre. The wardrobe mistress was waiting with the frock. I tore down my hair while running up the theatre lane. Somebody put a comb through it. A dry make-up was all I had time for: rouge and eyeblack. I was ready in two minutes, the orchestra having been told to keep playing the tunes over until I was.

The man whose wife I had helped to run away from him was in the wings to wish me luck. I flashed onto the stage just as the picnic party arrived at the stage door. They rushed for their lives in a car to beat the curtain, but I had the part.

As soon as we left Sydney I had it for always. After that night the parts came galloping in on me. It would be Sally Jellibrand, rising eighteen; the Countess of Something or Other, falling eighty; a serving maid with a song at the spinning wheel in *The Corsican Brothers* (the song especially written for my voice); the Widow Melnotte in *The Lady of Lyons*, and so on.

The Widow Melnotte was an anticlimax. I had played Pauline Deschaples—the Lady herself—in our dining room. And here was I playing the mere governess in *A Royal Divorce* after being a howling success as the Empress Josephine in our dining room. Now I had to stand by and hear our leading lady chuck away her points every night. It was frustrating to be a court lady, entirely silent in *The Prisoner of Zenda* after my domestic triumph in the dual roles of Princess Flavia and Antoinette de Mauban. Producers can't see a yard before their noses!

*That Fragile Hour: An Autobiography* (1990).

# Montague Grover

## (1870–1943)

*Monty Grover had an extensive career in journalism. He was foundation editor of the Sydney* Sun *(1910–16), editor of the* Sunday Sun *(1917) and its representative in London (1918–21), foundation editor of the* Sun-News Pictorial *(1922) and the* Evening Sun *(1923), magazine editor of the Melbourne* Herald *(1929–30), and first editor of the Sydney labour daily, the* World *(1931–32). He was also the author of plays and verse.*

That I ever became connected with press work is due very largely to the late editor of the *Bulletin*, J. F. Archibald. Like nearly every one of the past generation of Australian pressmen, I made my first appearance in the columns of the *Bulletin*. I forget what it was I wrote on that occasion, but I remember well receiving a letter from the editor which encouraged me to continue and persevere and forge my way ahead. That the editor of the most influential weekly in Australia should have taken the trouble to write to an unknown youth of no earthly value to his paper in those days struck me at the time as extraordinary consideration. After becoming an editor myself, I marvelled at it still more. The average editor has little time for even the courtesies of life. It is not surprising if people call him a boor. He has to be or his paper would never reach the streets. [...]

It was in 1890, I think, that I first made my appearance in the *Bulletin*. I was then serving articles to a Melbourne architect and, although both my parents had been connected with the weekly press, I had not the slightest idea of ever following journalism myself. It was my gradual development as a writer in the *Bulletin* which revealed to me that there might be pocket money in the game. I wrote more paragraphs and ventured an occasional story and verse. Many were posted but few were chosen. Still, the chosen brought sufficient to pay my expenses about town and, by the time I had come out of my articles, I was able to rely upon from fifteen shillings to a pound a week from my writings.

I emerged from my articles in the depths of Melbourne's depression of 1893, and was promptly discharged. When I started to trace the Greek orders, the office had comprised a manager, two draftsmen, a clerk, an office boy and myself. The depression had gradually stripped the office of its staff. For the final six months I was the sole survivor, and the boss decided that the business was not able to carry me a moment longer than the time specified in my articles.

I came to the conclusion that architecture and I must part—for a time at least. I knew nothing about bootmaking or delivering groceries. My knowledge of racing was confined to 'backing them', and experience had taught me that that was not sufficiently lucrative to be relied upon for a living. I had spent two years as an art student in the Melbourne National Gallery, but I had learned sufficient of art to realise that I was among the 'also rans'. Moreover, the future for the artist didn't seem any more rosy than the future for the architect. My ideas of burglary and garrotting were academic and hazy in those days and, anyhow, nobody in Melbourne had anything to steal during the depression. I turned to journalism.

Up to that time, my aspirations had been towards literature. Kipling and the bunch of wonderful short story writers which England produced in the early 1890s had just astonished the world and fired me along with the rest of the youthful Australians who dabbled in ink. This country itself had evolved a number of literary heroes whom we regarded with awe and admiration. At times, I had cherished furtive thoughts of forcing my way to fame as a story writer or a poet, but the possibility of holding any other relation to a newspaper but that of contributor never once occurred to me. [...]

Then, by the merest chance, I met a reporter. Herbert Power was one of the most capable men who ever put pen to paper. I was supremely interested when he spoke about his work. Hitherto, I had regarded reporters as a race of supermen, to whose ranks I dared not aspire. He disillusioned me. He explained that what the press wanted was not writers of superhuman ability. Anybody capable of writing a story fit for publication could write well enough to justify his billet as a reporter. What was wanted was a good all-round education, a knowledge of things going on, and common sense. His remarks made my heart bump. I had a good all-round education, a knowledge of things going on, and I was egotistical enough to believe, common sense. That night I went round to Cole's Book Arcade and bought Pitman's *Shorthand Teacher.*

At that time I was working on the survey of the northeastern Melbourne suburbs for the Metropolitan Board of Works, and when that job came to an end, I started out in real earnest on Pitman. For the first month, I put in twelve hours a day. Then I eased off and tried my hand at writing news articles. On the survey I had entered every backyard in North Carlton, North Fitzroy and Clifton Hill. I wrote my experiences in backyards and sent them to the Melbourne *Age*. They were printed. I sent another article of my art school life. That went off too.

I felt that my shorthand was now sufficiently good to take a chance. My mother, who was acquainted with David Syme, approached the great old man—for he was all that—and put in a word for me. Syme asked me to call. I went into his presence in fear and trembling, but I knew that any display of fear even in the presence of the prospective employer was not likely to recommend the displayer as a reporter. I put on as brave and confident an air as I could raise. Syme put a few questions to me. When he ascertained that I had not a university education I thought it was all up with me, and I hastened to remind him that I had already had two articles of a column and a half published in the Saturday *Age*. That settled all argument. He appeared to think that a man with the imprimatur of the *Age* on his copy had a more valuable degree than that of BA. He sent for G. F. H. Schuler, then chief of staff, later editor of the *Age*. I was introduced and Schuler was instructed to try me out with some casual work.

My first engagement, fortunately, was a football match. I turned out a first class half column. I have it by me still, and looking at it with the critical eye of age, I can say proudly that it was as good a football report as any editor could wish for.

It was just as well that I didn't get my second job first. This was a meeting of the Presbytery of Melbourne North. I went with a rather uneasy feeling. It was ten years since I had been to church or attended anything of a religious nature. As far as I can remember, the last function resembling a devotional character I had joined was a Sunday School picnic, and the reason I did so was that a certain young lady of the same age—twelve or thereabouts—had signified her intention of being present. Previous to that picnic, I had attended, or been required to attend, various churches—Anglican, Roman Catholic, Congregational, Wesleyan and one small sect which met in a hall about twelve feet square. It was, I believe, an offshoot of Plymouth Brethrenism, denounced as heretical by the parent body. I went there one luminous night to listen to a bewhiskered gentleman proving, by plans of the Pyramid of Cheops, that Queen Victoria had descended from Solomon and that we were all to be overwhelmed in a universal war. It was an impressive deliverance and kept me awake for several nights. Its memories stayed with me for years, but they were of little value in the Presbytery of Melbourne North.

I found myself suddenly in an atmosphere that was foreign as the proceedings of the Grand Lama of Tibet would be. Around me were parsons of a type I did not know existed. All the parsons I had previously encountered were mild men of peace. But the Presbytery of Melbourne North gave me something new in parsons. Every one of them was out for a fight. They spoke in strange Caledonian dialects that seemed to call for interpreters at times. Worse still Presbyterianism has a language of its own. When they appoint a parson to a church they 'moderate in a call'. They have a number of other weird phrases to describe everyday things. They did not come to blows. They never do, I found from subsequent acquaintance. But to the person who encounters them for the first time, each sentence seems likely to start violence which will end in a free fight. Every member of the Presbytery seems to suspect every other member of shocking and horrible things. He seems to hate him with the bitterness a Bulgarian feels towards a Turk.

I was new, of course; it was only their manner. The Presbyterians are just as kindly and considerate a crowd as the Anglicans or the Roman Catholics. But I thought the simulated vindictiveness real. I had enough journalistic instinct to know that if the moderator got a left hook home on the convenor, it would be good copy, but I feared my ability to do justice to the situation.

I took notes in my laboured shorthand, slip after slip, without the slightest idea of what they were talking about. I listened with the closest attention to try to gather the meaning of this strange language spoken in a stranger dialect. In vain. There was no other reporter in view, but I knew that the *Argus* could not have overlooked the meeting and I was afraid that the reporter must be taking his notes in some other part of the building.

My hand was trembling. The work of taking a verbatim note calls for wrist muscles and nerves that few possess. Even the experienced Hansard reporter often leaves the House with his hand shaking like a leaf. I worked at that Presbytery of Melbourne North till my fingers became paralysed and refused to move. I sat back, broken. My career in journalism was ended. Tomorrow I knew I would be passed out, disgraced, a failure.

Then a jaunty youth strolled down the aisle, seated himself at the table by my side, and asked casually, 'Done anything?' I tried to explain, but he cut me short. 'We don't want any of that tripe,' he said. He glanced at the notice paper of the meeting, said a few words to the clerk and started to write in longhand. When he had finished two and a half slips he scrawled his initials at the bottom and handed the slips to me. 'That's all the thing's worth', he remarked. 'It's no good our waiting here all night; there's a boshter girl at the Opera House now, I don't want to miss her turn'.

I read the two and a half slips, in which the skilled reporter who wasn't there had translated into sense the whole proceedings which were utterly unintelligible to the unskilled reporter, who wrote a paraphrase for his own paper. I had received my first lesson in practical journalism.

*Hold Page One: Memoirs of Monty Grover, Editor* (1993).

# Claude McKay

## (1878–1972)

*Claude McKay worked as a journalist in various towns in Victoria as well as in Brisbane and Sydney. With Sir James Joynton Smith and R.C. Packer, and aided by the ageing J.F. Archibald, he founded the popular newspaper,* Smith's Weekly, *and was editor or editor-in-chief in 1919–27 and 1939–50.*

How that first issue of *Smith's* ever came out has remained a mystery. Clyde Packer and Archie and I manufactured it somehow. A few friendly reporters on the dailies turned in news stories which their own papers wouldn't print but which they felt should be published. A social conscience, long stifled, had been awakening in newspapermen. We told them they could give it full play at last. We weren't interested in what then passed as important news—fires, murders, accidents.

'You don't expect to be murdered,' I would tell them, 'nor does anybody for matter of that. If there's a fire the premises are insured. And accidents are always what you read of as happening to somebody else. When, however, a man loses his job as a likely consequence he loses his home. If he's unjustly sacked, get the facts, give us the injustices! Give us not the murders of violence but cases of economic cannibalism. We want the daily lives of the people—where they live, how they live. We're interested in their affairs and so are they.'

All this sounds most commonplace now. But in 1919 it was a new note in journalism. And, what was very much to the point, it was music in the ears of Joynton Smith, on whose bank guarantee the paper was launched. In his patriotic fervour during the War Loan in which he participated so prominently he had made many promises of the way our troops would be treated on their return by a grateful country. He went far beyond governmental undertakings.

In a rather unconventional life he had come to regard his word as far more sacred than his signature. On being brought to the point of signing a document he would begin studying it to find a loophole. That he should be asked to sign anything was a reflection on his probity. To agree was to be irrevocably committed. His code was to shake hands on it. Recently I read again the first editorial in *Smith's Weekly,* which gave his views on the attitude Australians should assume following a victorious peace. The article was headed 'Why I Publish *Smith's Weekly*' and it bore Joynton Smith's name. It read:

Our men bought us anew with their blood. They made a new world, yet every day we are slipping back into the old. [...] Our promises are unfulfilled. We sanctioned the sacrifice. Let us meet our debt of honour. [...] It is for us to make democracy safe for Australia. To that end I would suggest a League of Citizens, every member pledged to a United Australia. [...] We have the freest franchise in the world. We can make Australia what we will. If we cannot make ourselves the happiest people and the world's most productive country the fault is only with ourselves.

So *Smith's*, hitched to a star, went forth as a twopenny broadsheet. The first poster was bannered 'Smith's Weekly', and instead of indicating the paper's contents it simply said: 'Buy It and See the Need for It!' There was mighty little news in its twenty-four pages, but it was charged with spirit and enthusiasm. There were warnings of what those could expect who stood in the way of light and full-statured nationhood.

Packer and I worked all through that first publication night at the insetting bench, and went to my flat at Randwick to have a bath and breakfast. We were far too excited to think of sleep, so we boarded a tram to the city. As we jolted from the first stop, Packer nudged me violently. I saw what he saw—a man, rather doubtfully, turning over the pages of *Smith's Weekly*. If ever anyone was the subject of anxious scrutiny it was he. We knew what was on every page he turned to. When he started to shake and then to laugh out loud we knew exactly where his eyes were. It was a joke of Archie's which Cecil Hartt had illustrated—little Patsy at his homework, the dead spit of his father; his mother, hands folded across her apron, gazing adoringly at her son. 'Please God,' she was saying, 'we'll make Patsy a praste.' And the husband, 'We'll make Patsy a praste, please God or not!'

Two more *Smith's Weeklys* came aboard on the tram run. They were read quietly. We saw nothing to indicate that barricades were about to be manned in the streets. We hadn't exactly started a revolution.

At our attic in Somerset House our few contributors were already there, each reading his own contribution. W. Bede Dalley, who had adopted us, affixing himself to the payroll *in loco parentis* to the Diggers, arrived before noon, *Smith's* under his arm. Patting his copy he remarked, 'John says she's a beauty!'

John, his brother, was an editorial writer on the *Bulletin*. He and another *Bulletin* staff man, 'Kodak', had written our social notes, a society burlesque credited to 'Maude de Plunke'. The Dalleys were both Oxford men, sons of William Bede Dalley, a plaque of whom in St Paul's Cathedral commemorates his part in sending the New South Wales contingent to the Sudan. Bill and John Dalley had eaten their dinners for the English Bar. Both had been in the war.

Bill's devotion to the Diggers was all embracing. He could magnify a minor grievance on their part into a national issue. One of them would come in with a minor complaint and after half an hour with Bill would be qualified for a whole chapter in Foxe's *Book of Martyrs*. When Bill wrote his story—into which he invariably introduced Dicey on the Constitution, or on the relation between Law and Public Opinion—it was a shrivelling indictment of callous government. It soon became apparent, however, that Bill was on the right track—that pensions and repatriation benefits were indeed on the scurvy side. He used the word 'cyanide' to meet this treatment. 'Cyaniding the Digger', was how he expressed it. Thus he conveyed that the victim was being deprived—by a process of extraction—of every particle of his rights. With Bill it was a declaration of wrongs. And he succeeded in being heard. There was a Federal election approaching and the soldier vote had to be reckoned with. When the parties took to the hustings Thomas Joseph Ryan jumped on to the Digger band-wagon. He acclaimed 'Billjim', so he called the Digger, as the saviour of his country, and avowed that nothing but the best was good enough for him. Archibald couldn't stomach Ryan in the role of protector of the returned soldier. He wrote that Ryan was more for 'Tomjo' than 'Billjim'. Hence, for campaigning purposes, *Smith's* always referred to Ryan as Tomjo.

I question if ever any two people, venturing into the uncharted seas of publishing, excited more prophecies of early disaster for their undertaking than did Packer and myself. Our first print of 40,000 was a 'sell out'. 'Curiosity sale' was the verdict of the prophets of doom. 'Truth in trousers' was another opinion given of *Smith's*. One of our early contributors was Frank Davison, father of Dalby. He came in after the sixth issue to tell me he made a collection of short-lived papers.

'I started to keep yours,' he confided, then, with a note of disappointment in his voice, added, 'but the damned thing will live.'

I knew that vicissitudes were in store. The first edition warned me that nothing would be taken by everyone as a joke. There was trouble in Ireland, and the politics of that most distressful country were imported here. We had been boycotted by the Irish Self-Determination League. Our drawing on making Patsy a priest brought down upon us the charge of raising the sectarian issue! A leaflet calling on all who had the true cause of Ireland at heart to boycott *Smith's Weekly* was widely distributed. We really had nothing to do with it; all the same, our second issue sold much better on account of the boycott. The Irish, being congenitally curious, wanted to read what *Smith's* was saying about them. As Packer remarked, 'Now if we could get a few more boycotts we'd be home on the bit.'

*This is the Life: The Autobiography of a Newspaperman* (1961).

# Lloyd Rees

(1895–1988)

*Lloyd Rees, one of Australia's best-known artists, worked in Brisbane and Sydney before making his first visit to Europe in 1923. From the 1940s he won numerous prizes and held frequent exhibitions. His light-filled paintings reflect his love of diverse regions and cities, including Paris and Chartres, Tuscany, the south coast of New South Wales, Sydney Harbour, the Bathurst region, central Australia, Tasmania, and early Canberra. He wrote two volumes of autobiography,* The Small Treasures of a Lifetime *(1969) and* Peaks and Valleys *(1985). In the extract below Rees's memory of St Paul's Cathedral was stimulated by his 1923 painting of the church.*

When I visited cities, the city itself and the architecture were always my first interests. (Of course, when I went to France and Italy I saw a lot of sculpture.) In London I wanted to see St Paul's. I had never seen a building of its size. There was nothing in Australia remotely approaching 400 feet in height. Wakelin was over in London and was there with his wife to meet the train when I arrived. The next day I went into London in a rather pearly, misty fog. You could see along Fleet Street towards Ludgate Hill. I looked up at a certain angle into the sky; I thought I should see the dome of St Paul's because I could see lots of other buildings through the mist. I was puzzled. Then I must have lifted my head; at about double the height up, I saw this great dome looming through the morning, misty air. It never looked so tremendous again—a wonderful thing.

It wasn't long before I went into St Paul's with my sketch block and started to draw. Very politely I was touched on the shoulder and a man said to me (a custodian), 'Have you a permit?' I said 'No'. 'Well you have to go in a certain office in Whitehall and write forms and get a permit'. I was later to find out that you couldn't even sketch in St James's Park without a permit. It was a war ruling that had not been rescinded. I received my permit and I was right: I could go back and draw St Paul's.

And I drew there. It was getting cold, coming on winter. I don't know if that was the motivation but I thought, I'd love to do a painting in here. And you know I had the cheek to go in there with my easel and set it up inside the main entrance, looking right down the nave to the dome. Now it was the dome that entranced me because in those days it was never devoid of blue haze. The fog could not get out of it and the sun would come through. The architecture was there, and the dome was silhouetted against the main arch of the nave, you see. It was so paintable. There was no great detail—you just got this misty blue, the firm shape of the arch and tonality of the architecture leading to it. I set up my easel there—not a big canvas, about 2 feet by 18 inches or so (Judge Edwards, a noted judge, later bought it)— and I proceeded to paint. Really the head custodian Mr Tanner should have complained, because of the danger of paint stains on their beautiful marble floor. Not a bit of it; I became accepted and I spent days and days there. I'd been trying to work in a room in Kensington—so cold—where the gas heater ate up bob pieces or two bobs that I couldn't afford. So there was another attraction. St Paul's was warm, beautifully warm. The huge windows had a unique quality: the building was never dark inside however dense the fog was outside, and apparently even through the fog that great window would bring in enough light in which to paint. But always the dome itself—I never saw the top of it and somehow I'm glad I never did. (After the clean-up in London, the last time I saw the dome, I saw some not-very-impressive, very, very faded paintings right up there.)

I'll never forget that man Tanner. One of my first mornings there he said, 'You don't need to cart all that material in the bus and then bring it back. Bring it to my office.' I worked on until the spring-time and tourists would come in and they used to flock around me. Tanner came out one day, saw the situation and said, 'We can't have that'. Those great buildings have a sort of fencing system of barriers that they can put down for royal occasions and such. Well every morning Mr Tanner would solemnly fence me in, so that the tourists had to look at me as though they were looking at royalty.

I look back and I have a marvellous sense of British understanding and courtesy. When the Lord Mayor's show was on, I was there in a box-seat at St Paul's—I could almost have touched the golden coach. But that was Tanner.

However, at a time when I was really blocking the way inside the entrance, there was a very pale-looking man—Dean Inge, notorious then as a great pessimist, and a great influence on English thinking—who passed me a couple of times in the morning and then came and said: 'Are you aware that you are working when there's a service on?' I replied (politely), 'Well, Sir, if I had to stop for every service I'd get nothing done', and 'Furthermore, I've got a permit to do it'. He said, 'Well if that is so, I won't notice you, I won't see you again'. He had me scared. Every morning his ghostly (he was ghastly white) big features used to go past me; I could feel his resentment. Anyway, I painted a couple of pictures of the aisle [...] and the main one with the dome which has never been traced. I was under this big window looking down the cathedral aisle after having painted the main nave, and one grey morning I looked across the cathedral to the balancing window and I saw it as a subject. I saw the aisle, the pews, and the great window with silhouetted buildings outside the window in the haze. That was a subject— very formal, but still a subject. And I thought: but it wants a relief, it wants a figure.

And what should happen, but this grim-faced man came along. He used to kneel and pray, and I remember the first morning he did it I said to myself 'I can't do anything about that'. Then I found that he came every day (this painting took me several mornings to complete). I said to myself, 'It's his habit; I'm going to paint him'. And I put him in, praying—this dark figure—and it did relieve the formality of the painting. Mr Tanner came along, looked at this picture and said, 'No mistaking who that is', and he walked off. Then I heard footsteps coming from the distant end: flop, flop, flop—I recognised them. I said to myself 'That's him'. And then he came. I was aware of him coming straight up and standing behind me. And I was, I admit, transfixed. I wondered what he was going to say, and then it came! 'Oh Sir, thank you, Sir. Thank you'—it was pathetic. And he went away and he recognised me every morning after that.

I asked Tanner about him; I said I thought he was the great Dean of the church. 'No', he said, 'He only sits in a box selling tickets for the Dome'. I used to be aware of a hacking cough resounding through that building and then I realised it was his. I spoke to Mr Tanner about it and he said, 'Yes, he shouldn't be here. He says, if he took a day off, he'd die'. I went down to Cornwall for a couple of weeks, and I came back and resumed painting, and there was no cough. I asked Tanner and he said, 'He took a day off, and he and his daughter went to the railway station and they sat down and he died'. It's a little thing that I can never forget. However there it was, that great building and the memories associated with it.

*Lloyd Rees: An Artist Remembers* (1987).

# Graham Richardson

## (1949– )

*Graham Richardson is an influential member of the Australian Labor Party and was a member of the Senate in 1983–94. He held several ministerial portfolios between 1987 and 1994, including health, social security, and transport and communication.*

Having seen a bit of party warfare first hand, in 1968 I was elected as a delegate to the Barton Federal Electorate Council, the party body dealing with federal affairs in the Barton electorate. It was here I learned another important lesson. In the Barton branch I moved what I thought was an obvious motion, condemning the 1968 Russian invasion of Czechoslovakia, confidently expecting it to be carried unanimously. Here it was that whatever shred of political innocence I still possessed disappeared forever. A Scotsman named Harry Wilson boldly informed us in his heavy brogue that Russian intervention had been necessary to prevent 'CIA infiltration'. His only evidence for this assertion was Dubcek's decision to allow the sale of *Time* magazine in Prague.

This was the first time I had heard mass murder defended, and however I thought such a defence might be mounted I had never contemplated anything like this. I was appalled to see this disgraceful effort compounded as the loyal comrades rushed to defend the legitimacy of the invasion. The uglier side of Australian communism, which had supported Stalin through tens of millions of murders, obviously had its share of supporters in the Labor Party. The Left was shockingly hardline in those days. Then and there I decided not simply to be a right-wing member of the ALP, but to become a tough and active one. My anti-communist resolution was eventually carried, but I had seen firsthand the tyranny of the Left which my father had fought all his life.

In 1970, I made one friendship that was to prove pivotal in climbing Labor's ladder of success, which I had now firmly decided to do. To climb such a ladder, you first have to know where it is, and there was no one better to point the way than Laurie Brereton. I met him in about mid 1970, and he impressed the hell out of me. It was in the old Randwick Labor Club, which was a real dump—I think they have pulled it down now. I was there with a bunch of students and in he walked, a young man in a magnificent suede coat. I'd never seen anything like Laurie. And in the year I met him, he was elected to the State Parliament, at twenty-three the youngest MP in New South Wales history.

This was the first time we had met, though we'd come across each other a couple of years before, when Laurie challenged my right to vote at the 1968 Young Labor elections. This apparently happened because I was suspected of having uttered friendly phrases in the direction of Frank Walker, and Laurie, who was pretty hardline Right, had never heard of my branch. In those days, Young Labor Council ballots were held in a dingy basement in Sydney's dingiest building, the Sydney Trades Hall. Laurie's intervention caused me to vote for Left candidates in some positions—the only time in my life I have been guilty of so heinous a crime. For the next few years Laurie and I did not cross paths and when I was finally introduced to him by Garry Johnston, then secretary of Young Labor, Laurie had forgotten our inauspicious first meeting.

Laurie knew everyone: unless you do, your capacity to go nowhere is greatly enhanced. Not only did he know everyone, but they listened to him. And because Laurie and I became firm friends, very slowly doors began to open. At the ALP office I met Kerry Sibraa, the office's liaison man with Young Labor, and even

Geoff Cahill the assistant party secretary in New South Wales. This was all pretty heady stuff.

I have never been politically ambitious and I certainly wasn't in 1970. Like so many of my colleagues who will appear later in this book, I was a political addict. If I couldn't get enough politics any other way, I'm sure I'd have injected it. So meeting the right people in the Labor Party was not part of a brilliant strategy carefully constructed by a youthful political genius. I wanted to meet them because everything they did fascinated me and I could get another fix of the stuff that was beginning to give my rather indolent life some purpose. And, while most people who attain positions of power may be reluctant to say so in these terms, the prospect of people deferring to me one day—in the way they deferred to the 'right people' I was beginning to meet—was pretty attractive.

*Whatever It Takes* (1994).

# 11

THINKERS, QUESTERS, AND STIRRERS

# Alexander Harris

## (1805–74)

*Alexander Harris was born in London and came to Australia in 1825 after deserting from the Guards. He worked at numerous occupations and underwent a religious conversion before returning to England in 1840. He published his first book,* Settlers and Convicts *(1847), under the pseudonym 'An Emigrant Mechanic' and followed it with an autobiographical account of his religious conversion,* Testimony to the Truth *(1848), and a fictional work,* The Emigrant Family *(1849). He died in Canada after becoming an American citizen. Harris's identity proved elusive for many years but was finally resolved by his grandson, Grant Carr Harris, then living in Canada. The extract below describes some of Harris's experiences and reflections while working as a sawyer.*

[T]here was nothing to prompt me, without religion as I then was, to exertion. I had conned the tale of the illustrious dead till I had ended in the reflection, What profit have they of all they knew, of all they did, now? The true evil with me was my scepticism of a God and a futurity. I had weighed *this* world well; I had measured it exactly. No conclusions about it, as the theatre of a mere material existence, could be more sound than mine were.

My error lay in the feeling so long paramount in my mind—whatever we may do, it will be all the same a hundred years hence. It is very true that my intellectual judgment was reforming on this great question; but not so, to any extent, the sentimental part of my mind. The feelings, the moral character, the will, are never, even to the day of our death, fully subordinate to logic. In early life, he is fortunate who can guide himself even in one-half that he does by the dictates of his reason. For my own part, rapid and conclusive as was my argumentation of these subjects, I must confess that my practice of what I reasoned out was most dilatory and discreditable.

The occupation I had adopted I found on the whole agreeable enough. I soon learned to work at it well. It was certainly, and especially at first, very laborious, but it invested me with an excellent appetite and general health. I slept, as the boys say, like a top. And it seemed as if I had found in it a sort of Briarean prerogative of gaining in strength just in proportion to the length and arduousness of the toil.

I recollect one evening, after supper, extending myself on a broad plank, which we had for a sort of rude settie at the door, watching the setting sun, repeating to myself that beautiful passage:

Slow sinks, more lovely ere its race be run,
Along Morea's hills the setting sun.

Probably I got half way through the canto before weariness and drowsiness overpowered me. The old couple had retired. Presently I slept. Presently also, it seemed, I awoke. I rose and turned into the hut, thinking to go to bed. At the instant, my mate reappeared from his chamber.

'You are before me, this morning,' he said.

I had slept all night, without moving a limb, till within a few minutes of sunrise. The clemency and loveliness of that climate may be partially comprehended when I add that I had on neither hat, nor coat, nor vest. My blood was unchilled; nor had the night air left a moisture on my garments.

In course of time I went to other parts of the country to work, sometimes with only a solitary comrade, working for a settler's farm buildings in woods many miles away from all other company; sometimes joining great camps of sawyers lumbering for Sydney timber merchants; now having an agreeable mate, now a bad-tempered one. It was the latter inconvenience that eventually produced in me an insuperable prejudice against the occupation.

There was, however, another particular of this mode of life which, from time to time, and always increasingly, biassed me against it—the vile habit of drinking universally prevalent among members of the craft. They have a saying among themselves that 'they earn their money like horses and spend it like asses.' And, verily, never was truth truer. At the lumbering stations there was always rum kept for sale. It was a very advantageous way of paying wages. Work was usually over for the week about noon on Saturday. The men who could not drive their way through a good week's work by that time, from when they commenced, were set down as no sawyers, though there was often a very startling inroad on the first part of the week made by the weekly 'spree'. That began on Saturday afternoon and lasted, often, all that night, all Sunday, and all Monday. Sometimes it was not over till Tuesday evening.

If at this period of my life I had not already come to feel a pretty strong aversion to great excess in drinking, I must have sunk ruined forever. But it happened that I had got well on in my upward flight. A few glasses—disgust—cessation—that was the usual course with me. Of the men I was associated with at that time, though full half of them were younger than myself, I suppose that there is not above one in ten alive now; and, certainly, of those deceased, one half, if not as much as three-fifths, were entirely the victims of liquor.

It will easily be seen that such a life, continued for a number of years, must gradually, surely, thoroughly throw thought to desuetude and obliterate sentiment. The customary forms of my mental being disappeared. If I thought at all, it was about the present and the visible; if I experienced any emotions, they were the ordinary and very reasonable results of common sense and passing events. I have long since learned to look upon this interregnum of the mind as one of the most important and valuable sections of my existence.

There was one subject, meantime, that was not by any means allowed to get into the category of oblivion. It was kept before me with a closeness and persistence which compelled attention. I know not where a more hopeless scholar to be made to comprehend the imminency of that hour which awaits all men, could have been sought for than I was. Yet I was made to comprehend it, and so comprehend it that it became at length the main object of my thoughts. From time to time I had such narrow escapes from *sudden* death—they were so numerous, they were so invariably reiterated when I began to forget their great lesson—as to leave me no alternative in the exercise of a strenuous and impartial common sense, aside from considering them the deliberate, purposeful acts of God. [...]

On one occasion I had let one of my mates work on the top of the log for a few days, and I worked in the pit. It was a pit dug in the ground, transoms across and our log on the transoms. We were cutting a piece of timber that weighed about three tons. The iron dogs had to be taken out to shift one of the transoms. The proper way is to put in a spare, or, as it is called, trap transom, whilst the regular one is being shifted. Otherwise the pitman's life would often be lost through the timber slipping off the point of the lever used temporarily to sustain it whilst the operation is being made. On this occasion I was hurrying forward to put in the trap transom when my mate prematurely knocked out the iron dogs; one of the halves of the log got off the back transom, and, being then nearly upright, breasted out the front one and fell into the pit just in front of me, almost brushing my face. One step further, one second more, and I should have been under it. Its weight was about a ton and a half.

Another time, I stood watching two men felling a large tree, till I got lost in a reverie and forgot where I was. They were not aware of my absence of mind, cut their tree through, and gave me not the slightest warning. Down it came, and when it was at an angle of about forty-five degrees, and not before, I saw my danger. When I observed it first, it was directly over my head, and the whole extent of its heavy limbs coming straight down on me. My movements, of course, were pretty speedy. I escaped; but the topmost branches actually touched my back as the ponderous mass thundered down on the earth behind me.

Again: I had risen early one summer morning and, having a newspaper in the hut, took a chair and sat down beside the hut, but opposite the door, to read. My feet were bare, and I had them on the front rail of the chair, the newspaper held with both hands in front of me. Hearing a noise at my feet, and thinking it was a little dog we had, I put down my feet to the ground without ceasing to read, and then, slowly bending forward, put down one hand. The dog not jumping up to my hand, I began to wonder why he did not, and removed the newspaper from before my face. There, between my bare feet, not four inches from either of them, coiled in circles, above which was elevated his head, the mouth wide open, the fork tongue quivering, sat a black snake, one of the most venomous species in the colony, and one of the largest in size I ever saw. He was about six feet in length.

In such circumstances I never feel any nervousness, though among the most nervous of human beings at other times. I knew instantly the exact course I must take. I looked at him fixedly as he looked at me, wondering all the time that he did not strike at my hand, which had got to within six inches or less of his open mouth. I drew back my hand very slowly, and he did not appear aware I was doing so, but was evidently uneasy under my steady, unflinching gaze.

We continued thus half a minute or more, the swaying motion he kept up with his head becoming feebler all the time At length, I began to have a feeling that he had had enough of my acquaintance and would be glad to get away. I turned my head so as to look back over my shoulder. Not a moment was past before I heard the odious rustling of his vile, scaly skin as he trailed himself out of the door. I followed with the shovel, caught him as he was half-way through a fence, and destroyed him. If he had bitten me, I might possibly have lived twelve hours. […] I see nothing strange in hairbreadth escapes occurring to me, any more than any other wanderer of land or sea. We all know that the lives of the backwoodsman and the mariner are full of such events. But I flatter myself that there would have been something very strange indeed in my overlooking the fact of its being quite possible—and, more, quite probable—that, sometime or other, there would arrive one which would not terminate so harmlessly.

I was not in the practice of casting out of my speculations on future events the most accredited doctrines which the experience of our race had furnished. In such a matter it needed no prompter to give me the generic axiom of the case: 'The pitcher that goeth oft to the well is broken at last.' I was likewise quite aware, that in a certain book, which, however, I had not expended much time on for many years, it was declared, 'He that being often reproved, hardeneth his neck, shall suddenly be cut off; and that without remedy.' *If* there was a God; *if* the Bible was His law, then most assuredly this was the part of it which I had most peculiarly to consider at this time.

Here were the warnings plain enough, and often enough; and about my taking very little 'reproof' from them—of that also there could be very little doubt. I was quite satisfied that one of my favorite notions—the simple materiality of the universe, the occurrence of all things by chance, the creatorship of 'the fortuitous concatenation of atoms' was an error, a very stupid one and a very perilous one. Possibly, also, my neglect to recognize a God might be another error. *Possibly* there might be a God. Certainly my not believing in Him would not unmake Him, if He existed. By stolid obstinacy I might make a fool of myself, but not make Him a nonentity.

It was a case which presented a sound demand on my attention, and I began to give it freely. My judgment was convinced that I ought to look fairly into the question and come to a rational conclusion about it.

'Religio Christi' (1858), reprinted in *The Secrets of Alexander Harris* (1961).

# Havelock Ellis

## (1859–1939)

*Havelock Ellis, the well-known British psychologist whose ideas on sex were both controversial and influential, spent four years teaching in Australia (1875–79). A year of that time was spent at a small school at Sparkes Creek, in the depths of the bush near Scone, New South Wales. It was a formative year for his intellectual and emotional development, if largely bereft of human contact. His novel, Kanga Creek, centres on his experiences at Sparkes Creek. He also describes the impact of this period on his life in his autobiography,* My Life *(1940), from which the extract below is taken.*

In a few days I was peacefully settled in my schoolhouse. The material basis of my new existence was swiftly established. It was, indeed, the easier by virtue of that vein of asceticism—sometimes, perhaps, a more Esthetic asceticism—which the life at Sparkes Creek doubtless confirmed in my disposition. Under the ordinary conditions of civilised life it might have remained for ever latent. My natural timidity with regard to taking the initiative in material matters, so altogether unrelated to my attitude in spiritual affairs, would probably have always held me back. But for my everlasting good fortune I was flung into the wide sea of Australian bush alone, to sink or to swim. Naturally I swam.

It was not a long list of simple material requirements that I made out, and I engaged one of the Barwick brothers for the day to go into Scone and obtain them for me from the Chinese dealer in everything there, one Charles Trogg. The Chinaman was equal to all my demands, and throughout my stay at Sparkes Creek

I never had occasion to buy anything from anyone else at Scone. For the rest, my bread and milk supplied from the household whence I had been ejected and brought every morning by one of the daughters, my pupil, a gentle silent girl who also sometimes brought me a present from her mother of a peach pie or the like dish. I had meat sometimes from one. Thus was settled, very easily and quickly settled, the physical basis of my life.

On this basis soon began the routine of my professional duties. That also was established with as little trouble as the physical mechanism of board and shelter. It was, indeed, the only phase of my uncongenial career as a school teacher that I controlled without effort, almost without thought. The instruction was of the most elementary kind, and its nature and methods were at every stage prescribed by the Council of Education. There was nothing left for me but to follow the simple routine in which I had been trained at Fort Street. The children, moreover, gave me no trouble. The girls, who were perhaps in the majority, were faultless. My predecessor told me he had some difficulty with the biggest ones; but I had none, nor ever have had in dealing with girls; it was with the boys I was apt to fail.

My walk over the hills several times a week brought fresh, delicious insights into Nature, such as now came to me for almost the first time in life. The fauna of this region was new and strange, more abundant than I had elsewhere seen. Round Carcoar I had chiefly observed snakes of various kinds, and many birds, including flocks of cockatoos, and families of parakeets. Here there were few snakes (the snake I chiefly recall, long and tawny, lived, I believe, beneath my verandah, for I once saw him lying on it) and not many birds. But there were many creatures of other kinds, huge jew lizards that lay motionless along branches of trees, and native bears, that moved away slowly, very slowly, if I approached them, and, above all, there were great kangaroos, that I was never able to approach, though I gazed at them with fascinated and admiring eyes as they would descend the hill slopes in large slow gracious bounds. It is one of the most beautiful modes of progression in Nature, and no one has seen a kangaroo who has only seen a captive kangaroo. The picture has always lingered in my memory with an intimate and peculiar charm. Of late I have wondered whether that charm may not lie in a resemblance of my own mental mode of progression to the slow deliberate curves of those resilient bounds which seemed to me so gracious and so appealing. Like the kangaroo, too, it may be that I live among a population of jew lizards and native bears who find my movements more fearsome or more impressive than they seem to myself. It was possibly Shelley who first helped me to inspire the exhilarating air which stimulated such a mode of intellectual movement. But Shelley was a poet and soared over men's heads. I am not a poet but a dreamer who is also a naturalist and a realist, and like the kangaroo, however vast the bounds I delight in, I can only achieve them by planting my feet firmly on the solid earth. A critic of my earliest book, *The New Spirit*, disparagingly said that its chief characteristic was a calm and matter-of-fact way of making daring revolutionary statements; I had never myself noted this, but the remark seemed to me acute. Now, when I look back, I am pleased to imagine a significance in the intimate appeal to me of those large silent bounds, so serene and so daring, of the kangaroo.

On the days when I went to my other school—two days of one week and three days of the next, for my time had to be divided equally between them—after I had had my breakfast of porridge and perhaps placed a saucepan containing meat and rice over the smouldering wood-fire in the hope it might be done (it was sometimes burnt) when I returned in the evening, and put in my pockets some biscuits and a flask of tea for lunch, I started on my walk across the range of hills which separated me from Junction Creek. The aspects of Nature were my only source of interest, beyond my own thoughts for there was no human dwelling within sight all the way, and I cannot recall ever having met a single person during all my year's walks. Yet it was a varied and delightful walk of which I never grew tired, and while I was often absorbed in my thoughts I was also always alive to the visions of beauty that were spread before my gaze. [...] In my hut I was almost beneath the shadow of another hill, indeed, a real mountain, which imparted no such pleasing emotions; gloomy and menacing, at night it seemed to be pressing and crushing me down, and I may perhaps trace to it the repulsion I feel towards mountains. [...] As I sat at my table on stormy evenings all my nerves were stirred by the prolonged rhythmic curves of gathered-up winds that rolled and tumbled and crashed through the trees among the hills like an ocean let loose. And once, on my return in the evening from Junction Creek, as I approached my hut and saw the blossoming roses that climbed the verandah posts, with their crimson splashes on the green background, a thrill of rapture went through me, and I saw roses as I had never seen them before, as I shall never see them again.

When in the morning I rose from my primitive couch and stood on my verandah—'en pissant vers les cieux,' as Rimbaud expresses it—the sense of Sabbath peace, the contact of the pure sunny air, would fill me with exhilaration. It was an admirable climate, seldom too hot or cold. I could not have led a more healthy life, and I had probably never before been so well. [...] At the same time my spiritual discontent and my emotional cravings attained a degree of calm I had not before known. Religious depression, such as I had sometimes experienced at Carcoar, had already left me at Grafton. But here at Sparkes Creek I was also comparatively free from definite emotional cravings. I was not within sight of any woman who could arouse the impulse of desire, and the memory of May Chapman was fading into a beautiful dream. Certainly I would feel at times the craving for love and the sense of my own unfitness to arouse it. I was, it seemed to me, so unattractive a person; I would sometimes look into the window-pane which served me as looking glass and wonder what sweet gracious woman, such as I desired, could ever love the image that met my sight. [...]

The craving for love was for me, at Sparkes Creek, so far as I consciously knew, an ideal need. When I took my bucket to the Barwicks' well, to obtain drinking water purer than the creek yielded, and hoisted up cool bright liquid, the lines of Swinburne I had lately learnt to know would come deliciously into my mind:

> Nothing is better, I well think,
> Than love; the hidden well water
> Is not so delicate to drink.

I had brought over Swinburne's *Songs Before Sunrise* from England and read it on the voyage with enjoyment. More recently I had picked up the first series of *Poems and Ballads* at Skinner's second-hand bookshop. [...] At Sparkes Creek I revelled for a time in *Poems and Ballads* more than in any other book, for its magnificent exuberance, its imaginative extravagance, seemed the adequate expression of my expanding self, and as I paced up and down my little patch of enclosed ground I would shout aloud the stanzas of 'The Masque of Bersabe.' The splendour of Swinburne's cerebral excitation at that time sufficed, as never later, to express my youthful desires.

Of physical desire I was as yet scarcely aware in any definite way except during sleep. That physical efflorescence of sex had begun with me early and often, as I have already told, at first usually without dreams, and it worried me because of the traces left behind. In time I understood what these manifestations meant and accepted them, methodically noting their occurrences in my pocket diary.

I endeavoured so far as possible to avoid anything likely to evoke them when asleep, and never, by any physical or mental procedure, sought consciously to produce them when awake. They had occurred indeed so frequently asleep that there was not much temptation to produce them when awake. But at Sparkes Creek, where my life, far from any kind of sexual stimulation, was simple and healthy and regular, these nocturnal eruptions probably ceased to give complete relief. At all events it was at Sparkes Creek that for the first time in my life I experienced the orgasm when awake. I was lying down on my simple bed, one warm pleasant day, reading something which evidently had in it for me some touch of erotic stimulation—I believe it was the *Dames Galantes* of Brantôme—and suddenly I became aware that the agreeable emotion aroused by the book, without any will or any action of my own, was becoming physically translated and fulfilled. I realised what had happened and felt no alarm; evidently there was nothing in the occurrence that was not natural and beautiful, though it was of course easy to imagine circumstances under which it would have been yet more natural and beautiful. It was not until after this event that I ever became definitely conscious of any stirring of physical excitement at the thought or the proximity of an attractive woman.

In this year of my solitary life, as never before or since, there was an immense thirst deep down in my youthful soul, a thirst of my whole being, though scarcely at all of my physical sex nature, for the revelation, in body and spirit, of a divinely glorious woman. My demand was large. There was no one anywhere who corresponded to it, who even more than faintly suggested it, not even among the women who had so far attracted me. And even if there had been, I should have felt myself completely unworthy of a boon so great that it would in my eyes at some moments have outweighed the whole world in the balance. I disdained the women who were within reach; the women I desired, hopelessly, it seemed, were women I had never seen or known. How inconceivable a miracle that life was indeed to bring me close to some of the noblest women in the world! [...] Whatever powers of love and tenderness I have acquired, whatever aptitude for delight in the bodies and souls of women, was all generated in those days of solitude.

Yet, I am well aware, the desire of love, the physical manifestations of sex, were both alike only rare interludes in my active and sunny life at Sparkes Creek. They were sufficiently acute, at all events the thirst for love, to represent in memory vivid moments of my life, but those moments were few. My desire for knowledge, if less acute, was more massive than my desire for love, and it was omnipresent. Moreover, it was a desire within my power to gratify. So I gratified it, freely and copiously, by means of books, books of all kinds, in English and French and German and Latin: poems, novels, theology, religion, subjects of almost every class, science, strange as it must seem, occupying the smallest place, if, indeed, any place at all, but in that phase I was eager to grasp the whole rather than the parts; it was synthesis I was drawn to rather than analysis. Though I bought every book I wanted, my books were selected carefully and deliberately. My mind was ranging freely, everywhere with a new power to grasp what it seized and to revel in its acquisitions. I had acquired the power of seeing the world freshly, and seeing it directly, with my own eyes, not through the dulling or disturbing medium of tradition and convention.

'My Life: The Australian Chapter' (1940), reprinted in<br>
Kanga Creek: Havelock Ellis in Australia (1989).

# Bessie Lee

(1860–1950)

*Bessie Lee was drawn into the temperance movement in 1883 and helped to pioneer the Woman's Christian Temperance Union (WCTU). After she made public her unconventional ideas on sex within marriage, she became alienated from the organisation and left its executive. Sponsored by the Victorian Alliance for the Suppression of the Liquor Traffic (1890–96), she travelled throughout the colony promoting the closure or reduction of hotels. As well as making speeches and taking pledges, she wrote for newspapers and the temperance press. When her husband, Harrison Lee, a railway worker, died in 1908, Bessie married Andrew Cowie, an affluent New Zealand farmer. In New Zealand she resumed office in the WCTU and was appointed a world missionary. After Cowie's death she finally settled in Pasadena, California, and conducted her last campaign in 1947. The narration of her autobiography shifts unpredictably between first and third persons.*

At the Convention of the WCTU many of the ladies objected to the advanced views put forward by Mrs Lee in these articles, and pleaded with her to utterly abjure such astounding theories. But she took her stand on the sentiment expressed so ably by Herbert Spencer, 'Whoever hesitates to utter that which he thinks the highest truth, lest it should be too much in advance of the time, must remember that while he is a descendant of the past, he is a parent of the future, and that his thoughts are as children born to him, which he may not carelessly let die.' She could not lightly take up such a solemn matter, nor lightly lay it aside; she believed that God had called her to do a work others shrunk from, and though her own nature recoiled from dabbling in dirt, she could not be one of God's good housekeepers and allow the dirt to remain. The broom and pan must be used to clear as much of it away as possible, even if so great a dust were raised in the process, that many would see only that, and not the cleansing that would follow. It was no wonder that some of the women condemned unsparingly this work for purity. They could not be blamed, for Mrs Lee's views to them were truly startling.

'You are injuring your own usefulness, Mrs Lee, by such advanced writings,' said one excited lady. (The writer winced, but bowed gravely.) 'Give up such a work, and keep to the Temperance Cause alone.'

'If I were to give up a work God has called me to, in deference to your wishes, you would be one of the first to despise me,' she answered, 'and I should feel for ever a coward cringing to the fear or favour of those I love. No, I will never give up the work till God tells me to. When He speaks, there will be no need for anyone else to say a word.'

'Mrs Lee was born a century before her time,' was the Hon. James Cambell's verdict, very kindly given.

'Well then,' she retorted, 'God needed me just 100 years before the world did, and I am willing to live, and work and suffer just when and where He wills.'

'You are bringing discredit on the whole union,' said one lady bitterly.

This was more than loyal flesh and blood could stand. While willing to suffer any opprobrium herself, she was jealous of the good name and fame of the WCTU, and eager for the progress of the whole Temperance Cause. To be a hindrance to the work so dear to her soul, was not to be allowed, so after many a sleepless night and troubled day a way out of the difficulty presented itself.

Only those who knew how very dear to her the Temperance Cause had grown could have any idea of what it cost to send to the WCTU Executive her resignation of the various offices with which they had honoured her. It was like cutting herself off from a glorious work, and from the comradeship of the noblest women she had ever known. It appeared to her as though her career had suddenly ended, when just begun, that henceforth she would be a woman with a life spoiled, by what many would call a 'fad', a 'caprice', and yet between God and her own heart at this time, was such a oneness, that she could trust even the shattered hopes, the disappointed longings, the crushed desires entirely to Him, knowing that the life apparently spoiled by perversity was still clay for the potter, and even if she never again appeared on a public platform to fight for a sober nation and an uplifted humanity, He yet could make of her some use somewhere in His great work of Redemption. The resignation was accepted by women who really loved her, but who honestly believed that she was mistaken and wayward in the work she was doing. [...]

She knew that she was a sore perplexity at this time to her beloved co-workers. They could not understand why the work she was so happy and successful in, should be given up, to go on with what could only bring pain and suffering; nor could she understand it herself. She only knew that she had to do just what she was doing, or be for ever condemned by God and her inner self. Why such a gigantic task should have been laid upon one so utterly incapable she did not know. Naturally timid and sensitive, she quailed from every sharp word, or disdainful look, and these were plentiful now. Averse to paining others, lo, she was causing pain to those she so dearly loved. Hating coarse words and writings, and everything that in the faintest degree savoured of impurity, she was now spoken of all over the colony as one who was advocating Malthusian doctrines, and injuring the young and innocent by pretending to fight against sensuality in its most subtle form. Was it any wonder that under this accumulation of perplexities, the frail body gave way, and she was again on a bed of sickness.

Angels came and ministered unto Christ, after His terrible time of temptation in the wilderness. Angels came again and ministered unto Him in Gethsemane's garden. God, ever mindful of them that are tempted, sent a ministering angel to His suffering disciple in the form of a little Scotch woman. Quaint, eccentric, and unlearned, the little woman was, nevertheless, an angel of light in this dark time. Her rugged Scotch tongue, her queer sayings were music sweet as any seraph's song to that tried soul.

'Cheer up, dear,' she would say, twinkling loving glances through her spectacles at the weak woman on the bed. 'We'll thrash the devil yet.' The one addressed didn't feel like thrashing any being so powerful as his Satanic majesty just then, but the confident tones and the cheery words were like balm of Gilead.

Soon came an additional blessing in the shape of a deputation from one of the most powerful Temperance bodies in Melbourne, asking her to accept the position of lecturer for them at a very good salary. Deeply touched, she thanked them gratefully, but firmly declined the honour.

'You see,' she explained, 'I get peculiar views and must express them; no matter how I try to keep myself in proper form, I angle out, and the angles rub roughly against each other. I can't bear to hurt individuals or organizations, so had better stand or fall alone.'

'We are willing to take you just as you are,' replied the kindly spokesman.

'Consider the "screw",' suggested his companion.

It was such a surprise that any one should imagine that money could weigh with her, that she was quite silent for a while, not knowing just how to explain without hurting their feelings. Then she gently said—

'If God directed me to take the position you so generously offer I would take it if need be for nothing, but ten pounds a week would not induce me to take up a work He has not called me to.'

She felt herself sinking in their estimation as she spoke, and, as the offer was never renewed, she concluded they thought such an unbusinesslike woman was really no great gain to their Society. As a matter of fact they did not try again, because they felt themselves powerless to influence one with such unworldly ways.

Next came the hearty invitation of Victoria's most powerful political body, the Victorian Alliance, but while willingly agreeing to help this organization, she utterly refused to become their lecturer and organizer.

Then came invitations from ministers and others in country districts, and after a very short interval she started out entirely free from any Society. For a year work crowded on her, and as day by day the mists cleared away, she found God's unerring Hand was guiding into avenues of greater usefulness than any before passed through.

*One of Australia's Daughters: An Autobiography of Mrs Harrison Lee* (1900).

# Arthur Lynch

## (1861–1934)

*Arthur Lynch was a son of John Lynch, one of Peter Lalor's captains at Eureka. He studied at the University of Melbourne before leaving for Europe. After a period of study in Berlin, he worked in London as a freelance writer, mixed in Irish circles, and became a powerful journalist for the* National Reformer. *By 1898 he was Paris correspondent for the* Daily Mail. *He was sent to report on the Boer War in South Africa but became involved as a participant. After his 'brigade' was disbanded Lynch was sent to the USA to promote the Boer cause. Meanwhile he had been elected for Galway as a Nationalist but was arrested at Dover in June 1902 before he could take his seat. Convicted of treason, he was released after a year following intervention by the King, Edward VII, and was pardoned in 1907. His later career included medicine, involvement in Irish politics, and contributions to controversy in various fields. He wrote more than thirty books.*

I went to South Africa unknown; in three weeks I was leading a troop at the Front. That statement is true as it stands, and even as I look back, the whole affair has to me something of the Arabian Nights atmosphere. But as I dislike the sophisticated style of writing in the larger scope of history, and as I do not desire to shine in any false glamour, I will endeavour in this small sphere to place the whole adventure in its proper light and setting.

[...]

For some years before the actual outbreak of the South African War I could see it coming, and my sympathies were entirely with the Boers. This was not altogether for their own sake, for I knew of them only through the vague pages of history and current literature, but because in relation to the great Imperial nation their situation seemed to me co-ordinate with that of my native country, Australia.

When the war actually broke out, I regarded the main issue as being that of a little Republic, which had the chance of expanding into a great future, being attacked and downed by an Imperial Power.

From the beginning I was anxious to go to South Africa to see the events close at hand. At first, however, I had no thought of actively participating. How was that possible? I had no experience of war, and my one individual arm would have been of little use, and it was absurd to think that I could act in any capacity as for instance, of command.

Here again what I say is perfectly true, and I could justifiably leave it there, but now comes in one of those extraordinary previsions which, without apparent foundation of reason have, from time to time swept across my mind, and inwardly and for my own special intention have given me an assurance of reality.

I would not have dared to mention this to anyone else, for the odds would seem ten thousand to one, but I felt certain that, somehow, I would get to South Africa, and that when I did reach the field of conflict, I was destined to exercise command.

Even to get there presented enormous difficulties, for the only newspapers that were at all enterprising at that time in Europe were the great London dailies, and such a paper as the 'Manchester Guardian;' and the French papers had not yet launched out into their more modern, adventurous scope.

However, to cut a long story short, at length I got a commission from the Paris 'Journal,' and then from 'Collier's Weekly,' of New York, and also from 'Black-and-White,' an illustrated weekly, of London.

I took my profession so seriously that I even bought a camera and practised with it, although without acquiring any particular skill. [...] When I arrived in Pretoria, General Botha had just come from the Front.

It was in Johannesburg, whither I had gone for a visit, that I met him. He had distinguished himself round Colenso, and already the eyes of the whole Boer forces were being turned towards him, recognising him as the coming man.

Certainly he was a great figure at that time: a man in the prime of life, tall, broad, and deep-chested, with all that air of health and great reserve of strength which I found to be characteristic of my new friends. The features were good and more animated than with the ordinary run of Boers. His figure was well set off by a plain but neat uniform; he was the first, in fact, of the Boer officers who wore a uniform. His eyes were blue, mild and kindly, but with an expression that glinted as of steel when the fighting was mentioned. He wore a small moustache and beard, and altogether looked a picture of a fine type of yeoman called upon to do military service.

When he offered his hand, that hand seemed to be heavy and strong as the paw of a lion, and when he smote on the table to give emphasis to a point, the gesture, again, gave evidence of enormous strength. Another point that I liked about Botha was his freedom from affectation. His manner was neither, as is some times found amongst the heroes of war, complaisant nor insipid; it was free and natural, and he laughed gleefully, and his eyes twinkled with delight, when his friends praised him.

I struck up a friendship with Botha on the spot, and—here comes in a fantastic stroke—proposed to him straight away that he should give me a command on his staff. He had already intimated that it would not be possible for me to carry on my correspondent's work. He said that if I were to send news or pictures, it would be almost equivalent to communicating directly from behind the Boer lines to the

Government in London. He said their resources were limited, and they had to conceal the disposition of their troops from the British.

He indicated to me that I could serve the cause of the Republic by helping in the 'organisation' of a troop which was then being got together in Johannesburg. It appeared that there was a great body of men, including some of the best fighting material, which was not incorporated in the regular Boer commandoes. These consisted of foreign elements, young Cape Colonists, or other young Afrikanders, and also of a certain number of Irish, who did not care to form part of the Irish Brigade under Colonel Blake which was already in the field.

A word or two may be said about the formation of that troop. At a noted London hotel, as I have already said, a small committee of Irishmen had met to consider the question of a propagandist paper. Amongst those who had attended was John MacBride, then a chemist's assistant in Dublin, an active and determined young man, ruddy of countenance and with reddish hair, with something of eagerness and determination and unflinching courage in his expression. [...]

At the outbreak of war he had recruited and organised the Irish Brigade, and had set up in command an Irish-American who had had some training at West Point as an officer and who, in appearance and style, suggested strongly the type of Buffalo Bill.

Colonel Blake was one of the most picturesque of the many dazzling figures I beheld in South Africa—a tall broad-shouldered man, with the open countenance of a Western cowboy rather than of an educated officer, dressed, moreover, with that curious combination of crude effects and brilliant display that delights the cowboy mind. A huge sombrero adorned his head, and round his neck was a white silk handkerchief, and beneath that a claret-coloured sort of tunic, displaying underneath a gorgeous vest. Corduroy breeches and huge boots and spurs completed the attire. 'Completed,' perhaps is not precisely the word, for Blake was not entirely Blake without a long lasso which he either wore round his body or carried on an upright standard in front of his Mexican saddle. Even then his figure in martial array was not complete. In his full splendour he rode a horse which was proportionately as tall and remarkable a figure as himself.

He was a brave man, and he had a way with soldiers, but if I were asked whether he were a good officer or not, I should be compelled to dive down into deep reserves. I well remember, by the way, my first meeting with Blake and MacBride. They were waiting for me at a certain spot, and I knew that they would be just as critical of me as I was of them, perhaps even more so for I felt quite friendly to both of them; and as they looked upon me as a town-bred type, forgetting that I was a country boy myself, I felt that they would scan my riding with very searching eyes. Therefore, as they stood reined upon a gently sloping rise, I set out in full tilt with all that air of vanity and show that seems appropriate to military display. I dashed up to MacBride after the style of the 'White Chief,' a hero of my boyhood from Captain Mayne Reid's wonderful stories of Mexico, and I showed no sign of halt even when a violent collision seemed inevitable. At the last moment I swerved slightly aside, reined up suddenly so as to attempt the White Chief effect, 'almost thrown on his haunches,' and then, with an air as if this were the normal manner of greeting, I put out my hand to MacBride. Inwardly I was laughing with great enjoyment, but MacBride, who at that time was an indifferent rider and who must have been really astonished, looked on with the immovable countenance of a stoical Red Indian and, without comment, introduced me to Colonel Blake. Blake, who was a good rider, looked upon this performance with gravity, but I could see that at least he admitted me to the circle of those who were beyond 'the Tender-foots and God-darned galoots, anyhow!'

[…]

I have given reason sufficient for joining the Boers, but I do not know that I have yet given the decisive reason and, when I do offer it, it may seem tenuous and incon-clusive. That is to say, if I were writing of the career of another, but all through my life I have respected certain ideas, cleaved to certain ideals, and even under the utmost pressure endeavoured to preserve intact my own clear visions of life, irre-spective of the motives that might sway others. Certain influences that have guided me may appear meaningless to many, others that have produced hundreds of years of the turmoil and bloodshed of our histories seem to me the dregs of insanity.

For long past I had been weaving out the web of my thoughts which later I destined to present in a formal manner. One may lead an intense life in this interior thought, and yet the suggestion may come again and again in bringing it to bear upon the passing show of realities that there is something unreal, something of a dream-like character in that existence.

Thoughts and ideals are despised by the strong 'common-sense' breed of men, especially by the 'strong silent man' of decadent poets of the Tennyson school or clever young women who excite the imaginations of the tweeny maids; and I have known philosophers, thinkers of a sort, who have contrasted unfavourably the work of the mind, even that of a man of science with the performances of 'men of action.' Now, I have known a number of these 'strong sons of men' and sometimes, in moments of crisis, have seen them trying to escape into ratholes; and I have noted the fallacy of the man of action in that so often his deeds have no meaning and lead to nothing, except perhaps the bolstering up of a false system, and the feeding of his little pomp and vanity.

What has this got to do with my taking up the rifle in South Africa? Simply this, that sympathising with their cause as I did I might well have supported them

otherwise, perhaps just as effectively, and with greater protection to myself, but—
and here comes in the little point towards which I have been driving: Was that little
world of thought which I guarded so religiously something of real meaning, was its
possession greater to me than all that I might have achieved in 'action' had I cast
these thoughts to the wind?

[…]

There, then, you have the deepest motive that influenced me. I was resolved to
show that I, a thinker, could ride with the boldest horsemen in the world and,
pitted with the 'men of action,' would set them a pace which would test their nerve
and call forth their every ounce of energy. This campaign was an episode of a
greater theme. […] Here also comes in something still more curious. It might be
said that, ethically, it was wrong, that if I believed my thoughts to be worth guard-
ing as superior, I should not have risked the extinction of these thoughts themselves
in such an adventure. But, to my mind, there was no risk of this sort, I had an
assurance, as if it had been written on high, that I would pull through, even amid
all sorts of perils, and with far richer experience. There was nothing supernatural
in this feeling of certitude, though to explore it would mean searching for the secret
of temperament and diving down into the recesses of psychology, and now is not
the time.

*My Life Story* (1924).

# E. L. Grant Watson

(1885–1970)

*Elliot Lovegood Grant Watson was born in England and educated at the University
of Cambridge. He visited Australia three times: in 1887, 1910–11, and 1912. On his
second visit he was a member of a scientific expedition led by the anthropologist,
Alfred Radcliffe-Brown. Daisy Bates and a Swedish cook, Louis Olsen, were the other
European members of the party. His Australian experience had a profound effect on
his thinking. He was the author of more than thirty books, including novels, works on
natural history, essays and some poetry. This extract concerns his second visit.*

Those first weeks that I spent in the bush were rich, not so much in outer, but in
inner experience. So far as outer experience went, they soon presented a very pleasant and happy monotony. The waking at early dawn in bitter cold, the relished

breakfast, as close to the camp-fire as I could squeeze, together with Jim Wickham and his men. The mine was not at that time more than a single shaft, some twenty feet deep with one short traverse. About twenty men were at work. These all extended to me, and to my ignorance of bush-ways, a kindly tolerance, though they were always telling me tall stories to see how much I would swallow. I, for my part, amused myself by seeing how much I could make them believe that I believed of the stuff they told. They discovered my simple artifice and were amused at my defence and ripost. They found amusement, too, in my activities, and in their times off would go hunting echidnas, bush-porcupines, those God-damn prickly B— as they called them. Of these I had about ten tethered to my tent pegs; I hoped to take them back, and ship them to England. The miners also brought me beetles and every kind of insect from mantis and phasmid to grasshoppers and crickets and ant-lions. I spent a good deal of my time collecting the thousands of beetles that are to be found lurking under the loose bark of the gum-trees, or that I could so easily beat from the low bushes into my Bignal beating-tray. I would wander solitary in the bush, but never very far from a wheel-track, for I had a keen apprehension of how easy it would be to get lost.

By ten o'clock the climate was so far changed that the morning sweaters were discarded. By eleven the sun was scorching hot, and at noon it were best to keep under cover. I was soon sun-burned, and my nose took on the appearance of a bright red blister. In the afternoon one could wander again, and at sundown was glad to pull on sweaters while the evening meal was in preparation.

This simple round, however, did not complete my experience: there was the bush and all that it stood for, and that was no small thing to cope with. I learned, and before long, how many men were distressed and indeed utterly destroyed by its strange power. A surveyor from Perth shot himself dead on the third day of his bush-sojourning. The miners took his death with no great surprise. 'It's the bush,' they said. 'Many men can't stand it. How about yourself, you Johnnie English-man?' I had been asking myself that question, or rather the ambiguous, veiled influences of the bush had been asking me.

In psychological interpretation, it is, I suppose, that the mild, innocent and aloof quality of that virgin territory appears as a symbol of the unconscious, as a symbol of all that civilisation has chosen to disregard. It is a vast interrogation mark, questioning itself, and more than consciousness can know of itself, or indeed of life. It says to man: 'Thou insignificant spark, where art thou? How is with thee in thy soul? Canst thou sustain my vast and indifferent regard? Or wilt thou shrivel into nothingness, rather than listen to my silences?'

So it was that day after day, the bush questioned me, as I wandered looking for beetles. One moment I might be happy enough, intent upon my hunt, but the next, the veil of time seemed drawn aside, and eternity gaped in the sun's glare, or in the cracking of a seed-pod.

There were times when I was frightened, but never too frightened to control myself. Death never stared threateningly at me. Already I seemed in a way to be familiar with this unfamiliarity, this unknown monster which whispered to me, 'I am the indefinite mother of good and evil. I transcend all things and am less than all things. I am the fullness and the void. I am both death and life. I am love and love's murder. Look not upon me for too long.'

Then I would turn away and seek the camp, and familiar human things, and be righted in my own esteem; and the next day perhaps, or some days later, the bush would speak to me again: 'Fear me. Do not hate me. Do not worship me. Do not resist me, nor presume to look for too long. Look aside and if you can, accept me.'

These feelings were not then so conscious as they have become for me in these later days, but as their result I came through my crisis, and in some measure learnt to accept those ambiguous prophecies, for towards the end of my visit to Bulfinch I had chosen to sleep out on the ground wrapped in my blankets, at a short distance from the camp rather than be under the protection of my tent. I liked it better that way. Liked to gaze at the stars until my eyes closed in sleep; woke with the false dawn, when all things stir in their slumber; slept again and woke again as the sun lipped the horizon, sending its slanting shafts to underline every bush and herb with a purple shadow. At such a time the sweet scent of the bush-blossoms would drift lightly in the frosty air. [...]

In reviewing memories of an expedition of this kind, there are many incidents which suggest themselves for recording. How we established contact with the shy and wild tribes from the interior, our methods of communication, or methods of work, and the aims that the expedition set itself; these, together with our personal contacts with the natives, and indeed, there might be added some personal adventures—all these things suggest themselves, but they fall outside the scope of a book which is seeking to separate, from the totality of the past, those events which seem to present an especial relevancy to the pattern of a life taken as a whole and carried so far as the brink of the present moment. There are numerous books recording the adventures of ethnological expeditions, in which men may read of the manners and customs of the Australian Aborigines. I seek for the essentials which bear on my own development, and so make no attempt at an historical picture, but rather to give the general impression received by this close contact with stone-age men, when, together with a few others of my race, I found myself falling within the subtle yet penetrating psychic aura of the Australian tribesmen.

Nietzsche has written: he who would hope to get an impartial view of contemporary affairs must separate himself by an act of will from the objects of his study, and place between himself and the present an interval of at least three hundred years. I did not need to make any such gigantic effort. This adventure of separating myself from the consciousness of my race, this feat was accomplished for me, whether I would or no, by the simple fact of being surrounded by aboriginal savages, and absent from civilisation in which I had been moulded. The process was slow and imperceptible yet it was sure. I entered the bush with a rationalistic, scientific bias. I thought magic to be a kind of infantile make-believe. It might appear real enough to savages, but to civilised people like myself it was not to be taken seriously. That was the initial attitude. The passing weeks and months changed this preconception.

I witnessed daily the power of magic. The social consciousness of these simple and friendly people was a concrete reality, and if I did not actively fear their magic I respected it, *and* I came to believe in it; and, as I came to fall under the spell of these people, so many thousands of years distant from our European conventions, so did those same European conventions suffer from an objective *devaluation*, if I may use such a phrase. I was coming to stand not only three hundred years, but perhaps three hundred thousand years away.

The process went so far during those fifteen months amongst the Aborigines (in one place or another) that I only just snatched myself back in time to be able to half-believe ever again in the conventions of Europe. I knew that magic could kill, and that magic, the man-made bending of the universal powers, could make ill or well. I had entered the animism of the savage mind, and had found within those mystical, sympathetic identifications the open doorways to the unconscious. I do not pretend that this was an altogether desirable experience, though I think it has been a useful one, seeing that I was able to balance, at a later date, its strong influence by five years of analytical psychology. It was in a way a unique experience, not so much understood or valued at the time, but valued and partly understood *afterwards*. It had lifted me, or perhaps sunk me, above or below the orthodox horizon of vision. Through no virtue or merit of my own this accident has happened to me. I have lived for a considerable number of months in the world of magic-sticks and stones, of totem animals, and if I have not actually met and conversed with the Alcheringa, animal ancestors, I have become convinced of their existence in the same way in which Dr Jung is convinced of the existence of the archetypes. That I have seen wild tribesmen trailing their silent, naked way through the unexplored bush-country still seems to me a possession of the soul. That I have seen stark young women streaming with the blood of a yet living turtle which they were laboriously dismembering with a stone knife, is a picture every bit as significant as the intellectual tea-parties I have attended at Lady Ottaline Morall's [*sic*]. Such experiences amidst primitive people contribute, perhaps, to odd visions which sometimes float before my eyes. If a conscious balance between such stark experiences and civilisation has not yet been attained, I am aware that it yet might be, and I view the portal of death as possibly leading to such a blending of conscious and unconscious values.

*But to What Purpose: The Autobiography of a Contemporary* (1946).

# *Thomas Keneally*

## (1935– )

*Thomas Keneally, one of Australia's best-known and most prolific novelists, was born in Sydney. At seventeen he began study for the Catholic priesthood but abandoned that vocation in 1960 and worked as a schoolteacher and clerk before the publication of his first novel,* The Place at Whitton, *in 1964. In this extract from the memoir of his child-hood Mattie is a blind schoolfriend, whom Keneally helped to study for the Higher School Certificate, Mangan is another close friend, who seemed bound for the silent order of the Trappists but who went to university instead, and Bernadette Curran is the girl whom Keneally had worshipped from a distance through the years of secondary school. GMH refers to Gerard Manley Hopkins, whose poems were Keneally's personal bible, carried constantly in his breastpocket. The Cardinal who had earlier attempted to persuade Keneally to train for the priesthood was Cardinal Gilroy.*

Coming back to Mattie's little bungalow on one of those first afternoons of know-ing about Mother Concordia and her impending death, I saw Curran and her well-dressed mother walking together down Shortland Avenue. Past the little suburban gardens they walked like two equals, intently discussing something. Bernadette Curran even wore her maroon Dominican Convent gloves, and Mrs Curran's gloves were white. They were two women dressed not so much to represent motherhood or daughterhood, but an impenetrable sisterhood. What they talked of was unguessable but, you couldn't doubt, marvellous. It occurred to me that whatever was going on there, my mother had been deprived of it in her two-boy, all-male family.

I told Matt, 'There goes Mrs Curran and Bernadette. They're dolled-up exquisitely!'

Matt gave a half chuckle. 'That must be pretty exciting for you, Tom,' he murmured.

I gave him a small nudge on the upper arm. But what they spoke of, the Curran women, transcended our chirping and banter. It had crux, it had weight.

Calling in at the Frawleys yet again, a household in which because of Mrs Frawley's kindness, Mr Frawley's serious purposes and the Frawley girls' genial mockery I felt appreciated, I found out what the Curran women had been discussing.

It was to do with Concordia, the matriarch of the Order. Like Mother Margaret, she had not borne earthly children. Yet this fact made all of them—the Frawleys, the Currans and all the rest—her children. In batteries, her daughters, class by class, girls small and large, in their impeccable maroon, had entered the Dominican chapel to pray for her deliverance or happy death. The Leaving Certificate girls were asked to come and go to the chapel only at their leisure, but come and go they did. A hush hung over their futures. Some may have even felt a pulse of an ambition to achieve in the end a death as notable, as reverberating as that of Concordia. Such a departure from the normal suburban or bush deaths of grandfathers and grandmothers!

The prefects of Santa Sabina were, I heard, admitted in a bunch into the large convent parlour, where Concordia's deathbed had been moved to allow for room for visitors. They saw the brave, rugged, sculpted face of Concordia, still cowled in the Order's regulation clothing for the sickbed at this supremest moment. They saw her lowered lids, and the effort of the discourse she pursued with God on earth's furthest up-jut, on land's end.

This was a death from an ancient and baroque tradition. Had there been what the Frawleys called 'some mad girl', some girl, that is, who was a temperamental echo of the mad boy I was, she might have been overly influenced, morbidly fascinated, inflamed by divine ambitions. But Curran was sensible, had no time—as I knew— for exorbitant responses. She should have come out safe from the visit to Concordia.

The full and potent magic of the death of the great Irish matriarch had not yet, however, been unleashed.

Imagine a room where the Honours English and History girls are at their desks, preparing for the coming public examination, when a messenger enters, a younger nun, and whispers to Curran. Mother Concordia wants to see Curran on her own. Walking out of the study, does Curran—who looks so settled in all life's circumstances—feel unsettled to be chosen to share some of Concordia's last seconds? She must not be totally at ease with such an excessive act of graciousness.

Here at last drama has found a way to penetrate Curran's matter-of-fact, nononsense, *Aussie* advance towards the greatness everyone agrees will mark her later life.

She approaches the sickroom where only the last watchers remain, the most senior nuns who have shared table and cloister with Concordia for years and who are now easing her on her way. Monsignor Loane is long gone from the bedside, with the canisters of holy oil with which he has anointed Concordia in the sacrament called Extreme Unction. Two nuns rise from their knees and take Curran by the elbow, bringing her forward to the deathbed. One of them touches Mother Concordia's shoulder. The old nun half opens her eyes. She tears her gaze away from Yahweh's long enough to say, 'Bernadette, I call upon you to become a Dominican nun and take my name, *Concordia*. I will pray for you and support you in the Presence of God.'

I still wonder if as Bernadette left the deathbed (and indeed the old nun would die overnight, eased of the question of the inheritance of her name) any nun said to her, 'Think closely about this. A command from Concordia is not necessarily a command from God!'

It had been after Concordia had made her severe bequest to Curran that I saw the Curran women speaking so earnestly on their way home and mentioned it to Matt.

It is wrong to surmise the decision was made for her by Concordia's deathbed edict. Sensible and democratic Curran was not so readily deprived of will as all that. But it must have had an effect in some scales of decision, and it seems she made the decision pretty quickly afterwards. She did not trumpet it though—I heard about it not from her lips. I had gone home with Matt to his house in Shortland Avenue, and his mother offered us tea and told us.

'Wow,' said Matt. 'What'll you do now, Mick?' Did he mean, how to top that? Or how to deal with it? I sat in a vacuum, my hands prickling. As soon as I could I left. It was as if this were a war, but all the maidens, not all the young men, were about to vanish. I walked bemused to the Frawley house in Broughton Road, and everyone was home except Mr Frawley the wiry grouper. Rose Frawley had answered the door with a half-smile.

'Have you heard the news?' all three women were asking. 'What will you do?' asked Rose. 'Join the Foreign Legion?'

[...]

I got home and my mother did not notice merely the phantom shape of GMH in the grey serge coat she looked after so arduously. She had met Mrs Frawley outside Cutcliffe's Pharmacy in Rochester Street and had been told.

'This shouldn't have any influence on what you decide,' she told me.

When my father came home from his store in Granville, he said the same thing. 'Just because everyone else is volunteering it doesn't bloody mean you have to.'

He knew whereof he spoke. He had been a volunteer in his day, and had not been fully happy in the service.

What was worst for me was that I could tell that whatever Curran was renouncing in the name of the Deity and Concordia it was not me. No messages or hints had been sent. There was no chance of a last hand-hold.

Nonetheless, amongst the quicksilver shifts of sentiment occurring to me, there now grew a desire to be associated with such a brave drama. Curran's sincere choice put the question to me in a lasting way the Cardinal had not been able to. On the one hand the sublime path. On the other hand, the chance of a normal university degree and a little double-fronted brick cottage in a suburban street. GMH had been a priest in his cell and had sung like an angel in his chains.

There were references of pure and sublime love as well: Eloise and Abelard, St Francis and St Clare. And then there was the other, Australian example Father Tenison-Woods and Mother Mary MacKillop. MacKillop the seraphically handsome woman, and Julian Tenison-Woods a priest like GMH, but a famed geologist rather than a poet. [...] They—Tenison-Woods, elegant Brit, former *Times* journalist, and MacKillop, colonial girl—had once been photographed side by side, and made a remarkable pair. Mother MacKillop's piercing, enormous eyes. No fainting mystic. A good, practical woman. Like Curran in that. Could there be some possible similar and future alliance between Curran and myself?

The following Sunday the Currans had us all up to their little brick house at Strathfield for an afternoon tea. It was a kind of celebration and farewell. I did not take my GMH, what was the point? As we drank the tea and ate the *Women's Weekly's* best sponge cake—it was still an era where women felt ashamed to serve cake from a cake shop—Curran did not make much of her decision, although Rose Frawley kept talking about it excitedly. [...]

Either Matt or Larkin the agnostic said, 'Which one of you will be Mother Superior first?' and we saw Mr Curran hide his face and turn his shoulder, which began to shudder. A shamed silence fell over everyone, and Mrs Curran went and laid a hand on his arm.

In that second I knew that I was going too. The sense of seeing the rituals from the *inside,* the way GMH had, overtook me again, but now it did not fill me with terror. It was in part a matter of crazily knowing that grief could not be avoided, and this grief displayed by the Curran parents was purposeful and noble. In the Currans' house at tea the richly-coloured skeins of motivation—a yearning for GMH's God, a desire to serve, a desire to instruct, a taste for drama, a preference for fleshless love, an exaltation in the Latin rites. I would never be bored by them, I knew. I would never listen surreptitiously in the confessional, between penitents, to the Saturday races.

*Homebush Boy: A Memoir* (1995).

# Sources and Acknowledgments

The editor and publisher wish to thank copyright holders for granting permission to reproduce textual extracts. Sources are as follows:

**James Armour**, *The Diggings, The Bush and Melbourne; or, Reminiscences of Three Years' Wanderings in Victoria*, G.D. McKellar, Glasgow, 1864, pp. 23–31. **Jimmie Barker**, *The Two Worlds of Jimmie Barker: The Life of an Australian Aboriginal 1900–1972*, Australian Institute of Aboriginal Studies, Canberra, 1977, pp. 88–97. **Bruce Beaver**, 'Flying' in *As It Was*, University of Queensland Press, St Lucia, 1979, pp. 35–9. **Gillian Bouras**, *A Foreign Wife*, McPhee Gribble/Penguin, Ringwood, Vic., 1986, pp. 61–3. **Stella Bowen**, *Drawn from Life*, George Mann, Maidstone, Kent, 1974, pp. 165–9. First published 1940. **Martin Boyd**, *Day of My Delight: An Anglo-Australian Memoir*, Lansdowne Press, Melbourne, 1965, pp. 74–8. **G[ordon] W[illiam] Broughton**, *Turn Again Home*, Jacaranda Press, Brisbane, 1965, pp. 60–6. **Vincent Buckley**, *Cutting Green Hay: Friendships, Movements and Cultural Conflicts in Australia's Great Decades*, Penguin Books, Ringwood, Vic., 1983, pp. 34–9. **Terry Burstall**, *A Soldier Returns: A Long Tan Veteran Discovers the Other Side of Vietnam*, University of Queensland Press, St Lucia, 1990, pp. 2–7, 9–10. **Ada Cambridge**, *Thirty Years in Australia*, Methuen, London, 1903, pp. 126–31. **Peter Conrad**, *Down Home: Revisiting Tasmania*, Chatto & Windus, London, 1988, pp. 216–21. **Jill Ker Conway**, *The Road from Coorain*, Minerva, London, 1992, pp. 41–51. First published London, Heinemann, 1989. **Eliza Davies**, *The Story of an Earnest Life*, Central Book Concern, Cincinnati, 1881, pp. 148–53. **Jack Davis**, *A Boy's Life*, Magabala Books, Broome, WA, 1991, pp. 82–6. **Alfred Deakin**, *The Crisis in Victorian Politics, 1879–1881: A Personal Retrospect* (ed. J. A. La Nauze and R. M. Crawford), Melbourne University Press, Carlton, 1957, pp. 24–34. **Robert Dessaix**, *Night Letters: A Journey Through Switzerland and Italy*, pp. 5–11, reprinted by permission of Pan Macmillan Australia, Sydney, copyright © Robert Dessaix 1996. **Havelock Ellis**, 'My Life: The Australian Chapter' in *Kanga Creek: Havelock Ellis in Australia* (ed. Geoffrey Dutton), Pan Books, Sydney, 1989, pp. 197–204. **Edward Eyre**, *Journals of Expeditions of Discovery into Central Australia and Overland from Adelaide to King George's Sound, in the years 1840–41*, London, 1845, vol. 1, pp. 394–402; vol. 2, pp. 1–4. **A. B. Facey**, *A Fortunate Life*, Penguin Books, Ringwood, Vic., 1981, pp. 254–6. **Kathleen Fitzpatrick**, *Solid Bluestone Foundations and Other Memories of a Melbourne Girlhood 1908–1928*, Macmillan, South Melbourne,

1983, pp. 30–3. **John Foster**, *Take Me to Paris, Johnny: A Life Accomplished in the Era of AIDS*, Minerva, Port Melbourne, 1993, pp. 112–15. **Mrs Arthur H. Garnsey** [Ann Stafford Bird], *Scarlet Pillows: An Australian Nurse's Tales of Long Ago* (facsimile edition), Hesperian Press, Carlisle, WA, 1984, pp. 59–66. First published 1950. **Montague Grover**, *Hold Page One: Memoirs of Monty Grover, Editor* (introd. and ed. Michael Cannon), Loch Haven Books, Main Ridge, Vic., 1993, pp. 35–41. **Barbara Hanrahan**, *The Scent of Eucalyptus*, Chatto & Windus/Hogarth Press, London, 1973, pp. 20–5. **Alexander Harris**, 'Religio Christi' in *The Secrets of Alexander Harris* (ed. A. H. Chisholm), Angus & Robertson, Sydney, 1961, pp. 187–91. First published anonymously in the *Saturday Evening Post* in 1858. **Eve Hogan**, 'The Hessian Walls' in *Selected Lives: Personal Reminiscences*, Fremantle Arts Centre Press, Fremantle, WA, 1983, pp. 104–9. **Joseph Holt**, *A Rum Story: The Adventures of Joseph Holt: Thirteen Years in New South Wales (1800–12)* (ed. Peter O'Shaughnessy), Kangaroo Press, Kenthurst, NSW, 1988, pp. 58–61. First published in London in 1838. **Donald Horne**, *Confessions of a New Boy*, Penguin Books, Ringwood, Vic., 1986, pp. 286–90. First published Viking, 1985. **Clive James**, *Unreliable Memoirs*, Pan Books, London, 1981, pp. 11–12, 22–4, 172–5. First published Jonathan Cape, London, 1980. **Kate Jennings**, *Save Me, Joe Louis*, Penguin Books, Ringwood, Vic., 1988, pp. 1–4, 12–14. **Ned Kelly**, *Ned Kelly being His Own Story of Life and Times*, Hawthorn Press, Melbourne, 1942 [n.p.]. **Thomas Keneally**, *Homebush Boy: A Memoir*, Minerva, Port Melbourne, 1995, pp. 160–7. **Bessie Lee**, *One of Australia's Daughters: An Autobiography of Mrs Harrison Lee*, Ideal Publishing Union, London, 1900, pp. 130–8. **Brian Lewis**, *Our War: Australia During World War I*, Melbourne University Press, Melbourne, 1980, pp. 33–8, 284–7. **William Linklater** with Lynda Tapp, *Gather No Moss*, Macmillan, South Melbourne, 1968, pp. 191–7. **Mary Rose Liverani**, *The Winter Sparrows*, Thomas Nelson, Melbourne, 1975, pp. 195–201. **Morris Lurie**, *Whole Life: An Autobiography*, Penguin Books, Ringwood, Vic., 1987, pp. 1–9. **Arthur Lynch**, *My Life Story*, John Long, London, 1924, pp. 151–4. **Graham McInnes**, *The Road to Gundagai*, Hogarth Press, London, 1985, pp. 266–8. First published Hamish Hamilton, 1965. **Claude McKay**, *This is the Life: The Autobiography of a Newspaperman*, Angus & Robertson, Sydney, 1961, pp. 130–3. **Mary Marlowe**, *That Fragile Hour: An Autobiography*, Angus & Robertson, Sydney, 1990 [n.p.]. **David Martin**, *My Strange Friend*, pp. 110–13, reprinted by permission of Pan Macmillan Australia, Sydney, copyright © David Martin 1991. **Roger Milliss**, *Serpent's Tooth*, Penguin Books, Ringwood, Vic., 1984, pp. 15–20. **Alan Moorehead**, *A Late Education: Episodes in a Life*, Hamish Hamilton, London, 1970, pp. 37–40, 50–6, 126–9. **John Frederick Mortlock**, *Experiences of a Convict Transported for Twenty-one Years* (ed. G. A. Wilkes and A. G. Mitchell), Sydney University Press, Sydney, 1965, pp. 129–34.

Ruth Park, *Fishing in the Styx*, Penguin Books, Ringwood, Vic., 1993, pp. 259–61. Hal Porter, *The Watcher on the Cast-iron Balcony*, Oxford University Press, Melbourne, 1963, pp. 57–62. Lloyd Rees with Renée Free, *Lloyd Rees: An Artist Remembers*, Craftsman House, Seaforth, NSW, 1987, pp. 17 18. Graham Richardson, *Whatever It Takes*, Bantam Books, Sydney, 1994, pp. 11–12. Henry Handel Richardson, *Myself When Young*, William Heinemann, London, 1948, pp. 54–62. Andrew Riemer, *Inside Outside: Life Between Two Worlds*, Angus & Robertson, Sydney, 1992, pp. 88–93. Barney Roberts, *A Kind of Cattle*, Australian War Memorial/William Collins, Sydney, 1985, pp. 34–40. Morley Roberts, *Land-travel and Sea-faring*, Lawrence & Bullen, London, 1891, pp. 17–31. Jessie Elizabeth Simons, *In Japanese Hands: Australian Nurses as POWs*, William Heinemann, Melbourne, 1985, pp. 11–21. First published as *While History Passed*, Heinemann, Melbourne, 1954. Emily Skinner, *A Woman on the Goldfields: Recollections of Emily Skinner 1854–1878* (ed. Edward Duyker), Melbourne University Press, Melbourne, 1995, pp. 63–9. Bernard Smith, *The Boy Adeodatus: The Portrait of a Lucky Bastard*, Penguin Books, Ringwood, Vic., 1984, pp. 8–13. Patsy Adam Smith, *Goodbye Girlie*, Penguin Books, Ringwood, Vic., 1994, pp. 27–35. Charles Stretton, *Memoirs of a Chequered Life*, Richard Bentley, London, 1862, vol. 3, pp. 2–13. A. Tiveychoc, *There and Back: The Story of an Australian Soldier 1915–1935*, Returned Soldiers and Sailors Imperial League of Australia, Sydney, 1935, pp. 221–5. Christos Tsiolkas and Sasha Soldatow, *Jump Cuts: An Autobiography*, Random House, Milsons Point, NSW, 1996, pp. 139–42. W[alter] J[ames] Turner, *Blow for Balloons being the First Hemisphere of the History of Henry Airbubble*, J.M. Dent, London, 1935, pp. 262–9. Glenyse Ward, *Wandering Girl*, Magabala Books, Broome, WA, 1987, pp. 101–9. Elliot Lovegood Grant Watson, *But to What Purpose: The Autobiography of a Contemporary*, Cresset Press, London, 1946, pp. 99–106. Thorvald Weitemeyer, *Missing Friends, being the Adventures of a Danish Emigrant in Queensland (1871–1880)*, T. Fisher Unwin, London, 1902, pp. 62–70, 199–208. Elisabeth Wynhausen, *Manly Girls*, Penguin Books, Ringwood, Vic., 1989, pp. 113–22.

Every effort has been made to trace the original source of copyright material contained in this book. The publisher would be pleased to hear from copyright holders to rectify any errors or omissions.

# Index